EVANGELICAL THEOLOGY IN TRANSITION

AMSTERDAM STUDIES IN THEOLOGY AND RELIGION
(AmSTaR)

The *Amsterdam Studies in Theology and Religion* (AmSTaR) is a peer-reviewed publication of VU University Press in cooperation with VISOR (VU Institute for the Study of Religion) and the Faculty of Theology. It publishes dissertations and scholarly monographs on a wide range of issues pertaining to theology and religion. The series is open to publications in English, German and Dutch.

Editorial Board

Prof. dr. C. van der Kooi
Dr. J.W. van Saane
Prof. dr. J.T. Sunier
Dr. P.G.A. Versteeg

Executive Editor

Dr. A.W. Zwiep

Volume 1

Evangelical Theology in Transition

Essays Under the Auspices of
the Center of Evangelical
and Reformation Theology (CERT)

Edited by

C. van der Kooi
E. van Staalduine-Sulman
A.W. Zwiep

VU University Press

VU Uitgeverij | VU University Press
De Boelelaan 1105
1081 HV Amsterdam
The Netherlands

E-mail: info@vu-uitgeverij.nl
Website: www.vu-uitgeverij.nl

© 2012 VU University Press
© 2012 cover design Heleen ten Voorde (VU Dienst Communicatie)

ISBN 9789086596003
NUR 700

All rights reserved. No part of this book may be reproduced, stored in a retrieval system, or transmitted, in any form or by any means, electronic, mechanical, photocopying, recording, or otherwise, without the prior written consent of the publisher.

In Memory of

*Stanley J. Grenz (1950–2005)
and
Clark H. Pinnock (1937–2010)*

Contents

List of Abbreviations ix

Preface xi

List of Contributors xiii

Introduction 1

1. Finding a Place of Holiness: Towards a Typological Characterization of Evangelical Churches in the Netherlands 15
   HENK BAKKER

2. The Evangelical Movement and the Enlightenment 40
   EVELINE VAN STAALDUINE-SULMAN

3. Distant Relatives: The Oxford Group
   and the Reformed Churches in Restored Union 68
   MAARTEN J. AALDERS

4. "A Banner That Flies Across This Land": An Interpretation and Evaluation of Dutch Evangelical Political Awareness Since the End of the Twentieth Century 86
   AD L.TH. DE BRUIJNE

5. Ecclesiology in Context: Urban Church Planting
   in the Netherlands 131
   STEFAN PAAS

6. The Impact of Liquid Church Discourse in Dutch Evangelical
   Churches: A Practical-Theological Analysis 148
   RENÉ ERWICH

7. Health, Wealth and Prosperity:
   A Biblical-Theological Reflection 164
   BERNHARD J.G. REITSMA

8. Creative Love Theism:
   The Doctrine of God in Reformed and Evangelical Theology...... 182
   CORNELIS VAN DER KOOI

9. John Wesley On Salvation, Necessity and Freedom 203
   ANTONIE VOS

10. The Wesleyan Quadrilateral Reconsidered:
    Wesley Meets Gadamer 223
    ARIE W. ZWIEP

Index of Authors 247

List of Abbreviations

Where possible, abbreviations of journals, monograph series etc. have been taken from Siegfried M. Schwertner, *Internationales Abkürzungsverzeichnis für Theologie und Grenzgebiete* (Berlin, New York: Walter de Gruyter, ²1992).

AncB	Anchor Bible
BCT	Bulletin voor Charismatische Theologie
BEC	Bronnen van de Europese cultuur
BHTh	Beiträge zur historischen Theologie
BKAT	Biblischer Kommentar zum Alten Testament
CB.NT	Coniectanea biblica. New Testament Series
CBETh	Contributions to Biblical Exegesis and Theology
COQG	Christian Origins and the Question of God
CRINT	Compendia Rerum Iudaicarum ad Novum Testamentum
DNK	Documentatieblad voor Nederlandse Kerkgeschiedenis na 1800
EHS.T	Europäische Hochschulschriften. Reihe 23, Theologie
GThT	Gereformeerd Theologisch Tijdschrift
GW	Gesammelte Werke
HUTh	Hermeneutische Untersuchungen zur Theologie
ICA	Initiations au christianisme ancien
ICC	International Critical Commentary
IJPR	International Journal
IJSCC	International Journal for the Study of the Christian Church
IJSTh	International Journal of Systematic Theology
IRM	International Review of Missions
JR	Journal of Religion
KeTh	Kerk en Theologie
KD	Karl Barth, Kirchliche Dogmatik
KG	Kritische Gesamtausgabe
LSJ	Liddell-Scott-Jones, Greek-English Lexicon
MisSt	Mission Studies
NCLS	National Character and Leadership Symposium
NESTTR	The Near East School of Theology Theological Review
NICNT	New International Commentary on the New Testament
NUStPEPh	Northwestern University Studies in Phenomenology and Existential Philosophy
NRSV	New Revised Standard Version
PhG	Philosophie und Geschichte
PhTo	Philosophy Today
PL	Patrologiae cursus completus. Series Latina

PrakTh	Praktische Theologie
PTMS	Princeton Theological Monograph Series
QJS	Quarterly Journal of Speech
RStRel	Routledge Studies in Religion
SABH	Studies in American Biblical Hermeneutics
SC	Sources chrétiennes
Sem.	Semeia
STAR	Studies in Theology and Religion
StHCT	Studies in the History of Christian Traditions
StRS	Studies in Religion and Society
TheolD	Theologisch Debat
TFil	Tijdschrift voor Filosofie
TNK	Tijdschrift voor Nederlandse Kerkgeschiedenis
TRE	Theologische Realenzyklopädie
TS	Theological Studies
TTh	Tijdschrift voor Theologie
UTB	Universal Taschenbücher
WBC	Word Biblical Commentaries
WeD	Woord en Dienst
WeZ	Wereld en Zending
WTJ	Wesleyan Theological Journal
WUNT	Wissenschaftliche Untersuchungen zum Neuen Testament

Preface

In 2003 plans were made for a Center of Evangelical and Reformation Theology (CERT) that would function as a platform to encourage critical reflection, research and publications pertinent to issues of Evangelical identity. What "Evangelical identity" exactly meant, turned out to be a matter of much debate from the start. In the mission statement of CERT it was taken in a broad sense to cover "Evangelical faith as rooted in the Reformation, Pietism and other renewal movements", and this is the definition used in this volume. Seven institutions located in the Netherlands participated in this project: Baptisten Seminarium (Bosch en Duin, now: Barneveld), Evangelische Alliantie; Evangelische Theologische Hogeschool (Veenendaal; originally part of the Evangelische Bijbel Scholen, now fully integrated with the Christelijke Hogeschool Ede / Ede Christian University of Applied Sciences), Evangelisch Werkverband, the journal *Soteria*, Tyndale Theological Seminary (Badhoevedorp), and VU University Amsterdam. The agreement on the launching of CERT was signed on 19 December 2003.

The first achievement was the establishing of a Master's course on Evangelical Theology at the Faculty of Theology of VU University. The master programme exists for seven years now and is fully integrated in the theological faculty. It consists of several specialized courses on Evangelical and Reformation Theology, focussed on the history of the revival movements, on modern forms of being church and church planting and so on.

A second achievement was the founding of the *J.H. Bavinck Chair for Church Planting and Church Renewal,* called after the missiologist Johan Bavinck (1895–1964) in 2010. Ede Christian University of Applied Sciences and the Protestant Theological University participate in the chair alongside VU University. Dr Stefan Paas, one of the contributors to this volume, held his inaugural address on 12 May 2011 on "Church Renewal by Church Planting: The Value of Church Planting for the Future of the Christian Tradition in Europe" ("Kerkvernieuwing door kerkplanting: de betekenis van kerkplanting voor de toekomst van de christelijke traditie in Europa").

Now that the educational needs started to be fulfilled, participants of CERT felt a growing desire to publish on typically Evangelical themes within theology. Research into these several themes had already been done in the context of various congresses and individual publications, but it had not led to a corporate project or book.

All the articles in this book have been extensively discussed in peer groups, the book as a whole has been subjected to an anonymous review procedure. We thank all reviewers for their input.

The plan for this volume was born in 2008. Subsidies were granted from the *Netherlands School for Advanced Studies in Theology and Religion* (NOSTER) and from the *VU Institute for the Study of Religion* (VISOR), for which we are truly grateful. This volume is its first fruit. We hope that it will contribute to a deeper understanding of Evangelical spirituality and theology in the Dutch context.

Thanks are finally due to Marjolein Turner-Prins for the translation of several of the articles in this volume and to Dr Creig Marlowe for his willingness to read through the entire manuscript in its final stage and giving many helpful corrections. We also appreciate the way in which Dr Jan Oegema of VU University Press has facilitated the publication of this book as the first instalment of the A*m*ST*a*R series. That many volumes may follow!

List of Contributors

DR. MAARTEN J. AALDERS (1954) studied theology at the VU University Amsterdam and worked as a Reformed minister in Woubrugge and Amstelveen. In 1990 he received his Ph.D. from VU University Amsterdam (under supervision of Prof C. Augustijn) on a study about the younger ethical theology, an important movement in Dutch theology, founding its opposition to "modern" (liberal) thought on the living faith of the Christian congregation, in the century between 1855 and 1955. Since then, he has published various articles related to modern church history in the Netherlands. Since his retirement in 2007, he is involved in a study on J.G. Geelkerken, a Dutch minister who was excluded from the Synod after a conflict in 1926. This contributed to the formation of the Reformed Churches in Restored Union.

DR. HENK A. BAKKER (1960), Licentiate Evangelische Theologische Faculteit Louvain (1987), Doctoral Studies at University of Utrecht (1990), and Ph.D. University of Groningen (2003), is Senior Lecturer in Baptist History, Identity, and Theology at VU University Amsterdam, and lecturer at the Dutch Baptist Seminary (Barneveld) and Ede Christian University of Applied Sciences. He is also fellow researcher at the Center for Patristic Research (Tilburg, Utrecht, Amsterdam). Among his publications are *Cyprian of Carthage: Studies in His Life, Language, and Thought* (2010, co-ed. with Paul van Geest and Hans van Loon), "Animosity and (Voluntary) Martyrdom: The Power of the Powerless", in: Fitzgerald, van Rensburg, van Rooy (eds.), *Animosity, the Bible and Us: Some European, North American and South African Perspectives* (2009), "Potamiaena: Some Observations About Martyrdom and Gender in Ancient Alexandria", in: A. Hilhorst, G.H. van Kooten (eds.), *The Wisdom of Egypt. Jewish, Early Christian and Gnostic Essays in Honour of Gerard P. Luttikhuizen* (2005), and *Exemplar Domini: Ignatius of Antioch and His Martyrological Self-Concept* (2003).

PROF. DR. AD L. TH. DE BRUIJNE (1959) is Professor of Christian Ethics and Spirituality at the Theological University of the Gereformeerde Kerken (vrijgemaakt) in Kampen. Previously he has been a minister in Nijverdal and in the center of Rotterdam. In 2006 he received his Ph.D. at the University of Leiden with a study about the political theology of Oliver O'Donovan entitled *Levend in Leviatan: Een onderzoek naar de theorie over 'christendom' in de politieke theologie van Oliver O'Donovan* (Kampen 2006). Among his other publications is a study about the relation between ethics and spirituality, *Affect en effect: De betekenis van een bijbelse spiritualiteitvoor de christelijke ethiek in een(post-) seculiere tijd* (Kampen 2010). His fields of interest, on which he also published many articles, are the relation of church and society, sexual ethics and hermeneutics.

DR. RENÉ ERWICH (1964), theological studies Utrecht University (1988) and Doctoral Studies in Switzerland (Rüschlikon), Ph.D. Utrecht University (1999), is professor (lector) of Spiritual Leadership at Ede Christian University and assistant professor of Practical Theology at the Evangelische Theologische Faculteit Leuven. Dr. Erwich headed the Evangelische Theologische Hogeschool (ETH) from 2005–2010 (Ede) and is the former rector of the Dutch Baptist Seminary. He is an ordained minister of the Dutch Baptist Union and worked in three Baptist Churches. Dr. Erwich served as assistant professor in missiology at the International Baptist Theological Seminary (IBTS) in Prague from 1999–2002. Among his publications are *Het gaat om mensen* (Zoetermeer 1999, diss.) and *Veelkleurig Verlangen* (Zoetermeer 2008).

PROF. DR. STEFAN PAAS (1969), Ph.D. Utrecht University (1998), is J.H. Bavinck Professor of Church Planting and Church Renewal at the VU University Amsterdam, and lecturer in Missiology at the Theological University of the Free Reformed Churches in Kampen. Previously, he has worked as a missionary consultant and as a church planter in several Dutch cities. Among his publications are *Jezus als Heer in een plat land* (2001), *De werkers van het laatste uur* (2003), *Creation and Judgement* (2003), *Vrede stichten* (2007), and *Onder spanning* (2011, editor and co-author). Currently, he is working on a research project Christian Mission in Post-Christian Europe.

List of Contributors

PROF. DR. CORNELIS VAN DER KOOI (1952), editor, theological studies at the VU University Amsterdam (1980), Ph.D. VU University Amsterdam (1985), was minister of the Reformed Church in Leimuiden fron 1984–1992. He currently holds the chair of Western Systematic Theology at VU University Amsterdam and is director of the Center of Evangelical and Reformation Theology (CERT). He wrote his dissertation on the development of the early theology of Karl Barth, *Anfängliche Theologie. Der Denkweg des jungen Karl Barth* (Munich 1987). Among his publications are *As in a Mirror. John Calvin and Karl Barth on Knowing God* (Leiden 2005), and *Tegenwoordigheid van Geest. Verkenningen op het gebied van de leer van de Heilige Geest* (Kampen 2006). He is co-editor of Barth's *Der Römerbrief (Zweite Fassung 1922)* in de *Karl Barth Gesamtausgabe* (Zurich 2010). He published extensively in the field of christology, pneumatology and neo-calvinism.

PROF. DR. BERNHARD J.G. REITSMA (1965), Doctoral Studies, Utrecht University (1991), Ph.D. Leiden University, is Extraordinary Professor for the Church in the Context of Islam at VU University Amsterdam, senior-lecturer at the Ede Christian University. From 1998–2005 he worked as lecturer at the Near East School of Theology and at the Arab Baptist Theological Seminary in Beirut, Lebanon. His publications include *Geest en Schepping* (Zoetermeer 1997, diss.), *Wie is onze God: Arabische Christenen, Israel en de aard van God* (Zoetermeer 2006), which is currently being translated into English and a variety of articles concerning Christian theology in the context of Islam.

DR. EVELINE VAN STAALDUINE-SULMAN (1964), editor, theological studies, Evangelische Theologische Faculteit Louvain (1985) and Protestantse Theologische Universiteit Kampen (1995), Ph.D. Theologische Universiteit Kampen (2002), was lecturer at Ede Christian University of Applied Sciences, is assistant professor of Old Testament and researcher of Targum at VU University Amsterdam. She is coordinator of CERT and one of the editors of the journal *Soteria*. Among her publications are *The Targum of Samuel* (Leiden 2002), *Critical Edition of Targum Samuel* (http://www.targum.nl/KritischeEditie/critical.aspx) and "De Evangelische Beweging en de Verlichting", *TheolD* 5/2 (2008), 4–14.

PROF. DR. ANTONIE VOS (1944) took his Ph.D. from Utrecht University in 1981 on *Kennis en Noodzakelijkheid* (Knowledge and Necessity). After having taught as a teaching assistant in philosophical studies for a couple of years, he lectured in philosophy: semantics, epistemology and philosophy of religion, and the history of philosophy, including medieval philosophy in particular (1969–1984), and in theology: systematic theology, church history and medieval thought (1984–2009). Since 2008, he acts as part-time research professor of Post-Reformation Studies at the Evangelische Theologische Faculteit Louvain. He published several works in philosophy and the history of philosophy, and on systematic theology and he lectured at several institutions in Europe and the United States. Vos founded the research groups John Duns Scotus and Reformed Scholasticism. He published *Contingency and Freedom* (Dordrecht 1994), *Duns Scotus on Divine Love* (Aldershot 2003), *The Philosophy of John Duns Scotus* (Edinburgh 2006), *Reformation and Scholasticism* (Grand Rapids 2001), and *Reformed Thought on Freedom* (Grand Rapids 2010).

DR. ARIE W. ZWIEP (1964), editor, Licentiate (1987) and Doctoral Studies, Evangelische Theologische Faculteit Louvain (1990), Ph.D. University of Durham, UK (1996), is assistant professor of New Testament and Hermeneutics at VU University Amsterdam and lecturer at Ede Christian University of Applied Sciences. From 1996–2004 he was dean of studies and vice-director of the Evangelische Theologische Hogeschool (Veenendaal, now Ede). He is one of the initiators of CERT. Among his publications are *The Ascension of the Messiah in Lukan Christology* (Leiden 1997), *Judas and the Choice of Matthias* (Tübingen 2004), *Tussen tekst en lezer: een historische inleiding in de bijbelse hermeneutiek* (Amsterdam 2009, ²2010), and *Christ, the Spirit and the Community of God* (Tübingen 2010).

Introduction

1. *Transitions and Fusions*

This volume explores recent developments in the Evangelical movement in the Netherlands. We have defined these developments in terms of transitions and fusions. By transitions we refer to internal changes within the Evangelical movement itself, in response to external transformations within Dutch society. In new cultural and societal circumstances, Evangelicalism is changing and this raises new questions and provides new answers. One of the typical changes of the last decades is that, in the Netherlands, Evangelicalism is no longer a marginal phenomenon but a factor of influence in a number of ecclesiastical and societal domains. As a result, both the need for academic reflection and the will to participate in the academy seems to increase. This volume is one specimen of this transitional path. It describes various transitions not only from a neutral, outside perspective, but also from within, that is, by contributors who label themselves as Evangelicals or who are at least sympathetic with the concerns of Evangelicalism.

By fusions we refer to a mutual process of change: the Evangelical movement is not only undergoing a transformation, but it also affects its conversation partners. In particular, a mutual influence between the larger Protestant domain and the Evangelical movement is visible. Several contributions in this volume describe the effects of the changing Evangelical movement on Dutch Protestantism and vice versa. We could well speak of an osmosis that causes transformation on both sides. Also, Pentecostal theology and practices are involved in a similar process of causing changes in and being changed by the Evangelical movement. This process is less well worked out in the present volume, although it is clearly reflected, for instance, in the contribution of Bernhard Reitsma. This volume, however, focuses first and foremost on Dutch Evangelicalism in its Protestant context.

2. *Evangelical: Defining a Concept*

Before we discuss some trends and developments, we will describe what we mean by the Evangelical movement, especially in connection with and in contrast to Reformed Protestantism. Taking these movements as different streams of spirituality and theology will inevitably raise the question whether it is legitimate to make such a sharp distinction. An obvious sign of the close relationship between "Reformed" and "Evangelical" traditions is found in the book on *The Modern Theologians*, edited by David Ford.[1] The Dutch theologian G.C. Berkouwer, internationally renowned for his *Dogmatic Studies*[2] and his *The Triumph of Grace in the Theology of Karl Barth*,[3] is here described and discussed not as Reformed theologian, but under the category of "The Evangelical Theology". For a Dutch readership this is remarkable, if not astonishing, since more conservative Evangelicals in the past tended to regard Berkouwer as a liberal, especially because of his two-volume study on *Holy Scripture*.[4] Evangelical and Reformed theology are still sharply distinguished within the Dutch context as two different ways of doing theology and as stemming, sociologically speaking, from different contexts. In Germany, the terms *evangelisch* and *evangelikal* may historically have the same root, but these too refer to two different contexts of doing theology. In the English-speaking world, however, *evangelical* encompasses a much broader range, including a wide variety of mainline Protestant theology.

What does Evangelical mean? This volume reflects the ongoing debate on what historically and phenomenologically can be labelled as Evangelical. Particularly the contributions of Henk Bakker, Eveline van Staalduine-Sulman, Maarten Aalders and Ad de Bruijne address this problem in some detail and they take different positions. On the one hand, there is the position, historically and substantially, that the Reformed and Evangelical traditions are not entirely different branches of Protestant theology. Together they belong to the religious delta that originates in the Reformation of the sixteenth century. According to this position, Evangelical spirituality and practice are the outcome of a long history, of which Puritanism, German pietism, Methodism, revivalism and the holiness movement are the most important building stones and markers of distinct practices, spirituality and theology. This positioning of Evangelicalism within the stream of the historical Re-

---

[1] Ray S. Anderson, "Evangelical Theology" in: David F. Ford (ed.), *The Modern Theologians: An Introduction to Christian Theology in the Twentieth Century* (Oxford: Blackwell, 2001), 480–498.
[2] Gerrit Cornelis Berkouwer, *Dogmatische Studiën* (Kampen: J.H. Kok, 1949–1972); Eng. transl. Grand Rapids: Eerdmans, 1952–1976).
[3] Gerrit Cornelis Berkouwer, *De triomf der genade in de theologie van Karl Barth* (Kampen: J.H. Kok, 1954); Eng. transl. Grand Rapids: Eerdmans 1956).
[4] Gerrit Cornelis Berkouwer, *De Heilige Schrift* (DS; Kampen: J.H. Kok, 1966–1967), 2 vols.; Eng. transl. *Holy Scripture* (Grand Rapids; Eerdmans, 1975).

formation can be motivated by a systematic-theological observation: Evangelical theology for its greatest part is dependent on theological reflection within the Reformed tradition. As to Trinitarian theology, the Christological dogma, the doctrine of creation and providence, and the doctrine of justification, Evangelical theology is to a large degree indebted to Reformed theology.

Nevertheless, there is ample reason not to downplay the differences. Although many Evangelicals feel attracted to Reformed and even Calvinistic types of theology, a number of Evangelicals would describe their identity in outright opposition to Reformed theology and identify themselves with "Arminian" and Wesleyan concerns, not to forget the large number of Roman-Catholics who share an Evangelical attitude. In the Netherlands this broader type of Evangelicalism has sometimes been termed an "ecumenism of the heart" (Arie van der Veer), that is, as an attempt to transcend ecclesiastical and theological boundaries and reconfigure classical (premodern) distinctions. In the Netherlands, a large number of present-day Evangelicals are former members of Reformed churches. Interestingly though, there is also a trend of Evangelicals turning back to mainline churches (i.e. to the established Protestant churches), as the research by Otto de Bruijne, Peter Pit and Karin Timmerman has recently shown.[5]

Evangelicalism is a movement which, according to Stanley Grenz, can be qualified by three major characteristics or focal points: convertive piety, sanctification and mission.[6] Each of these elements has to do with the human response to God. A common feature, not only of Evangelical practices and spirituality but also of its theology, is the interest taken in the active role of the human subject. The focus on mission and outreach in the Evangelical tradition is a clear sign of this, but it also applies to the emphasis on applicable (read: relevant) exegesis and practical theology. The qualification of Grenz somewhat differs from another well-known description of Evangelical piety, that of David Bebbington, who defines Evangelicalism in terms of conversionalism, activism, a high view of Scripture as the Word of God and "cruci-centrism" (cross-centeredness).[7] Bebbington links the beginning of the Evangelical

---

[5] Otto de Bruijne, Peter Pit, Karin Timmerman (eds.), *Ooit evangelisch: de achterdeur van evangelische gemeenten* (Kampen: Kok, 2009).

[6] Stanley J. Grenz, *Renewing the Center: Evangelical Theology in a Post-Theological Era* (Grand Rapids: Baker 2000), 17.

[7] David W. Bebbington, *Evangelicalism in Modern Britain: A History from the 1730s to the 1980s* (Grand Rapids: Baker, 1992), 2–3.

movement to the pragmatic Enlightenment ideal of John Locke. Henk Bakker, in his contribution to this volume, casts doubt on the affirmation that this historical dependence belongs to the core of the Evangelical movement, in contrast to Eveline van Staalduine in her article.

In the contributions of Bakker and De Bruijne we find another way to define the identity of the Evangelical movement, namely a phenomenological one. They argue that the Evangelical movement is characterized, phenomenological speaking, by a strong contrast between the kingdom of God and the earthly realm. Whatever institution arises in this world (state, church, school), it can never be identified with the kingdom of God. The eschatological orientation of classical Evangelicalism is, according to these authors, an indissoluble element of a much older tradition that reaches back to the early church. Evangelicalism, in their view, is not a historically fixed movement but a protest movement that accompanies a church that tends to forget its expectation of the kingdom. De Bruijne issues a warning that the present-day Evangelical movement is in imminent danger of losing its "Anabaptist" flavour. This warning concurs with other contributions, such as those of Paas and Reitsma, who all stress that the Christian community is characterized as a counterculture.

In sum, in this volume we take the word "Evangelical" in its broad sense as a counter-movement accompanying the church at large, including the Reformed Churches. This includes not only churches and para-churches that explicitly call themselves Evangelical, but also other movements in history that demonstrate similar critical and eschatological concerns with an appeal to the Gospel. This implies that the Evangelical movement sees itself, almost by definition, as a critical minority, as especially Bakker, Van Staalduine and Paas argue.

3. *Evangelicalism in a Dutch Context*

The contributors to this volume are from Dutch origin and their contributions relate mostly to the situation in the Netherlands. Hence, as one of our reviewers remarked, the title of this volume might well have been *Evangelical Theology in Transition in the Netherlands*. We are much aware of the fact the results of our research cannot be easily generalized or applied to other contexts. However, that does not mean that readers from other geographical and cultural contexts cannot profit from this particular context. We like to think of these essays as "case studies" in which the applied methodologies can be applied to other ecclesial and cultural backgrounds. Still, the observations and analyses are made from a contemporary Dutch perspective. In the last decades, Dutch culture has undergone profound changes. From a position of cultural dominance, the Christian churches have waned in number and influence. Institutional involvement in Christian churches and organizations has decreased dramatically.[8] A frequent remark is that religious institutions have lost the authority and power to dominate and define the lives of believers.[9] People have come to deal with life issues in an individualistic and subjective way, very often much unrelated to a religious worldview. In this new multi-cultural and multi-religious context, Evangelicalism has been a movement coloured by strong commitment that brought about vitality, new initiatives for mission, and a new song culture.

Although difficult to describe, one can at least say that Evangelicals can be found in very different places. One can, of course, locate them as members of independent Evangelical and Pentecostal churches, but perhaps greater numbers and impact can be found within the established churches.[10] The Evangelical influence in the churches might be demonstrated by the increasing impact of the Evangelisch Werkverband (a coalition of Evangelical pastors within the Protestant Church of the Netherlands), by a growing acceptance of an Evangelical song culture in the worship services of local churches and by the popularity of the so-called Alpha Course (an introductory course to the basics of Christian faith). In terms of numbers, the Evangelical movement is difficult to estimate. Its character as a network of independent initiatives, organizations and individuals makes it impossible to give exact figures. However, the estimated numbers in the last decade go from 3,1 % to 11 % of the total population in the Netherlands.[11] In light of a total estimate of 39% being affiliated with a religious movement or organization, this range of the percentage of Evangelicals is impressive.[12]

In the Netherlands, the Evangelical movement did not only have an impact in renewal movements such as Youth for Christ, the Navigators and new independent churches. It became also very visible in the

---

[8] J. de Hart, "Postmoderne spiritualiteit", in: G. Dekker, T. Bernts, J. de Hart (eds.), *God in Nederland* (Kampen: Kok, 2007), 118–192.
[9] Johan Roeland, *Selfation: Dutch Evangelical Youth Between Subjectivization and Subjection* (Amsterdam: Pallas, Amsterdam University Press, 2009), 24.
[10] Miranda Klaver, Peter Versteeg, "Evangelicalisering als proces van religieuze verandering", *PrakTh* 34 (2007), 169–182.
[11] Roeland, *Selfation*, 27.
[12] Roeland, *Selfation*, 24.

foundation, in the years 1965–1970, of a new broadcasting company, the *Evangelische Omroep* (EO). This media company, being itself already a "bricolage" of different, cooperating Evangelical and Reformed people, became a notable example of cooperation between Reformed and Evangelical (free-church) believers. Starting as a voice against liberal theology and biblical criticism of that time, and aiming at the evangelization of society, its rapid growth has shown the necessity of responsible academic reflection. Whereas Evangelicals were strong in action, they were often poor in reflection, theologically and politically. Although this remains true for a significant portion of the Dutch Evangelical world, it is also true that the need for critical reflection is increasingly acknowledged and has now resulted in a cautious move by Evangelicals into the academic world. As examples of this movement to a more reflective style one can point to the theological journal *Soteria*, founded in 1984, the Evangelische Theologische Hogeschool (ETH), now integrated in Ede Christian University of Applied Sciences (Christelijke Hogeschool Ede, CHE), the Evangelical Theological Faculty (ETF) at Leuven and the Center of Evangelical and Reformation Theology (CERT), launched in 2004 at VU University Amsterdam. This very awareness is a sign that somehow a transition is being made from a rather anti-intellectual attitude towards a more cooperative engagement in theological debates.

The growing awareness for the need of critical reflection is not to deny that there was no critical reflection at all in earlier times. But as a critical countermovement, much energy was spent on apologetics and in regard to personal involvement in practical activities. Evangelical activism was a time- and energy-consuming factor that fuelled mistrust concerning academic work. In the postmodern mindset, however, some aspects of Evangelical spirituality link up easier with the dominant culture. The strong individualism, the high esteem of an empirical approach in contrast to purely theoretical reflection (see Paas), and the distinction between the Bible and one's interpretation of it (see Zwiep) are examples of a growing affinity with contemporary culture. Many authors in this volume emphasize and acknowledge the postmodern flavour of the Evangelical movement (Bakker, Erwich, Van der Kooi, Zwiep, Van Staalduine).

4. *Free Will and the Concept of God*

It is often said that Evangelical interest in the human subject is much closer to modernity than many other strands in Protestant (Reformed) theology. Evangelical theology, in this view, should be regarded as a translation of orthodox Protestantism to modern culture. The stress on active involvement of the human subject in conversion, the appeal for continuous transformation and sanctification of the individual and the urge to missions in a secularized world, are all evidence of a focus on active involvement of the human being. However, in this process of translation more is involved than this notion of the human subject. It has also a bearing upon themes or loci that at first sight do not have any relation to the appropriation of Christian faith.

Arguably the strong emphasis on human response also results from themes that were popular in Methodist and revivalist theology. In these circles, the emphasis on free will, and the belief in the possibility of transforming one's life in accordance with the will of God, were strongly defended and propagated. This stress on the free will caused a kind of so-called "Arminianism" in the Evangelical branches of Protestant theology that affected, for example, their doctrine of God. A number of Evangelicals strongly opposed the Calvinistic doctrine of election and (double) predestination. In recent times, the debate on open theism (Clark Pinnock) made clear that the doctrine of God is also deeply affected by this stress on human response and responsibility.[13] In this volume some of the contributions investigate the way the Evangelical translation has caused a twist in the Reformed heritage. By "updating" Reformed orthodox theology to the concerns of modernity, some far-reaching shifts have taken place. One example is the debate on free will and grace. The emphasis on free will has traditionally been stressed in the Methodist and Evangelical tradition. But is it really true that an emphasis on God's Lordship in human history is detrimental to the notion of human responsibility? The contributions of Antonie Vos and Kees van der Kooi in this volume deal with this intricate debate.

5. *Practices and the Role of the Church*

The definitions of Evangelical identity discussed above have in common that they focus on concepts and beliefs, not so much on practices and habits. This one-sided focus on concepts and ideas is also visible in this volume, although a transition is visible towards a pursuit of theol-

---

[13] Clark H. Pinnock, with Robert C. Brow, *Unbounded Love: A Good News Theology for the 21st Century* (Downers Grove: InterVarsity Press, 1994); Clark H. Pinnock, *Most Moved Mover: A Theology of God's Openness* (Grand Rapids: Baker, 2001).

ogy that takes its starting point for reflection in practices and acknowledges the need for empirical research. Theology does not only consider ideas and beliefs, but also reflects on practices. These practices must be broadly defined: how we relate ourselves to reality does not only come to expression in concepts and words, but also by means of our imagination, our feelings and our senses.[14] We could say that, next to the discursive domain, the non-discursive domains must be engendered. A new perspective for doing theology is greatly needed. Although not the main topic of this volume, this need for a reorientation is noticed especially in the contributions of Stefan Paas, René Erwich and, from a somewhat different angle, Arie Zwiep. It means that research into Evangelical and charismatic practices may ultimately effect theology. The way many Evangelicals relate to their context and modern culture may very well give a distinct feature to the way they live these beliefs. The specific contribution of Evangelicalism to the renewal of Christendom may be this impetus from a cognitive mode of Protestantism to a more expressive and experiential mode of Christianity, in which a range of semiotic fields of signs and meanings play a constitutive role.[15] In some of the contributions about the Church (Paas, Erwich) and the public domain (De Bruijne) the importance of starting with practices in real life comes explicitly to the fore.

Another important issue is the changing role and concept of the church. Evangelicals have been renowned for their critical attitude against the structures of the mainline churches; many of them started their own "free churches", free in actual practice, meaning "free from the dominant, established churches with their suffocating structures". In their call for authentic faith Evangelicals tended to be revivalist and even reactionary, looking back to (and longing for) biblical times, especially to the early Christian communities as examples of authentic faith. To date, the fascination with the early church is even growing (Bakker), although at the same time much attention is given to new forms of the Christian communities (Paas, Erwich). Church planting, emerging and liquid church are only a few designations of the movement and changes that are going on in the field of ecclesiology. They can be related to postmodern tendencies, in which the traditional ways of being related to a church are fading or at least are accompanied by other means of

---

[14] See Miranda Klaver, *This Is My Desire: A Semiotic Perspective on Conversion in an Evangelical Seeker Church and a Pentecostal Church in the Netherlands* (Amsterdam: Amsterdam University Press, 2011), 25.

[15] Klaver, *This Is My Desire*, 20–21, 404–405.

affiliation and involvement. One of the challenges for future research is how to assess these seemingly contrasting ways of being church. Is the fascination with the earliest forms of Christianity a form of restoration theology (a Romantic ideal)? Are the new ways of being church dangerous genuflections to postmodern cultural relativism?

Evangelical theology and practices have also had an impact in contemporary Reformed practices and theology. Examples of this influence can be found in various areas. One example is baptism. The modern preoccupation with the role of the human subject and the formation of the self has a bearing on the debate and the practice of baptism. In the Reformed tradition infant baptism is still a stronghold of religious practice; but that this practice is increasingly subject to debate is also clear, especially since it is, according to Evangelicals of a Baptist persuasion, built on cultural premises that no longer hold in our current situation, namely the idea of the Reformed (*Hervormde*) Church as a state church. Reformed theology is urged to rethink its own practices and theological justification of these practices. Directly related with baptism is the idea of the church as a religious community. In theological terms, ecclesiological questions belong to the main focal points of Evangelical spirituality and have been addressed in recent years. In the Netherlands, attention to new forms of ecclesial community, labelled as Emerging Church, has begun among Evangelicals and has subsequently launched initiatives in the established Protestant churches.

6. *Short Overview of the Contributions*

One of the transitions that runs like a red thread throughout this volume is that one of the classic distinguishing marks of Evangelical theology, an anti-academic stance especially against historical-critical study of the Bible, is on the wane. The authors of this volume are convinced that this older identity-marker of Evangelicalism, some kind of Biblicism or fundamentalism, has to be overcome and in fact has turned out to be disastrous. The classical debates about the so-called "inerrancy" of Scripture, for example, were stamped by outright *modern* presuppositions, such as the conviction that revelation should be identified with propositional truth and that the trustworthiness of the Gospel depended on an infallible Bible. All these debates were founded on typical modern notions, including the philosophical notion of "hard-core" foundationalism. The contribution of Arie Zwiep bears ample evidence of a transition to a context in which critical biblical scholarship does not necessarily have to distance itself from the Christian faith, but can be done in an attitude of scholarly integrity and personal involvement. Honesty requires us to admit that many Dutch Evangelicals, including many pastors and theologians, still regard biblical scholarship (and academic study in general) as an enemy rather than an ally of Christian faith.

The first part of this book provides a quest for the identity of the Evangelical movement. Bakker enters a plea for a phenomenological definition. A historical description would have been possible, but he considers that too shallow an approach to establish what he thinks Dutch Evangelicalism stands for: a prophetic movement that accompanies the church and that by definition holds a minority position. Eveline van Staalduine's contribution also relates to the identification of the Evangelical movement in the Netherlands, with a special focus on the role of biblical studies. She argues that the relationship between Evangelicalism and modernity is much more complicated than some scholars think and much closer than most fundamentalists want it to be.

The increasing contribution and visibility within the public domain is another item of discussion. This transition is the core of the article of Ad de Bruijne. He exposes a political awakening among Evangelical Christians, who often stood aloof in the political arena as a matter of principle. A significant number of them, concentrated in the political party *ChristenUnie*, shifted to a more neo-Calvinistic position. Whereas notions such as sojourning (following Jesus) and a dispensationalist conception of history ("This World is Not My Home, I'm Just a Passing Through") deterred classic Evangelicals from active participation in the public sphere, it appears that these theological elements are less stressed among a large group of contemporary Evangelicals in the Netherlands. They devote themselves more explicitly to social justice and this means that they actually annex a more neo-Calvinistic opinion. One of the factors that have led to this increasing participation is the swift secularization of society. This caused what Hijme Stoffels calls an "awareness of crisis".[16] Anxiety about various undesirable developments in the public sphere (especially in ethical matters) roused Evangelicals to a sense of responsibility towards society. Whether this is a radical change, depends on one's definition of Evangelicalism and to which part of its history one compares the actual situation. Considering its roots in the Reformation, in Puritanism and Methodism with their stress on con-

---

[16] Hijme C. Stoffels, *Wandelen in het licht: waarden, geloofsovertuigingen en sociale posities van Nederlandse evangelischen* (Kampen: Kok 1990), 34.

version, Bible, individual holiness and mission, this is hardly a significant change. Puritanism and Methodism had no fundamental hesitation whatsoever to engage in politics. Neo-Calvinism fits within this broader definition of Evangelicalism. The situation is completely different when one considers the political ideas of the Anabaptists and the Baptist movement. The left wing of the Evangelical movement must be seen against the background of an ongoing Anabaptist stream that stresses the opposition between the kingdom of God and the earthly realm. De Bruijne argues that Evangelicals should not turn away from these critical notions, because he doubts whether the pluralism of neo-Calvinism will last in the end.

Two articles address the observation that Evangelical trends in the Netherlands often begin abroad but somehow find a soil for growth in the Low Countries. Maarten Aalders observes this in the history of the Oxford movement. He argues that the Evangelical movement in the Netherlands is not a phenomenon arising after the Second World War, as some historians think. Aalders shows that the revival movement from Wales affected churches and theologians in the Netherlands in the interbellum. It came to an end, because it ended up in ethical conflicts. Bernhard Reitsma also draws attention to transitions elsewhere in the world that seem to have affected the situation of the Dutch Evangelical churches. In Christian communities, mostly of Pentecostal background, living at the edge of society or even endangered in their existence, the features of "cruci-centrism" and mission come together in an intriguing way, giving Christian life and theology an entirely new twist. A good part of the Evangelical world in such places has embraced some kind of "prosperity gospel". Although living in a Western society where this emphasis on a blessed and blossoming life can too easily fall under a debunking verdict, it is argued in this article that "cruci-centrism" not only relates to individual salvation, but has also implications for community life at large.

The trend to start a fresh discussion on what church is, already hinted at above, is the main denominator of the next contributions to this volume. The broader Evangelical tradition can be characterized as a movement in which the critical distance between established churches and their institutions has always been great. It might even be said that the Evangelical world typically does not want to be incorporated in larger ecclesial or institutional bodies. Some leaders immediately retreat when they envisage organisational incorporation or the start of a new organization. They claim to be "new" or "authentically biblical" in their appeal to the biblical past. Apart from that, there is also a vast attention to and reflection on new faith communities or practices to be church. Intriguing is the practice-orientated reflection and its applications to missions. The missionary impulse has been characteristic for the Evangelical movement from the start and it will remain so. In his contribution, Stefan Paas delineates the transition in the role and the function of the church from a monopoly position towards a minority position in the religious marketplace. This, he argues, should be accompanied by a marketing strategy (1) from a congregational understanding of the church to a network church, and (2) from an emphasis on confessional foundations to an emphasis on missions and values. This strategy is, according to Paas, fundamental to thinking properly about the origin and existence of the church in all its diversity. Furthermore, he feels that new church models should not be supported by the extant authorities, but should engage themselves with the margins of society. That means that a new model should be based on a voluntary and egalitarian structure. This practice-orientated encounter is also visible in the contribution of René Erwich. He argues that the definition of church is less based in the theological concepts we have, but rather in its practices. In his article he undertakes empirical research into some recent Evangelical communities in the Netherlands that claim to be practitioners of what has come to be known as *Liquid Church* (Pete Ward), a development which is of course not restricted to the contemporary Dutch context.

The last three contributions consider the inherent theological contents of Wesleyanism. The theology of John Wesley has always been influential in Evangelicalism, although his impact seems to be underestimated. The same goes for Arminianism. Although many Evangelicals have full-blown "Arminian" sympathies, in practice the appeal to Arminius and Wesley often functions simply as a "identity-marker", without knowledge of the historical and theological context that have shaped these identities. Many Dutch Evangelicals that left the Reformed churches quite well remember the steady warning against Arminianism and, on the rebound, call themselves Arminian without ever having read a single word in his writings. Antoon Vos states in his theological-historical essay that a sharp distinction should be made between Arminius and Wesleyanism, even though Methodism, standing in the tradition of Wesley, is often qualified as Arminian. Whereas Arminius' own ideas are totally governed by a strong notion of "necessity" (in a philosophical sense) and therefore suppose a neutral divine will at one point, the context of Wesley's concepts is quite different. The commitment for the individual human being, for his questions, his despair and economical and social tragedy is described in this contribution as the practical commitment of the Methodist tradition. It is about humans, about their healing and salvation. In its focus on the surprise that God's contingent will holds for the human, the Evangelical movement maintains the biblical message. Also Cornelis van der Kooi's contribution encompasses theological subjects. The debate on open theism, as it was launched, among others, by the late Clark Pinnock, may have reached its peak. The theme of this debate offers an important opportunity to discuss and move beyond traditional controversies between orthodox Christianity and the Evangelical world. He traces some dilemmas caused by contrasting the acts of God and the freedom of humans, as if these were two equal parties. Van der Kooi tries to find a way out by turning to biblical theology and by giving systematic theology a more modest place. The contribution of Arie Zwiep regarding Evangelical hermeneutics fits in the transition towards the academic domain, and tries to bring in some helpful insights from Wesleyanism to advance the contemporary debate on biblical hermeneutics in Evangelical circles. He leaves the traditional distrust against biblical studies and contemporary hermeneutics (or against hermeneutics as such, for that matter!) behind and argues for a more open attitude to contemporary biblical scholarship. Zwiep creatively combines the so-called Wesleyan Quadrilateral with Gadamer's hermeneutics.

This volume is dedicated to the memory of Stanley Grenz and Clark Pinnock, two Evangelical thinkers who were a source of inspiration to many of us and whose intellectual and spiritual legacy we wish not to be forgotten.

The Editors

Chapter One

Finding a Place of Holiness:
Towards a Typological Characterization of Evangelical Churches in the Netherlands

Henk Bakker

1. Introduction

The Dutch Evangelical movement is often regarded as the missionary fruit of a wave of ecclesiastical activities and influence from North America to North Western Europe after World War II, which was fed mainly by a negative assessment of the existing churches in the Netherlands and its surrounding countries. In the Netherlands, the breeding ground for this unease and desire for transformation evolved from as early as the nineteenth century. Then, between the two World Wars and even more so after the Second World War, this spiritual ground was ploughed extensively, especially through the influence of writings in which the established churches were firmly placed in an apocalyptic framework, e.g. those of Johannes de Heer and Hal Lindsey. From the 1960s onwards, the Netherlands were affected by waves of church planting and church renewal activities. Some of the resulting churches and organizations were completely new, others were built on the withered remains of existing churches and organizations.[1]

In this chapter we will aim to achieve, first, a description of Evangelical churches in the Netherlands, second, an analysis (based on empirical research) of some transitions that can be observed in recent Dutch Evangelicalism and, third, a discussion of several fusions and other relationships between Evangelicalism and other currents in Dutch (Protestant) Christianity. We will conclude with some reflections on the future of Evangelicalism in the Netherlands.[2]

---

[1] Gerrit Noort, Stefan Paas, Henk de Roest, Sake Stoppels (eds.), *Als een kerk (opnieuw) begint: handboek voor missionaire gemeenschapsvorming* (Zoetermeer: Boekencentrum, 2008), 84–88.

[2] In 2005, Olof de Vries and Henk Bakker wrote a draft text for a possible typology

2. Description

In 2006 it was believed there were 890 Evangelical congregations in the Netherlands, with a combined membership of about 148.000.[3] Within the Protestant churches, including orthodox Reformed churches, the influence of Evangelicalism was growing. The percentage of Evangelicals within the existing traditional churches is estimated to be about 10%. Around the year 2020, an expected 72% of the inhabitants of the Netherlands will have no affiliation with any religion, and of the remaining 28%, 10% will be Catholic, 8% Muslim, and 11% will be Reformed, Evangelical or "other". Assuming a population of about 16 million in 2020, this means we may then have about 500.000 Evangelically minded Christians in the Netherlands, both inside and outside Reformed circles. An estimated 20% of those will faithfully attend church every week.[4]

The question is of course whether these figures present a situation in the Netherlands very different from the rest of Europe and whether there is a distinctly unique Dutch situation. This is arguably the case. In 2000, 60% of the population of the Netherlands was unchurched, and the Netherlands took the lead in the secularization of Western Europe.[5] The cause can be found in the way the churches and the Evangelical movement in the Netherlands were rooted in the nineteenth-century zeitgeist. And the question of the origins of the Dutch Evangelical movement leads to the time of *le Réveil*. The shifts that took place during that time have determined the way in which the churches in the Netherlands responded to Modernity as it emerged in the nineteenth

---

of the Evangelical movement for the ERT (Evangelical and Reformation Theology) programme at the VU University of Amsterdam; this programme is part of CERT (Center of Evangelical and Reformation Theology). This article is based on a revised edition of that text, entitled "Typering en positionering van de evangelische beweging", written at the request of CERT (2005/2006, Vrije Universiteit).

[3] See in: W.B.H.J. van de Donk, A.P. Jonkers, G.J. Kronjee, R.J.J.M. Plum (eds.), *Geloven in het publieke domein: verkenningen van een dubbele transformatie* (Den Haag: Wetenschappelijke Raad voor het Regeringsbeleid, 2006), 107.

[4] See the reports *Religie aan het begin van de 21^e eeuw* (Centraal Bureau voor de Statistiek, Den Haag/Heerlen, 2009), and *Identificatie met Nederland* (Wetenschappelijke Raad voor het Regeringsbeleid; Amsterdam: Amsterdam University Press, 2007). Cf. Jos Becker, Joep de Hart, *Godsdienstige veranderingen in Nederland: verschuivingen in de binding met de kerken en de christelijke traditie* (Sociaal Cultureel Planbureau; Den Haag, 2006), and Henk Tieleman, "Ecclesia, quo vadis?", *KeTh* 58 (2007), 22–32.

[5] Cf. Theo Schepens, "Nederlandse katholieken en Rome: wie is er vreemd?", in: Rein Nauta (ed.), *Vreemd! Varianten van verscheidenheid*, 15–28. See also Antonie Vos, "Ligt Europa in Holland? Naar aanleiding van Dr. B. Wentsel en de crisis in de cultuur van Europa", *Kontekstueel* 15/4 (2001), 26–35.

and twentieth century. The development of the Evangelical movement in the Northern parts of the Low Countries, as well as its agenda, were determined by the many discussions about faith and thought that took place both inside and outside the churches in the Netherlands during the nineteenth century.[6]

At this point, we will proceed by moving to a review of the phenomenological character of the Dutch Evangelical movement. With regard to the subject of this article, our questions concern the concretization of a particular movement. What is the most elementary characteristic of its Evangelical nature, what is its "specific gravity"? We will focus on three issues: Evangelicalism as a Christ-centered movement, Evangelicalism as a prophetic movement, and Evangelicalism as a caring movement.

2.1. *Christ-Centered Visibility*

In a phenomenological sense, the Evangelical movement can be described as having a self-manifestation in which Christian groups and individuals urge the existing main church to return to its normative beginnings in the circle of Christ and early Christian tradition, i.e. to its pre-Catholic gestalt. The specific gravity of the Evangelical movement is determined by the manifestation of God's coming to us in Christ, the *missio Dei*. This is its central theme. The person of Jesus Christ and the Gospel take central stage in this return, turn-around or even conversion of the church. Stanley Grenz follows Donald Dayton in using the term "convertive piety" (1991).[7] Convertive piety is an ever returning

---

[6] See Isaäc da Costa, *Bezwaren tegen de geest der eeuw* (Bleiswijk: Tolle Lege, [1823] 1974), Arie L. Molendijk, "Tegen de tijdgeest: Isaäc da Costa's *Bezwaren*, het Réveil en de Verlichting", in: F.G.M. Broeyer, D.Th. Kuiper (eds.), *Is 't waar of niet? Ophefmakende publicaties uit de 'lange' negentiende eeuw* (Jaarboek voor de geschiedenis van het protestantisme na 1800, vol. 13; Zoetermeer: Boekencentrum, 2005); G. Groen van Prinsterer, *Ongeloof en revolutie* [eds. Koert van Bekkum and Herman Selderhuis] (Klassiek licht; Barneveld: Nederlands Dagblad, [1847] 2008), and Vos, "Ligt Europa in Holland?". Cf. the following research papers: Arend Kagchelland, Michiel Kagchelland, *Van Dompers en Verlichten: een onderzoek naar de confrontatie tussen het vroege protestantse Réveil en de Verlichting in Nederland (1815-1826)* (Delft: Eburon, 2009); J.G. Barnhoorn, *Amicitia Christiana: Da Costa en Groen van Prinsterer in hun briefwisseling (1830-1860)* (Bunnik: De Banier, 2009); W. van der Zwaag, *Réveil en afscheiding: negentiende-eeuwse kerkhistorie met bijzondere actualiteit* (Kampen: De Groot-Goudriaan, 2006). See also Allard Pierson, *Oudere tijdgenoten* (Amsterdam: Ton Bolland, [1888] 1982) and especially Gert Mink, *Op het tweede plan: evangelisten in de tweede helft van de negentiende eeuw* (Leiden: J.J. Groen en Zoon, 1995). Cf. also G.A. Wumkes, *De opkomst en vestiging van het baptisme in Nederland* (Sneek: Osinga, 1912) and A.L. Constandse, *Geschiedenis van het Humanisme in Nederland* (Den Haag: Kruseman, ³1980).

[7] Stanley J. Grenz, *Renewing the Center: Evangelical Theology In a Post-Theological*

form of God-centred visibility, of "being a visible saint".[8] The main phenomenological characteristic of the Evangelical movement can be summarized as consistently bringing up the Gospel message as a critique of everything that exists. Evangelicals bring up Christ in order to create corrections in (and the conversion of) the existing spiritual, ecclesiastical and social order.

Theologically speaking, this Christ-centred manifestation can therefore be interpreted as a manner of incarnational thinking. In the same way that Christ, the eternal Word of God, became flesh, His followers are urged to translate God's words into deeds and to be the manifestation of Christ in this world: "As the Father has sent me, I am sending you" (John 20:21). Incarnation is not only the pattern of our salvation, it is also the pattern of the way in which the church should live and experience salvation. Mission implies incarnation, because it is in the notion of incarnation that we see how close Christ came to humanity and even sin. The Apostle Paul states in Romans 8:3 that Christ arrived in the likeness of sinful man (Greek: *en homoiōmati sarkos hamartias*).[9] He was not far removed from sin, but lived very close to it. Human likeness also means likeness to the world. After all, Jesus took on human nature in its fallen form.[10] He entered a sinful world but it did not enter Him. According to Bonhoeffer, Jesus came in the gestalt of abomination, he became the worst sinner (*peccator pessimus*) and it was difficult to distinguish between him and sin.[11]

Era (Grand Rapids: Baker Academic, 2000), 44–50; Ian Randall, *What a Friend We Have in Jesus: The Evangelical Tradition* (London: Darton, Longman and Todd, 2005), 25–41.

[8] Cf. W. van 't Spijker, W. Balke, K. Exalto, L. van Driel, *Spiritualiteit*, 273–339; Grenz, *Renewing the Center*, 26–66, especially 46 n.94.

[9] Romans 8:3, Gr. *ho theos ton heautou huion pempsas en homoiōmati sarkos hamartias*.

[10] C.E.B. Cranfield, *The Epistle to the Romans* (ICC; Edinburgh: T.&T. Clark, 1975), 1:379–382. Cf. James D.G. Dunn, *Romans 1–8* (WBC 38; Dallas: Word, 1988), 421: "Whatever the precise force of the *homoioma* [transcription HB], it must include the thought of Jesus' complete identification with 'sinful flesh'"; John Murray, *The Epistle to the Romans* (NICNT; Grand Rapids: Eerdmans, 1959), 1:280: "He is concerned to show that when the Father sent the Son into this world of sin, of misery, and of death, he sent him in a manner that brought him into the closest relation to sinful humanity that it was possible for him to come without becoming himself sinful".

[11] Dietrich Bonhoeffer, *Wer ist und wer war Jesus Christus? Seine Geschichte und sein Geheimnis* (Stundenbuch 4; Hamburg: Furche-Verlag, 1962), 31 ("Jesus Christus ist … in der Gestalt des Ärgernisses"), 116–117 ("Er ist wirklich für uns zur Sünde gemacht und als der peccator pessimus gekreuzigt" […] "Seine Taten … sind nicht sündlos, sondern zweideutig").

Through the Holy Spirit the missionary church is, like Christ, fully part of this world. Some measure of similarity to the world is therefore unavoidable. The calling of the church starts with incarnation. It starts when the church takes on human, sinful flesh in a contextual sense. A church that follows Christ will want to be as close as possible to sin (Latin: *similitudine carnis peccati*) in order to pick it up and reconcile it with God. This is its all-important priestly calling, to give flesh and bones to the life of Christ in an intrinsically human context. The church should follow Christ's example and be close to sin without becoming sinful. And as the church becomes the flesh of Christ, it enters the culture and assimilates it transformatively, i.e. it makes the world into God's Kingdom wherever possible. In following God's incarnation in Christ, the church is obliged to aim for creative and sometimes daring forms of contextualization.[12] In reality, however, the church often does not get any further than proclamation, even in the Dutch Evangelical movement. Churches and organizations hardly manage to cause a transformation in existing structures.

One of the necessary and daring challenges for the modern Evangelical mind is bringing a full apology of the Christian faith to the forum of public rational thinking by using its very secular words and semantics.[13] First Christian apologists like Justin, Tertullian, Minucius Felix, Athenagoras and others, felt responsible for doing exactly this, viz. crossing the borders of early-Christian narrative, rhetoric and vernacular, and entering the pagan mind-set with an outsider-oriented, deeply contextualized Gospel of Christ. It was their peculiar way of becoming "close to sin" even at the risk of compromising the unique and exclusive character of early Christian confession and revelation. Becoming incarnational meant becoming apologetically relevant for public life and culture.

Paradigmatic for the Evangelical movement is the incarnational yearning for Christ-related corrective revitalization or missionary incarnation. This main characteristic can be observed in the church time

---

[12] Eddie Gibbs, Ian Coffey, *Church Next: Quantum Changes in Christian Ministry* (Leicester: InterVarsity, 2001) 55. Cf. B. Wentsel: "Op de incarnatie rust mede het beginsel van de contextualisatie van het christendom in een eigen gestalte in de cultuur" ("On the incarnation rests, among other things, the principle of the contextualization of Christianity so as to have its own gestalt in the culture"), in: B. Wentsel, *Dogmatiek 3b: God en mens verzoend. Incarnatie, verzoening, koninkrijk van God* (Kampen: Kok, 1991), 208.

[13] Cf. Ivana Dolejšová, *Accounts of Hope: A Problem of Method in Postmodern Apologia* (EHS.T 726; Bern: Peter Lang, 2001).

and again throughout its history. Some examples are the mystagogic figures of Tertullian,[14] Antony the Great,[15] Francis of Assisi, Martin Luther, John Wycliffe, William Tyndale, Geert Grotius, Thomas à Kempis, George Whitefield, John Wesley, Isaäc da Costa, Groen van Prinsterer, and Billy Graham. In their own way, they all "brought up Christ correctively" and aimed for Evangelical presence, i.e. Christ-centred visibility in the church and the world.[16] From a phenomenological viewpoint, the Evangelical movement can therefore be characterized as a reactionary and revitalizing movement. The church has nearly always found such a group of Christians inside, near or opposite itself,[17] and in saying "opposite itself" we are describing the Evangelical movement as a prophetic counter-voice addressing both the church and the world.

2.2. *The Hermeneutics of Distrust*

The movement that originated with the person of Christ and in the context of the Jewish nation, can certainly be characterized as a prophetic, revitalizing movement. Christ and his followers saw it as their task to speak Words of God against the existing temple cult.[18] These words were usually of a corrective nature. From the perspective of religious anthropology, both priests and prophets are needed for the continuation of religious practice. The prophet's task is focussed on warning the religious establishment. The prophet therefore works in an area of tension between tradition and original intention on the one hand, and into what they have developed on the other. The prophet's main task is to correct the priest (and the king) and to call them back to the source.[19] The priestly office represents the *mysterium tremendum et fascinosum*.

---

[14] See H.A. Bakker, "*Ze hebben lief, maar worden vervolgd*". *Radicaal christendom in de tweede eeuw en nu* (Zoetermeer: Boekencentrum, ³2007), 23–141.

[15] See G.J.M. Bartelink, *De bloeiende woestijn: de wereld van het vroege monachisme* (BEC 11; Baarn, 1993), 67.

[16] Cf. Stephen D.C. Corts, *Particularism As an Evangelical Response to Religious Plurality* (Diss. Southern Baptist Theological Seminary, 1991), 354: "The theological orientation of the Evangelicals is clearly Christocentric".

[17] Cf. Olof de Vries, *Gelovig gedoopt: 400 jaar baptisme, 150 jaar in Nederland* (Kampen: Kok, 2009), 24–27.

[18] Mark 14:58. It is interesting that both Stephen and Paul continue this tradition, and are arrested for the same reason as Christ, see Acts 7:48; 17:24 and 21:28–30.

[19] Pieter Boersema, "Het belangrijke onderscheid tussen priester en profeet: een religieus-antropologische reflective", in: Pieter Boersema, Mart-Jan Paul, Maria Verhoeff (eds.), *Gezag in beweging: kerkelijk leiderschap tussen tekst en context* (Heerenveen: Protestantse Pers, 2008), 114. Cf. Günter Lanczkowski, *Einführung in die Religionsphänomenologie* (Darmstadt: Wissenschaftliche Buchgesellschaft, ³1992), 87–89.

As such, it has a tendency to strengthen its power, and in doing so to separate religion from its service to God and its God-given initiative. This is why prophets are more often accused of conservatism than of modernism.

The prophetic movement takes an assessing and critical stance toward an institutionalized religion that looks conservative, but essentially no longer is. If the prophet allows himself to be incorporated into the system, the prophethood becomes a new structure, and one in which the prophet becomes a proclaimer of the word, like the priest. He takes over the work of the priest and is assimilated into the religious structure. He becomes a part of the institutionalized religion and his original task will be taken over by the scholar.[20] If the ministries of priest and prophet are combined in this way, the prophet is essentially being silenced and encapsulated into the religious system. He may produce his own noise, but it will be a sound that comes from within the system and has been adapted to be more acceptable. A prophet who has been integrated into the official religious structure is a compromised prophet who has abandoned his original calling and role in opposition to the existing structure.[21] With regard to the Evangelical movement in the Netherlands, its prophetic fervor was partly lost when its prophetic anti-structure was turned into independent denominations. This is why it is now called *salonfähig*, sits down with the ecclesiastical leadership, and is losing its prophetic power. Pieter Boersema writes:

> A prophet points out shortcomings in religious practice, but he does not offer a new power structure; that is part of the priestly role. As the prophetic movement turns into an institution, it loses its power.[22]

The Scottish religious sociologist Steve Bruce labels structural adaptation to the surrounding culture as ecclesiastical suicide. Anyone who repeatedly adopts contemporary symbols from his surroundings and presents them in the church, essentially puts himself under the authority of those surroundings and creates the impression that he believes in the status quo and even subscribes to it.[23] We must note here that

---

[20] Boersema, "Het belangrijke onderscheid", 117.
[21] Boersema, "Het belangrijke onderscheid", 120.
[22] Boersema, "Het belangrijke onderscheid", 122: "Een profeet geeft tekortkomingen in de cultus aan, maar komt niet met een nieuwe gezagsstructuur, want dat hoort bij het priesterambt. Als de profetische beweging zich institutionaliseert is ze haar kracht kwijt". Cf. Stoffels, "Tussen Alpha en Omega", 3 juni 2002.
[23] See Steve Bruce, in an interview with J.R.A. Dekker in the Reformed newspaper *Reformatorisch Dagblad* of 16 February 2006.

Bruce is an ardent proponent of the secularization thesis and that he sees a gulf between religion and modernity that cannot be bridged. To him, faith and church are strange fossils that belong in some sort of "faith reservation" (hence the term "reservation Christianity"). This way, not only the church but also the unbeliever is faced with two worlds, and the unbeliever will need to step out of his own world in order to gain access to the symbols used in the church. Although Bruce may be right from a strictly sociological point of view, this is a viewpoint that cannot be maintained from a theological point of view. The Christian who strives for transformation should have reservations (difference of opinion) about the cultural clichés that surround him, but he should not end up in a mental reservation (restrictive place). A movement for spiritual renewal that only trusts and accepts the symbols of the world and does not understand the "hermeneutics of distrust" of the Scriptures and the Holy Spirit,[24] will only be able to nod to this world on behalf of Christ, and has lost its prophetic impact.

2.3. *Dutch Evangelicalism as a Polymorphous Caring Movement*

In his study on Dutch Evangelicalism, Pieter Boersema classifies the Dutch Evangelical movement as a movement that not only provides resistance and renewal, but also transforming conversion and care, a movement that goes along with cultural developments and uses contemporary language and symbols.[25] It opposes the existing culture and knows how to take in that culture to a certain degree and how to use it to build God's Kingdom. People look at the Dutch Evangelical movement for comforting gestures and meaningful solidarity to help them survive in a world that is generally harsh and complex. For this reason the ecclesiastical culture is focussed—both liturgically and pastoral-theologically—on "soft" notions such as being loved, being accepted and meaningfulness, and there is a real risk that the quality of this polymorphous care will eventually disappoint people and that the spiritual fabric of the church community will at times be found to be too fragile. In places where leaders use power to prevent the spiritual fabric holding the church together from breaking, the loving atmosphere can change into a threatening and suffocating one.

---

[24] A. van de Beek, *Ontmaskering: christelijk geloof en cultuur* (Zoetermeer: Meinema, 2001), 9–12.

[25] Boersema, *De evangelische beweging in de samenleving*, 19.

Using a minimum of "essentials" that bind them together, various Evangelical churches and organizations often work together to reach both believers and unbelievers with the love and care of the Gospel of Christ. The Evangelical movement is assimilating by nature, for example when it enters churches as an ecumenical fellowship of the heart, uniting Christians. Therefore the Dutch Evangelical movement can be typified as a trans-denominational network of collaborating Christians, a network that often takes a pragmatic and idealistic stance (e.g. by being "seeker-sensitive" and market-oriented), and therefore turns out to be less principled as a movement. Because of this pragmatism, Evangelical networks are often hard to define, and they are often concentrated around Evangelical campaigns, spiritual renewal programmes, visionary leadership, conferences and demand-driven "products". They are consumer-oriented, as with the Evangelical broadcasting company *Evangelische Omroep*. There is an Evangelical "Yellow Pages", a guide with names and addresses of Evangelical churches, organizations, bodies, agencies, etc. At the same time, this polymorphous but sometimes amorphous face of the Dutch Evangelical movement seems to make any typology impossible.

3. Transitions in Dutch Evangelicalism

Recently, some important changes can be observed in the Dutch Evangelical movement. In this section we mention two of them. Both can be explained as examples of a transition towards a more "institutional" or "established" stage on the part of Dutch Evangelicals.

3.1. Less Protest, More Flexibility

Recent research among 282 Evangelically-minded pastors from about 24 groups and denominations in the Netherlands (with an average response rate of 34%), has shown that Evangelical churches today feel little need to be opposed to other churches.[26] Less than half a century

---

[26] Henk Bakker, Teus van de Lagemaat, "De evangelische voorganger in beeld. Landelijk onderzoek naar de opvattingen van evangelische voorgangers in Nederland", Lectoraat Gemeenteopbouw Christelijke Hogeschool Ede (Ede, 2008). This research was carried out among pastors in the Unie van Baptisten Gemeenten (Union of Baptist Churches in the Netherlands), Alliantie van [onafhankelijke] Baptistengemeenten en CAMA gemeenten (Independent Baptist churches and C&MA churches), Leger des Heils (Salvation Army), Kerk van de Nazarener (Church of the Nazarene), and Verenigde Pinkster- en Evangeliegemeenten (Association of Pentecostal and Assemblies of God churches in the Netherlands; these were approached and questioned in limited

ago this was different. Evangelical churches were characterized more by protest, revitalization and restoration than by care.[27] Moreover, more than 80% of the pastors questioned indicated that they had a clear, written statement of faith that includes God, Christ, the Holy Spirit and describes the calling and mission of the church. Interestingly, 46.5% of these leaders indicated that in the past they had been members of a traditional Protestant denomination, 21% of another Evangelical church. Only 27% grew up in the same denomination where they are now leaders. In other words: Evangelical pastors now seem to regard the terms "Evangelical" and "Protestant" more as complementary than as opposing terms.

Evangelical pastors value their own church history, but they also have a strongly valued awareness of their connection with other churches and denominations and with the "Church of the ages".[28] Evangelical churches often lack a clear view on the role of the pastor, but his author-

---

numbers). 282 were directly approached, 180 responded, and 127 completed the questionnaire. It is estimated that there are another 300 Evangelical pastors in the Netherlands who are not part of the orthodox Protestant churches. The results of the questionnaire are based on the responses of 282 pastors, but these are typical—or certainly not atypical—for the roughly 300 who were not approached.

[27] See Sipco J. Vellenga, *Een ondernemende beweging. De groei van de evangelische beweging in Nederland* (Dissertation VU; Amsterdam: VU Uitgeverij, 1991), 238: "De secularisatie dringt het georganiseerde christendom in Nederland verder terug. Christelijke groeperingen kunnen op deze ontwikkeling verschillend reageren. We hebben onderscheid gemaakt tussen vier houdingen: afwending, protest, aanpassing en integratie ... De evangelische beweging is te beschouwen als een protestbeweging tegen deze ontwikkeling; zij verzet zich er tegen door vooral missionaire activiteiten te organiseren, waarin ze haar traditionele boodschap op een eigentijdse en zeer persoonlijke manier aan onkerkelijk opgevoede en seculier denkende mensen probeert over te dragen." (Translation: "Secularization pushes back organized Christianity in the Netherlands even further. There are different ways in which Christian groups can respond to this development. We have distinguished four attitudes: turning away, protest, adaptation and integration ... The Evangelical movement can be regarded as a movement of protest against this development; it resists by organising mainly missionary activities aimed at communicating its traditional message in a contemporary and very personal way to people who have no church education and who think in a secular way.") In 2004, thirteen years after Vellenga's research, Pieter R. Boersema observes that the Evangelical movement is developing into a caring movement, see *De evangelische beweging in de samenleving: een antropologisch onderzoek naar religieuze veranderingen in de Evangelische Beweging in Vlaanderen en Nederland gedurende de periode 1972–2002* – Dissertation defended at the Catholic University of Louvain, Belgium, Faculty of Psychology and Pedagogic Studies, Department of Social and Cultural Anthropology).

[28] 74.0% are very aware of the history of their own church; 70.1% judge having links with non-Evangelical churches as "good", 29.9% believe there are not enough links; 65.1% feel linked to the Church of the ages, and 34.1% believe that even these links could be stronger.

ity—as a desired situation—is subscribed to relatively strongly.[29] 54% of Evangelical pastors rate the Sunday service as the most important church activity, 33% as the second most important. Interestingly, and in discordance with the past, there is room for different opinions about, for example, the historicity of certain Biblical stories (Adam and Eve, Jonah in the fish), ethical issues (homosexuality, cohabitation), theological markers (baptism, speaking in tongues, view on Israel and Judaism), but the pastors fully agree on what they regard as "essentials" such as: (1) personal conversion, (2) the experience of Christ's presence in meetings, (3) the authority of Scripture in teaching and life, and especially (4) the need for flexible mission (i.e. building bridges with groups in their own culture and geographical area).[30]

We observe a diverse range of spiritual catchwords that take the function of group passwords among Evangelicals. A rhetorical sociological analysis will throw up a general picture of how group passwords create social cohesion and which passwords are being used. These are terms that reflect a rhetorical view on religious experience, and summarize it in short phrases. In some cases they take the shape of a motto (a catch phrase or slogan) or an ideograph. Ideographs are normal words or phrases that are used to express normative ideological positions. Examples are *glasnost* [openness] during the time of president Gorbachev, and *yes we can* as used by president Obama. Language can thus become a powerful carrier of religious values and self-descriptions. Ideographs are particularly useful as expressions of a common conviction or emotion when ordinary language is used in a particular context, or to distinguish insiders from outsiders. Ideographs tend to shape the common opinion of the denominations where they are used. They have also been described as "hot buttons" that are dropped during conversations, and as "one term sums of an orientation" that can be sung or chanted.[31] Even though there is no official, normative Evangelical theology, themes and views concerning Scripture, the Second Coming of Christ, being filled with the Spirit, the use of spiritual gifts etcetera, carry a strongly dogmatic and ideographic authority. A term such as *Mara-*

---

[29] 45–60%.
[30] 87% of the pastors questioned feel that it is essential that Christians can point at a clear moment of conversion in their lives; 76% feel that a service is successful only if there is a strong awareness of Christ's presence; 95% feel that the church in all its parts should try to "find the lost" and preach the Gospel to the unchurched and semi-churched. Openness toward culture and environment is therefore of vital importance.
[31] Michael Calvin McGee, "The 'Ideograph': A Link between Rhetoric and Ideology", *QJS* 66 (1980), 1–16.

natha carries great meaning in some Evangelical circles, but hardly at all in others (The emphasis on the End Times, which was prevalent in the Netherlands during the previous century, has almost disappeared). The same can be observed with regard to catchwords and phrases such as *witnessing, Israel, falling in the Spirit, ministry, anointing,* and *the Father Heart of God*. Evangelicals can be observed to make a distinction between "essentials" and "non-essentials", a distinction that is also reflected in the authority ascribed to each ideograph.

In summary, nowadays the Dutch Evangelical movement includes churches and Christians who do not necessarily share exactly the same doctrinal views, but who still confess the same missionary passion and are spreading the Gospel in an often flexible way.[32] Generally, Evangelicals know how to make use of the zeitgeist. God's Spirit is looking for new ways of reaching current generations of the unchurched and semi-churched with the Word of Christ. Methodological flexibility combined with focused missionary behaviour can be regarded as a common pattern for all Evangelicals. It can therefore also be subjected to sociological research. As such, the Dutch Evangelical movement has been able to create a distinct profile for itself in recent years, which is still getting stronger.[33]

3.2. *The Dutch Evangelical Movement's Back Door*

One of the signs of the increasing "institutionalization" of the Evangelical movement is that, at the start of the twenty-first century, it is less critical of the prevailing culture than it was in the second half of the twentieth century. It is changing from the inside, under the influence of neighbouring orthodox (Reformed) churches on the one hand and the prevailing culture of Late Modernity on the other.[34] The decreasing distance between other churches and the surrounding general culture is

---

[32] Generally, the same can be said for Evangelicals in the United Kingdom and the United States; see Randall, *What a Friend We Have in Jesus*, 146–164.

[33] Ton Bernts, Gert de Jong, Hasan Yar, "Een religieuze atlas van Nederland", in: Van de Donk et al. (eds.), *Geloven in het publieke domein*, 108. See see also recent research by Johan H. Roeland, *Selfation: Dutch Evangelical Youth Between Subjectivization and Subjection* (Amsterdam: Pallas, Amsterdam University Press, 2009); Peter G.A. Versteeg, *The Ethnography of a Dutch Pentecostal Church: Vineyard Utrecht and the International Charismatic Movement* (StRS 70; Lewiston, NY: Mellen Press, 2010), and Miranda Klaver, *This Is My Desire: A Semiotic Perspective on Conversion in an Evangelical Seeker Church and a Pentecostal Church in the Netherlands* (Amsterdam: Amsterdam University Press, 2011).

[34] Hijme Stoffels, *Wandelen in het licht: waarden, geloofsovertuigingen en sociale posities van Nederlandse evangelischen* (Kampen: Kok, 1990), 140.

demonstrated in Christians who are leaving Evangelical churches and organizations through the back door. Also in this respect Evangelicalism in the Netherlands is looking more and more like other churches.

The book *Ooit Evangelisch* ("Evangelical some time"), published in 2009, shows the results of research carried out by Otto de Bruijne c.s.[35] There were 136 respondents, 103 of whom qualified for the research. The respondents had been involved in a total of 168 Evangelical churches—this is at least 10% of the Evangelical Churches in the Netherlands—before leaving them. For the purposes of De Bruijne's research, "Evangelical churches" were defined as the full spectrum of free churches in the Netherlands, including Brethren, Baptist, Pentecostal, Full Gospel, Charismatic, Vineyard and like-minded churches.[36] The three criteria for qualification for the research were: (1) the respondent has left this type of church for good, (2) the respondent has previously been going to this type of church for at least two years, and (3) the respondent has consciously stayed away from this type of church for a minimum of two years.

Although the response was rather meagre and the respondents were generally highly educated (78% held a university degree or similar), the research offers sufficient scope for conclusions about the culture within Evangelical churches that leads people who have been wholeheartedly involved in their church for an average eighteen years, to leave through the back door with pain in their hearts. The main reason given for their departure was the stifled atmosphere in Evangelical churches.[37] That which was once the strong side of their church, i.e. the offer of a sense of safety and intimacy, enthusiasm, room for emotions, a flexible structure, and the outspoken assurance that faith offers, was regarded after many years as oppressive, because it was replaced by superficiality, obligation, and feelings of lack of safety and capriciousness.[38]

What troubled the respondents most was the unspoken doctrine of the infallibility of the leader.[39] Due to a lack of clear structures, situations in which the leadership tried to maintain control tended to end in painful confrontations. One respondent describes this type of conflict

---

[35] Otto de Bruijne, Peter Pit, Karin Timmerman (eds.), *Ooit evangelisch: de achterdeur van evangelische gemeenten* (Kampen: Kok, 2009).
[36] De Bruijne, *Ooit evangelisch*, 13: "de breedte van Vergadering der gelovigen, Baptisten, christengemeenten, Pinkster en Volle Evangeliegemeenten, Rafaël, Berea, Vineyard en soortgelijke gemeenten".
[37] De Bruijne, *Ooit evangelisch*, 87
[38] De Bruijne, *Ooit evangelisch*, 88.
[39] De Bruijne, *Ooit evangelisch*, 89.

as a "collision of realities" involving manipulation. The respondents felt that their church was living in a bubble that did not match their daily reality, and that the congregation was expected to keep quiet about this apparent lack of authenticity and to keep believing in the church's spiritual narrative, out of loyalty to the chosen leadership.

> Anyone who thinks ahead and can see that certain things are going wrong, is not regarded as an ally but as a traitor. The theology, the views, ideals and norms of the church clash with people's worldviews and lives.[40]

The closedness of the Evangelical religious system and the leadership structures that have developed as part of it, apparently leave no room for criticism. Minor issues grow into major problems, and can even lead to suspicion and mind control. As suspicion mounts, these Evangelical churches grow into what could be called "greedy communities" or "intensive faith farms", claiming all the time, energy and loyalty of their members.

Most respondents indicated that once they severed their ties with their Evangelical church, the door was slammed closed behind them. They were accused of wrongdoing and in some cases Old Testament style curses were spoken over them. As a consequence, 22 respondents decided they no longer wished to be involved with any Evangelical church and switched to a non-Evangelical church. Around 35 respondents switched to another church that was also Evangelical in its outlook. Around 20 respondents continued without any church, and 9 respondents turned away from the Christian faith altogether.

Looking at these results, De Bruijne makes the general remark that suspicion of intellectualism and rationalism gives the Dutch Evangelical movement a social and theological disadvantage. The researchers point at the lack of theological vision and depth as the lasting negative experience that was mentioned most often by the respondents.[41] Also the "climate of suffocation" in some Evangelical churches can be identified as an undesirable factor, especially because it can cause church members to see God as a suffocating God.

4. *Fusions? Relationships between Evangelicalism and Other Churches*

The Evangelical movement in the Netherlands lives in close symbiosis

---

[40] De Bruijne, *Ooit evangelisch*, 90: "Degene die meedenkt en zaken fout ziet gaan, wordt niet als bondgenoot, maar als verrader gezien. De theologie, de eigen visies, idealen en normen botsen met de werkelijkheid en het leven van de mensen".
[41] De Bruijne, *Ooit evangelisch*, 129.

with other Protestant (mostly Reformed) denominations. This means, on the one hand, that its missionary success is very limited: most members of Evangelical churches have their background in other Protestant churches. On the other hand, Evangelicalism exerts a great deal of influence on older churches. Sometimes it is even seen as a solution for spiritual drought in those churches. In this section we discuss these issues pertaining to the close and dynamic relationship between Evangelicalism and other churches.

4.1. *Incorporation into Existing Dutch Churches*

The Dutch Evangelical movement is a fast moving platform of Christians who wish to bring culture, Gospel and people together, whereby the involvement of culture is felt to be a means to an end and not an end in itself. The Dutch Evangelical movement consciously searches for contemporary means of explaining the Gospel to both Christians and non-Christians in a compelling manner. The organization Youth for Christ, for example, has used the motto *Anchored to the Rock, geared to the times* for many decades as a summary of its policy. Although not all Evangelical groups are happy with this "assimilation" as they see it, the Dutch Evangelical movement is generally very open to its surrounding culture and therefore also to the individualistic zeitgeist.[42] According to Hijme Stoffels, professor of Religious Sociology, the unchurched are now seeing the Dutch Evangelical movement less and less as "different" as a result of this, and large groups of orthodox Protestants are being led into postmodernity.[43] In the early 1990s the Dutch Evangelical movement appeared to recruit mostly people who had grown up in a strong Christian environment. This growth can be explained mainly by the weakening of the organizational structure of the orthodox Protestant world, which started in the 1960s. (Examples of this are the breaking down of religious and sociopolitical barriers in the Netherlands, as well as liturgical unrest and renewal.) Dissatisfaction with spiritual developments in Dutch society and their churches grew, and large groups of people transferred to denominations that were more Evangelical in their outlook and maintained their traditional moral principles. The Evangelical outlook was generally communicated in a clearer and more relevant way, and there was more focus on personal religious experi-

---

[42] Cf. Wil van den Bercken, *Tegen de religieuze behaaglijkheid: een onvroom pleidooi voor het christendom* (Baarn: Ten Have, 2003).

[43] Hijme Stoffels, "Tussen Alpha en Omega: de evangelische beweging op weg naar het einde", a lecture delivered to Evangelische Alliantie, Driebergen, 3 June 2002.

ence. Moreover, there was a general expectation that the existing ecclesiastical market would keep shrinking as a result of the ongoing secularization, and that the Dutch Evangelical movement would have to integrate deeply into the prevailing culture and personal experience of people in order to ensure its own survival.[44]

The continued growth of the Dutch Evangelical movement even now can be attributed to the transfer of individual protestant believers, or even whole protestant families, to Evangelical circles, and by the speedy "Evangelicalization" of existing Protestant churches.[45] In both cases the following description of children from orthodox protestant families applies, as observed by Peter van Rooden while walking to his local train station:

> As I walk to the train station in the city of Leiden in the morning, I come across the children of this small socioreligious group, students at a newly opened auxiliary branch of one of these neo-orthodox secondary schools. They are easy to spot, especially the girls in their long skirts without any hint of make-up. They are the future members of the Evangelical movement, I say to myself. When they are a little older, they will leave their parents' church and join an Evangelical church. They will long for an intense, personal faith, that does not give them a separate social identity. They will want to live in a modern part of town, wear jeans, have barbecues on Sundays, and be a Believer in Christ. This is exactly what the Evangelical Movement offers.[46]

During the 1980s and 1990s, secularization in the Netherlands peaked and the Evangelicalization of existing churches took off, as shown by the fact that the Evangelical songbook *Opwekkingsliederen* was used more and more in the established churches. The growing Evangelicalization of orthodox Protestantism resulted in the gradual incorporation of the Dutch Evangelical movement into the established churches. Although the movement was growing as a result of people transferring

---

[44] Vellenga, *Een ondernemende beweging*, 224–238.

[45] See the discussion in the special issue "Evangelicalisering binnen de gevestigde kerken", Henk de Roest, Sake Stoppels (eds.), *PrakTh* 34/2 (2007), 163–296.

[46] De Roest, Stoppels, "Evangelicalisering in de gevestigde kerken", *PrakTh* 34/2 (2007), 164: "Wanneer ik 's morgens naar het Leidse station loop, kom ik de kinderen uit dit nieuwe zuiltje tegen, die een net opgerichte dependance van een van deze neo-orthodoxe middelbare scholen bezoeken. Ze zijn onmiddellijk te herkennen, vooral de meisjes in hun lange rokken, zonder enige make-up. Daar lopen de aanstaande leden van de evangelische beweging, denk ik dan. Wanneer ze wat ouder zijn, zullen ze de kerk van hun ouders verlaten, en lid worden van een evangelische gemeente. Dan willen ze een innig, persoonlijk geloof, dat geen aparte sociale identiteit met zich meebrengt. Ze willen dan ook in een vinexwijk wonen, een spijkerbroek dragen, op zondag barbecuen, en een "Christusgelovige" zijn. Dat is wat de evangelicale beweging biedt".

from orthodox circles, there was little or no transfer from the secular world. This is undoubtedly a result of the way in which the Dutch Evangelical movement communicated. In many ways the Evangelical faith looked attractive to the conservative churches, but as a social movement[47] in the Netherlands it stood almost completely separate from its intellectual and scientific environments.

Evangelical churches and organizations are still rarely involved in scientific research, such as the study of culture, ethics, history and theology. And in so far as Evangelical churches engage in theological reflection, this is nearly always driven by missionary, denominational or ecumenical interests. Explicit theological concepts and creeds are being reviewed and recalibrated, but again mainly in the interests of the progress of the Gospel. Wide-ranging accounts and apologias, in which the Gospel is compared with science and culture, are a rarity. As a consequence, the Dutch Evangelical movement has to this day not been taken seriously as a social interlocutor (with the exception of the ChristenUnie, a Christian political party, and the Evangelische Omroep, the Dutch Evangelical broadcasting company). In the national debate of ethical, social and pastoral issues, the Dutch Evangelical movement does not offer any new insights. Evangelicals often parrot the existing culture and politics without consulting their religious traditions.[48] As a consequence, the Dutch Evangelical movement has not gained any real ground with regard to the Christianization of people, culture and society, especially not since the start of the twenty-first century.[49] At the moment, Evangelicals do not play a significant role in the public domain, except in the area of care. Evangelical care has managed to put itself firmly on the Dutch map in the past three decades. In many cases it enjoys wide recognition. Two examples are *Stichting De Hoop*, which offers social and psychiatric care, and the social work carried out by Youth for Christ.

---

[47] Vellenga, *Een ondernemende beweging*, 233: "In onze optiek is de evangelische beweging te beschouwen als een nieuwe sociale beweging" ("As we see it, the Evangelical movement can be regarded as a new social movement").

[48] For American Evangelicalism, see in this regard Mark A. Noll, *The Scandal of the Evangelical Mind* (Grand Rapids: Eerdmans, 1994) and R.J. Sider, *The Scandal of the Evangelical Conscience: Why Are Christians Living Just Like the Rest of the World?* (Grand Rapids: Baker, 2005).

[49] Pieter R. Boersema, "The Evangelical Movement in the Netherlands. New Wine in New Wineskins?", in: Erik Sengers (ed.), *The Dutch and Their Gods: Secularization and Transformation of Religion in the Netherlands Since 1950* (Hilversum: Verloren, 2005), 166–167.

4.2. McGrath and the Netherlands

It is typical for the Dutch church situation that the Dutch Evangelical movement was accepted by long-established Protestant denominations and was even incorporated into its ranks. The speedy incorporation of Evangelical faith in existing churches during the 1980s and 1990s has raised the question how this was possible. Alister McGrath assumes that because Protestantism makes a clear distinction between the holy and the secular, between the sacred and the profane, it carries within itself the seeds of subjectivism and atheism.[50] Secularization will therefore continue to spread in Protestant circles, unless the trend is reversed through the influence of Evangelicalism. It is partly through the Dutch Evangelical movement that alternatives have been found for the "dead ends" of Protestant liberalism and horizontalism. According to McGrath, Protestantism will only survive within the boundaries of Evangelicalism.[51] At a global level, the future of the Christian religion is up to Roman-Catholicism, Eastern Orthodoxy and charismatically minded Evangelicalism, because it is only here that the desacralization of creation and the world has made little advance. The removal of the divine and the spiritual from the visible world has not only led to the removal of spirituality from society—resulting in exploitation, activism and capitalism—it has also led to the removal of the sacred from the ordinary. The ordinary as a location of the extraordinary was abandoned.[52] In other words, the ordinary narrative of life, the *petit histoire*, has disappeared behind the rationally correct discourse of the scholastic Protestantism in Modernity.

According to McGrath, the awareness of the sacred in the world has been kept alive in Roman-Catholic circles, but also in the Pentecostal and charismatic movements. Their churches have a resacralizing effect on their environment, in the same way in which eighteenth-century Pi-

---

[50] Alister McGrath, *The Twilight of Atheism: The Rise and Fall of Disbelief in the Modern World* (New York: Doubleday, 2004); cf. Govert Buijs, Herman Paul, "Het einde van het protestantisme", interview with Alister E. McGrath, *Beweging* (autumn 2003), 29–34.

[51] Alister McGrath, *Evangelicalism and the Future of Christianity* (Downers Grove: IVP, 1995).

[52] Cf. Meerten B. ter Borg, "Het gewone als vindplaats van het bijzondere. Religie van alledag of waarom poets ik mijn tanden", in: Rein Nauta (red.), *Vreemd! Varianten van verscheidenheid en verschil in godsdienst en kerk* (Publickslezingen Departement Religiewetenschappen en Theologie 12; Nijmegen: Valkhof Pers, 2009), 108–118, and H.C. van der Meulen, *De pastor als reisgenoot: pastoraal-theologische gedachten over geestelijke begeleiding* (Zoetermeer: Boekencentrum, 2004), 117–153.

etism, as "internal Mission", passed on the connection with the sacred at a time of a strong emerging ideal of Enlightenment. The modern Dutch Evangelical movement knows how to combine a minimum of orthodoxy (right teaching), missionary orthopraxy (right living) and authentic orthohexy (right attitude or inner competency, Gr. *hexis*), anchoring people's faith in their experience and daily life. This is the attractive part of Evangelicalism, and also its *pièce de résistance*.

McGrath's remarks have not remained unopposed in the Netherlands. Especially the ease with which he uses the term "Protestantism" as a general term and almost de-historicizes it, is open to criticism. McGrath seems to believe that "undogmatic" Protestantism is the only true, legitimate form of Christianity. In this regard he agrees with several well-known dogma historians from the German Liberal School (such as Harnack, Loofs and Seeberg) of the late nineteenth and early-twentieth century.[53] However, Harnack's Protestantism is not undogmatic. His form of Christianity is loaded with strong modernist prejudices and one-sided liberal dogmatism. Besides, Protestantism exists in many shapes and gestalts. Especially in the Netherlands, the way in which the Reformed Churches have developed throughout the centuries is unique. Dutch church history is complex and strongly linked to the way in which Protestant churches in the Netherlands today—whether or not influenced by the Evangelical movement—hold their heads high and face the future with an attitude of hope.[54] This is why Antonie Vos wrote the following passionate response to McGrath:

> A theologian needs to take the whole history of the global church and of all parts of the world seriously. If anyone ignores the European continent, he does not work with a true picture of Christianity and Protestantism.[55]

The relationship between Protestantism and Evangelical faith (*evangelisch*) in the Netherlands differs from that in the United Kingdom, Germany (*evangelikal*) and France (*évangelique*).[56] The highly contingent,

---

[53] Antonie Vos, "Is 'het einde van het protestantisme' het einde?", *Beweging* (summer 2004), 5–9.

[54] Cf. Henk de Roest, *En de wind steekt op! Kleine ecclesiologie van de hoop* (Zoetermeer: Meinema, 2005).

[55] Vos, "Het einde", 8: "Een theoloog moet echter de gehele geschiedenis van de wereldkerk en alle werelddelen ernstig nemen. Wie aan het Europese vasteland geen boodschap heeft, werkt niet met een reëel beeld van christendom en protestantisme".

[56] The term "Evangelical" does not carry a strong denominational and theological meaning in the Netherlands. This is different in the UK and in North America, even with several Reformed denominations there who have created a strong profile for themselves. In North America the term "Evangelical" carries an even more po-

sometimes bizarre history of the church in the Netherlands could actually be a reason for hope and expectation, because it indicates that Protestantism in the Netherlands will survive with or without help from the Dutch Evangelical movement. It can stand on its own feet, or in other words: its renewal, vitality and survival are found in its own history, tradition and gestalt.

If we search the most recent centuries of Dutch history, looking for tangible moments and periods when the free flow from the ordinary to the sacred was put under pressure, we observe that in the Netherlands the change took place halfway through the nineteenth century, when Modernism emerged, strongly dividing and partly paralyzing the churches of the Netherlands.[57]

4.3. Bebbington and the Netherlands

Modernity can be described as the belief that there is only one universal rationality linking people from all times and places together, which can be understood and applied anywhere in the world. The Modernist outlook distanced itself from the realm of imagination (including the arts), and was fully convinced that the world can be understood and controlled by way of reason and scientific experiment. It was believed that all details and dimensions of human existence can be explained, even the questions that seem impossible to solve. Mankind was thought to be able to dissect reality. The modernist outlook can therefore be compared with a panoptic point from which every subject can be observed, studied and controlled. In the modernist view, nothing can escape from the all-seeing eye of reason. Modernists believed that they had found the vantage point from which the whole world can be understood and explained. In this context, Dietrich Bonhoeffer quotes Archimedes in his letters from prison: "Give me a place to stand and I will move the earth" (*dos moi pou stō kai kinō tēn gēn*). To Bonhoeffer, this monomanic rationalist attitude was *hubris*, an exponent of the reasoning of Modernity, announcing the failure (and possible death) of the church.[58]

---

lemic and denominational orientation than in the UK. In Germany, "Evangelikal" is a variation of "Evangelisch" (Protestant), though much more defensive of the so-called (orthodox) fundamentals of the Christian faith.

[57] According to McGrath, the turning point for all of Europe was 1840–1870. Cf. J.N. Bakhuizen van den Brink, J. van den Berg, W.F. Dankbaar, *Handboek der Kerkgeschiedenis* (Leeuwarden: De Tille, ⁴1985), 4:141–197.

[58] See Christian Gremmels, Eberhard Bethge, Renate Bethge (eds.), *Widerstand und Ergebung. Briefe und Aufzeichnungen aus der Haft* (Werke 8; Gütersloh: Chr. Kaiser Verlag, 1998), 368–369 and 557.

According to British historian David Bebbington, the international Evangelical movement had a clearly identifiable historical beginning, namely in the 1730s in England, during the Evangelical Revival in London, with John Wesley and George Whitefield, and also in New England in Northampton, with Jonathan Edwards.[59] Bebbington claims that this movement distinguished itself from Puritanism by its activist accents. This activism was given a strong rational basis in the dogma of assurance of salvation. It was possible to establish whether someone was saved by checking their personal experience. In this, theologians such as Edwards and Wesley were influenced by their zeitgeist and had introduced John Locke's pragmatic Enlightenment thinking into their systematic theology. A person was now able to have assurance of his salvation (hence the term "Methodism"). This opened the door to mission and activism as a way in which this assurance of salvation was experienced, worked out and shared.[60] Empiricism cleared the path for activism, and thereby witnessed the birth of the global Evangelical movement.

The Bebbington thesis, although welcomed as plausible by many experts, has also met with some opposition. It is debatable whether there was much difference between the sixteenth- and seventeenth-century Puritans and the eighteenth-century preachers in their teaching of assurance of salvation. In fact, it can be argued that there is a lot of agreement between Puritans and revival preachers in this area.[61] Although the Evangelical movement carried new elements, such as Methodism as a practical movement, a certain amount of continuity between the Age of Puritanism and Evangelical Revival (1560–1660)

---

[59] Cf. David Bebbington, *Evangelicalism in Modern Britain: A History from the 1730s to the 1980s* (London: Unwin Hyman, 1989). Bebbington claims that the Evangelical Movement emerged from the eighteenth-century trans-Atlantic revivals as a new phenomenon. He also claims that the new movement did not develop an antithetical attitude towards the Enlightenment, but instead took over certain elements of it. See the discussion in the compilation of articles in: Michael A.G. Haykin, Kenneth J. Steward (eds.), *The Emergence of Evangelicalism: Exploring Historical Continuities* (Nottingham: Apollos, 2008). Cf. Mark A. Noll, *The Rise of Evangelicalism: The Age of Edwards, Whitefield and the Wesleys* (A History of Evangelicalism; Leicester: IVP, 2004). Cf. David W. Bebbington, *The Dominance of Evangelicalism: The Age of Spurgeon and Moody* (A History of Evangelicalism; Leicester: IVP, 2005). Cf. Henk Bakker, *Draads en tegendraads: leren van de puriteinen* (CHE Reeks; Zoetermeer: Boekencentrum, 2006), 89–122. Cf. Grenz, *Renewing the Center*, 15, 44, 49, 250.

[60] Cf. Teun van der Leer, "Evangelisch dankzij de Verlichting?", *Soteria* 27/2 (2010), 46–50.

[61] Michael A.G. Haykin, "Evangelicalism and the Enlightenment: A Reassessment", in: Haykin, Steward (eds.), *Emergence of Evangelicalism*, 37–60, especially 51, 55–56, 60.

can be observed.⁶² According to Bebbington's classification, both Puritanism and the Reformation can be described as forms of Evangelical renewal,⁶³ and also the *Nadere Reformatie* ("Further Reformation") in the Netherlands during the seventeenth and eighteenth century.⁶⁴ According to several of Bebbington's critics, activism on the grounds of the experience of assurance of salvation existed as early as the sixteenth century. Moreover, the distinction between Puritanism and Revivalism was never made in the nineteenth century. It was invented as late as the twentieth century.⁶⁵ In short, the thesis that the spirit of Enlightenment brought forth and characterized the world-wide Evangelical movement is still controversial. In the original spiritual DNA profile of the notion "Evangelical", the spirit of Enlightenment does not necessarily need to take top position, although it cannot be denied that human ratio does play an important role.

To a certain extent, this is also true for the historical origins of the Dutch Evangelical movement. The first references to the Dutch Evangelical movement are found in the nineteenth century, at the time of *le Réveil*, when the Dutch church tore apart at grass root level, like a field that was ploughed and prepared for a wider, popular "Evangelical" movement that can be regarded as the direct spiritual ancestor of the current Dutch Evangelical movement. The Dutch lived through the nineteenth century with its emerging Modernism in their very own way. So far no thorough analysis has been made of what has been called "revived Pietism" in the Netherlands, i.e. the influence of nineteenth- and twentieth-century Atlantic and transatlantic revivals on the churches in the Netherlands.

5. Concluding Reflections

The Dutch Evangelical movement is at a historical crossroads. Historically, sociologically and also anthropologically it stands in the tradi-

---

[62] John Coffey, "Puritanism, Evangelicalism and the Evangelical Protestant Tradition", in: Haykin, Steward (eds.), *Emergence of Evangelicalism*, 252–277.

[63] Garry Williams, "Enlightenment Epistemology and Eighteenth-Century Evangelical Doctrines of Assurance", in: Haykin, Steward (eds.), *Emergence of Evangelicalism*, 345–374.

[64] Joel R. Beeke, "Evangelicalism and the Dutch Further Reformation", in: Haykin, Steward (eds.), *Emergence of Evangelicalism*, 146–168.

[65] Ian J. Shaw, "The Evangelical Revival Through the Eyes of the 'Evangelical Century': Nineteenth-Century Perceptions of the Origins of Evangelicalism", in: Haykin, Steward (eds.), *Emergence of Evangelicalism*, 302–323.

tion of the prophetic anti-structure, which urges church and nation to return to convertive piety and Christ-centred visibility. If it adapts too much to existing systems and structures, it will be difficult to keep calling it Evangelical in the phenomenological sense of the word.

Using recent figures and research, we have shown that Evangelical pastors see the Dutch Evangelical movement less as a protest movement and more as a caring movement that has no need to oppose the established churches.[66] Late-modern Evangelicals do not take a principled stance in opposition to creeds and tradition. They even leave a lot of room for dogmatic differences and tolerance. This large openness toward the surrounding culture causes the Dutch Evangelical movement to generally use a postmodern framework without offering any answers to complex questions of life and faith, thought and confession, science and reality. Statements of faith generally have ideographic meaning only, and it should be noted that the view on leadership and loyalty is sometimes unspoken and can easily lead to a stifling atmosphere.

Research has also shown that from the 1980s onwards, Evangelical churches and organizations in the Netherlands have increasingly manifested themselves towards the surrounding churches and culture as a polymorphous caring movement. There is a strong focus on the "soft" notions of the Christian faith, such as acceptance, healing, fulfilment and other forms of spiritual care. The "hard" notions that characterized the last century until well into the 1980s—orthodoxy, morals, urgency—seem to matter less. The Dutch Evangelical movement now behaves less like a protest or converting movement, and seems to be able to flexibly adapt both to the existing churches and to its surrounding culture of experience, for the sake of its missionary purposes. Evangelicals connect with church and world in an assimilating ecumenical transfer. They have shifted from challenging the churches and culture around them to being assimilated into them and making themselves comfortable. They also have a growing sense of historical awareness, a growing interest in their own traditions, and they distinguish between "essential" and "non-essential" beliefs, although Evangelicals still hold on to group passwords for internal use.

---

[66] Cf. Olof de Vries, *Gelovig gedoopt*, 230–269. The recent history of the Dutch Baptists also shows that Baptist churches are positioned in between church and movement, and that as soon as "churchification" sets in, a counter movement emerges. For example, post-War ecumenical Baptism was halted between 1963 and 1986. The churchification and ecumenicalism of the Dutch Evangelical movement also elicit opposition.

Because of its largely flexible, time-focussed attitude and comfort-mindedness, the Evangelical movement as a product attracts the interest of the un-churched in a way both significant and limited. In their missionary transfer into existing Christian churches and organizations, Evangelical Christians have brought with them the symbols of the expressively individualistic culture. Outsiders now do not need to leave their own comfort zone when they enter Evangelical culture, and as a result they hardly feel challenged to experience Christian spirituality as "different".

This means that the Evangelical movement has a limited market. It also loses members due to its largely anti-academic (or low-academic) image. It is therefore debatable whether the views of Alister McGrath and David Bebbington hold water for the situation in the Netherlands. Was the Evangelical "flavour" the salvation or the replacement of Dutch Protestantism, and was the Evangelical movement in the Netherlands caused by "enlightened" Modernism? Moreover, how essential is it for the Evangelical movement, indeed, how self-evidently does it match the core values of the Evangelical movement of the "low countries" to be held accountable for a serious and solid *apologia* at the forum of the public world?

Therefore, it is debatable whether the Dutch Evangelical movement can be regarded as the lifebuoy of secularized Protestantism. The Bebbington thesis has definitely not been sufficiently researched and confirmed, at least not for the Dutch situation. When Bebbington states that the Evangelical movement emerged from the rationalism of the Enlightenment's empiricism, he probably has mainly the eighteenth century situation in the United Kingdom and North-America in mind.[67] It is questionable whether an Evangelical theology has been developed in the Netherlands that can safely contain the Evangelical movement as a place of holiness,[68] either at a spiritual or at a rational level. Even in a time of renewed spirituality and resacralization, the Evangelical movement cannot lead Christianity in the Netherlands back to a sense of "première naïveté" (Ricoeur), or even to a second naivety. Once naivety is lost, it's lost forever, and all Christians in the West have, simply by becoming an educated Atlantic citizen, irreversibly moved beyond the

---

[67] Bebbington, *Evangelicalism in Modern Britain*, 74: "The activism of the Evangelical movement sprang from its strong teaching on assurance. That, in turn, was a product of the confidence of the new age about the validity of experience. The evangelical version of Protestantism was created by the Enlightenment".

[68] Cf. Lanczkowski, *Einführung in die Religionsphänomenologie*, 37–44.

possibility of credibly adhering to any uncritical mind-set whatsoever.

Finally, a matter of debate also is whether Dutch Evangelical churches should be ready to take on themselves the role of caring churches, and suffer severe decline in their authentic prophetic role. "Evangelical" essentially means: bringing up the Gospel as a critique of everything that exists. Evangelicals proclaim a prophetic, revitalizing message, and the prophet must avoid taking over the priestly task of proclamation. It is therefore questionable whether the Dutch Evangelical movement should take up the role of a caring church. Would it not be better if it kept its prophetic role in opposition (even in Evangelical politics, but there only in a limited way), if it attempted to both explain and bridge the historical gap between itself and modernity for the sake of the proclamation of the Gospel? We can only observe that Dutch theology is lagging behind in this regard.

Chapter Two

The Evangelical Movement and the Enlightenment

Eveline van Staalduine-Sulman

1. Introduction and Occasion

The Enlightenment started off as a European movement, which soon found its way across the Atlantic.[1] It was linked to various aspects of society, such as urbanisation, industrialisation, and the structure of politics, culture and philosophy, but also to the way in which social life was structured. It influenced all these aspects, but not in the same measure and manner for every group in society and every nation on earth. "Far-reaching variability developed even within the West—within Europe itself, and above all between Europe and the Americas—the USA, Latin America, and Canada".[2] This was partly because the Enlightenment was not developed from one basic idea by one group of people. Right from the start it consisted of various ideas and presuppositions that were all developed further.

> The civilization of modernity as it developed first in the West was from its very beginning beset by internal antinomies and contradictions, giving rise to continual critical discourse which focused on the relations, tensions, and contradictions between its premises and between these premises and the development of modern societies.[3]

Within these modern societies, I should like to focus on Evangelical

---

[1] Adapted from E. van Staalduine-Sulman, "De Evangelische Beweging en de Verlichting," *TheolD* 5/2 (2008), 4–14.
[2] S.N. Eisenstadt, *Fundamentalism, Sectarianism, and Revolution: The Jacobin Dimension of Modernity* (Cambridge: Cambridge University Press, 1999), 198.
[3] Eisenstadt, *Fundamentalism*, 198–199. See also Isaiah Berlin, *Het kromme hout waaruit de mens gemaakt is: episoden uit de ideeën geschiedenis* (Kampen: Kok Agora; Kapellen: Pelckmans, 1990), 191–217, and the description of the intellectual counter-movements against the radical Enlightenment in Jonathan I. Israel, *Radical Enlightenment: Philosophy and the Making of Modernity 1650-1750* (Oxford, New York: Oxford University Press, 2001), 445ff.

churches and trends—which for the purposes of this article we will call the "Evangelical Movement"—and their relationship with various aspects of the Enlightenment. We will concentrate on the situation in the Netherlands,[4] where the Evangelical movement consists of many small groups and churches wedged in between larger denominations in a secularising society. Especially because secularization in the Netherlands took place in a way that was relatively radical and intensive, many people seem to be under the impression that the appearance of Evangelical churches and groups is a return to pre-Enlightenment ideas and practice. In their view, Evangelicals are behind and still need to be brought into conformity with this intellectual consensus. We will look at two examples of this attitude and then delve deeper into it.

In his book *Een kerk met karakter* (Eng. *A Church with Character*), Gerben Heitink wonders what current times have to offer to churches, and what the church has to offer to current society.[5] He briefly describes the developments in the Protestant churches in recent years, often revealing his own attitude towards the Evangelical movement. This can be seen in a statement such as:

> The problem is, however, that many modern believers do not feel at ease with it [the Evangelical movement, EvS], because as children of the Enlightenment they understand faith less as joy and certainty, and more as doubt and uncertainty; this leads to a very different kind of spirituality.[6]

This implies—and I refer not just to this quote, but also to the rest of his book—that Heitink does not see the Evangelical movement as a child of the Enlightenment, but that he believes the Evangelical movement is stuck somewhere in the seventeenth or eighteenth century.[7] This, I will

---

[4] For this reason I quote mainly from Dutch literature about church, fundamentalism and Evangelical trends.

[5] G. Heitink, *Een kerk met karakter. Tijd voor heroriëntatie* (Kampen: Kok, 2007).

[6] Heitink, *Een kerk met karakter*, 167: "Het probleem is echter dat veel moderne gelovigen zich hier [= de Evangelische Beweging, EvS] niet bij thuis voelen omdat zij als kinderen van de Verlichting het geloof minder verstaan als blijdschap en zekerheid en meer als twijfel en aanvechting, wat ook een heel andere spiritualiteit met zich meebrengt". There is a similar claim on pp. 315-316: "Charismatische en evangelische groepen lijken het meest greep te hebben op die geïndividualiseerde beleving ... Maar andere gelovigen [sic] die door de Verlichting zijn heengegaan zullen zich hier in veel gevallen niet bij thuis voelen." (Translation: "Charismatic and Evangelical groups seem to have a better hold of this individualised experience.... But other believers, who have gone through the Enlightenment, will often not feel at ease with this.")

[7] This also implies that everyone who allows himself to be influenced by the Enlightenment by definition turns liberal, Heitink, *Een kerk met karakter*, 66: "Ook in de Gereformeerde Kerken drong de Verlichting door en wel met zo'n typisch gere-

argue, is definitely not a tenable position.[8]

There are also other areas in which established theology enters into debate with the Evangelical movement. Siegfried Zimmer observes in his book *Schadet die Bibelwissenschaft dem Glauben?* (Eng. *Do Biblical Studies Harm Faith?*) that when it comes to our stance on the Bible, there is a deep gulf running through Christianity.[9] In his book Zimmer attempts to bridge this gulf from the historical-critical side. He questions the way in which Evangelicals use the Bible, and in his approach he largely ignores all distinctions between Evangelicals, Fundamentalists and Orthodox Protestants. Perhaps the German *Evangelikal* is more fundamentalist than the Dutch *evangelisch*. Zimmer is right when he states that faith "from cover to cover" goes together with a very selective use of the Bible. He also describes getting the impression, especially from reading the Chicago Statements,[10] that the Evangelical movement ascribes as much authority to the Bible as it does to God. His defence of the historical-critical method consists of a long list of arguments why the book of Job is not historical, but only a play.[11] Nowhere in his book does he manage to explain the relevance of this stance, and as a result his book seems to prove that the fundamentalist prejudice against historical criticism is justified: historical criticism does indeed harm faith! It is as if Zimmer attempts to bridge the gulf by shouting to those on the other side that they are wrong.

---

formeerde ijver dat zij in vrijzinnigheid de Hervormde Kerk naar de kroon staken". (Translation: "The Enlightenment also penetrated into the *Gereformeerde* Churches, even with such typically reformed zeal, that they became even more liberal than the *Hervormde* denomination.")

[8] A few fundamentalist Evangelicals may wish to remain "unblemished", but from the non-fundamentalist side they will be told that their theology has also been influenced by rationalism, see Siegfried Zimmer, *Schadet die Bibelwissenschaft dem Glauben? Klärung eines Konflikts* (Göttingen: Vandenhoeck & Ruprecht, 2007), 47. Charles Taylor, *A Secular Age* (Cambridge & London: Harvard University Press, 2007), 60–61, remarks that pre-modern ideas are often defended with Englightenment arguments. Eisenstadt, *Fundamentalism*, 1–38, unapologetically categorises fundamentalism as "modern".

[9] Zimmer, *Schadet die Bibelwissenschaft*, 1.

[10] Written in 1978 and 1982 by about 300 Evangelical leaders. About the infallibility of the Bible, see N.L. Geisler (ed.), *Inerrancy* (Grand Rapids: Baker Academie, 1980), and about hermeneutics, see E.D. Radmacher, R.D. Preus (eds.), *Hermeneutics, Inerrancy, and the Bible. Papers from the International Council on Biblical Inerrancy Summit II* (Grand Rapids: Zondervan Academie, 1984).

[11] Zimmer, *Schadet die Bibelwissenschaft*, 167ff.

2. The Approach of This Article

In this article, we will look at the approaches we have just identified, and respond to them. First we will look at the general relationship between the Evangelical movement and the Enlightenment, and we will see that this relationship is complex. In some aspects, Evangelicals agree with other, mainly Protestant, churches. In other aspects, the Evangelical movement is ahead or acts like a countermovement. We will take a closer look at Zimmer's criticism, especially at the position of Biblical Studies, and mostly my own field, the Old Testament. We will then see how one-sided both Zimmer and his opponents are and that it is high time for a different approach.

Before looking at the Evangelical movement, we need to make a few preliminary remarks. The Evangelical movement is a broad movement. I have chosen to use a relatively vague definition: the Evangelical movement is the movement that emphasises the life-changing, individual, personal relationship with God, as accomplished by the life and suffering of Jesus Christ. The Evangelical movement seems to be growing broader. The borders between Evangelical and Pentecostal churches on the one side, and between Evangelical and orthodox Protestant churches on the other, are becoming more vague.[12] Within the Evangelical movement itself, there are differences between those who are very close to Calvinism and those who are outspoken Arminians, between fundamentalists and creative thinkers, between strict conservatives (such as the Southern Baptists) and happy-go-lucky progressives (the so-called Liquid Church movement). Finally, outsiders often measure the average Evangelical believer by the standards of the highly-trained Protestant theologian, which is an unfair comparison.[13] We will need to keep these difficulties in the back of our minds as we discuss our subject.

3. The Term "Going through the Enlightenment"

Every person is a child of his times, of his culture, and his local environment. That does not mean, however, that everyone thinks the same way or even has a same mind-set. Everyone's mind-set or paradigm

---

[12] See movements such as the *Evangelisch Werkverband* inside the *Protestantse Kerk in Nederland (PKN)* and the *Charismatisch Werkverband Nederland*. Bart Wallet, "Pinksteren in de kerk", *Wapenveld* 58/1 (2008), 7, writes that the influence on the Reformed should not only be labelled as Evangelicalization, but also as a Pentecostal influence.

[13] Jurgen van den Herik, "Een dampende vrijage", *WeD* 57/7 (2008), 26–27, esp. 26, points this out as well.

is constructed from various elements in his culture and surroundings. Knowledge is not simply heaped up in our minds, it is framed within these paradigms.[14] That research and conclusions drawn from its findings will be influenced by the researcher and his mind-set, especially in the less exact sciences such as history and theology, is therefore inevitable. Arguments are considered within the researchers' paradigms and within each paradigm they will be assigned a different value.

The picture of "going through the Enlightenment," as used by Heitink a number of times, seems incorrect. The Enlightenment is not a tunnel one can crawl through in order to come out at the other end with the truth in hand. It is not simply a road from primitive to developed ideas. If it was, the Enlightenment would be something outside ourselves, a road we could walk up and down. The Enlightenment is more of a broad, general cultural movement with various elements; and that has seeped into us, shaping us all in different ways.[15] The Evangelical movement is not standing outside a tunnel, afraid or unwilling to enter. It happily walks alongside other Enlightenment movements, but choosing its own route from premodern to postmodern.[16]

Let us, in response to Heitink, take a look at the roads that the Evangelical movement has walked and the direction it is taking. The following description of the Evangelical movement is my own as I have come to know it. My impression of the Evangelical movement has largely been influenced by people who used to be Reformed and turned Evangelical, and also by the larger Evangelical denominations, but less so by non-denominational groups. I shall not attempt to prove that some Evangelical theologians are working within the parameters of scientific ideals of modern theologians such as Heitink or that others have been accepted by their liberal colleagues as equals in their field. I could do that by giving a long list of names, but then I would fall into the same trap as Heitink by using a picture that only allows for one route from the Enlightenment to the present. In these postmodern days we can see that there are (and have been) several routes, that our understanding is limited and that we are critical of our own knowledge and potential.

---

[14] Walter Brueggemann, *Texts under Negotiation. The Bible and Postmodern Imagination* (Minneapolis: Augsburg Fortress, 1993), 7. See also Taylor, *A Secular Age*, 36.

[15] Eisenstadt, *Fundamentalism*, 196, talks about "the multiplicity of modern cultural programs and ... their continuous dynamics". See also his *Multiple Modernities* (New Brunswick: Transactions, 2002).

[16] There is also a difference in the speed of response to cultural trends. One group can be faster than others in taking up a particular aspect, but lag behind in another area. See Taylor, *A Secular Age*, 29.

4. Characteristics of the Enlightenment in All Churches

As a child of the Enlightenment, the Evangelical movement has a number of characteristics that can also be found in other Protestant churches. I shall mention five, and it should be borne in mind that these aspects of the Enlightenment have not necessarily been adopted more deeply by the Evangelical movement than by the Reformed Churches in the Netherlands.

The first characteristic, *continuous individualism coupled with the principle of equality*, has found its way into all Protestant and Evangelical churches. None of these churches have a complementary structure, they are all structured as congregations in which all members are in principle equals. Complementarity[17] was a characteristic of the Medieval Catholic church. Different groups of people had different roles in the church. New Testament calls to leave everything behind or to stay unmarried were not equally applied—either literally or allegorically—to all people. Only the clergy were expected to fully take up these calls. They also had to ensure the salvation of the laity. This principle was abandoned in all the churches of the Reformation, including the Evangelical movement, but the latter went further than the first. In the area of faith and life each church member was expected to make a personal choice for Christ and subsequently to be fully devoted.[18] Evangelical ecclesiology usually does not allow for passive members or the semi-churched. At a formal level we often observe congregationalism as opposed to a presbyterial-synodal system.

In some parts of the Evangelical movement, especially non-denominational groups, the leadership tends to be charismatic (with a small "c"), and as a result the principle of congregationalism will at times be put on the back burner. In extreme cases, leaders are regarded as "anointed" in the same way that kings David and Saul were, and therefore untouchable. Yet even this phenomenon is not premodern or complementary, but more like the position of a charismatic politician or a deejay with a faithful following.[19]

---

[17] This term is used by Taylor, *A Secular Age*, 44–45.
[18] All those who have no affiliations with any groups in modern society are still members of society, cf. Taylor, *A Secular Age*, 210, and similarly all Evangelical Christians without any affiliation to any church or group are still members of Christ's body.
[19] Or like modern forms of spirituality and neo-paganism which also have "their authoritative gurus", cf. J.H. Roeland, *Selfation: Dutch Evangelical Youth Between Subjectivization and Subjection* (Amsterdam: Pallas, Amsterdam University Press 2009), 207.

A second characteristic of the Enlightenment is *the implementation of the separation of church and state*. The *Nederlands Hervormde* Church, which was the official state church in the Netherlands for a long time, has had to get used to this, as judged by the slow way in which the "silver cord" between state and popular church was severed.[20] In the Evangelical movement this separation took place in a much more radical way, starting from the time of the Reformation. In contrast with the theocratic picture of the church in the Reformation, the Anabaptists saw the church as an entirely separate congregation of true believers, an institution that was completely removed from all power institutes in society.[21] This conscious "minority theology" led to a number of elements that are relatively typical for the Evangelical movement: (a) adult baptism, because child baptism was part of state Christianity;[22] (b) a devaluation of the Old Testament,[23] because it could be used to support claims to power if the church decided to manifest itself as a nation as did the children of Israel; and (c) pacifism, as a way of obeying the Sermon on the Mount, coupled with the abandonment of any cultural mandate.

Naturally, not every church within the Evangelical movement believes in minority theology or in pacifism as much as the Anabaptists. In times and places where Evangelical churches formed a majority or at least a large minority, the relationship with power has at times been different. And the lack of vision for society as a whole has led to many responses, including the current *Micha-campagne* (Micah Challenge).[24] In the Netherlands, Evangelical Christians have always been in the minority. The cultural mandate that Heitink describes[25] will not be met with any recognition in the average Evangelical church in the Nether-

---

[20] See W.H. den Ouden, *De ontknoping van de zilveren koorde: De geschiedenis van de rijkstraktementen in de Nederlandse Hervormde Kerk* (Zoetermeer: Boekencentrum, 2004).

[21] Christopher J.H. Wright, *Old Testament Ethics for the People of God* (Leicester: InterVarsity Press, 2004), 396–397

[22] An important exception in the Netherlands are the *Vrije Evangelische Gemeenten* (Evangelical Free churches in the Netherlands, who founded the *Bond van Vrije Evangelische Gemeenten* in 1881).

[23] Wright, *Old Testament Ethics*, 397: "The strength of Anabaptist conviction on this matter [baptism, EvS], coupled with the intense heat and severe cost of the controversy, probably led to a sharper devaluation of the Old Testament than would have been intended otherwise."

[24] See www.michacampagne.nl. An example of an earlier counter-reaction is C.F.H. Henry, *The Uneasy Conscience of Modern Fundamentalism* (Grand Rapids: Eerdmans, 1947).

[25] Heitink, *Een kerk met karakter*, 351.

lands, even though there are culturally and politically active Christians even here. As a rule, Dutch Evangelicals believe in a different mandate, *viz.* that of winning followers of Christ and helping them to grow in their faith and commitment. Where Heitink starts his subchapter about culture by writing: "The cultural climate in which we live is still arid," the Evangelical will respond: "It has always been arid for us."[26]

A third characteristic of the Enlightenment is *the ideal of spirit above body*, of spirituality above rituals, of inner obedience above outward appearance, as introduced by humanism.[27] This too is a characteristic of both Reformed and Evangelical churches. In some areas the Evangelical movement has gone less far in this, when we think of its efforts for the abolition of slavery or its fight against alcohol abuse. The work of the Salvation Army is at times very physical. In other areas it was much more radical than the Reformed churches. Communion and baptism are barely recognised as sacraments, and the Salvation Army has even abandoned these two.[28] Some traditional characteristics of the Reformation—Sunday rest, attendance at Sunday services, wearing nice clothes on a Sunday—are seen as outward appearance in Evangelical churches.

As of late, however, a reactionary trend has been observed, and even more so outside the church. A total lack of attention for the body is now regarded as unnatural. The same trend is becoming visible in the church, for example in Biblical-theological writings about the physical suffering of the Psalmist.[29] Also the emphasis on healing within the Evangelical movement fits into this shifting mind-set.[30] Evangelicalism on the whole is taking the same route back towards the body and to experience as modern society does, in contrast to the more established protestant churches.

> Evangelicalism is an experiential religion, which is particularly visible in the way its worship service is designed. The worship service contains a

---

[26] It needs to be pointed out that Heitink has recent secularisation in mind, and the Evangelical his continuous position in the minority. The impact of secularism on the latter is smaller than on the first.

[27] See Taylor, *A Secular Age*, 72 for the humanists and 141ff. for the Enlightenment.

[28] Further to the discussion about fasting in Isaiah 58, some say that the Salvation Army has communion when its members are handing out soup to the homeless.

[29] E.g. in: D.L. Migliore, *Arguing with God: Resistance and Relinquishment in the Life of Faith* (Kamper Oraties 18; Kampen: Theologische Universiteit Kampen, 2001).

[30] For instance in Kees van der Kooi, "Het zuchten van de Geest: De omgang met grenzen in de bediening tot genezing", *BCT* 54 (2004), as quoted by Willem J. Ouweneel, "Theologische vragen rond ziekte en genezing", *BCT* 59 (2008), 2–13, esp. 4.

number of sensational forms (pop music, an atmospheric setting, words and bodily practices) and a discourse on the presence of God. Taken together, these aim to evoke a strong sensory and emotional experience of God. [...] In its way of addressing the embodied subject, evangelicalism differs to those established reformed Protestant traditions which mainly speak to the ear and encourage an intellectual understanding of the sacred.[31]

A fourth characteristic of the Enlightenment is *the emergence of a new view of creation*. Where God, angels, demons, people, animals and objects were still part of the cosmic unity during Medieval times, the Enlightenment has separated God from his creation.[32] A distinction was made between the natural and the supernatural. The difference between God's good intention and how evil crept in was emphasised and evil was viewed as an unnatural phenomenon. The "shapeability" or "malleability" (*maakbaarheid*) of society and humankind was increasingly emphasised. Education and training became important with this regard. They can all be found in the church, including Evangelical churches. God as Creator, separate from creation, is a notion also embraced by Evangelicals. So is evil as an unnatural phenomenon. Education—in an Evangelical theological setting—is playing an increasingly important role in the weekly meetings of church members: Bible study, prayer times, support groups, etc. Especially Methodism is well-known for this.

The last characteristic of Evangelicalism we will look at is *the disappearance of Neo-Platonism from theology and hermeneutics*. Let me mention one example: the exposition of Song of Songs.[33] Until well into the Enlightenment this book was explained as an allegory, partly because of the influence of the Neo-Platonism that has characterised our culture for so long. The book could also be interpreted as describing physical love between man and woman, as pointed out by Theodore of Mopsuestia. His exposition was however rejected at the Fifth Council of 553 AD:[34] the real message was "of course" not about earthly life in

---

[31] Roeland, *Selfation*, 205. See Miranda Klaver, *This Is My Desire: A Semiotic Perspective on Conversion in an Evangelical Seeker Church and a Pentecostal Church in the Netherlands* (Amsterdam: Amsterdam University Press, 2011).

[32] Taylor, *A Secular Age*, 152.

[33] Gillis Gerleman, *Ruth, Das Hohelied* (BKAT 18; Neukirchen-Vluyn: Neukirchener Verlag, 1965), 43–51.

[34] Another attempt at an earthly interpretation was also crushed. Sebastian Castellio (1515–1563), a humanist, was told to leave Geneva because of his literal interpretation. Calvin avocated an allegorical interpretation, as did Luther.

the here and now, but about true love between God and his church. The abandonment of Neo-Platonism did not immediately lead to change. Not until well into the nineteenth century, when Johann Gottfried Herder wrote a book about Song of Songs and applied it to marriage between man and wife, did the earthly interpretation become common.[35]

On this point, the Evangelical movement has needed more time to get into step with historical exegesis—and even now there are still many preachers who read the book Song of Songs within the context of God's love for the Church.[36] Still, during my years as a lecturer at the *Evangelische Theologische Hogeschool* (2001–2007) nearly all the students I met felt that Song of Songs was "of course" only applicable to earthly love and thought it was "silly" to read allegorical sermons about it. Also fundamentalist Bible readers, with their emphasis on the historical truth of each verse, find it strange to read the allegorical expositions of the Church Fathers. They may think that Fundamentalism is the continuation of the old universal theology, but this is not entirely true.[37]

5. *The Evangelical Movement Ahead*

The Evangelical movement made the journey from premodern to postmodern at its own speed, and at times was radically progressive. The notions of individuality, and the separation between church and state, entered the Evangelical churches at an earlier date and are still more strongly present than in the other Protestant churches. Because of this radicalism, Evangelical churches also have a larger interface with current secular society in all three meanings of the word "secular": (a) there is separation between church and state, (b) believers are in the minority, and (c) both faith and the absence of faith are options.[38] It is for this reason that the Evangelical movement does not regard secularization as a terrible loss, as some Protestant churches do.

Also in other areas the Evangelical movement has been more radical in its journey to modernity. Take, for instance, the abolition of special

---

[35] J.G. von Herder, *Lieder der Liebe: die ältesten und schönsten aus Morgenlande: nebst vier und vierzig alten Minneliedern* (Leipzig: Weygand, 1778).
[36] They can now appeal to the "canonical approach", which considers what those who put together the Canon had in mind when they included this book. In any case the greatest Jewish proponent of Song of Songs as a holy book, Rabbi Akiva, read it basically as an allegory.
[37] See M. Sarot, "Fundamentalisme als theologiehistorische categorie", *TNedK* 13/2 (2010), 57–63, esp. 58.
[38] See Taylor, *A Secular Age*, 1–3, for the three definitions of secular.

times and places.[39] In Medieval times, and within Protestantism also in the centuries thereafter, there was a distinction between the sacred and the profane, that was applied to objects, places, times and people. Sunday rest is Protestant—in a stronger measure in the Netherlands than in the countries surrounding us—but not Evangelical. Special regard for church buildings is definitely not Evangelical. Evangelicals often meet in schools or theatres. Evangelical clergy do not wear clerical dress during church services. Certain Evangelical groups do not even celebrate Christmas. Similarly, the Apostolic times are given equal treatment. Many see them not as exceptional—even though they are held to be normative—but as a time of beginnings. Tongues, healing and supernatural signs are not regarded as limited to those days, as in traditional Protestant theology, but as continuing in our days.

The combination of individuality and minority thinking has also led to more emphasis on personal interpretation of the Bible without regard for tradition, which is seen as "unnecessary ballast". The traditional organ can be replaced by a band. Evangelicals read an eclectic choice of theological and devotional books from a variety of traditions and countries. Because of the radicality of the Evangelical movement, there is no separate Evangelical youth culture. And because of the absence of firm ties above the local level, there is also more room for globalizing trends. Dutch Evangelical Christians often feel equally connected with Evangelical churches in China as with Baptist churches in the Netherlands.

Before and immediately after the Second World War, the Netherlands were characterised by the compartmentalization (*verzuiling*) of society. The breakdown of these sociopolitical compartments was regarded by the Protestant churches partly as liberating, partly as destructive. New organisations that did not fit into one of the societal compartments but overlapped with several instead, were welcomed. The use that the Evangelical movement made of decompartmentalization (*ontzuiling*) was one of the aspects in which it was going with the times. Para-church organisations such as Youth for Christ, the Evangelical broadcasting company *Evangelische Omroep*, *Stichting Opwekking*, the Navigators and Campus Crusade for Christ, as well as para-church youth and family conventions such as *EO Jongerendag*, *EO Familiedag*, *Flevofestival*, and finally the mega youth churches, fit in with the recent trend to attend mass meetings. They create an ecumenical "fellowship of the heart" without the need for churches to merge or formally collaborate.

---

[39] Taylor, *A Secular Age*, 54–59, discusses the shift from special times, places and objects to their equalization.

Some Evangelical characteristics that were regarded as "odd" in modern times, are suddenly becoming strong points in our postmodern days. The absence of systematic theology in sermons, combined with the emphasis on personal experience, is appreciated by a lot of young people. Maintaining the notion of a personal God[40] and the literal interpretation of the miracles in the Bible fit with the current renewed interest in the mysterious and supernatural.[41] The "old-fashioned" emphasis on sin, the powerlessness of people to develop or redeem themselves and the acceptance of God as transcendent and humankind as knowing little about Him, fit with the end of positivism.[42] The radical message and the simple evangelistic approach are effective in the religious market: it is clear what the Evangelical movement stands for.

Another area in which the Evangelical movement is ahead is the social aspect of church life. Many Evangelical churches can be found in medium-sized and large towns and cities. They have a structure that fits the social needs of town dwellers. Evangelical churches are as good as—and sometimes better than—Reformed churches at meeting social needs. Kuitert gives the following description:

> ... what emigrants in foreign countries experience in the church and what country people experience in town: a sense of belonging, of having and finding acquaintances in a place where one only meets strangers: a village in a city. The Christian church is not the only institution that offers this quality of living, but it is offering it, and it is well equipped to do so.[43]

Kuitert believes this social aspect is only a secondary task of the church, but his impression is that it is becoming more significant:

---

[40] However, there are also liberal theologians who maintain the view of a personal God; see, for instance, Eginhard Meijering in an interview with Dick Schinkelshoek, "Verlangen naar een volle kerk", *Nederlands Dagblad* (1 maart 2008), ZOZ 5. He says that an impersonal view of God does not help to make the likelihood that God exists more convincing: "Ook als mensen daarvan overtuigd zijn, hebben ze nog steeds geen behoefte aan Hem." (Translation: "Even if people are convinced of that, they still do not have a need for him.")

[41] See Coert H. Lindijer, *Op verkenning in het postmoderne landschap* (Zoetermeer: Boekencentrum, 2003), 94–111. Think, for instance, of the revival of the *Narnia* books by C.S. Lewis, *The Lord of the Rings* by J.R.R. Tolkien, the success of series such as *Harry Potter* and *Twilight* and all kinds of horror films.

[42] See Lindijer, *Op verkenning*, 24–25.

[43] H.M. Kuitert, *Jezus: nalatenschap van het christendom. Schets voor een christologie* (Baarn: Ten Have, 1998), 283: "... wat emigranten in den vreemde aan de kerk beleven en plattelanders in de grote stad: ergens bij horen, bekenden hebben en bekenden krijgen in een oord waar enkel onbekenden je pad kruisen: een dorpje in de grote stad. De christelijke kerk is niet de enige instantie die voor deze bewoonbaarheid zorgt, maar ze is er ook, ze is er zelfs goed voor geëquipeerd".

That may well be a secondary task of the church, in actual practice it is becoming more and more of a practical main task, the most attractive aspect of being church.[44]

In Evangelical ecclesiology, however, this does not appear to be a "secondary task". Passages about the body of Christ (Rom. 12; 1 Cor. 12), the unity of the church under the headship of Christ (Eph. 4) and the church as a family (Eph. 2), are not just seen as by-lines, but emphasised instead. The church is the body of Christ and as such it has a social task,[45] as expressed in various church structure models.[46]

6. *The Evangelical Movement as a Counterculture*

If the Evangelical movement is a modern or postmodern movement in so many ways, then why do so many theologians describe it as old-fashioned? Van der Herik wonders: "Why is there no thorough analysis of the question why Evangelical theology appears to hit us where it hurts?"[47] This question can be approached from at least two sides. In my opinion, we first need to look at the emotional side of this issue. Many modern theologians come across elements of the Evangelical message that resemble what they have only recently conquered themselves: the positivist assurance and certainty of faith that met with so much resistance in the 1950s and 1960s, and pietistic godliness with all the fretting that it always seems to cause.

Many theologians have a disdain for Evangelical joy and radicalism. It seems in flagrant opposition to their own position of entanglement in the tentacles of secularization. Where Protestant and Catholic theologians from Europe allow the appeal of secularization to penetrate into their own lives so that they too experience the pain of doubt, they see an emerging ease within the Evangelical movement, which is partly fed by American optimism and at times also from other foreign countries. While they themselves are caught in a painful disorientating process,

---

[44] Kuitert, *Jezus*, 284: "Dat mag honderd keer een bijfunctie van de kerk zijn, ze is in de praktijk, ik durf wel te zeggen: hoe langer hoe meer, een praktische hoofdfunctie, de meest aantrekkelijke, aansprekelijke factor van het kerkzijn".

[45] This social aspect was of great importance to people from other churches who converted to Evangelicalism, see Otto de Bruijne et al., *Ooit evangelisch: de achterdeur van evangelische gemeenten* (Kampen: Kok, 2009), 33–34.

[46] For the latest trends, see the special issue "Ecclesiologie" of *Soteria* 27/3 (2010).

[47] Van den Herik, "Een dampende vrijage", 27: "Waarom ontbreekt deugdelijke analyse over de vraag hoe het toch komt dat evangelicale theologie blijkbaar soms op een pijnlijke plek drukt?".

Evangelicals seem to happily throw themselves into a phase of orientation or reorientation.[48] It seems that the pain of secularization in all its facets has not penetrated into the lives and thoughts of Evangelical believers and theologians.

"Ordinary" members of the Reformed churches, however, are attracted to Evangelicalism because of this pain. In their own church they miss the certainty of faith, the intense piety of radicality and the joy that they observe in Evangelical churches.[49] I found a sympathetic description of this painful reality as observed from the more liberal viewpoint, in the novel *The Promise* by Chaim Potok, where the main character, Reuven, says about the gulf between himself and ultra-orthodox Jews: "I wish they weren't so afraid of new ideas". His father answers by asking, "You want a great deal, Reuven. The Messiah has not yet come. Will new ideas enable them to go on singing and dancing?" "We can't ignore the truth, abba." "No," he said. "We cannot ignore the truth. At the same time, we cannot quite sing and dance as they do." He was silent a moment. "That is the dilemma of our time, Reuven. I do not know what the answer is."[50]

Probably, the emotional rejection of the Evangelical movement also contains an element of impatience. Many modern theories of the 1950s and 1960s claimed that, given time, everybody would embrace all aspects of Western society.[51] This may not have been expressed explicitly, but it was implied in statements such as, "They are not ready yet", and, "We are ahead in this". It must indeed be painful for them to observe now, fifty years later, that not everyone has modernised in equal measure and that they are not ahead in the sense that everyone is following. It would perhaps be better to observe that different groups have modernised in different ways, and that within modernity there is a lot of scope for variety.[52]

Perhaps, the Evangelical movement within the Protestant Churches appals theologians by not being "politically correct" anymore. They seem to reject the Enlightenment ideals and culture, which were care-

---
[48] For the terms orientation, disorientation and reorientation within spirituality, see Walter Brueggemann, *Spirituality of the Psalms* (Minneapolis: Augsburg Fortress, 2001).
[49] C.f. also the reasons that people gave when asked why they left their original church and transferred to an Evangelical church: De Bruijne et al., *Ooit evangelisch*, 32–33.
[50] Chaim Potok, *The Promise* (New York: Anchor Books, 1969, 1977), 312.
[51] See Eisenstadt, *Fundamentalism*, 196.
[52] See my first section.

fully achieved. They do not consider every opinion as equal, they claim to be right. They do not ask for a dialogue with other religions, they choose to evangelize. They do not want to restrict themselves to the official Songbook, the *Liedboek voor de Kerken*, although these songs are textually and musically justified. They sing songs of the worst sort! In spite of all the beautiful words and poetical phrases in the protestant churches, people can amazingly be touched by the rhythm and the simple language of Praise Songs. This phenomenon runs partly parallel to the popular political parties in the Netherlands, who also do not want to be politically correct anymore. They are done with continuous correctness and with not saying what they still feel inside. They are post-Enlightenment parties.[53]

A second part of the answer lies in the rational realm. At some points, the Evangelical movement did not go with the flow of modern times, but positioned itself as a counter-movement, especially with regard to rationalism and historicism. Rationalism uses human rationality as a tool and calibration point in its acquisition of knowledge. This movement accepts very little that does not need any rational underpinning. That has led to what is currently called "foundationalism",[54] and to investigating everything within its historical context.[55] In opposition, fundamentalism emerged at the other end of the spectrum, both within and outside the Evangelical movement. Marcel Sarot describes this as "not the holding on to a traditional position", but rather as "a reaction to foundationalism".[56] He defines fundamentalism as a rationalist movement:

> Fundamentalists are modern through and through: they are foundationalists who accept the Enlightenment axiom that our knowledge needs to be built on reliable foundations. They go against the flow of modernity with their assumption that the Scriptures as God's *infallible, inerrant* Word can be such a foundation. This position is however not premodern. It was born from modern influences. We can therefore define fundamentalists as modern foundationalists who accept religious presuppositions as their basic propositions or fundamental knowledge."[57]

---

[53] Described by Bas Heijne, "Het populisme keert zich tegen de Verlichting—niet geheel onterecht", *Opinie & Debat, bijlage bij NRC Handelsblad* (31 Dec. 2010/1 Jan. 2011), 1–3.

[54] Sarot, "Fundamentalisme", 60.

[55] Albeit with the exception of their own statements. This contrasts with postmodernism, which places everything, including the subject itself, in its historical context.

[56] Sarot, "Fundamentalisme", 62.

[57] Sarot, "Fundamentalisme", 62: "Fundamentalisten zijn door en door modern: het zijn funderingsdenkers die het Verlichtingsaxioma accepteren dat het gebouw van

Traditional and fundamentalist rationalism also have elements in common. Both have left the church and its authority behind. Fundamentalism sees the Bible as the ultimate authority—often without realising that its interpretation is also determined by ecclesiastical authorities—whereas historical criticism sees reason as the ultimate authority—sometimes without realising that new authorities have been introduced, such as men with titles and togas.[58] Both start from the written text. Stanley Hauerwas even states that fundamentalism and historical criticism are two sides of the same coin at this point: "Both change *Sola Scriptura* into "sola text". They think they can read a text without moral leadership and spiritual education."[59]

With regard to Biblical studies, the Evangelical movement—its fundamentalist branch included—takes a different position from historical criticism, as it is based on different presuppositions and interests. Where historical criticism asks for the historical reality behind the text, the Evangelical movement takes the equality of believers and its view of the Bible as "a letter from God to you" as its starting points.[60] In that sense it is a closer match with pietism, romanticism or existentialism, because of its emphasis on individual experience and the longing to the return to paradisical harmony between God and humankind. This difference in presupposition fits the interests of both sides. Theology as taught in universities wants to be taken seriously and feels compelled to follow the rationalistic interpretation of history.[61] It needs to carry

---

onze kennis op betrouwbare fundamenten moet worden opgetrokken. Zij roeien tegen de hoofdstroom van de moderniteit in met hun aanname dat de Schrift als Gods onfeilbaar (*infallible*) of foutloos (*inerrant*) Woord zo'n fundament kan zijn. Toch is deze positie niet premodern. Zij zelf onder invloed van de moderniteit ontstaan. Wij kunnen fundamentalisen dus definiëren als moderne funderingsdenkers die religieuze uitgangspunten als basisproposities of fundentele kennis accepteren".

[58] Brueggemann, *Texts under Negotiation*, viii. He writes about the authorities of historical criticism: "Thus the new intellectual hegemony of male certitude (unencumbered by the body) fostered a political-economic hegemony, whereby the 'disinterested', 'objective' ones at the center could dominate the margin. That 'objective' control was supremely masculine in its perception and domination" (4–5) and about objectivity in science: "an agreement of everyone in the room", whereby he notes that not everyone was allowed in (8).

[59] Stanley Hauerwas in an interview with Herman Paul and Bart Wallet, in: *Wapenveld* 58/1 (2008), 24–25.

[60] See the beautiful description of Bible Study in Evangelical circles, including his points of critique, in: A.W. Zwiep, "Onderweg naar morgen: hermeneutische bespiegelingen vanuit een 'post-conservatief Evangelical' perspectief", in: G.C. den Hertog, C. van der Kooi (eds), *Tussen leer en lezen: de spanning tussen bijbelwetenschap en geloofsleer* (Kampen: Kok, 2007), 33–54.

[61] Brueggemann, *Texts under Negotiation*, calls the historical-critical method the

out its research while leaving God and divine intervention out of the equation. Only what can be observed by humans counts. Theology has become part of the study of *Humanities*, forced to use the methods of other subjects.[62] It also wants to be free from ecclesiastical interests and therefore needs to question tradition.[63] Currently there is also the financial impetus from subsidizers—such as NWO, the Dutch Organization for Scientific Research—to take a descriptive-historical or textual approach, rather than a normative, dogmatic, Biblical-theological or ethical one.

The Evangelical movement, however, serves the interests of the "ordinary people" rather than those of rationalism.[64] Because it feels that each person should be able to have a personal relationship with God and needs to be educated through Bible study to become a follower of Christ, it has a strong requirement for a Bible that can be read and understood by all and for all believers to be taken seriously. Evangelicals are also more convinced of the sinfulness of humankind, including its ability to reason.[65] The fruits of nineteenth-century positivism, when the Evangelical movement emerged as an independent movement in Europe, were not all good. More knowledge did not lead to a better life. Science turned against the Bible. Enlightenment politics did not lead to more peace, but to a twentieth century filled with warfare.[66]

The Evangelical movement has found an interface with "positive thinking", an American movement that attempts to lift people out of their problems by having them think positively. This fits in with the American culture of freedom and self-fulfilment, the "American dream".[67] Freedom is expressed by informality and lack of official documents and traditions, but also by talking about one's own choice for

---

"practice of modernity" (viii) which is as much culture-bound as all other trends (p. 1).

[62] See Israel, *Radical Enlightenment*, 200, 208, 388.

[63] How onesided this approach is, is clear from the general overview of approaches in Old Testament studies, as listed in the back of Richard N. Soulen, R. Kendall Soulen, *Handbook of Biblical Criticism* (Louisville: Westminster John Knox Press, ³2001).

[64] See also K.R. Trembath, *Evangelical Theories of Biblical Inspiration: A Review and Proposal* (New York, Oxford: Oxford University Press, 1987), 74–75.

[65] Against thinkers like Lodewijk Meyer, who considered philosophy as the "infallible" and only criterion for interpreting Scripture; see Israel, *Radical Enlightenment*, 197ff. And against branches of reformed Protestantism "which distrust the body, the senses and the emotions as means of accessing the sacred", cf. Roeland, *Selfation*, 205.

[66] See also Brueggemann, *Texts under Negotiation*, 6–7.

[67] A lot of information about the Evangelical subculture can be gleaned from Charles Groenhuijsen, *Amerikanen zijn niet gek* (Amsterdam: Balans, ²2007).

Jesus and one's own spiritual life and convictions.⁶⁸ With respect to self-fulfilment, "evangelicalism accepts and even nourishes a lifestyle orientation that is bound up with a popular culture which is defined by the moral ends of pleasure, happiness and self-fulfilment."⁶⁹ It does not focus on painting a ponderous picture of reality, like European Enlightenment theologians tend to do, but on imagining a counter-reality—and this is straight from the Bible—a different way of looking at reality as it is and at reality as one would like it to be.⁷⁰ This imagination is often a part of American rhetoric. Unfortunately, however, both fundamentalists and their liberal opponents tend to take this rhetoric literally.⁷¹

The continuous stream of mutual criticism has hardened both movements. In that regard fundamentalism can be seen as the "unpaid bill" of the unlimited adaptation of scientific theology to the cultural requirement to doubt everything, including what the Bible says. Evangelical young people were even discouraged by their peers from studying theology, even if they had a real desire to do so.

7. Biblical Studies

Let us now look at the gulf between the Evangelical movement and historical criticism that exists in the area of Old Testament studies. When young Evangelicals decide to study theology—and these days they are no longer an exception—they will often listen to their Old Testament lecturers in bewilderment. At home they have learned to look at the text in its entirety (the *Letztgestalt*) and in its canonical context, and not to split it into different sources. In sermons in their home churches, preachers try to derive the author's message from his line of thought or

---

⁶⁸ "...one's involvement is described as a choice and one's religious stance as one's own conviction." Roeland, *Selfation*, 207. See also the contributions of Van der Kooi (chapter eight) and Vos (chapter nine) in this volume.

⁶⁹ Roeland, *Selfation*, 208-209; see also 212.

⁷⁰ Although he is not an Evangelical, Walter Brueggemann says something similar about the "counterworld of evangelical imagination" in *Texts under Negotiation*.

⁷¹ For instance, liberal preachers in "Pleidooi voor orthodoxie en vrijzinnigheid", *WeD* 57/5 (2008), 20-21, take statements by M. Zandbergen, an Evangelical pastor, literally without putting him into context: "Ons baart zorg dat men er zelfs trots op is niet in gesprek te zijn met wetenschap, cultuur en technologie." (Translation: "We are concerned that people are even proud of not conversing with science, culture and technology") However, Zandbergen responds to people who allow themselves to be dictated by culture and science too much. The situation is comparable to the current discussion about Islam that is taking place in Dutch society. Both Muslim fundamentalists and fierce opponents take every word of imams literally. The rest of the world—Western and non-Western—only regard them as good or bad rhetoric.

from the direction the story takes, even though this message may be presented in a fragmentary or dogmatic way. Evangelicals who study theology hope to find a scientific entry point into the meaning of the texts, preferably one that is better than they have heard in their churches. They hope to be offered methods of interpreting those texts and of finding responsible applications in the present.

At university, all this seems to be rather irrelevant. Students are often presented with something quite different: a historical-critical approach to texts that makes them wonder what relevance the outcomes have for Bible reading in church and private devotions. Old Testament studies will look for the facts behind the text. Their methods of interpreting Scripture resemble the methods of investigating any other ancient text.[72] The texts themselves—the *Letztgestalt*—are often overlooked, and very little attention is paid to their rhetoric.[73] Jan Fokkelman, not himself an Evangelical but wrestling with the same questions, writes about this:

> This approach (...) used to focus on the question, "Where does the text come from?", and it often carried an undertone of suspicion. There was a strong conviction that one can only interpret a text after a reconstruction of its genesis has been made that is as complete as possible. The result was that for more than two centuries [theologians] have speculated about questions such as: how many hands have worked on this text, what sources were available to the author (rather than the editor), and what were his influences. It is now becoming ever clearer that "the mountain has brought forth a mouse": the answers vary more and more, and a consensus about the genesis of most texts is further removed from us than ever. The results of this research remain completely hypothetical, and they fill up fat and especially dull commentaries that have discouraged many users, even to this day. The research into the history behind the texts has some degree of legitimacy—after all, asking questions does not harm anyone—but it has become misleading because no time was given to the central question of Bible exposition.[74]

---

[72] Spinoza suggested that the method of interpreting Scripture should not differ from the method of interpreting nature; see Israel, *Radical Enlightenment*, 242–257. Meanwhile, we see a difference in degree between sciences and humanities with regard to interpreting patterns and statistics; so R. Bod, *De vergeten wetenschappen: een geschiedenis van de humaniora* (Amsterdam: Bert Bakker, 2010), 433–435

[73] Brueggemann, *Texts under Negotiation*, 5–6, about this field: "[W]ith its practice of historical criticism, it has sought validation in facticity behind the text. The outcome of such procedure is that the texts themselves are largely dismissed, and words themselves do not count for much. So there is in modernity a resulting dismissal of rhetoric as 'mere rhetoric' and the discounting of speech."

[74] Jan Fokkelman, "Algemene Inleiding: Oog in oog met de tekst zelf", in: Jan Fokkelman, Wim Weren (eds.), *De Bijbel literair: Opbouw en gedachtegang van de bijbelse geschriften en hun onderlinge relaties* (Zoetermeer, Kapellen: Meinema & Pelckmans,

Brueggemann may be gentle with his remark that the lack of consensus is caused more by the ability (or lack of it) of the Bible writers than of "scholarly confusion",[75] but we should really consider whether a method that leads to various different answers is valid, or whether scholars within the historical critical approach use the same method at all. Moreover, hardly any researchers offer conclusions about the meaning of the text as a whole or the meaning of particular texts for today's reader. The gulf between then and now seems absolute. Also the Reformed churches that had their preachers educated at state universities came to the conclusion that the gulf between a historical-critical reading of the Old Testament and day-to-day ecclesiastical work is widening. This has led to counter-movements—and not only in Evangelical circles—such as the so-called *Amsterdamse School*, and to the introduction of terms such as "second naiveté"[76] and the flight to forms of spirituality that have no historical basis.[77]

8. *The Other Side of the Gulf*

In the Evangelical movement, Bible exposition has followed a differ-

---

2003), 11: "Deze benadering (...) stelde de vraag centraal 'waar komt de tekst vandaan?' en dat had meestal een ondertoon van wantrouwen. Men was er heilig van overtuigd dat je pas tot interpreteren van een tekst in staat bent als je eerst een zo volledig mogelijke reconstructie van zijn wordingsgang hebt gemaakt. En dat had tot gevolg dat men meer dan twee eeuwen fanatiek gespeculeerd heeft over vragen als: hoeveel handen hebben aan deze tekst gewerkt, welke bronnen had de schrijver (eerder een redacteur) tot zijn beschikking, en onder welke invloed stond hij? Het wordt thans steeds duidelijker dat de berg een muis heeft gebaard: de antwoorden liepen steeds verder uiteen, en een consensus over de ontstaansgeschiedenis van de meeste teksten is verder weg dan ooit. De resultaten van dit onderzoek blijven louter hypothetisch, en ze vullen dikke en vooral dorre commentaren die vele gebruikers hebben ontmoedigd, tot vandaag de dag toe. Het onderzoek naar de voorgeschiedenis heeft een zekere legitimiteit—vragen staat immers vrij—maar het werd misleidend omdat men in wezen niet meer aan de centrale vraag van het Bijbel uitleggen toe kwam".

[75] Walter Brueggemann, *David's Truth in Israel's Imagination and Memory* (Philadelphia: Fortress Press, 1985), 121 n.8.

[76] See Heitink, *Een kerk met karakter*, 242. See also M.I. Wallace, *The Second Naiveté. Barth, Ricoeur, and the New Yale Theology* (SABH 6; Macon: Mercer University Press, 1990, ²1995).

[77] Kick Bras, "De Bijbel lezen met je hart," *Bodem* 1 (Feb. 2008), 17–21, esp. 18: "De wetenschap lijkt zich nogal eens te verliezen in de reconstructie van historische gegevens die ver af staan van ons huidige leven. De "gewone" gelovige die inspiratie zoekt en versterking van zijn of haar spiritualiteit voelt zich nogal eens in de kou staan." (Translation: "Science seems to often lose itself in the reconstruction of historical data that are too far removed from our current lives. The "ordinary" believer looking for inspiration and the strengthening of his or her spirituality, will often feel left in the cold.")

ent route. It was more a matter of Bible use and giving meaning to it, than of exegesis.[78] However, over the past few decades there have been numerous attempts to couple traditional individual Bible use by Evangelicals to scientific methods.[79] Subjects such as linguistics, philosophy of language, hermeneutics, literary or structural analysis of stories, and the historical context of Bible passages all are addressed in Evangelical theology, as demonstrated by, for example, the articles that have recently appeared in the Dutch quarterly for Evangelical theological thought *Soteria*.

It remains important, however, that the "ordinary" believer should benefit as well; that historical-critical results can be incorporated in our faith. In that regard the Evangelical movement is still a counter-movement. To take but one example, in the special edition "Bijbel en bijbelgebruik" ("Bible and the way it is used") of *Soteria* (2008), De Vries opens with the statement that words do not have a permanent single meaning, but that the meanings of words develop throughout time. He goes along with linguistic philosophy, but also with the Evangelical habit of addressing the ordinary reader:

> Biblical words travel through the history of salvation, on their way to fulfilment in the Eschaton. On the way there, the meanings of those words will try to find their realisation in each new historical context. The reader/hearer of the Bible text also has his place in this history. While he is reading, he needs to understand his own place in that history. Once that happens, the text becomes meaningful to him.[80]

Two responses to this article point to other issues within the Evangelical movement. An article entitled "Can historical research and charismatic exposition go together?", the believer's experience is introduced

---

[78] See the examples in Olof de Vries, "Méér dan de letter: Over de viervoudige Schriftzin, heilshistorisch verstaan", *Soteria* 25/1 (2008), 7–17.

[79] By, amongst others, Gordon Wenham, Richard Bauckham, Robert Gordon, Hugh Williamson, Gordon McConville, John Stott, Alister McGrath, Anthony Thiselton, Tom Wright, Miroslav Volf, Stanley Grenz, James McClendon jr., Kees van der Kooi, Arie Zwiep, Henk Bakker, Stefan Paas.

[80] De Vries, "Méér dan de letter", 15: "Bijbelwoorden reizen door de heilsgeschiedenis, op weg naar hun vervulling in het eschaton. De betekenis van die woorden zoekt onderweg een verwerkelijking in elke nieuwe historische context. In deze geschiedenis heeft ook de lezer/hoorder van de bijbeltekst zijn plaats. We moeten zeggen: al lezend moet hij zijn specifieke plaats in die geschiedenis leren verstaan. Wanneer dat gebeurt, krijgt de tekst voor hem betekenis". This claim matches that of Cees Houtman, *De Schrift wordt geschreven: Op zoek naar een christelijke hermeneutiek van het Oude Testament* (Zoetermeer: Meinema, 2006), who also shows more interest in the history of a text within the faith community.

as helpful in understanding the texts: "The true meaning only becomes clear once we experience the reality described here for ourselves".[81] At a theoretical level, this matches the approach of other theologians. At a practical level, however, they will describe a different kind of experience. Brueggemann talks about obedience as a way of finding knowledge,[82] Ratzinger writes that the meaning of a word can best be understood by looking at people who have been deeply affected by that word and have shown its meaning by the way they live their lives.[83] The input of personal experience—and this is also the position of reader-response criticism—is of great importance for today's meaning of a text.

The relationship between personal experience and the scientific approach sometimes reminds me of the following picture. A car driver will know from experience how far away from the traffic lights he will have to start braking in order to stop at the white line. A mathematician in the passenger seat may be able to explain how to calculate the braking power, but this is of no use to the driver, even though it is reliable and true. On the contrary, if he were to try and calculate the distance next time he approaches a traffic light, he can be sure he will have passed it before completing the calculation. Similarly, every believer uses his faith, and theology is only a rational, and therefore one-sided, way of thinking about that faith. To continue our picture, it may be useful and even necessary to do the calculations before the start of the production process, but they will not determine and drive our faith on a practical and day-to-day level.

The second reviewer in *Soteria* discusses the historical background of the Bible and the gulf between then and now. And he too takes the believer living with this gap into consideration:

> But in my view, to really honour history means that we first honour the difference, and that we are amazed and at times dumb-struck at how things were different in Biblical times. The Word became *flesh*. Let historical-critical research show that. For the believer that really does not mean that it is best for the book to remain closed. After all, it was the *Word* that became flesh.[84]

---

[81] Gijs van den Brink, "Kunnen historisch onderzoek en charismatische uitleg samengaan?" *Soteria* 25/1 (2008), 18–23, esp. 22: "De ware betekenis wordt pas duidelijk wanneer wij de beschreven werkelijkheid zelf meemaken".

[82] Walter Brueggemann, *The Creative Word: Canon as a Model for Biblical Education* (Philadelphia: Fortress Press, 1982), title of Chapter 5.

[83] Joseph Ratzinger Benedictus XVI, *Jezus van Nazareth. Deel 1: Van de doop in de Jordaan tot de Gedaanteverandering* (Tielt: Lannoo, 2007), 93.

[84] Ad van der Dussen, "Dankzij de letter", *Soteria* 25/1 (2008), 24–29, esp. 29: "Maar

Zimmer tries to bridge the gulf between Evangelicals and non-Evangelicals at this point by saying that his side is right. But the gulf can only be bridged if both sides are ready to take a critical look at their own positions. Both sides will have to do some self-inspection: what is my interest in theology? Why do I practice it this way? Why do I reject more of what the other says than is really necessary? Both sides should be able to take a further step into postmodernism by being less rigid in assuming that they are right. After all, we know we are only human, and that therefore we are not always absolutely right.[85] Both sides ought to admit that the reconstruction of historical events leading to the Biblical texts is only hypothetical—in the fundamentalist camp it rests on tradition, and in the historical-critical camp on the imaginary power of the theologian.[86] Both sides ought to take a further step in Biblical studies by not getting stuck in the historical reconstruction as the only thing that gives meaning to a text, but to explore other aspects of the texts in rhetoric and cognition[87] throughout the centuries and in the various faith communities. The resulting small histories will entice people more in our postmodern days than the big hypotheses.[88]

9. The Book of Job

Zimmer concludes his book with a chapter about Job, as approached from a historical-critical viewpoint. In seven points he explains why it is likely that the book is a literary device, a made-up story, and he points out that these seven points have been accepted by Bible scholars since the nineteenth century. He finishes by claiming that fundamentalists who maintain the historical nature of the story, concentrate on

---

echt recht doen aan de geschiedenis betekent mijns inziens toch, dat je eerst het verschil honoreert, en vol verwondering en soms verbijstering leest hoe anders het toeging in de bladzijden van de Bijbel. Het Woord is *vlees* geworden. Laat het historisch kritisch onderzoek dat maar uitwijzen. Voor de gelovige betekent dat echt niet dat het boek maar beter gesloten kan blijven. Immers: het *Woord* is vlees geworden".

[85] See Lindijer, *Op verkenning*, 24.

[86] Cf. C.J. Galipeau, *Isaiah Berlin's Liberalism* (Oxford: Clarendon, 1994), 27: "Berlin argues that the adequacy of historical writing is determined by two things. (...) The second test of adequacy is how well the model of human nature and society used to explain action 'fits' with our sense 'of what human beings, as we understand the term, could have felt or thought or done'." Galipeau refers to Berlin's *Concepts and Categories* (London: Henry Hardy, 1978), 139–40.

[87] See, amongst others, the general approach of Ellen van Wolde, *Reframing Biblical Studies: When Language and Text Meet Culture, Cognition and Context* (Winona Lake: Eisenbrauns, 2009), 1–50.

[88] See Lindijer, *Op verkenning*, 41–60.

"other things" and overlook the signs in the book that its story is not historical.[89] This approach seems to me to have little value for the current debate. And history confirms this. An average Evangelical reading Zimmer's chapter about Job will answer the question in the book title by saying, "Do Biblical studies harm faith? Yes, because as we can see he says it is all a made-up story." This is because first, Zimmer ignores the content, the story of the book of Job, and secondly because he does not offer a theology in which questions about faith can be linked to a made-up story. This way, Christians on both sides of the gap keep shouting "yes it is" and "no it isn't" at each other.

I believe it would be more useful to leave the debate about historical constructions for the time being, or to be postmodern about it and "postpone" it for now. After all, only a small part of the meaning of the text depends on it. Reconstructions cannot be proven, only made more or less convincing. We cannot repeat history in a double-blind study. So let us concentrate on other things. I do not mean that historical research should be abandoned. Comparisons with Babylonian wisdom literature will reveal elements of the meaning of the book of Job, although here too we must criticise historical criticism by saying we should not only look at the similarities but also at the differences, and that the extra-Biblical parallels are not always more important than intra-Biblical ones.[90]

With regard to the book of Job we still have a lot of linguistic work to do. The grammar books provide some insight into the syntax of the prose used from Genesis to Kings, but research into the syntax of poetry is lagging behind. The meaning of certain sentences is still unclear, if only at a syntactical level. More research should also be invested in the poetical form. What does it mean that most thoughts are expressed in parallel phrases? How does the syntax determine the meaning of the sentence in this book?[91] Let us look for historical data that can place the theology of Job's friends, Job's questions and God's questions in the right context.[92] Dating is of course of some importance here, at least

---

[89] Zimmer, *Schadet die Bibelwissenschaft*, 169–183, esp. 181–182. Admittedly, free scientific research is not appreciated within the Evangelical movement, and certainly not within fundamentalist circles within the Evangelical movement.

[90] See the tenor of E. van Staalduine-Sulman, "Between Legislative and Linguistic Parallels: Exod. 21:22–25 in Its Context", in: R. Roukema et al. (ed.), *The Interpretation of Exodus: Studies in Honour of Cornelis Houtman* (Contributions to Biblical Exegesis and Theology 44; Leuven: Peeters, 2006), 207–224.

[91] See my article, "Structuren en vormen in Hebreeuwse poëzie", *Soteria* 25/1, 62–74.

[92] Like Pieter van der Lugt, "Job", in: Fokkelman, Weren, *De Bijbel literair*, 333–355.

theoretically. What can we assume the author knew? But practically there is not that much difference. The Babylonian parallels are mostly a lot older than any of the possible dates for this book. Biblical texts that also address this issue will be used anyway. And even people who date Job somewhere in the days of Moses use the intertextual method in order to find the meaning of the text.

After linguistics and structural analysis, we should look at rhetoric:[93] What is being said? Who is using what arguments? What purpose do the introduction and the conclusion serve in the *Letztgestalt* of the text? What does it mean that God condemns Job's friends? And in doing this I should like to leave the reality of the story as it is for as long as possible. In the rhetorical analysis, a number of points will need to be addressed that Zimmer also mentions in his chapter: repetition, the use of numbers, etc. And here we would look not at their historical but at their rhetorical value, and then we might well find the reason why these numbers were included in the text.

Only after doing all of this, we should start wondering why not everything seems to fit. For instance, who is Elihu, and what is his speech doing in between Job's and God's? The standard answer is, of course, that it is a later addition. To some ears, the answer "That is an addition put in by the author of the second edition" sounds a lot more Evangelical. It is not the end of the answer to the question, however, because it does not explain anything about the content. Is the content of the book different without Elihu's contribution? And if not, then why would anyone have wanted to add it?

A discussion about the nature of Scripture would not be out of place here. The classical historical-critical methods often viewed additions as mutilations of the original text. Until well into the 1960s, many commentators would study the original passages, but not the passages they regarded as additions.[94] Likewise, every verse in the Bible that one could prove to be culturally determined was no longer considered valid for our times. This created the impression among fundamentalists that historical critics simply created their own Bible. All passages they did not like were labelled as additions or as culturally determined and left out of the study. Thus the Bible lost its position as *Gegenüber* ("opposite").

---

[93] According to the order in Eep Talstra, *Oude en Nieuwe Lezers: Een inleiding in de methoden van uitleg van het Oude Testament* (Ontwerpen 2; Kampen: Kok, 2002).
[94] Houtman, *De Schrift*, 86–87.

A more sympathetic approach can be found with Cees Houtman.[95] He views additions as "actualisation and re-writing" and leaves them in place as part of the Scriptures.[96] Also his modesty in saying that the composition of Bible books cannot be traced "in detail" sounds more sympathetic in comparison to authors who believe they can provide detailed proof.[97] It seems to me that this is a better way of attempting to bridge the gap than Zimmer's book. Arguably, the Evangelical side needs to consider that if Christ speaks in the form of parables, perhaps God can also speak in the form of a play. Why not accept that not only psalms, prophecy and historical writings, but plays too can be written under the guidance of the Holy Spirit in order to enhance the faith of the Christian community? Again, we need a theology in which questions of faith are linked to the outcomes of historical investigation.

As we look at the Old Testament, we see that many Evangelicals need to learn to understand it as it is, and not only from the perspective of the New Testament.[98] It seems to me that we are only halfway done, however, because the Old Testament did not only have a historical meaning within the Israelite cult, but also in Judaism and Christianity. As an Evangelical Christian I am still very interested in the way this book was received in the New Testament. Why is its culture so strongly saturated with the link between sin and punishment (see John 5)? And why does Christ go against this? Is His reason linked to the problems addressed in the book of Job? How did the book of Job with the issues it discusses end up in church history? At what times did it play any role and when was the link between sin and punishment regarded as all-important? In looking at this, I would not only like to see the answers that we would find as historical data, but also accept the writers of those times as fellow-Christians. Their thoughts and experiences count. Why did they emphasise or choose not to emphasise certain theological notions at the time?[99]

---

[95] In line with Is. Berlin's search for "a certain humility": "in the light of the limited range of our knowledge and even of our imperfect understanding of individuals and societies"; M. Jinkins, *Christianity, Tolerance and Pluralism: A Theological Engagement with Isaiah Berlin's Social Theory* (RStRel 9; London, New York: Routledge, 2004), 121.
[96] Houtman, *De Schrift*, 87.
[97] Houtman, *De Schrift*, 85.
[98] Also Chris Wright, an Evangelical, warns about this in *Jezus leren kennen door het Oude Testament* (Apeldoorn: Novapres, 1992), 36–37.
[99] See, amongst others, Arie W. Zwiep, *Tussen tekst en lezer: Een historische inleiding in de bijbelse hermeneutiek 1: De vroege kerk–Schleiermacher* (Amsterdam: VU University Press, 2009, ²2010).

We will need to conclude our research by looking at our current culture. What does it have to say about these issues? These days we tend to show less solidarity, and we take a "he had it coming" attitude in relation to health problems linked with smoking or obesity. How can we link those attitudes to the book of Job? What is the meaning of the suffering of persecuted Christians? What can we do with the book of Job at pastoral level? Can we transfer the meaning of the book to today in our sermons? And if so, how?

Ending up in our time looks like an unscientific approach, at least from the viewpoint of traditional modernism. Yet I believe that this will eventually become of at least some importance for Old Testament studies as a discipline, and also for theology in general. The number of Evangelicals who study theology in the Netherlands is growing, and their interests still lie with the "ordinary" believer. Moreover, the current policy of subsidy providers in the Netherlands is getting more focussed on the benefit of a particular discipline for society. The objectives of the pure historical-critical method will turn out to be harder to "sell" to those subsidy providers if they keep ignoring the meaning of texts for discussions that are going on today.

10. *And Finally....*

The Evangelical movement is not a movement that is stuck in the days before the Enlightenment. It is in step with the times, albeit in its own way. In some respects it is ahead, in others it is slightly behind, and sometimes it is going with the flow as much as all others. With regard to rationality it is a counter-movement. It refuses to be like other theologies, but determines its own direction. This direction is partly determined by its interests, which lie with the "ordinary" believer. However, Evangelical believers are slowly becoming more historically aware. Does that mean that the Evangelical movement is crawling through the tunnel of Enlightenment after all? No, that picture is wrong. The Enlightenment is too diverse. The Evangelical movement is going in the same direction, from premodern, via modern, to postmodern, albeit choosing its own paths. Moreover, we no longer live in a modern, but in a postmodern culture. That also means that the history of the Evangelical movement will be different from that of established theology. History never really repeats itself.

If we look at Biblical studies, especially within the field of the Old Testament, and look at the differences between the traditional historical-critical method on the one hand and the Evangelical and sometimes fundamentalist approach on the other, it is clear that both sides serve their own interests. It is good to realize that about the others and to know that a different interest will need a different approach. It is even better to realise the same thing about ourselves and to recognize that our own methods also have their relativities. The controversy about the historicity of certain stories has only pushed both sides further apart. The gulf cannot be bridged by putting even more emphasis on the truth or otherwise of a particular Bible passage. It can only be bridged by taking on a self-critical and modest approach and by taking a step forward in postmodern times. The small histories of all meanings that a text has provided throughout the ages, together with their meaning for discussions taking place today, could be enriching for both sides.

Chapter Three

Distant Relatives: The Oxford Group and the Reformed Churches in Restored Union

Maarten J. Aalders

1. *Introduction*

In 1926, the actions of Dr J.G. Geelkerken, pastor in South Amsterdam, caused a split in the Reformed denomination known as the *Gereformeerde Kerken in Nederland* (to which we shall refer as "GKN"). It was the eruption of a conflict that had been smouldering for many years. One of the themes of the conflict was spirituality. A group called *Beweging der Jongeren* ("Young People's Movement") was unhappy about the rationalist climate in the GKN, and their call for a reformation was heard ever more frequently.[1] In their youth, many of the ministers had been engaged in the revival movement that spread from Wales across the world (1904–1905).[2] In 1926 a new denomination, named *Gereformeerde Kerken in Nederland (in Hersteld Verband)* or Reformed Churches in Restored Union, was born.[3] (We shall refer to this new denomination as "RU".)

In a certain way the RU can be seen as a late fruit of the revival of Wales. Therefore, that devotion was an important theme in *Woord en Geest* ("Word and Spirit", 1925–1941), the journal of Geelkerken and his friends, is no surprise. Illustrative is the series of articles about the confession, written by C. Vermaat, one of Geelkerken's allies, which

---

[1] For more information about this, see D.Th. Kuiper, "Gefnuikte vernieuwing", in: D.Th. Kuiper, *Tussen observatie en participatie: twee eeuwen gereformeerde en antirevolutionaire wereld in ontwikkelingsperspectief* (Hilversum 2002) 123–152.

[2] M.J. Aalders, "Geestelijke bewegingen in het interbellum", in: George Harinck (red.), *"Steek elke pastorie in brand!" Honderd jaar dwarsverbindingen tussen Pinkstergemeenten en protestantse kerken* (Amsterdam 2008 = Ter Lezing, deel 3), 9–20.

[3] About this church, see M.J. Aalders, "Een handjevol verkenners? Het Hersteld Verband opnieuw bezien", *DNK* (December 2010), 26–41, and the source literature listed there.

appeared during its first year.[4] But there was also interest in and admiration for the Salvation Army (as expressed by J.G. Geelkerken, J.J. Buskes), there was interest in Möttlingen and in J.C. Blumhardt (as expressed by C. Vermaat, P.A.E. Sillevis Smitt, and E.L. Smelik), as well as attention for the Fellowship Movement (J.C. Aalders), and for personal devotional life (G.W. van Deth).

2. *Frank Buchman and the Oxford Group Movement*

Frank N.D. Buchman (1878–1961) started his career as a Lutheran minister in Philadelphia, where he worked in one of its poorest areas.[5] After a conflict with the board of the orphanage under his management, he travelled to Europe to consider his future. In 1908 he attended the Keswick Convention. Here, Buchman was touched by a sermon by Jessie Penn-Lewis, who during the years of the Welsh revival had worked closely with Robert Evans, the driving force behind the revival. Her sermon about Christ's death on the cross proved to be a turning point in Buchman's life.[6] The young pastor decided to resolve the conflict with his former employer, and it was during this time that he decided to dedicate his life to evangelism. He became involved in evangelistic work among students at Penn State College, which flourished, partly as a result of his input. In 1915 he took part in missionary work in India, and in 1916 he became Assistant Professor of Evangelism at the University of Hartford. During these years he developed a preference for personal pastoral care as a means of evangelism, in contrast to the more usual evangelistic rallies. He adopted John Mott's idea of focussing on "key men", leading figures in a community, with the aim of achieving what he called "national salvation" through them. In 1922 Buchman decided to leave Hartford and go his own way "in faith and prayer". He built up an influential network and created subsidiaries in several countries.[7] Among others, at the University of Oxford he had many fol-

---

[4] C. Vermaat, "Confessionalisme I–V", *Woord en Geest*, 6, 13, 20 and 27 November, 4 December 1925. About him, see J. Exalto, "De ambtelijke lijdensweg van Cornelis Vermaat (1874–1960): dominee tegen het formalisme", *TNK* 2 (1999), 3–12.

[5] About him, see Garth Lean, *Frank Buchman* (London 1985).

[6] Jessie Penn-Lewis was a friend of Robert Evans, the driving force behind the Welsh revival. Evans stayed with her and her husband in Leicester for many years. See J.W. van Dijk, *De opwekking te Wales 1904–1905: Vergeet de arbeiders niet* = Church History paper 2007, RUU.

[7] The story goes that Buchman's address book contained about 2 million addresses. See H.D. de Loor, *Nieuw Nederland loopt van stapel: de Oxford Groep in Nederland, een sociale beweging van het interbellum* (Kampen 1986), 48.

lowers. That is how the movement received its name. In 1929 Buchman visited South Africa, where he helped to improve the tense relations between the English and Boers. The idea that national problems can be solved through personal evangelism was strengthened here. In Canada the same approach led to the lifting of a general port workers' strike. Later he held large-scale campaigns in Norway (1934), Denmark (1935), and the United Kingdom (1936). In 1937 he held a campaign in the Netherlands, entitled *Nieuw Nederland loopt van stapel* ("the launch of the New Netherlands"). This seems to have been another turning point, at least for Buchman's popularity in the Netherlands. What had started as an "old-fashioned" revival movement, seemed to have become a victim of its own success. The personal aspect disappeared in the background, the movement lost some of its Christian character, Buchman's grip on the movement as a whole became stronger, and the name was changed from *Oxford Group* into *Moral Re-Armament*.

Frank Buchman's first contacts with the Netherlands date from 1923, when he came into contact with the Van Heeckeren van Kells, a noble family in De Steeg, whom he visited in 1924. This visit led to the first *house meeting*, a gathering of thirty to forty people where testimonies were given of lives that were changed by the Christian faith. A second house meeting took place in 1927. A decisive factor in the developments in the Netherlands seems to have been the move of G. Baron van Wassenaer van Catwijk and his wife from Oxford to The Hague in order to support Buchman's work there. They visited all clergymen in The Hague and witnessed to them of the change they had experienced in their lives. The only clergyman who was interested at the time was Rev. Creutzberg of the Duinoord Church.[8] Together with H. van Schothorst, who was a theology student at the time, Creutzberg and the Van Wassenaer van Catwijks became the main pillars of Buchman's work and movement in our country. Another pillar was M. van Rhijn, a lecturer at the Theological Faculty of the University of Utrecht.[9] In 1928, he and his wife attended a house meeting, and in 1932 he promoted the movement in the weekly *Algemeen Weekblad voor Christendom en Cultuur*.[10]

---

[8] The records of this church make no mention of its link with Buchman. See C.B. van Haeringen, *Vijf-en-twintig jaren Duinoordkerk: 17 december 1920–17 december 1945* (The Hague, 1945).

[9] According to De Loor, *Nieuw Nederland*, 175, it was thanks to M. van Rhijn that the OGM rooted more strongly in churches that were interested in Ethical Theology ("Ethische theologie", a central theological movement in the Dutch Reformed Church from the middle of the nineteenth century until the middle of the twentieth century).

[10] M. van Rhijn, "De Groep-beweging", *Algemeen Weekblad*, 8, 15 and 23 April 1932.

In the ensuing years the work grew in scope and size, and as a result the Oxford Group received more attention from the ecclesiastical press.

Frank Buchman and the Oxford Group Movement ("OGM") can also be seen, like the RU, as an outcome of the Welsh revival. More than other denominations in the Netherlands, the RU was almost predisposed to welcome the OGM with open arms. This article focuses on the question how the RU has reacted to Buchman.[11]

The most important source to help us answer this question is the weekly *Woord en Geest*, that was published from 1925 until 1940. This weekly was not written exclusively for members of the Restored Union, and from 1935-1936 onward some of the editorial staff—K.H. Miskotte, D. Tromp and J.A. van Nie—were members of yet another Reformed denomination, the *Hervormde* Church. (We shall refer to this denomination as "NHK".) Nonetheless, it was the one journal to which RU ministers contributed. I have also checked the RU's denominational journal, but this was much less outspoken about the OGM, both in terms of news reports and of expressed opinion.[12]

3. Positive Reactions from Within the Restored Union Churches

The first article about the OGM written by an RU member came from Rev. G.W. van Deth, and was published in the 1933 issue of *Jaarboek voor de Gereformeerde Kerken in Nederland (in Hersteld Verband)* ("Year book for the Reformed Churches in Restored Union in the Netherlands").[13] Van Deth had been a guest at a house meeting (but did not stay for the whole event), and also had several acquaintances who

---

At the end of that year, he wrote about E. Brunner and the Group Movement, see *Algemeen Weekblad*, 11, 18 and 25 November 1932. Earlier, The Hague clergyman D.A. van den Bosch wrote an article about the OGM in *Stemmen des Tijds*, entitled "De Buchman-beweging", 19 (930) 388-410.

[11] For historical information about the spread of the OGM in the Netherlands, see De Loor, *Nieuw Nederland*, 57-171. Also H.J.Ph.G. Kaajan, "Voor en tegen 'Nieuw Nederland'. Protestantse reacties op de Pinkstermanifestatie van de Oxford-beweging in Utrecht en haar nasleep (1937-1939)", *DNK* 14 (1991), no 35, 63-71.

[12] *Het Kerkblad voor de Gereformeerde Kerken in Nederland zooals die samenleven in hersteld verband*. Rev. H.C. van den Brink and H.A. van den Hoven van Genderen were the editors. The OGM was discussed very ocasionally, and then only briefly. For an example, see the article by Van den Hoven van Genderen, in *Het Kerkblad*, 6 October 1935, "De betekenis van de doop", about Miskotte's rejection of the OGM, and 16 August 1936, H.C. van den Brink, "Karl Barth over de Oxfordbeweging".

[13] G.W. van Deth, "De Groep Beweging", in: *Jaarboek voor de Gereformeerde Kerken in Nederland (in Hersteld Verband)* 6 (1933), 162-170. According to the postscript, Van Deth wrote it in December 1932.

were influenced by the OGM. He argued that it was no longer a movement that limited itself to aristocratic circles, but that a wide variety of people could be found at the house meetings. About 60–70 people were present at the party that Van Deth attended. Those who wanted to speak were invited to do so, but everyone was free to contribute or not. Van Deth also attended an evening where a passage from the Bible was being discussed as a group. He commented, "[I]k [g]eloof, dat velen hier, de Bijbel leerden lezen als een boek dat speciaal ook voor hen geschreven was." ("I believe that many who were present learned to read the Bible as a book that had also been written especially for them.")[14] Further on in the article, Van Deth discusses several themes that are central to the OGM. He explains the term Quiet Time, and writes that OGM members discuss specific sins and confess them to a trusted acquaintance or in a small group. A fourth point he describes is the complete surrender of our being to Christ. Finally he mentions the obligation to share about religious experiences. Van Deth had some objections to the OGM, especially regarding their economic, social and political naivety (as he saw it). "Toch is het zeker, dat we hier staan voor een werk van Gods Geest, en dat we niet anders kunnen dan met dankbaarheid dit erkennen." ("Yet it is certain that we are here confronted with a work of God's Spirit and that we cannot do anything but thankfully recognise it.")[15] He felt that the OGM was one of the signs that "nieuw leven uit Christus naar voren breekt" ("new life from Christ is bursting forward"). He detected the same phenomenon in his denomination, where plans were being made for a conference in the first half of 1933, with the aim of reviving people's spiritual lives.[16]

We see more caution with E.L. Smelik, who was an RU minister in Rotterdam, and who wrote in *Woord en Geest* about the comparison between Swiss theology (K. Barth among others) and the OGM early during the year of 1933.[17] He saw significant differences. For example,

---

[14] Van Deth, "De Groep Beweging", in: *Jaarboek Hersteld Verband* 6 (1933), 167.

[15] Van Deth, "De Groep Beweging", in: *Jaarboek Hersteld Verband*, 6 (1933), 169.

[16] He is slightly more critical in his review of A.J. Russel, "Alleen voor zondaars" (Amsterdam 1933), *Woord en Geest*, 26 May 1933. His criticism concerns the strong emphasis on guidance by the Holy Spirit. He does, however, admit "dat we hier te doen hebben met een verschijnsel, waarvan we niet anders kunnen zeggen, dan dat het te danken is aan het werk van den Heiligen Geest" ("that we are confronted here with a phenomenon about which we can only say that it is owing to the work of the Holy Spirit").

[17] E.L. Smelik, "Zwitsersche theologie en House-party-beweging", *Woord en Geest*, 17 February 1933, in response to A.J. Russel, "Alleen voor zondaars".

the OGM focussed on the drawing rooms of the wealthy, and Swiss theology on social struggle. One was a lay movement, the other one of theologians. With the one there was no room for deeper reflection, with the other it all revolved around the system. The one was about a direct experience from God, whereas Swiss theology was characterised by an emphasis on the anti-mystical and paradoxical nature of revelation. One was not connected with the church, the other was. Smelik realised that a meeting between the two would lead to passionate discussions, but felt that this was no reason to avoid it. He pointed out that E. Brunner's judgement of the OGM was positive, albeit not without criticism. Smelik concluded by expressing his hope that the Oxford Group would provide some fresh input in the churches.

This was also the wish of I.N.Th. Diepenhorst, mayor of the town of Epe and probably a member of the Restored Union, who wrote three articles about the OGM in *Woord en Geest*.[18] He had several points of criticism, but also had high expectations of the OGM. The same issue contains a short article by J.R.R. Schmal, member of the Restored Union in The Hague, in which he quotes several critical remarks made by a former supporter but does not add any comments.[19]

When, in the autumn of 1933, the international student magazine *The Student World* devoted an issue to the question whether it is possible to know Gods' will, Smelik wrote a critical response.[20] All kinds of people had been asked for their opinion, he argued, but this made the magazine inconsistent, and the terms under discussion had not been clearly defined either. The most significant differences came to light in the articles by E. Thurneysen, a Swiss theologian, and David Cairns, a theology student strongly drawn to the OGM.[21] Thurneysen warned against overestimating one's own experience of faith and argued that we will never experience anything that is equal to the experience of Biblical characters. By stating this, he directly opposed the fundamen-

---

[18] I.N.Th. Diepenhorst, "De Oxford Groep Beweging", *Woord en Geest*, 19 and 26 May and 2 June 1933. He was the son of P.A. Diepenhorst, a lecturer at the Free University of Amsterdam and member of the Reformed Union.

[19] J.J.R. Schmal, "Bezwaren tegen de Buchmanbeweging", *Woord en Geest*, 26 May 1933, a summary of the objections of a certain Rev Commons. It contains an apology by the editorial team with regards to the series by Diepenhorst. In general, the editorial team (Geelkerken) would hesitate before refusing to include an article. Schmal was a productive contributor to *Woord en Geest*.

[20] E.L. Smelik, "Leiding", *Eltheto* 88 (1933–1934) 93–99.

[21] David Cairns translated books and brochures by E. Brunner into English, includin *Die Kirchen, die Gruppenbewegung und die Kirche Jesu Christi* (Berlin 1936).

tal principle of the OGM. Smelik felt that Thurneysen was too bookish and grim. He referred to the Epistle of James, where the Old Testament prophet Elijah is described as "a human being, even as we are. He prayed earnestly that it would not rain, and it did not rain on the land for three years."[22] He thought that it was not implausible that the apostle, when measured against the theological plan, was working outside the dialectic order.[23]

Smelik decided to discuss this theme more extensively in a brochure,[24] in which he provided what he felt was lacking in *The Student World*: a careful consideration of the various aspects of God's guidance in daily life. The brochure extensively discusses God's divine providence, the commandments, and the question whether we can know God's will in specific situations. The brochure does not deny that we can, but is also reserved and points out what were Smelik's perceived dangers in the OGM. In response, his colleague Sillevis Smitt wrote that perhaps Smelik saw God's providence too much as "unchanging" and warned that this might lead to fatalistic resignation.[25] Where Smelik distinguishes between God's general and His specific guidance, Smitt agrees with him. But he also believes that Smelik was too afraid of letting go of personal responsibility. According to Smitt, neither Thurneysen nor Smelik can escape from the thought that God's revelation is complete. After all, the great fact of salvation is that Jesus Christ is still alive, and therefore modern-day Christians have the same advantage as the first Christians. If our experience is different from theirs, it is our own fault, Smitt argues. In his opinion, Smelik takes the dilemma too lightly.

Woord en Geest was always reasonably positive about the OGM during this year. Some booklets received positive reviews, J.C. Aalders pleaded for K. Barth and Buchman to join forces.[26] There is an article about a campaign in London, taken from the *NRC* national newspaper,

---

[22] James 5: 17.
[23] E.L. Smelik, "Leiding", *Eltheto* 88 (1933–1934) 96.
[24] E.L. Smelik, *Leiding van God* (Baarn 1934).
[25] P.A.E. Sillevis Smitt, *Woord en Geest*, 3 August 1934, in response to E.L. Smelik, *Leiding van God* (Baarn 1934).
[26] J.G. Geelkerken, a review of G. Allen, *Hij die komt* (Amsterdam 1933), *Woord en Geest*, 19 January 1934; J.C. Aalders, "Barth en Buchman. Dialectische theologie en Groep-beweging", *Woord en Geest*, 29 June 1934; idem, review of J. Kitchen, *Ik was een volslagen heiden* (Nijkerk 1934), *Woord en Geest*, 10 August 1934, G.W. Van Deth, *Woord en Geest*, 24 August 1934, review of H. Begbie, *Vernieuwde menschen* (Utrecht 1934). *Woord en Geest*'s issue of 10 August 1934 contains a favorable report about an OGM campaign in East London, taken from *Het Vaderland*'s issue of 29 July.

that is slightly more critical.[27] The author of this article does not doubt the sincerity of the movement, but regards it as a movement that benefits from some people's rejection of the intellect.

4. Critical Responses

Until 1934, *Woord en Geest* hardly published any articles in which the OGM was criticised, and *Het Kerkblad* did not mention the movement. Any criticism from within the RU had the character of critical remarks rather than that of fundamental criticism. Only during the year 1934-1935 this seems to have changed.

The change started on 11 January 1935, with an article by J.J.R. Schmal, who—as we saw earlier—had been critical about the OGM before. He included an interview with Professor Karl Vold, lecturer at the Free Theological Faculty of Oslo, in order to make clear to the readership that some within the church in Norway were dismissive of the OGM. Vold pointed out that the OGM was after moral rather than religious conversion, and that Buchman's name was heard within the OGM more frequently than the name of Jesus.[28] The following week, however, the editorial team published a positive article, written by Norwegian scholar S. Mowinckel, about his experiences with the Oxford Group. He wrote that his spiritual life had been dull and half-dead for many years, but that through the work of the OGM God had become a living reality to him.[29]

Some time later, the editorial team published a very critical article by N.G.J. van S (short for N.G.J. van Schouwenburg), who had attended a meeting in the Bach room at the Amsterdam conservatory, and decided on the basis of this meeting that Frank Buchman was a loudmouth. "Hij moet schreeuwen omdat hetgeen hij zegt niets betekent, in elk geval niets bijzonders inhoudt." ("He needs to shout, because what he says

---

[27] "De Oxford-groep-beweging", *Woord en Geest*, 16 February 1934, taken from the NRC newspaper, 10 February 1934. According to De Loor, *Nieuw Nederland*, the article appeared in the *Het Vaderland* issue dated 11 February 1934, but these two claims are not necessarily mutually exclusive.

[28] "De Groepsbeweging in Noorwegen", *Woord en Geest*, 11 January 1935. The interview appeared in the *Kristeligt Dagblad*.

[29] S. Mowinckel, "Mijne ontmoeting met 'Oxford'", *Woord en Geest*, 18 January 1935. Translation of an article in *Den kristne Buddhistmission*. The readers of *Woord en Geest* had been able to read in the previous issue that Karl Vold wondered whether the radical Old Testament scholar Mowinckel was going to take back what he written about the Old Testament in the past. He did not mention his scientific insights.

does not mean anything, or at least nothing out of the ordinary.")[30] The article provoked several negative responses.[31] Even Buskes and Tromp were at the meeting of 17 January, and according to Rev. H. Sasse, minister of an NHK church in Amsterdam and a loyal activist within the OGM, they too were very disappointed.[32]

De Loor believes that the meeting of 17 January 1935 in the Bach room in Amsterdam was a turning point in "the eyes of dialectic theologians".[33] Buchman had been unmasked as a charlatan, he argued, and from this point onwards no more discussions with the OGM took place. De Loor does not show any proof for his proposition, however, and his conclusion is wrong when it concerns the "Barthians" who contributed to *Woord en Geest* at the time.

Buskes was probably critical even before the infamous meeting in the Bach room. In the *Kerk en Vrede* issue of 20 January 1935, published a few days after the meeting, Buskes utters some sharp criticism of the idea that people within the OGM did not unanimously choose against armament within the OGM because not everyone had received the same guidance on this point.[34] He denies that people receive individual

---

[30] "Een bijeenkomst van de Oxord-Group", *Woord en Geest*, 25 January 1935.

[31] Mr. G. Ruys (HV?), "De Oxford-Group", *Woord en Geest*, 1 February 1935; J. Bentinck, "Hoe vinden wij de waarheid?", *Woord en Geest*, 15 February 1935. This article prompted the editorial team to announce that it had not yet decided what its opinion about this movement was. One of the editors had announced he would soon write about the OGM, see *Woord en Geest*, 15 February 1935. Also C. Muns responded: "De Oxford Groep beweging", *Woord en Geest*, 15 February 1935. The same issue contained a response from N.G.J. van S(chouwenburg) to responses he had received. See "Een bijeenkomst van de Oxford Group", *Woord en Geest*, 15 February 1935.

[32] De Loor, *Nieuw Nederland*, 85, interview with Rev. H. Sasse. Earlier, Buskes had sharply criticised his GKN colleague W. van 't Sant. See J.J. Buskes, "De Buchman beweging", *Woord en Geest*, 5 May 1933. He rebuked his GKN colleague W. van 't Sant for speaking out against the OGM at a meeting for GKN clergymen, only on the basis of what he had read. He praised his colleague J.G. Fernhout from Bandoeng, who spoke about his personal experiences with the Oxford Group. About this, see J.G. Kunst, "Verslag van de 22ste Algemeene Vergadering van de Vereeniging van Predikanten van de Gereformeerde Kerken in Nederland op woensdag 19 en donderdag 20 april 1933 in het Jaarbeursgebouw te Utrecht", *GThT* 34 (1933–1934), 249–268. See also W. van 't Sant, *Beproeft de geesten: een nadere toetsing van de Buchman-beweging* ('s Gravenhage 1934). R. van Deemter wrote a response to Van 't Sant, *Oxfordgroep en christendom* (Delft 1934), in the *Woord en Geest* issue of 7 September 1934, which was reviewed by G.W. van Deth. He wrote that it was "ontstellend en bedroevend" ("outrageous and sad") that Van 't Sant had dared to write his brochure without having had any personal contact with the group.

[33] De Loor, *Nieuw Nederland*, 84–84, 179.

[34] *Kerk en vrede*, 10 (1935), 20 January 1935, in an editorial note with an article by C.M. Top, "Nogmaals: De Oxfordgroep en de Oorlog". It is unclear whether Buskes

orders from God, except when it concerns the content of the Gospel message. "Dat zou het meest noodlottige individualisme beteekenen." ("That would mean the most fatal form of individualism.") It would mean arbitrariness. He also argues that God does not give conflicting orders. He believes that a choice for or against war is unavoidable and that Buchman will need to speak out. Otherwise "de grote massa van de Buchman-menschen bereid blijken om oorlogsdiensten te verrichten in de overtuiging, dat God hun dit voorschrijft. Hoe lang hinkt gijlieden op twee gedachten?" ("the large majority of Buchman's people will show themselves to be willing to perform acts of war in the belief that God orders this. How long will you dither?")

In later days, Buskes and other Barthians were to discuss the OGM again. But that does not negate the fact that the infamous meeting in the Bach room had damaged Buchman's cause. After a flurry of articles about the OGM at the start of 1935 the discussion in *Woord en Geest* went quiet for a while, until the end of that year.[35] One reason for this was undoubtedly that supporters of the OGM avoided all discussion about church and theology. Buskes, however, did publicly speak out.[36] The immediate occasion was a book by E. Brunner about the renewal of the church.[37] Buskes agreed with Brunner in seeing the OGM as an extension of the church, which provided pastoral care and witness where the church had failed to do so. The OGM was right in emphasising the priesthood of all believers, they argued. Buskes also saw some dangers. It is possible for people's own stories to be given more importance than God's Word, and witness is not the same as proclamation. But that does not mean that we can dismiss the OGM as pietistic and dangerous, Buskes argued. Every believer is a missionary, and missions are needed more than ever in a Europe that is taking off its mask. Buskes had many questions about the OGM, which he saw primarily as a movement that God was using to send a message to the church. To Buskes, the OGM was a call for the church to get its act together.

Over time, more critical articles appeared in *Woord en Geest*.[38] One

---

wrote his comments before 17 January 1935. It seems almost impossible, and Buskes does not refer to the OGM meeting in the Bach room that took place on that day.

[35] De H., "De Oxford-Groep op het verkeerde pad", *Woord en Geest*, 20 December 1935, a venomous article.

[36] J.J. Buskes, "Een vraag van de Buchmanbeweging aan de kerk", *Woord en Geest*, 24 January 1936.

[37] E. Brunner, *Um die Erneuerung der Kirche. Ein Wort an alle die sie lieb haben* (Bern 1934). The second chapter was entitled "Die Gruppenbewegung als Frage an die Kirche".

[38] J.M.Ph. Uitman, "De Oxford Groep. Idealisme of levens-echt?", *Woord en Geest*,

was written by Danish clergyman R. Prenter, who wondered whether the OGM's message was indeed as biblical as it claimed to be, and asked what the OGM was really offering.[39] He felt that the people in the OGM regarded their own needs and experience as their highest authority, and took this as a sign of decline in the church. Prenter preferred to emphasise the Word and Sacrament as means of grace, not people's own changed lives. After all, false gods and the antichrist also offer supernatural experiences. What we need, argued Prenter, is a revival that builds on the means of grace.

Prenter's view was not characteristic of the direction of the journal. When psychiatrist S.T. Heidema, who had been involved with *Woord en Geest* for many years, albeit not very actively, and who was a member of the Restored Union, wrote approvingly about public confession of sin such as was customary in the OGM, his article was included in the journal.[40] A year later, in July 1937, the editorial team accepted a positive article by the retired NHK clergyman J.A. Hoek, about the question how it was possible that Brunner had joined up with the OGM. This was undoubtedly a question about which the editorial team and other contributors to *Woord en Geest* had been wondering, and Barth's rejection must certainly have influenced the opinions of many clergymen in the Restored Union.[41] *Woord en Geest* was still not of one mind concerning the OGM. Even Buskes as a Barthian found something useful in the OGM's teaching.

---

17 January 1936. See also "De Oxford-beweging bekritiseerd", *Woord en Geest*, 14 August 1936, a critical writing by a Catholic, taken from *Het Schild*.

[39] "Oxford", *Woord en Geest*, 8 May 1936. Prenter was a minister at Hvilsager in Jutland. His article appeared in *Studentenkredsen*. The staff translator had included it in the journal in order to demonstrate that not everyone in Scandinavia was enthusiastic about the OGM.

[40] S.T. Heidema, "Geweten en schuldgevoel", *Woord en Geest*, 3, 17, 24 and 31 July and 7 August 1936. During that time, Heidema requested a letter of recommendation so he could defect to the NHK. See SAA, Archief Amsterdam-Zuid, inventory number 22, Minutes of the church council, 2 September 1936. Heidema was Clinical Director at the Valerius Clinic, and after World War II he was involved with the Pentecostal Movement. His wife attended an OGM summer camp in Holten, 1938. See De Loor, *Nieuw Nederland*, 126, who also reported that this couple sympathized with the NSB, the Dutch national socialist party, during World War II. Curiously, De Loor calls Heidema's wife "mevrouw Van Heidema" ("Mrs Van Heidema").

[41] About the Barth-Brunner controversy regarding the OGM, see J.W. Hart, *Karl Barth vs. Emil Brunner. The Formation and Dissolution of a Theological Alliance 1916–1936* (New York etc. 2001).

5. A Change of Climate in the Restored Union and in Woord en Geest

The Restored Union was never a church for the *Beweging der Jongeren* ("Young People's Movement") only. Others were welcomed as well. But these "Young People" were present in the RU, even if they were unable to make a permanent mark on its churches. An important factor was undoubtedly that Vermaat retired early and stopped writing, and that Aalders had transferred to the NHK and published fewer articles in *Woord en Geest*. When Sillevis Smitt died in a traffic accident in June 1937, the more "spiritual" wing within the RU lost much of its influence, whereas the influence of the "Barthians" in the RU (such as Buskes, Nieuwpoort, Diepersloot) was growing.

A similar shift had taken place in *Woord en Geest*. The influence of theologians of a Barthian persuasion had grown. At the start of the 10th year of publication (1935–1936), the Board of the *Woord en Geest* foundation deliberately included a number of NHK theologians in its editorial team and in the group of contributors, most of whom were Barthians. They had noticed that the journal was languishing and the interest from people in the Restored Union was dwindling. They hoped to stem the decline by giving more space to Barthian theologians.[42]

This did not mean that they only included critical articles about the OGM from then on. The articles by Heidema and Hoek are ample proof. But the fact that the popularity of the OGM with clergymen in the Restored Union was smaller than a year earlier, is clear from a response written by Rev. G. Ubbink, who was a member of the RU, to the big Pentecost Campaign organised by the OGM in 1937, *Nieuw Nederland loopt van stapel* ("the launch of the New Netherlands").[43] He had attended the meetings for pastors, and had noticed that many clergymen in the GKN were positive about the OGM, in spite of their official publications, but that most clergymen in the RU were against it. He himself preferred to give the movement the benefit of the doubt. It was reaching out to many people who were outside the reach of the church, and he felt that as long as the OGM did not reject the church, the church should not reject the OGM. Geelkerken was skeptical, but

---

[42] From Geelkerken's personal archives, 85, *Woord en Geest* records, the minutes of the executive committee of the *Woord en Geest* foundation, 27 June 1935.

[43] G. Ubbink, " Nieuw Nederland loopt van stapel", *Woord en Geest*, 14 May 1937. Ubbink was a minister of churches in Utrecht and Tienhoven. In the same issue, Schmal mentions "Een Roomsch oordeel over de Oxford-groepsbeweging" ("A Catholic judgement on the Oxford Group Movement").

did not entirely reject the OGM.[44]

Towards the end of 1937 a renewed polemic started in *Woord en Geest,* when NHK theologian J. Koopmans wrote a critical article about the OGM in response to a booklet about the Oxford Group written by NHK theologian J.F. Beerens. Amongst other things, Beerens mentions the dejection of dogma and the naive separation of Word and Spirit, as he sees it. Koopmans responds to the argument about the many people outside the reach of the church who were being reached by the OGM by questioning whether the OGM really leads people to Christ. Koopmans argues that Beerens leaves his readers out in the cold and does not answer the question of what the church's opinion should be of the OGM.[45] W. Dirkse wrote an emotional response, in which he asks why the church was always so negative about the OGM.[46] Koopmans added a postscript, in which he refers to the first Epistle of John, where the church is told to test the spirits.[47] The issue at stake is obedience to God's Word, not people's attitude towards the OGM, Koopmans argued, and where Christ's confession is unclear, people should not appeal to the Holy Spirit, because He is the Spirit of Christ. This triggered a response by Hilbrandt Boschma, who argued that we should not endlessly ask for a confession of Christ in the flesh.[48] His response prompted Geelkerken to write an editorial in which he argues that Koopmans is right in questioning the Christian character of the OGM as a way of testing the spirit behind the OGM. Apparently Geelkerken was now of the opinion that the OGM was a little too vague in stating its basic principles.[49] Less than a month later, editorial secretary Dr. A. van Deth, RU member and brother of G.W. van Deth, responded by warning the readers against being over-critical. He argued that many had come to faith through the OGM, and that God's ways are not always our ways. We would prefer to use a different approach, he wrote, but that should remind us of our own shortsightedness and perhaps make us less criti-

---

[44] J.G. Geelkerken, "Over de Oxford-Groep beweging", *Woord en Geest,* 28 May 1937. In response to C. Rose, *Als de mensch luistert* (Amsterdam 1937), and E. Brunner, *De kerken-de Groepbeweging en de kerk van Jezus Christus* (Amsterdam 1937).

[45] J. K(oopmans), review of J.F. Beerens, *Kerk en Groep* (Putten 1937), *Woord en Geest,* 19 November 1937.

[46] W. Dirkse, "Aan de reactie van *Woord en Geest*", 3 December 1937.

[47] 1 John 4: 1–3.

[48] H. Boschma, "Over de belijdenis van de Oxfordgroep", *Woord en Geest,* 24 December 1937. Also from Boschma's hand was *De Oxford-beweging en de Vredes-beweging* (Ruurlo ca 1938).

[49] 24 December 1937, editorial note with the article by H. Boschma.

cal. Evidently, the debate about Koopmans's review had irritated him

The new editorial team and the changes to the group of contributors during the year 1935–1936 did not immediately lead to a more critical attitude towards the OGM. But the resistance in RU circles was probably stronger than before, as we can deduce from Ubbink's article about the large-scale Pentecost Campaign in 1937. Ubbink was still an important exception, however, and even Buskes admitted that although he had many critical questions, he too could learn from the OGM. By the end of 1937, Geelkerken seems to have finally yielded to the more sceptical side,[50] whereas A. van Deth defended the OGM. In short, *Woord en Geest* allowed its contributors to have different opinions.

6. Rejection

Although some within the Restored Union were critical about the OGM from an early stage, the rejection became clearly visible in 1938, when the movement changed its direction and also its name. From then on it was called Moral Re-Armament (MRA), and the organisation as such entered a new phase.[51] From then on there was more direction, given from one central point, with no room for local variations and initiatives, and no more house meetings. National moral re-armament was emphasised as the only possible defence of the world peace that was so seriously under threat at that time. To quote Buchman, the issue at stake was no longer a "nice comfortable awakening, a nice armchair religion," but the question of "how to save a crumbling civilisation." He was especially worried about communism.[52] Revival alone was not enough, a revolution was needed.[53] The crisis that Europe was in, Buchman argued, was a moral crisis. To Van Wassenaer and others this was the beginning of the end of their involvement, because they no longer regarded it as a Christian campaign. [54]

When a call for moral re-armament was published in the *Times* newspaper of 10 September, a similar call was issued in the Netherlands.[55] Among its signatories were P.J.M. Aalberse, a senior government adviser, F. Beelaerts van Blokland, another senior government

---

[50] See also his neutral review of two brochures by T. Spoerri, *Bevrijdend geloof* (Amsterdam 1938) and idem, *De weg tot de daad* (Amsterdam 1938).
[51] De Loor, *Nieuw Nederland*, 122–124
[52] De Loor, *Nieuw Nederland*, 125.
[53] De Loor, *Nieuw Nederland*, 140.
[54] See also De Loor, *Nieuw Nederland*, 127–128.
[55] See De Loor, *Nieuw Nederland*, 128–141.

adviser, R. Feith, president of the highest-ranking court in the Netherlands, and P.J. Oud, former Minister of Finance.[56] Several weeks later they announced that their call had met with a lot of response, even from Queen Wilhelmina.[57]

In the issue of *Woord en Geest* in which their call was announced, there is also an article by A. van Deth, in which he assesses it. He points out that the Dutch call is less of a call for conversion than the British one. The Dutch call mentions "groote zedelijke krachten, die aanwezig zijn in het Nederlandsche volk" ("significant moral powers that are present in the Dutch nation"). Although the second publication contains a stronger emphasis on a personal attitude to life, he argues that it offers no clear definition of the spiritual attitude that should enable us to fight the social wrongs of selfishness, concealment and suspicion that the movement speaks out against. He also argues that any call for moral re-armament needs to go together with a radical condemnation of the existing social order, as this is based on "de winstzucht van de enkeling, het veel verheerlijkte particuliere initiatief" ("the individual's lust for profit, the often lauded individual initiative"). A third point of criticism concerns the expression "moral and spiritual re-armament", which he judges to be misleading. "Door luid geroep en propaganda komt geen geestelijke herbewapening tot stand, maar door bekeering en ootmoed." ("Spiritual re-armament is not initiated by shouting and propaganda, but by conversion and humility"). There is no other way than the way of the Gospel of peace. Its very radical call is a call to overthrow the national and international order. It is essentially a call to fight the realm of Satan, the realm of sin, argued Van Deth, who wondered whether the public was sufficiently aware of this.

There were others too, who contributed articles to *Woord en Geest* in which they uttered criticism of MRA.[58] The pastor of the RU church in the city of Leeuwarden, J. Diepersloot, believed that the appeal for a *moral* re-armament was unbiblical, that it was too focussed on the mor-

---

[56] The call appeared in the *NRC* issue of 19 September 1938, as well as other newspapers, and was also published in *Woord en Geest*, in its issue of 21 October 1938.

[57] *NRC*, 8 October 1938, taken over in *Woord en Geest*, 21 October 1938. See also "Een persoonlijk woord van de koningin", *Woord en Geest*, 21 October, taken over from *NRC*, 10 October 1938.

[58] De Loor, *Nieuw Nederland*, 140. P.H. Muller, "Moreele Herbewapening", *Woord en Geest*, 28 October 1938; Vigilax, "Zóó kan de wereld worden", *Woord en Geest*, 25 November 1938; *Woord en Geest*, 16 December 1938, which extensively quotes from a critical article in *De Oud-katholiek* dated 10 December 1938; G.H. Slotemaker de Bruine, "Herbewapening", *Woord en Geest*, 17 February 1939.

al level, and not really interested in religion.⁵⁹ He felt that the church's task is to protect the Gospel from being diluted with "allerlei vaag idealisme" ("all kinds of vague idealism") and spoke out against the "naïeve zelfvoldaanheid" ("naive self-congratulatory attitude") with which the MRA presented itself. Our fundamental need is that we have lost God, argued Diepersloot.⁶⁰ The strongest criticism came from Buskes, who wrote a cynical article about the MRA, in which he tore it to pieces and called it moral deception of the worst kind.⁶¹ He even attacked prince Bernard, the husband of the crown princess of the Netherlands, as well as all student unions. Prince Bernard, who had been Head Scout in the Netherlands since early 1938, had stated that what the scouts aimed for was fully within the spirit of MRA. The student unions had uttered their support for the MRA in language that was entirely secular. Especially the student's union at the Free University of Amsterdam was attacked, even though Buskes had been a member in his younger days. Buskes continued his article with a reference to something Barth had said in 1934 about the conflict within the German church. The starting point had been the Christian rather than Christ himself, and this would lead to taking the pious person, the spiritual person, the moral person, the natural person, and finally the pagan as a starting point. He asked when people's eyes would ever be opened, and concluded by arguing that the church should "not take another drop from this cup".⁶²

On 8 December 1939, Geelkerken wrote an article along the same lines.⁶³ He stated that he did not wish to deny that the Oxford Group

---

⁵⁹ "Geloof in Jezus Christus of geestelijke herbewapening", *Woord en Geest*, 31 March 1939; Leeuwarder Courant, 22 March 1939. De Loor, *Nieuw Nederland*, 131, speaks of Christian humanity. About the development within the MRA, see De Loor, *Nieuw Nederland*, 147–170.

⁶⁰ *Woord en Geest*, 14 April 1939, contains an article by Diepersloot, which shows the *Leeuwarder Courant* newspaper, from which the editors of *Woord en Geest* had taken this news, had not included Diepersloot's criticism of Queen Wilhelmina. He had argued that the Queen should not have used the words God, Christ, and Holy Spirit.

⁶¹ J.J. Buskes Jr., "Geestelijke en moreele herbewapening", *Woord en Geest*, 21 April 1939; J.J.R. Schmal, "Zwendel?", *Woord en Geest*, 19 May 1939. As far as I know, Buskes did not respond.

⁶² Several weeks later, when NHK clergyman H.A. Visser published a critical article about the MRA, which his colleague P. Fagel described as callous, the editorial team responded by stating it agreed with Visser, and that the MRA's message is not the same as the church's. H.A. Visser, "Herbewapening en kerkelijke zielszorg", *Woord en Geest*, 12 May 1939; P. Fagel, *Woord en Geest*, 2 June 1939; "Naschrift", editorial team of *Woord en Geest*.

⁶³ J.G. Geelkerken, "Kerkelijk leven", *Woord en Geest*, 8 December 1939. He refers to an MRA meeting in the Apollo Hall in Amsterdam, on 1 December 1939. About this,

had been a means that God had used to bring many to Christ, but that he also felt very strongly that it was using well-sounding but empty slogans such as "Nieuw Nederland loopt van stapel" ("the launch of the New Netherlands"), and "God heeft een plan" ("God has a plan"). To illustrate his point, he quotes a radio message given by Buchman, which he described as superficial and humanistic, "hard en onverteerbaar als scheepsbeschuit" ("as hard and indigestible as hardtack").[64] In a pamphlet entitled *De weg tot de gouden eeuw* ("The way to the Golden Age"), there is no mention whatsoever of Christ.[65] Geelkerken was convinced that Buchman and his followers had good intentions, but that in the face of the real, deep need and culpability, it sounded like "oppervlakkig gepraat" ("superficial chatter"), and that, to Geelkerken, settled the matter.[66]

7. Conclusions

The Restored Union initially welcomed the OGM as something positive, and there were high expectations of it. In the light of the background of some of the people in the Restored Union, this is not surprising. However, critical points were uttered from the very beginning. There was something of a turning point at the start of 1935, after Buchman's meeting in Amsterdam, although articles by Heidema (1936), Ubbink (1937) and Geelkerken (1937) show that not everyone in the RU had rejected the movement by then.

The actual rejection of the OGM by the Restored Union was still to come. It was not linked with the discussion between Barth and Brunner (which came into the open in 1936), nor with the change of climate within the Restored Union, nor even with the new editorial team of the *Woord en Geest* journal. It was only when the OGM changed direction that the RU clergy were no longer able to support it. In 1938, when the OGM changed its name into MRA as well as formulating a new objective and taking on a new approach, many felt that the movement had lost its Christian character. The OGM/MRA had lost its popularity within the Restored Union, and there was no more reticence in the

---

see De Loor, *Nieuw Nederland*, 162–164.

[64] This was an expression taken from an unnamed paper reporting on Buchman's radio lecture.

[65] I have as yet been unable to locate this pamphlet.

[66] The last, and partly critical, news item in *Woord en Geest*, 5 January 1940, "Moreele en geestelijke herbewapening", taken over from the *De Groene Amsterdammer* issue of 23 December 1939.

condemnation of the OGM/MRA. Van Deth, Buskes, Diepersloot and Geelkerken spoke out very clearly. In the light of Ubbink's statements (1937) we may assume that their attitude was representative of all clergy in the Restored Union. It is not known what ordinary churchgoers within the RU felt about this, and there is no way of finding out.

It meant that the OGM/MRA had made itself unpopular. A different strategy, a clearer link with Biblical witness and less American optimism might have led to a more profitable exchange between the OGM and the churches in the Netherlands, especially the churches of the Restored Union. Because of their origins, they would have been natural allies of Frank Buchman and his followers. But the latter missed their opportunity to bless the Dutch churches.

Chapter Four

"A Banner That Flies Across This Land":
An Interpretation and Evaluation of Dutch Evangelical Political Awareness Since the End of the Twentieth Century

Ad L. Th. de Bruijne

1. Introduction

During the run-up to the parliamentary elections of 2006, Dutch TV viewers were presented with a striking scene. At a local party meeting of the *ChristenUnie* ("Christian Union"),[1] a Christian political movement deriving from the Neo-Calvinist Reformed tradition initiated by Abraham Kuyper, the leaders of this party appeared on stage with evangelical fervour. Campaigning to attract the Evangelical voters among immigrants from non-Western nations, their public appearance involved a great deal of hand-clapping and apportionment of praise. This scene illustrates the political awakening of Dutch Evangelical groups since the second half of the twentieth century.[2] Several of them distanced themselves from particular tendencies, which were frequently regarded as "Anabaptist," to embrace the long-established Reformed tradition of Christian politics. In this essay, I wish to interpret and evaluate this transition in Dutch Evangelicalism.

To avoid confusion, I shall first define what "Evangelical" means in this context. In terms of this transition, it refers to an "Evangelical Christian" in a narrow sense, as distinct from other orthodox Christians, such as those belonging to reformed churches. Defined in this limited sense, Evangelicals are to be found in the Netherlands among such groups as the Pentecostals, Baptists, Plymouth Brethren, and a series of free, sometimes charismatic churches that do not operate within

---

[1] For the sake of clarity, we will hereafter use the original Dutch name of the party.
[2] http://www.sanderchan.com/2006/02/christenunie-op-campagne-in-de-bijlmer_25.htm; NOS Journaal 26–02–2006 (8.00 PM); Ewout H. Klei, *"Klein maar krachtig, dat maakt ons uniek": Een geschiedenis van het Gereformeerd Politiek Verbond, 1948–2003* (Dissertation Theologische Universiteit Kampen 2011), 284–288, 328f.

organized denominations. The characterization "Evangelical" is also applied to a wider group of Christians, even including reformed believers. This broader Evangelical tradition will not be absent from my argument. The concrete case that provides a focus for my research is however concerned with Evangelicals in the narrower sense.³

At first glance, the observed transition might seem to announce a strengthened Christian contribution to the public sphere. Evangelicals offer a new pool of voters and potential public representatives.⁴ However, the new collaboration between Reformed and Evangelical Christians also generates tensions. Such a flare-up occurred when Yvette Lont, an Amsterdam Evangelical politician of immigrant background, regarded her position in the *ChristenUnie* as an opportunity to fulfil her missionary ambitions. Her activity conflicted with the tradition of genuine political activity within the party.⁵ It is furthermore intriguing that some Christians in the Reformed tradition move in the opposite direction. They believe that the existing political strategy insufficiently reflects the post-Christian Western context and the corresponding minority position of Christianity. They therefore make a plea for "resourcing", and seek inspiration from precisely the same "Anabaptist" tendencies that Evangelicals have been renouncing.⁶

This raises the question of how the increased political awareness among late modern Dutch Evangelicals should be interpreted and appreciated. To find an answer, I shall first analyse the indicated transition among Evangelicals (§ 2). I will then interpret this phenomenon in light of the relationship between Evangelicals (now also in the broader sense) and politics (§ 3). Subsequently, I offer an evaluation of this transition in the light of recent developments within late modern political theology (§ 4). To provide sufficient material, I shall make regular comparisons with the American situation when relevant to my arguments.

---

3   For further information, see the introductory chapter of this book.
4   Dick Schinkelshoek, "Bestuurslid Bert Niehof over de onrust binnen de Christen-Unie", *Nederlands Dagblad* 28-10-2008. Of the five seats in the Dutch House of Representatives that the party has held since the election of 2010, two are occupied by members from the Evangelical tradition.
5   Yvette Lont, "CU moet erfenis van paars feller bestrijden", *Nederlands Dagblad* 27-09-2008.
6   Ad de Bruijne, "Christelijke politiek in een niet-christelijke samenleving", in: Wolter Huttinga, Geert-Jan Spijker (red.), *Macht en overtuiging: debat over de fundering van de ChristenUnie* (Amersfoort: G. Groen van Prinstererstichting, 2007), 30–39; James Kennedy, *Stad op een berg: de publieke rol van protestantse kerken* (Zoetermeer: Boekencentrum, 2009); Stefan Paas, *Vrede Stichten: politieke meditaties* (Zoetermeer: Boekencentrum, 2007).

2. A Transition Among Evangelicals

2.1. Political Reticence

Cees Stavleu, one of the Evangelicals active in the *ChristenUnie*, plays down contentions about some innate reluctance among Evangelicals to participate in politics.[7] We shall see that he is partly right. Still, the mere fact that an "Evangelical Work Group" has existed in this party since 2006 indicates that more can be said. This work group aims to increase "the political awareness of Evangelicals and their involvement in Christian politics" and to develop "an Evangelical perspective on politics".[8] Unfortunately, the group itself provides insufficient material for analysis. Such analysis however becomes possible if we go a little further back in time. The participation of Evangelicals in the Reformed political tradition actually started in one of the forerunners of the *ChristenUnie*, the *Reformatorische Politieke Federatie* (RPF). In the 1980s and 90s, prominent Evangelicals joined this movement and publicly explained their motives to do so, as an effort to persuade still more Evangelicals to become politically involved. In the collection of essays entitled *Vreemdelingschap en politiek* ("Resident Aliens and Politics") 1994), they explained why they should trade in their political detachment for political involvement.[9]

The contributors first of all explain why many Evangelicals are against political participation. I summarize their anti-political sentiments in four key points: (a) a very pronounced two-kingdom doctrine, (b) dispensationalist future expectations, (c) a spirituality in which the "spiritual" prevails, and (d) an emphasis on an individual's free will.

(a) Many evangelicals contrast God's heavenly kingdom with the earthly realm, which, according to them, is particularly encapsulated in the political sphere. Sin dominates in the earthly realm and the associated sphere of politics is necessarily permeated with violence and dishonesty. Christians are citizens of the heavenly kingdom and so

---

[7] Cees Stavleu, "Evangelisch christendom en maatschappelijke verantwoordelijkheid", in: *Denkwijzer: studieblad van het wetenschappelijk instituut en de bestuurdersvereniging van de Christenunie*, 2/4 (2002), 12–14.

[8] http://www.christenunie.nl/nl/werkgroepevangelischen (22–12–2009).

[9] Johan J. Frinsel sr. *et al.*, *Vreemdelingschap en politiek: christen en politieke verantwoordelijkheid* (Nunspeet: Marnix van St. Aldegondestichting, 1994). See also Willem J. Ouweneel, *Het koninkrijk Gods en de staat* (Nunspeet: Marnix van St. Aldegondestichting, 1995). No Evangelical influences existed within the *Gereformeerd Politiek Verbond* (*Dutch Reformed Political League*), the parent organization that was strongly affiliated with a single denomination.

strangers on earth. They have the mission of embodying the style of God's kingdom and not to be directly responsible for what transpires in the earthly realm. This opposition to the worldly is illustrated by the action of an Evangelical who passed on all the candidates on his ballot and then wrote down "I choose Jesus".[10]

(b) Many Evangelicals have dispensationalist future expectations. They expect the emergence of an ideal future earthly state but not within the existing dispensation. In particular, the pre-millennialists among them believe that this earthly realm of the future shall only appear after a first return of Jesus Christ. This undermines the relevance of Christian political commitment in the existing dispensation.[11]

(c) The Evangelical spirituality often places priority on "spiritual" activities such as Bible study, prayer, worship, congregational activities, and missionary engagement, all of which is performed in the "private" sphere. As a result, social and political tasks are at least secondary. Quite a few churches and Evangelical congregations have relatively little focus on social and political domains. Spirituality also puts emphasis on victory. It is precisely a theology of glory that makes practical politics difficult. The partial solutions and provisional orders that characterize the political sphere fall short of the ideal of radical and profound renewal.[12]

(d) Evangelicals argue that every religious decision must be made voluntarily and individually. Christian politics has however always been striving for legislation that contains Christian values. This implies accepting a collective means of resisting bad practices and promoting good conduct, that operates from the outside and does not require inner conviction.[13]

2.2. *Changing Attitudes*

In the transition to the tradition of the *ChristenUnie*, some Evangelicals have abandoned these objections. Instead, they began to make arguments for the principle of becoming engaged in Christian politics. This switch can also be detected in the 1994 collection of essays and may be

---

[10] Frinsel, *Vreemdelingschap*, 9f., 12, 34, 40, 56.
[11] 10, 42, 22 26; R. Holvast in: P. Boersema, R. Holvast, J. Hoek, *Evangelisch of Reformatorisch: duel of duet* (Ede: Christelijke Hogeschool Ede, 2005), 20.
[12] Frinsel, *Vreemdelingschap*, 10, 20, 25v. In addition, see the analysis of J.B. Elshtain in: J. Budziszewski *et al.*, *Evangelicals in the Public Square: Four Formative Voices on Political Thought and Action* (Grand Rapids: Baker Academic, 2006), 196f. 199.
[13] Frinsel, *Vreemdelingschap*, 43.

summarized in the following three points: (a) a softening of the two-kingdom doctrine, based on the kingship of Christ, (b) new insights into the specific nature of the political sphere, (c) a sense of social urgency due to aggressive secularization.

(a) Following the example of Neo-Calvinist or Reformed Christians, politically awakened Evangelicals emphasize the fact that Christ's kingship governs all areas of life. This view qualifies the contrast between the earthly and the heavenly kingdoms. Christians now everywhere are called to follow Christ and be his witnesses. They are not only citizens of the kingdom of God, but of the earthly realm as well. Moreover, these Evangelicals are not insisting that sin infects the field of politics to a fundamentally greater extent than other spheres such as the business community. Evangelicals have been participating in this community for ages.[14]

In connection with this transition, there is a greater appreciation of creational structures. The Evangelical theologian and philosopher Willem Ouweneel adopts, for example, the distinction between structure and direction deriving from Reformational philosophy. This distinction has to do with the appreciation of creation and its structures, which characterizes the Reformed Neo-Calvinist tradition. According to Ouweneel, we may not perceive the decay due to evil as a corruption of the structures of existence itself. Evil lies in the heart. The decisive factor is therefore the direction in which these structures are developed. As a result, we may not bring the political sphere itself into disrepute. As one of the creational structures, it can, in principle, be developed in the right direction. Some of these Evangelicals furthermore even appeal to the characteristic Neo-Calvinist notion of the cultural mandate.[15]

(b) Some Evangelicals see their new political participation primarily as an opportunity to witness and to evangelize. However, others develop more genuinely political objectives. In their view, Christ's rule over the political sphere deals with the organization of public life. Government does not affect the private sphere but the public dimension of existence, where it should maintain law and social peace. As part of their engagement, Christians cannot ignore such areas of common shared interest, as they also benefit, for example, from family allowance legislation or suffer the consequences of decisions about traffic and transport. Avoidance of this sphere as a matter of principle would be contrived.

---

[14] Frinsel, *Vreemdelingschap*, 13, 22, 35, 38.
[15] Frinsel, *Vreemdelingschap*, 25, 34, 37, 39.

An examination of the nature of the public domain also undermines the objection that Christian political engagement imposes moral restraints on non-Christians against their free will. As long as the government keeps to its task and does not disturb the private sphere, no one is compelled to accept Christian norms. No objection can be raised based on the possibility that a legislator influenced by Christianity may impose a noticeable Christian turn on public life. Such an objection would apply to every persuasion that a majority government or a society might exhibit. Influential interests constitute an inherent part of public life in a democracy and should not be a reason for preventing any Christian incursion into politics.[16]

(c) Finally, the transition to politics among Evangelicals has evidently been strongly incited by the rapid secularization that has been going on since the 1960s. Evangelicals see the increase in anti-Biblical legislation regarding, for example, abortion, euthanasia, equal treatment and marriage, as evidence of the nation's loss of its Christian nature. Motivated from deep concern for this development, they assemble and mobilize all the opposing forces at their disposal. Important decisions about the direction of society are taken especially in politics. Moreover, Christian politics proves to be strategically important in providing practical support for various Christian social actions. While most Evangelicals have never opposed this social activism, some of them now move on to a more political ideal, namely "a new Netherlands based on Biblical principals".[17]

3. Evangelicals and Politics in the Netherlands

3.1. Without Restraint?

To properly appreciate the outlined transition among Evangelicals in the Netherlands during the 1990s, we need to have both a better understanding of the Evangelical movement and its relationship to politics. The above-mentioned collection of essays gives the explicit impression that Evangelicals are naturally reticent about entering the political sphere. This makes their transition striking and challenges them to account publicly for their changing views. However, this does not apply to all Christians who characterize themselves as "Evangelical". Stavleu argues that Evangelicals have traditionally distinguished themselves for

---

[16] Frinsel, *Vreemdelingschap*, 14f., 22, 27, 42ff.
[17] Frinsel, *Vreemdelingschap*, 16ff., 31, 41.

their civic and social engagement, and have not remained aloof from public life.

This discrepancy reflects differences in the manner in which the term "Evangelical" is defined. For Stavleu, it is a tradition that derives from a combination of Reformation, Puritan and revival movements.[18] This view is supported by the sociological and systematic theological analysis by other researchers.[19] Such studies characterize Evangelical as a combination of, for example, orthodox, experience-based, interested in revival, missionary and eschatological tendencies.[20] For others, Evangelicals are characterized by the emphasis that they place on the individual, conversion, the Bible, Jesus and the Holy Spirit.[21] Another view mentions the Bible, personal conversion and mission.[22] Still another refers to the Bible, gospel, cross, substitution, righteousness, conversion, sanctification (showing the image of Christ), and witnessing.[23] Neither the Puritan nor the revivalist traditions have indeed any fundamental reticence about participation in public or political life. Both have paid a great deal of attention to the renewal of society and the need to correct social evils such as slavery. Nor is political responsibility avoided. It is regarded as one possible way to serve Christ. An example was provided by the nineteenth-century European movement of the *Réveil*, which formed one of the most influential factors to inspire Dutch Christians to political involvement, especially under the guidance of Guillaume Groen van Prinsterer.[24]

---

[18] Stavleu, "Evangelisch". In addition, see Mark A. Noll, *The Rise of Evangelicalism: The Age of Edwards, Whitefield and the Wesleys* (A History of Evangelicalism 1; Downers Grove: InterVarsity, 2003).

[19] For further information, see Chapters one and two in this collection, and Robert E. Webber, *The Younger Evangelicals: Facing the Challenges of the New World* (Grand Rapids: Baker, 2002), 23-42.

[20] H.C. Stoffels, *Wandelen in het licht: waarden, geloofsovertuigingen en sociale posities van Nederlandse evangelischen* (Kampen: Kok, ²1991), 40ff.

[21] Pieter R. Boersema, "The Evangelical Movement in the Netherlands: New Wine in New Wineskins?", in: Erik Sengers (ed.), *The Dutch and Their Gods: Secularization and Transformation of Religion in the Netherlands Since 1950* (Hilversum: Verloren, 2005), 163-179, 170. On the other hand, Boersema typifies Evangelicalism as "amorphous" and therefore difficult to define.

[22] Teun van der Leer, "Wat heeft 15 jaar evangelische theologische bezinning ons gebracht en hoe gaan we verder?", *Soteria* 12/4 (1995), 2-7, 5.

[23] O.H. de Vries, "De flexibiliteit van de Evangelischen: een bespreking van de mogelijkheden die de Evangelische Beweging heeft om te reageren op veranderingen in de cultuur, blijkens Derek J. Tidball, *Who are the Evangelicals*", *Soteria* 12/4 (1995), 30-39, 32 (referring to Stott).

[24] W.G.F. van Vliet, *Groen van Prinsterers historische benadering van de politiek* (Hilversum: Verloren, 2008).

An even broader conception of "Evangelical", such as the one that is often prevalent in the Anglo-Saxon world, further reinforces this conclusion.[25] In this conception, all orthodox Christians are Evangelical, including those who are associated with the Reformation but do not to any extent belong to the traditions of Puritanism or the revival movements. For Lutherans, Reformed, Anglicans and Presbyterians, there is almost never any question about the legitimacy of Christians being politically active. They often exhibit rather theocratic attitudes that hold the state to be officially Christian and that grant the church a recognized public function. For instance, the recent study by Budziszewski and others into the roots of political attitudes among American Evangelicals deals with the "Reformed" Abraham Kuyper in addition to "Evangelical" (in the narrower sense) thinkers such as John Howard Yoder and Carl F. Henry.[26] Stephen Lazarus includes the Neo-Calvinist James Skillen in his typology of Evangelical views on politics.[27] He discerns four attitudes toward political life among Evangelicals. Some wish Christianity to dominate the public domain. Lazarus recognizes this attitude among the followers of the "Christian Coalition" and the "Moral Majority" in the United States. Others deliberately distance themselves from this strategy and retreat from such a position. The book *Blinded by Might* by Cal Thomas and Ed Dobson is an example of this second view.[28] A third group accepts Christian public responsibility but in a more subdued manner. Lazarus identifies this more reserved position with the contemporary followers of Augustine. Finally there are those who see political participation as a positive calling to serve Christ and stand up for what they as Christians have learned to view as good. It is in this group that Lazarus places Skillen. Other typologies of Evangelical attitudes to politics do not significantly contradict this view.[29]

---

[25] Ronald J. Sider, *Toward an Evangelical Public Policy: Political Strategies for the Health of the Nation* (Grand Rapids: Baker Books, 2005); Russel D. Moore, *The Kingdom of Christ: The New Evangelical Perspective* (Wheaton: Crossway Books, 2004), 19vv; Christian Smith, *What Evangelicals Really Want* (Berkeley: University of California Press, 2000), 15ff., locates Evangelicals in the overlapping area between three categories: members of conservative Protestant churches, those who call themselves "evangelical", and those who regard themselves as "fundamentalist".

[26] Budziszewski, *Evangelicals*, 10ff.

[27] Stephen Lazarus, "Evangelicalism and Politics", in: Craig Bartholomew, Robin Parry, Andrew West (eds.), *The Futures of Evangelicalism: Issues and Prospects* (Leicester: InterVarsity, 2003), 316.

[28] Sider, *Toward*, 25ff. 29; Cal Thomas, Ed Dobson, *Blinded by Might: Can the "Religious Right" Save America?* (Grand Rapids: Zondervan, 1999).

[29] For instance, Boersema provides three categories: conservative, assimilating, and

3.2. Reservation with Multiple Backgrounds

The above mentioned typology nevertheless also implies that there are Evangelicals who traditionally remain detached from politics on principle, as well as many other Evangelicals who accept the possibility of Christian public responsibility in theory but were often rather reluctant to undertake it in practice. Among this group, the attention paid to personal spirituality, Christian community life and the missionary calling was much greater than their concerns for social or political issues. This is, for example, readily revealed by a survey of the topics that dominate Evangelical publications. An investigation of the records and issues of the Dutch Evangelical theological journal *Soteria* shows that, since the early 1980s, relatively few articles have any political tinge to them. Further illustrative is the appearance of a treatise on political theology written by the leading American evangelical theologian Wayne Grudem, which was announced and experienced as a special event and, in a certain sense, a change of course. Moreover, even in this work, Grudem spends a great deal of energy in convincing Evangelicals who are less politically aware.[30] Lazarus therefore rightly observes that political and social reflection is often not a priority with Evangelicals.[31]

This scarcity of Evangelical political involvement has several causes. This is due in part to the fact that the Evangelical way of believing bears, in many ways, the hallmark of modernity and the Enlightenment.[32] This is not so much the case in questions of doctrine but all the more with respect to the atmosphere of faith. Just as the Enlightenment, Evangelicalism often embraced, for example, a foundationalist theoretical model, and a strong empirically based common sense approach. We also recognize the tendency of the Enlightenment to privatize religion and drop all emphasis on the personhood of the individual believer.[33] This quickly gives rise to a duality with a private sphere where religion

---

transformational ("Movement", 170, 176).

[30] Wayne A. Grudem, *Politics According to the Bible: A Comprehensive Resource for Understanding Modern Political Issues in the Light of Scripture* (Grand Rapids: Zondervan, 2010); cf. http://adrianwarnock.com (22–12–2010); http://www.christian.org.uk/grudemtour/(22–12–2010); http://www.christiantoday.com/article/wayne.grudem.tackles.how.when.and.why.christians.should.engage.in.politics/25864.htm (22–12–2010).

[31] Lazarus, "Politics", 316. His essay on politics constitutes the last contribution to a collection of essays on Evangelicals and reveals that political involvement is certainly not the most prominent identifying feature.

[32] De Vries, "Flexibiliteit", 33f., 36; Boersema, "Movement", 174, 177.

[33] Lazarus, "Politics", 316.

flourishes opposing a public sphere, where faith has almost no role. Quite a few Evangelicals remain caught in this duality, even if they are not politically disengaged. Their political affiliations or involvement are hardly affected by their Christian beliefs, if at all. In Dutch elections for example, Evangelical voters have often voted for non-Christian parties without giving much thought to such a choice.[34]

Another element underlying a great deal of political reticence among Evangelicals involves a development that occurred at the beginning of the twentieth century, discernible in both the Anglo-Saxon and the Dutch contexts.[35] In the second half of the nineteenth century, there arose an intellectual and religious conflict between orthodox and liberal Christian denominations. It concerned the identity of the (then still) Christian society. The dispute was about whether this identity should be adapted to modernity or else remain in line with traditional Bible-based faith. This fight meant that both modernism and fundamentalism became more strongly entrenched. Especially in America, Evangelicals (the heirs of the revivalist traditions), Reformed and Presbyterians joined together in the battle.[36] As part of this alliance, Evangelicals constituted a large group in the United States, unlike in the Netherlands, where they were a minority and where the same struggle was mainly carried out by Christians from the Reformed tradition. In effect, a similar religious alliance developed in the Netherlands only at the end of the twentieth century, when this struggle against modernity was reinvigorated.[37] In the United States the early twentieth-century culture war was narrowly won by the modernists. As a result, many conservative Christians withdrew from the public domain. They concentrated more on the individual believer and the church. In America this retreat included both "Evangelical" and Reformed Christians.[38] In the Netherlands on the other hand, the Reformed became dominant as a result of the emancipation movement around Abraham Kuyper.

---

[34] Frinsel, *Vreemdelingschap*, 24; Eduard Groen, "Pas op voor de overheid!", in: William den Boer, Teun van der Leer (red.), *Calvijn, de Baptisten en de gemeente van morgen* (Apeldoorn: Theologische Universiteit, 2010), 45–53.

[35] Sider, *Toward*, 17–20; De Vries, "Flexibiliteit", 31, 37; Boersema, "Movement", 165; H. van den Belt *et al.*, *Evangelisch en reformatorisch: een wereld van verschil?* (Kampen: De Groot Goudriaan, 2010). Stoffels, *Licht*, 86, notes a reduction to the individual, starting in the second half of the nineteenth century. See also Webber, *Younger Evangelicals*, 25ff.

[36] Moore, *Kingdom*, 20f.

[37] Boersema, *Duel*, 1.

[38] Sider, *Toward*, 19f.

Although, for many ordinary Christians, this involvement occurred within the pillarization (*verzuiling*) model of Dutch culture, often without producing any direct public activities, the activities of leaders and representatives meant that the religious pillar as a whole displayed a great deal of Christian public influence. To the extent that a similar retraction to that in the States took place in the Netherlands, it was therefore mainly the originally publicly active Evangelicals that undertook it.

Moreover, the increasingly pessimistic cultural climate played a role in this retraction movement in the early twentieth century. The skepticism surrounding the modern belief in progress also weakened the ambitious political goal of achieving a better earthly situation and the ambition to change society. The result was a conservative backlash and a corresponding strengthening of the eschatological undertones in Evangelical spirituality. Moreover, this transformed the frequently underlying post-millenniarist model into a pre-millenniarist model. There were no longer any expectations about an earthly kingdom of peace resulting from our history and our activities within history. At first, a catastrophe would occur, after which Jesus would return. Only then there would be a new ideal age for the earth.[39]

The developments during this period had two additional consequences for the relationship between Evangelicals and politics. Fundamentalism was accompanied by a Biblicist turn, which made a Christian political vision difficult. For a while in micro-ethics, many thought it possible to reach straightforward conclusions from directly normative Biblical texts. In macro-ethics (including politics), this turned out to be more problematic.[40] Moreover, the motif of the "kingdom of God" fell into disrepute. Liberal opponents placed a great deal of emphasis on the kingdom, such as the American Social Gospel Movement around Walter Rauschenbusch. As a result, the concept of the kingdom came to be regarded by many Evangelicals with an appropriate degree of suspicion. This further reduced the attention paid to the broader scope of God's work and confirmed the one-sided focus on the personal.[41]

3.3. *The Anabaptist Stream*

The preceding section has shown that much of the aloofness of many Evangelicals to the public domain has primarily external motivations.

---

[39] De Vries, "Flexibiliteit", 31, 37.
[40] Stoffels, *Licht*, 69, 86, 109.
[41] Budziszewski, *Evangelicals*, 44ff., 124vv (on Carl F. Henry).

Still, the Evangelical tradition also has sub-streams in which the problem cuts deeper. By this, I mean the traditions of the Baptist movement and especially Anabaptism. These are sometimes wrongly overlooked in definitions of what is Evangelical. If we primarily think of the Evangelical movement as a product of the Reformation, Puritanism and revivals, the Baptists appear rather separate. With ninety million members, this group constitutes, however, one of the largest church denominations in the world, second only to Roman Catholicism, and it occupies a central position in the Evangelical world.

Nor should the Baptist movement and Anabaptism simply be equated. The Baptist movement arose from the early Calvinist Puritan movement, while Anabaptism went its own way from the start in the sixteenth century. Anabaptist thought is fundamentally dualist, while Baptist thought is not.[42] However, there are also similarities. They include, for instance, the vision of holiness and imitation as well as the separation of church and state, by which both want to guarantee freedom of the individual conscience.[43] There was also some historical influence. In his study into the roots of the Baptist movement, Bakker reveals the role played by earlier Anabaptism. De Vries explores this tradition even further when he also includes dissident movements within the pre-Reformation Catholic Church among the forerunners to both Baptists and Anabaptists. Typical of many of these movements was a certain renunciation of the Constantinian *corpus Christianum*.[44] Discussions of the relationship between Baptists and Anabaptists are sometimes motivated by more than just historical interest. For example, Bakker emphatically tries to revalue the Anabaptist roots and use them to strengthen the contemporary identity of the Baptist movement. Important for our aim in this article is the fact that he also applies this accent to the field of politics. Other contemporary Baptists have also valued the cultural links with the earlier Anabaptists.[45]

---

[42] Gerard den Hertog, "Brengt het einde van het 'Constantijnse tijdperk' ons op één lijn?", in: William den Boer, Teun van der Leer (eds.), *Calvijn, de Baptisten en de gemeente van morgen* (Apeldoorn: Theologische Universiteit, 2010), 55–65, 58f.

[43] Groen, "Pas op voor de overheid!", 47; Olof H. de Vries, "Het verschil tussen een soteriologie 'van voren' en 'van achteren,'" in: idem, 107–118.

[44] Henk A. Bakker, *De weg van het wassende water: op zoek naar de wortels van het Baptisme* (Zoetermeer: Boekencentrum, 2008), 248; De Vries, "Flexibiliteit", 31, even identifies mediaeval currents such as the Franciscans Hussieten and Waldenzen; further see De Vries, "Verschil".

[45] James McClendon, *Ethics* (Systematic Theology 1; Nashville: Abingdon Press, 1986).

By such cultural means, Anabaptism has also influenced other Evangelical and even Reformed sub-traditions. Even without personal knowledge of the writings of the Anabaptists themselves or conscious adherence to Anabaptist views, various typical conceptions have remained alive through the centuries. They came to the fore again in the wake of several revivals, reform movements and secessions of the eighteenth and nineteenth centuries.[46]

In such a cultural way, traditional Anabaptism contained at least two sub-traditions.[47] Both are based on a fundamental duality between God's kingdom and the earthly realm, while locating politics in this latter domain. In one sub-tradition, this view of politics motivates a militant approach aimed at conquest. As the earthly kingdom opposes the kingdom of God, it must be conquered and replaced by the church, which constitutes an initial rudimentary form of the kingdom of God. There is no hesitation to exploit political means, even including violence, as is demonstrated in the experiment on the German city of Münster. Another group argues that, in this dispensation, the church alone represents God's kingdom. This view leads, for example, to powerful church discipline, but explicitly refutes any involvement in the formation of government, state and society. Although God, in his hidden providence, uses these elements to temporarily order the earth as long as the kingdom itself is still absent, Christians should respect government but bear no direct responsibility for governing. In this old world, they form a new community of peace, and may therefore not use any means that does not fit into the kingdom of God (e.g., power or violence). Their task is peaceful coexistence. In addition, they will find that this entails suffering and oppression for them. This second approach has become dominant in the history of Anabaptism. Its associated conceptions have discernible effects throughout the sub-streams of the Evangelical movement as well as in Reformed practices. Interestingly enough, we recognize several of these Anabaptist features in the early days of one of the forerunners to the *ChristenUnie*, the *Gereformeerd Politiek Verbond*.[48] Insofar as Evangelicals have inherited these conceptions from

---

[46] For example, Anabaptist practices are visible in some forms of Pietism, Labadism, Darbism and Adventism, but also in the school around H.P. Scholte in the Dutch tradition of secession; see also Richard J. Mouw, *The God Who Commands* (Notre Dame: University of Notre Dame Press, 1990), 141–146.

[47] W. van 't Spijker, *Gereformeerden en Dopers: gesprek onderweg* (Kampen: Kok, 1986).

[48] For example, see J. Francke, *De Kerk en het sociale vraagstuk: enkele beschouwingen* (Haarlem: Mannenbond op Gereformeerden grondslag, 1950). Initially, no political

the Anabaptist tradition in a conscious or indirect manner, they are in principle reticent about Christian bearing responsibility in the public sphere or participating in politics. It is therefore noteworthy when, in our time, such groups nevertheless engage in political participation and activity. This cannot be trivialized by the general observation that the Evangelical tradition is not always as detached as is often claimed.

Nor can any objection about the largely theological nature of this analysis remove this conclusion. Still, a more sociological approach might reveal different reasons for the conversion of Dutch Evangelical Christians to public participation. Since the 1960s, the Evangelical movement in the Netherlands has grown strongly due to new converts from the larger established churches. It seems likely that the public orientation to which they always have been accustomed is not automatically abandoned when they become Evangelical. As they begin to dominate in numbers, Evangelical groups will of course correspondingly adopt even more of the features of the established churches. In fact, this seems a persuasive additional explanation for the shift to the public domain among late modern Evangelicals.[49] However, further empirical research is needed to determine the extent to which such a movement has actually occurred. After all, there are also many other former practices that ex-Reformed Christians have radically abandoned. But even when granting the plausibility of such sociological explanations, we have to conclude that they still remain insufficient. Individuals in Evangelical circles who defend and justify their new political awareness are not particularly these later converts but classic Evangelical leaders such as Ouweneel and Frinsel. They also explicitly testify to a change in their vision. The considerations that they repudiate often contain readily discernible Anabaptist features, especially with regards to the sharp contrast between the kingdom of God and the earthly realm, along with the unquestionable positioning of politics in this earthly realm. This leads to the conclusion that the transition of Evangelicals to the reformed political tradition means abandoning some basic beliefs of the Evangelical tradition. This raises the question of what is motivating people to makes such radical changes.

---

program was desired, actions were antithetical and the political activity in question entirely concerned the church, Klei, *Klein,* 56, 62–68, 87; A.A. van Ruler, *Theologisch Werk* (Nijkerk: Callenbach, 1971), 3:98–163; J.G. Woelderink, *De gevaren van de doperse geestesstroming* (Barneveld: Nederlands Dagblad, 2009).

[49] For this suggestion, I would like to thank Dr Stefan Paas.

3.4. Response to Secularization

The above shows that the shift of Evangelicals into politics at the end of the twentieth century is, for some, a rediscovery of an element that already existed in the Evangelical tradition and, for others, involves an emphatic abandonment of another important element of that same tradition. It seems likely that the incentive for such a move was the same in both groups of Evangelicals. The rapid secularization at the end of the twentieth century led both to the awakening of Evangelicals from the eighteenth and nineteenth century revival traditions and a more radical transition of Evangelicals who had been embracing Anabaptist ideas.

This view is plausible if we place this political awakening in a broader context. After World War II, the entire Western world experienced a renewed struggle for the Christian character of modern society.[50] With the memory of the fascist derailment in Christian Europe fresh in memory and in view of a secular progressive ambition being advocated by some Christians, many people sought guidance and perspective in a new public role for the Christian tradition, but in a more derived and indirect cultural form. That the roots of the dominant Christian Democratic movement in Europe run back to those years is significant. In addition, from the outset there has been a focus on the connection between Christian tradition and the pursuit of European integration. Even though Evangelical Christians, as indeed the more orthodox Reformed Christians, often shared little with European Christian democratic ideals and even less with European integration, they apparently shared revived interest in the Christian character of the public domain, if in different ways. This is demonstrable in both the Dutch and the American context.[51]

---

[50] Ad de Bruijne, "*Levend in Leviatan:* An Investigation Into the Theory of 'Christianity'", in: *Oliver O'Donovan's Political Theology* (Kampen: Kok, 2006), 184, 191ff; Mary Anne Perkins, *Christendom and European Identity: The Legacy of a Grand Narrative since 1789* (Berlin, New York: Walter de Gruyter, 2004); Callum Brown and Martin Greschat, in: Hugh McLeod, Werner Ustorf (eds.), *The Decline of Christendom in Western Europe, 1750–2000* (Cambridge: Cambridge University Press, 2003), 18, 138; J.H. Oldham, *The Resurrection of Christendom* (London: Sheldon Press, 1940); Robert Song, *Christianity and Liberal Society* (Oxford: Clarendon Press, 1997), 130–133, 155; Vigen Guroian, *Ethics after Christendom: Toward an Ecclesial Christian Ethic* (Grand Rapids: Eerdmans, 1994), 12f.; William Temple, *What Christians Stand for in the Secular World* (London: SCM, 1944).

[51] Budziszewski, *Evangelicals*, 16; Boersema, "Movement", 165v; Stoffels, *Licht*, 40vv, De Vries, "Flexibiliteit", 31.

For example, this is clearly evident in the activity of the "Neo-Evangelical" theologian Carl F. Henry in the United States. He created public organizations and think tanks (e.g. the *National Association of Evangelicals*) and also founded the famous magazine *Christianity Today*. His appearance caused an initial upsurge of public and political momentum among Evangelicals.[52] In the Dutch context, there was at first only an increase in outreach activities, such as the massive and successful meetings that Billy Graham organized in the 1950s. Still, these also had an indirect social effect, if only in the growing self-awareness among Evangelical Christians. A further step has been taken since the sixties. The Netherlands has undergone rapid changes, including from a spiritual and moral perspective. These changes have been increasingly accompanied by Evangelical efforts to combat social decay, a campaign in which the Christian identity of the Netherlands was evidently at stake, and which was epitomized in disputes concerning ethical issues like abortion, euthanasia and sexuality. Sociologist Hijme Stoffels indicates that a consciousness of crisis among Dutch Evangelicals of the time stimulated them to undertake social and political commitment. For example, he points to the One Way Days of Pentecostal pastor Ben Hoekendijk. To his evangelizing call for personal conversion, he added an urgent moral appeal to the nation. The organizers sent telegrams to government and Queen exposing the lawlessness and moral decay of the Netherlands. Land and people as a whole were called to repentance.[53] However, this activity was not very political in nature. In a certain sense, Evangelicals regained the public and socio-moral dimension in their missionary strategy that had been present at the time of the revivals. What begins with the individual and involves personal conversion will, in the end, have an impact on society and the nation as a whole.[54]

At the same time, that the struggle for a public domain that reflects Christian values might sometimes become more independent from evangelizing activities is not surprising. Interesting in this context is a 1981 action in which Evangelicals were called to vote for Dries van Agt, the leader of the largest Dutch Christian Democratic Party (*CDA*). Unlike what contemporaneous Evangelicals in the United States considered important, the emphasis was not placed on whether a politician was personally "born again" or how explicit he referred to the gospel.

---

[52] Budziszewski, *Evangelicals*, 16, 19, 124–139.
[53] Stoffels, *Licht*, 34, 38; Boersema, "Movement", 173.
[54] Stoffels, *Licht*, 37f.

The goal was more limited; it might indeed be possible to reverse the nation's moral decay through a political election.[55]

A similar movement occurred around some new or renewed organizations in which Evangelicals collaborated with Reformed Christians. Secularism was contested through institutions such as the *Evangelische Alliantie* (Evangelical Alliance), *Evangelische Omroep* (Evangelical Broadcasting Company), the *Evangelische Theologische Hogeschool* in Veenendaal, now part of the *Christelijke Hogeschool Ede* (Ede Christian University of Applied Sciences) and the *Evangelische Hogeschool* (Evangelical College) in Amersfoort. These organizations embodied an effort to fight secularism and defend a public sphere that remained stamped with Christianity. In addition to the evangelizing purpose, attention was first of all paid to moral issues. Later, social objectives were given separate attention. Eventually, this led to politically tinged activities, which sometimes even diluted the evangelizing purpose.[56]

This new social and sometimes political momentum among Evangelicals in the Netherlands is similar to contemporaneous movements in the United States. The "Moral Majority", the "Christian Coalition" and later the "faith-based" public initiatives display similar development. In America, the political influence of Evangelicals behind the scenes is great and sometimes decisive.[57] However, a difference between the United States and the Netherlands is discernible here, one that can throw some light on the course of affairs in the Netherlands. We saw that, in America, both Evangelical and Reformed Christians withdrew from the public sphere at the beginning of the twentieth century. The political re-awakening in the second half of the century, and especially after the 1960s, therefore also included both traditions. Interesting is that the Dutch Neo-Calvinist tradition was an important source of inspiration for both strands of this political activation. Even some sub-traditions connected with a more Anabaptist background displayed an interest in Neo-Calvinism. Apparently, this Dutch tradition was considered to be a motivating and fruitful tradition in the struggle for a Christian-influenced public domain. Many were eager to repeat what Kuyper had tried to do in the Netherlands. In the Netherlands itself, the

---

[55] Stoffels, Light, 34. Budziszewski, *Evangelicals*, 15ff., thinks the problem with the political participation of Evangelicals is not so much a principle of renunciation, but rather a kind of "common sense pragmatism" with a clear lack of vision, and also a too one-sided personal interpretation of the belief that Jesus is Lord.
[56] Boersema, "Movement", 166–169.
[57] Budziszewski, *Evangelicals*, 17; Lazarus, "Politics", 334ff.

situation was different. Dutch Reformed Christians had never actually retreated from public life and the Dutch Neo-Calvinist tradition had also maintained a presence in politics. As a consequence, the political awakening in response to the 1960s did not so much involve Dutch Reformed Christians as Dutch Evangelicals (in both broader and narrower senses). Just as in America, they discovered the potential of the Neo-Calvinist tradition to combat secularism and fight for a Christian Dutch society. This explains why some groups are even willing to give up some Anabaptist tendencies.

3.5. *Radical Evangelicalism*

In addition to the struggle against secularism, the growing political awareness among Evangelicals has another root. A more progressive and radical version of Evangelicalism developed in response to liberation theology and emphases in the World Council of Churches. Three major conferences, (Lausanne 1974, Wheaton 1983, Lausanne II / Manila 1989) strongly urged that personal conversion and evangelism must not occur in isolation. Commitment to social justice as well as better social and political structures is also necessary. Nico van der Leer described the focus on the gospel of the kingdom and the realization that this implies a union of evangelism and social action as a relatively new item for Evangelicals.[58]

These radical Evangelicals in America can be found in organizations such as Crossroads and Sojourners, and are exemplified by such theologians as Jim Wallis, Ronald Sider and Stanley Grenz. The British organization *Tear Fund* became active in the Netherlands, while the *RPF* grew both a right and a more or less left-wing and a left-leaning *Evangelische Volkspartij* (Evangelical People's Party) was also founded.[59] Evert W. van de Poll was able, for example, to put environmental issues on the Evangelical agenda as early as the eighties. He also added a cultural mandate to missionary duties and stressed that God's kingdom and government are already effecting transformation in the world. Empowered by the Holy Spirit, Christians must work for justice.

Such left-wing Evangelical trends contained recognizable Reformed and Neo-Calvinist views. Van de Poll was not out of line when he noted in 1990 that increasingly more Evangelicals were agreeing with Re-

---

[58] Nico van der Leer, "Het Lausanne II congres 1989: een eerste reactie op het Manila-manifest", *Soteria* 7/1 (1990), 13–24, 16.
[59] Sider, *Toward*, 29f.; Stoffels, *Licht*, 29, 36f.; Webber, *Younger Evangelicals*, 38ff.

formed Christians in the belief that God's kingdom has traces running through the present world.[60] Van de Poll however continued to hold more reservations about the connection between Christians and political power than the Dutch Reformed movement did.[61] Nevertheless, the field of politics certainly garnered attention among these Dutch Evangelicals, including some debate on the Evangelical political task with regard to European integration.[62]

But apart from Reformed and Neo-Calvinist overtones, this more radical evangelical approach also strikes some activist notes, reminiscent of the more militant sub-tradition within classical Anabaptism. In addition, the inspiration that left-wing Evangelicalism derived from theologies of liberation and revolution augmented this influence. These theologies are sometimes said to continue the more activist variant of Anabaptism.[63] The existing terrestrial realm is claimed, figuratively and sometimes literally, assaulted and, wherever possible, renewed in the name of God's kingdom. It must be noted that such radical and militant overtones may also be found within the broader Evangelical and Reformed traditions, and therefore are not necessarily connected to Anabaptist strands of thought. Sometimes they are just metaphors expressing a missionary enthusiasm and optimism. Often, they are, to a certain extent, played out against a theocratic backdrop in which the kingdom of God is more or less linked to a geographical earthly nation. Recognizing these contexts does not however obliterate the more specific Anabaptist background to such ideas in liberation theology, which are frequently current among left-wing Evangelicals as well. Of course those other contexts might help to explain why such militancy sometimes not only attracts radical but also moderate Evangelicals and even

---

[60] Klaas Runia, *Evangelisch en gereformeerd: verkenning en herkenning* (Driebergen: Evangelische Alliantie, 1992), 8; E. W. van de Poll, "Theologische bezinning bij het conciliair proces: het koninkrijk en zijn gerechtigheid", *Soteria* 7/1 (1990), 2–12, 4f.; Wout van Laar, "Valt er te leren van de Latijnsamerikaanse bevrijdingstheologie?", *Soteria* 5/4 (1988), 31–39.

[61] Evert van de Poll, Janna Stapert, *Als het water bitter is: Evangelisch denken en de milieucrisis* (Sliedrecht: Merweboek, 1988); Evert W. van de Poll, "Cultuuropdracht en milieuzorg: wissels om in het westerse denken", *Soteria* 6/2 (1989), 10–23; idem, *Op gespannen voet: Geschiedenis en actualiteit van Romeinen 13 en Openbaring 13* (Kampen: Kok, 1985).

[62] Cees J. Verharen, "De hele kerk en het hele evangelie voor het nieuwe Europa", *Soteria* 9/3 (1992), 36–40, 39f.

[63] Nigel Goring Wright, *Disavowing Constantine: Mission, Church and the Social Order in the Theologies of John Howard Yoder and Jürgen Moltmann* (Carlisle: Paternoster Press, 2000).

Reformed Christians. Moreover, the appeal of such militant Evangelicalism was emerging precisely at the time when charismatic spirituality was gaining ground. In charismatic spirituality, the emphasis is often placed on winning the spiritual battle and militantly proclaiming "victories".

These radical traits within Evangelicalism are visible in more than one way. For instance, some orthodox Christians in the 1970s adopted the instrument of demonstrations which was originally considered as typically "left". In the United States, there were Evangelicals advocating civil disobedience in opposition to abortion, while anti-abortion activities in the Netherlands (e.g. the founding of *Schreeuw om leven*, "Cry for Life") became harder and more confrontational.[64] Notable is the renewed use of military metaphors for evangelical activities, such as "march" and "crusade". Marches were held "for Jesus" or "for life" in which reference is made to the biblical conquest of Jericho.[65] Personally, I remember the militant mass meetings of the Evangelical pastor Ben Hoekendijk. During one of the One Way Days, he sent our young audience to the centre of Utrecht in order "to conquer Utrecht for Jesus". Immediately outside the conference hall, the first battle consisted in a verbal confrontation with the gay movement that was waiting for us. Homosexuality was regarded as a clear symptom of the social decay caused by the forces of secularization that had to be overcome.

The obvious conclusion is that Evangelicals were mobilized to combat secularization and, because of that objective, adopted the existing Neo-Calvinist ideal of the Netherlands as a Christian society. They reiterated and thus lengthened the social pillarization structure that Reformed Christians had implemented earlier in the twentieth century. However, they did so with a touch of Anabaptist pro-active radicalism that acted contagiously on some Reformed Christians and renewed activist tendencies in the Reformed tradition. Evangelicals and Reformed Christians were increasingly able to sing together revivalist songs that spoke of a "country" that would be "conquered" or an "enemy" who had to be "fought". The feeling is prominently expressed in a popular

---

[64] John Piper, "Rescue those Being Led Away to Death", in: David K. Clark, Robert V. Rakestraw, *Readings in Christian Ethics 2: Issues and Applications* (Grand Rapids: Baker Books, 1996), 444–446; http://www.schreeuwomleven.nl/ (22-12-2010).

[65] http://www.schreeuwomleven.nl/ (22-12-2010); William Thomas, *An Assessment of Mass Meetings as a Method of Evangelism: Case Study of Eurofest '75 and the Billy Graham Crusade in Brussels* (Amsterdam: Rodopi, 1977). The history of the church and particularly the mission is replete with a long tradition of military and conquest-oriented metaphors.

revival song, which was written as the theme song of the "Global march for Jesus" in 1996. Both the militant mood of the melody and the highly activist text are well suited to the political awakening among some Evangelicals that was going on at the time: *Wij willen dat Jezus wordt verhoogd / zodat hij gezien wordt in ons land/ (...) Dit willen wij/ En bidden wij/ (...) Stap voor Stap/wordt 't land veroverd/langzaam, maar zeker gaan wij door/elke muur wordt afgebroken/door gebed, vallen ze neer en neer en neer en neer...* [We want to see Jesus lifted high/ a banner that flies across this land (...) We want to see (...) Step by step we're moving forward/ little by little we're taking ground (...) Strongholds come tumbling down and down/ And down and down].[66]

3.6. A Constantinian Mindset

In the foregoing, I have argued that the transition of Evangelicals to the Neo-Calvinist *RPF* and (later) *ChristenUnie* was born from the struggle against secularization. As a result of being affiliated with this struggle, Evangelicals embraced the long-standing Neo-Calvinist re-Christianization agenda.[67] For the Evangelicals from the Puritan tradition, the change did not involve any amendment of principal but merely a shift in practice. But Evangelicals with ideas deriving from the Anabaptist tradition sometimes abandoned crucial fundamental beliefs in negotiating this transition.[68] Moreover, the Reformed movement was itself changed by its acquisition of new allies. Its spirituality became more evangelical. Its social and political action was clearly associated with missionary ambition. Its attitude was sometimes more radical.

In addition to the common front against secularism, there were other reasons why the two groups came into contact and influenced each other. The classic closed vertical pillars (social compartments) which had long characterized the Netherlands have now nearly all been demolished. A horizontal open network society has been created, which is characterized as having multidimensional channels of communication. It facilitates new encounters and leads naturally to the acquisition of insights and practices from other traditions. At first, the pillars were

---

[66] Theo van Essen *et al.*, *Opwekkingsliederen: nummers 423–570* (Putten: Stichting Opwekkingslektuur, 2006), nr. 468. The author and composer of the original English song is Doug Horley, see http://www.gospelmusic.org.uk/v-z/we_want_to_see_jesus_lifted_high.htm (22–10–2010).

[67] A.A. van der Schans, *Kuyper en Kersten: ijveraars voor herkerstening van onze samenleving* (Leiden: Groen, 1992).

[68] See section 2.2 above.

widened and then later disappeared entirely.

The fact that Anabaptist-oriented Evangelicals embraced the Neo-Calvinist struggle for a Christian Netherlands is remarkable. They belong to the traditionally anti-Constantinian variant of the universal Church.[69] Ernst Troeltsch characterizes them as churches of the "sect" type.[70] Unlike "established" churches, they do not identify themselves with the existing power and structures of a society. They hold that God's kingdom is opposed to the earthly kingdom. However, we are inclined to conclude that, despite such beliefs, these Evangelicals actually have leaned more heavily on the Christian character of Dutch society than their doctrine allows. The aforementioned consciousness of crisis among them seems to clearly indicate this inconsistency. In many ways and perhaps unbeknownst to them, they benefited from the synthesis between religion and society or politics, as well as from the Christian connection to earthly power that they fundamentally reject. They also experienced a society where Christian values were established along with a public morality that supported the Christian lifestyle apparently as a matter of course. Only such reliance on a given social context could explain the alienation that they also apparently experienced due to the rapid secularization at the end of the twentieth century. Only through such deep roots in an outwardly Christian society is it possible for even basic principles of faith to be abandoned in exchange for ideas that seem better suited to the reversal of the general loss of faith. Adopting an apt characterization by Stuart Murray, we might state that these Evangelicals, despite their Anabaptist conceptions, displayed the *mindset* of Constantinianism or Christendom.[71]

---

[69] John Howard Yoder, *The Politics of Jesus, Vicit agnus noster* (Grand Rapids: Eerdmans, 1972), 17f., 110, 155 n. 13; Stanley Hauerwas, "A Christian Critique of Christian America" (originally 1986), in: John Berkman, Michael Cartwright (eds.), *The Hauerwas Reader* (Durham, London: Duke University Press), 459–480, 470, 472; Stanley Hauerwas, *After Christendom: How the Church is to Behave if Freedom, Justice, and a Christian Nation are Bad Ideas* (Nashville: Abingdon Press, 1991), 15f., 18, 25, 72f., 88f.

[70] Ernst Troeltsch, *Die Soziallehren der christlichen Kirchen und Gruppen* (Tübingen: Mohr Siebeck), 3-1923, 733–737, 790–794; Arie L. Molendijk, *Zwischen Theologie und Soziologie, Ernst Troeltsch Typen der christlichen Gemeinschaftsbildung: Kirche, Sekte, Mystik* (Gütersloh: Gütersloher Verlaghaus, 1996).

[71] Stuart Murray, *Post-Christendom, Church and Mission in a Strange New World* (Carlisle: Paternoster Press, 2004), 3, 8, 17, 19, 21f., 184, 200. 259; http://www.anabaptist-network.com (22-12-2010).

4. The Challenge of Contemporary Political Theology

Based on the above interpretation, I shall now offer an evaluation of the transition to political participation among Evangelicals associated with the *ChristenUnie*. This would appear to reinforce the existing (Neo-Calvinist) tradition of political involvement. The ancient battle receives new impetus, while a possible missionary and spiritual deficit is replenished. However, I think that the reality is different. Some Neo-Calvinists are now even searching for an alternative. They do this because of the same de-Christianization movement, that led some Evangelicals to adopt the classical Neo-Calvinism. Therein lies a paradox, one made all the sharper because of the fact that these Neo-Calvinists sometimes find solutions with characteristics similar to the ones that Evangelicals have renounced. Here we face, therefore, a profound difference of opinion as to whether the existing Neo-Calvinist and Anabaptist strategies are still adequate in the late modern context. While some Evangelicals have exchanged their Anabaptist-influenced approach for Neo-Calvinism, some Reformed Christians have done exactly the opposite.

It is also my belief that the Neo-Calvinist tradition at least needs to be improved and that Anabaptist notions are indispensable. Unfortunately, the Constantinian mindset of some Evangelicals leads them to prematurely abandon features of their own tradition that may be simply beneficial. To defend this view, let me first examine why the Neo-Calvinist tradition requires improvement. I will then make it clear that the Anabaptist approach possesses a key position within the current and on-going politico-theological debate.

4.1. Neo-Calvinism Needs Renewal

The need to improve Neo-Calvinism in order to make it better suit the current context is made readily apparent by some often forgotten elements in the concept of its creator, Abraham Kuyper. It is further demonstrated by developments subsequent to Kuyper.

Kuyper Today
The political theology of Abraham Kuyper is an ingenious construction intended to ensure that the Netherlands remained or became again a Christian country, and that the gospel and church continue to have a public role, even after the separation of church and state. Kuyper's model exists by virtue of some specific theological beliefs. Kuyper believed, for example, that every nation is allotted a unique identity and

historic mission as part of God's eternal counsel, and this divine allotment is revealed by history. He also distinguishes God's common grace by a constant and a progressive variant. Based on the latter, he was able to describe the Netherlands as a country to which God gave a Calvinist spirit and in which the society should be based on God's creation orders as well as on a few basic Christian options, such as giving public honour to God, prohibition of public profanity and observance of Sunday as a public day of rest. According to him, even non-Christians could understand the value of these principles. Moreover, his distinction between the church as organism and as an institution helps him to meet the demands of the Enlightenment. Although he accepts that the institution no longer has a direct public function, his notion of the organism still allows him to override the Enlightenment. Thus, he mobilizes the church to uphold the Lordship of Christ in all areas of life.[72]

Apart from his theological convictions, Kuyper's analysis of his own age is especially crucial for his Christian ambitions in the public sphere. This prophetical element is an element frequently given inadequate attention in the interpretation of Kuyper. His analysis shows that Kuyper's ideal of a Christian Netherlands was related to his immediate context and cannot be viewed, as later Neo-Calvinists or contemporary admirers do, as a generally applicable political strategy. Between the lines, Kuyper even indicates a period when this ideal should be abandoned. At the end of history, the public value of Christian truth shall seem to vanish. There will be a final battle in which all the fruit of progressive common grace will seem lost. The church then survives as a persecuted minority in a society that it can no longer influence with Christian values. To pass through this last storm of time, Christians will retreat back into the shelter of the institution.

Kuyper seriously considered the possibility that this final battle may have already begun with the Enlightenment. In this case, a political re-Christianization ideal would be misplaced. Based on the Bible, he believed, however, that the final battle would be religious in nature. According to him, the Enlightenment did not have any religious principle; instead, it was a parasite of the Christian tradition to which it reacts. Moreover, the final battle would only occur when progressive common

---

[72] A. Kuyper, *Het Calvinisme, Zes Stone-lezingen in october 1898 te Princeton (N.J.) gehouden* (Kampen: Kok, ²1925), *passim*; idem, *De Gemeene Gratie* (Kampen: Kok, 3-1931/2), 1:254, 86, 503f.; 2:247, 665, 673, 689; 3:425; idem, *Pro Rege of het koningschap van Christus* (Kampen: Kok, 1911/2), 2:354; 3:16f., 70. 189ff. 193v; idem, *Ons Program* (Amsterdam: Höveker & Wormser, ⁵1907), 101, 103f., 303, 405.

grace was at its peak and the performance of the cultural mandate was completed. For Kuyper, this state had nearly been reached because Calvinism represented the highest stage of development. But Calvinism itself was not yet fully mature. The journey of God's common grace over the world only would be completed after progressive common grace first spread across the North-American continent and reached the West Coast of the United States. Kuyper then expected that the religious final battle would be one in which Calvinist America opposed Eastern religions and Islam. Therefore, as long as Calvinism was still growing in America, it could still bear fruit in the Netherlands. Kuyper's commitment to a Christian Netherlands existed by the grace of this speculation about the meaning of America in the contemporaneous context.[73]

We are not doing justice to Kuyper when we apply his model automatically to other eras and contexts. Such re-application at least requires a theological analysis of the new context. We may even suspect that Kuyper himself would make different choices if he were dealing with the Netherlands of the late twentieth century. Looking back at the century, he has been remarkably accurate. Calvinism initially underwent a prolonged boom in the Netherlands. Neo-Calvinists were able to introduce many Christian elements into the public realm by incorporating them in laws.[74] However, a new wave of secularism rolled over the country after the Second World War and especially after the 1960s. Unlike the nineteenth century, this secularist trend affected not just the top layer of society but also the masses. Unlike Kuyper's time, there were no longer any extensive latent identity-defining Christian forces existing among the people that could be mobilized politically. Meanwhile, new "culture wars" were erupting in the United States. Moreover, the a-religious form of secularism passed its peak and we began

---

[73] Kuyper, *Calvinisme*, 62, 156ff. 171. 181f.; idem, *Gratie* 1:426; 2:220v; idem, *Pro Rege* 1:32, 43f., 70, 279; 2:45ff., 49; 3:171. 225f., 311f., 350–353; *Ons Program*, 76; Chris van Koppen, *De Geuzen van de Negentiende Eeuw, Abraham Kuyper en Zuid-Afrika* (Wormer: Inmerc, 1992), 65f., 214–217; Heslam, *Creating*, 63, 73, 79. Jeroen Koch points out that the expectation of a future dominance of Asia in early twentieth-century Europe was a result of the victory of Japan in Russia *(Abraham Kuyper: een biografie,* Amsterdam: Boom, 2006, 519ff.; Heslam, *Creating*, 226f., 244). According to Dekker, Kuyper eventually gave up his ideal of re-Christianization (in: C. Augustijn, J.H. Prins, H.E.S. Woldring (red.), *Abraham Kuyper: zijn volksdeel, zijn invloed* (Delft: Meinema, 1987), 202).

[74] Kuyper, *Rege* 2:388; 3:203, 388; John Bolt, *A Free Church, a Holy Nation: Abraham Kuyper's American Public Theology* (Grand Rapids: Eerdmans, 2001), xv; Luis E. Lugo, *Religion, Pluralism, and Public Life: Abraham Kuyper's Legacy for the Twenty-First Century* (Grand Rapids: Eerdmans, 2000), 88, 268, 271, 280, 301.

to experience a new religiosity, as a matter of fact primarily in oriental dress.[75] Also notable was the growing polarization between the West and Islam. Kuyper would recognize all this as precursors of the final battle. According to his theory, such events indicate that the era of the ancient Neo-Calvinist ideal had passed. It was no longer appropriate to engage in an interim struggle for the identity of culture. Christians must now primarily survive and, for this purpose, they must temporarily retreat and strengthen the institutional church.

These Kuyperian lines of thought remind us strongly of the traces followed by contemporary post-Constantinian political theologians, such as Stanley Hauerwas. In the present context, Kuyper himself would likely adopt typically "Anabaptist" characteristics. The political awakening of Evangelicals around the *ChristenUnie* would have, for him, come one hundred years too late. He would regret that, by adhering to his Neo-Calvinism, his contemporary heirs would maintain a context-less application of the old ideal. It would frustrate the adaptation of the theory that he deemed necessary to suit a changing context.

Enforced Updates
The need to adapt the Kuyperian model has been demonstrated by its subsequent development. This history of revision shall be exemplified by two modernising versions of Neo-Calvinism from the mid-twentieth century and by two more recent variants.

Two Updates Halfway: Zuidema and Schilder
In mid-twentieth century, Reformed theologian and philosopher Sytse Zuidema defended Neo-Calvinism against criticism from some proponents of dialectical theology. He abandoned a few specific Kuyperian notions, while he simultaneously maintained the guiding political ideal of a Christian Netherlands.[76] Dialectical theology contains criticism of the struggle for a Christian culture and Christian organizations. Attention is given to the missionary and public mission of the institutional church itself. An approach in which creation, history and continuity were key notions was abandoned and followed by an eschatological emphasis and attention to discontinuity. God's kingdom and the

---

[75] Charles Taylor, *A Secular Age* (Cambridge, MA: The Belknap Press of Harvard University Press, 2007), 507ff., 513–522, 534f.
[76] S.U. Zuidema, *Einde van het Christendom?* (Den Haag: Centraal Comité van AR kiesverenigingen, 1949), 66ff., 71f., 80, 83f., 88; idem, *De christen en de politiek* ('s Gravenhage; Antirevolutionaire partijstichting, 1951), 9f., 12., 15f., 23f., 36, 61f.

earthly realm were placed in sharper contrast. Dialectical theologians perceived a fracture in European culture and spoke in the wake of Kierkegaard and Nietzsche of the "end of Christendom".[77]

For Zuidema, however, the permanent mission was to employ Christian political action to ensure that the Netherlands was and remained a Christian country. Unlike Kuyper, he did not base this view on any speculation about the progress of common grace throughout the history of mankind or an analysis of the situation in the Netherlands. In effect, he did not support his views with the concept of an outwardly Christian culture. Instead, his views are based on timeless scriptural principles. According to Zuidema, the above-mentioned mission follows, for example, from the fact that Christ's rule is related to and may have a noticeable impact on history, already before the eschatological future. Christ claims submission in all areas of life. Moreover, God's commandments and ordinances suit the structures of creation and hence are persuasive for non-Christians as well. Finally, like Abraham, Christians are urged to help their neighbours share in the blessings that they themselves have received. Zuidema refuted the dialectical emphasis on the institutional church and defended the idea of a variety of areas of life in which Christian organizations are the suitable instruments to promote God's kingdom.

The school around Klaas Schilder displayed greater sensitivity to the challenge of dialectical theology. This group was also firmly committed to the struggle for a Christian culture, Christian organizations and to the political ideal of a Christian Dutch state. In this view, however, "Christian" is a quality that (unlike Kuyper and Zuidema assert) does not relate to common grace but (as Barth claims) results from Christ's redemptive work. According to Schilder, this work also involves maintaining the creation as God's work in the beginning and performing the cultural mandate. The institutional church and its members are cooperative in this respect. All Christian action in society therefore originates in the church. Although, according to Schilder, non-Christians sometimes also detect the value of the law of God as a kind of robe that perfectly fits creation, he harboured no great expectations with re-

---

[77] C.J. Dippel, *Kerk en wereld in de crisis: een appèl tot christelijke solidariteit in een democratisch-socialistische politiek en maatschappelijke omwenteling* (met een Ten Geleide van K.H. Miskotte; 's-Gravenhage: Boekencentrum, 1947); Martien E. Brinkman, *De theologie van Karl Barth: dynamiet of dynamo voor christelijk handelen: De politieke en theologische controverse tussen Nederlandse Barthianen en Neocalvinisten* (Baarn: Ten Have, 1983).

gard to this possibility. Due to the antithesis between church and world, Christian input appears marginal and only recognizable as a building block for the new creation through faith. Work on Christian culture (including Christian political commitment) shall not achieve the ideal during the course of history. It remains a truncated pyramid that Christ must come to complete.[78]

Both mid-twentieth century variants suffer from similar defects. They direct the course of Christian politics by means of an ideal that grates with the existing context. As secularization progresses, the pursuit of a Christian society becomes increasingly unrealistic. This can eliminate the space for more realistic political goals in a society that is no longer Christian. The question then arises whether the Kuyperian ideal can, with any justification, be extracted from the foundation on the basis of which Kuyper developed it. The overly general theological principles that later became decisive for this approach imply that Christians everywhere and in all historical circumstances should be aiming for a Christian society. For anyone confronting the situation in countries without a Christian tradition where Christians are a tiny minority (e.g., Egypt), it soon becomes obvious that this ideal is crippling. Any Christian political involvement in such societies would obviously have other priorities. The old ideal therefore only exists by the grace of a very specific context in which the Christian tradition has been influential and does not survive a change of context.

Judeo-Christian Humanism
At the end of the twentieth century, we see how the various heirs to the Kuyperian tradition are increasingly politically committed to preserving what they characterize as "the Judeo-Christian" or "Judeo-Christian-humanist" tradition in the Netherlands. The same is happening in

---

[78] K. Schilder, *Christus en cultuur* (Franeker: Van Wijnen, ⁶1988); J. Douma, *Algemene genade: uiteenzetting, vergelijking en beoordeling van de opvattingen van A. Kuyper, K. Schilder en Joh. Calvijn over algemene genade* (Goes: Oosterbaan & Le Cointre, ²1974); J. Douma, "Christus en cultuur", in: J. Douma, C. Trimp, K. Veling (red.), *K. Schilder: aspecten van zijn werk* (Barneveld: De Vuurbaak, 1990), 169–201; A.J. Verbrugh, *Universeel en Antirevolutionair. Toelichting bij de richtlijnen voor de nationaal-gereformeerde dat is universeel-christelijke en antirevolutionaire politiek I–III* (Groningen: de Vuurbaak, 1980–1985) 1:80ff., 3:22; J. van der Jagt, A.J. Verbrugh, *Politiek mozaiek: opstellen aangeboden aan dr. A.J. Verbrugh, na 52 jaar werken aan nationaal-gereformeerde politiek* (Barneveld: De Vuurbaak, 1992), 211–222; R. Kuiper, A.J. Verbrugh, *Gelukkig is het land: naar een gemotiveerde samenleving* (Barneveld: De Vuurbaak, 1996); G.J. Schutte, *Er zit meer achter dan je denkt: enkele achtergronden van hedendaags politiek denken* (Bedum: Woord en wereld, 2002).

other Western countries. This prevalent view is not only perceivable in the domain of Christian politics but also within other political orientations, such as conservative and nationalist movements. Insofar as this new adage has been adopted by Christian Democrats, we should recognize it as an adjusted and watered-down version of the ancient ideal of a Christian Netherlands.[79] The more far-reaching option of a society that acknowledges God and takes His commandments as a guide has been abandoned. Instead, these Christians are readily satisfied with some key values that have, in part, historical Christian roots. These include freedom, individuality, equality, rationality, and a public role for religion in general.[80] Christian content has been translated into general principles. Discernibly underlying this change is the transformed social context resulting from ongoing secularization. Evidently, the old Kuyperian ideal may not be applied to new circumstances without being revised.

In the light of the original Kuyperian commitment, this revision, is however, problematic. First, it exactly agrees with the liberal approach of many nineteenth-century Christians. They sought a middle way between the classical Christian tradition and modernity, and readily stressed the usefulness of Christian-inspired values and virtues for the purpose of creating good citizens. In fact, Neo-Calvinism started out as an alternative to this approach. This late modern adaptation therefore reverses its own development.

Secondly, it has become apparent that the present ideal of a Judeo-Christian-humanist tradition is not neutral. It serves as an exclusion mechanism and operates as an instrument of power.[81] Not without reason has it become especially popular as a means of keeping Islam at

---

[79] Jan Jaap de Ruiter, *De statistieken der religies: Beschouwingen over de joods-christelijk-islamitische traditie van ons land* (Budel: Damon, 2005((he notes a possible development in which Islam is also included); Marcel Poorthuis, Theo Salemink, *Een donkere spiegel: Nederlandse katholieken over joden, 1870-2005; Tussen antisemitisme en erkenning* (Nijmegen: Valkhof Pers, 2006), 697, 748, 756, 770-773, 781-784; Sidney E. Mead, *The Old Religion in the Brave New World: Reflections on the Relation Between Christendom and the Republic* (The Jefferson Memorial Lectures 1974; Berkeley, Los Angeles, London: University of California Press, 1977), 2, 18, 60-64, 76f., 84, 88f., 128ff.; Martin E. Marty, "A Judeo-Christian Looks at the Judeo-Christian Tradition", in: *The Christian Century* (October 5th 1986), 858-860; Leroy S. Rouner (ed.), *Civil Religion and Political Theology* (Notre Dame: University of Notre Dame Press, 1986); Ian S. Markham, *Plurality and Christian Ethics* (Cambridge: Cambridge University Press, 1994), 98-106. 107-126, 193ff.; H.E.S. Woldring, *Politieke filosofie van de christendemocratie* (Budel: Damon, 2003); Richard John Neuhaus, *The Naked Public Square: Religion and Democracy in America* (Grand Rapids: Eerdmans, ²1986).
[80] Perkins, *Christendom*, 1-5.
[81] Poorthuis, *Spiegel*, 783.

bay. We cannot say that this necessarily conflicts with Kuyper's original intention. Although he allows space in the public sphere for different religious traditions to coexist, this space is not unlimited. These traditions are all rooted in the Dutch (Christian) history and national character. It remains to be seen whether Kuyper would, for example, accept Islam simply as another pillar in addition to the existing ones, such as several of his descendants are proposing. However, the ideal of an updated "Judeo-Christian-humanist" tradition is risky. In Kuyper's day, this general Christianity encompassed virtually all the then existing groups within society, who were all influenced by the Christian history of the nation in one way or another. Today, this is no longer the case. Both followers of other religions and radical secular citizens refuse to consider this historical background as their own. Therefore, this ideal is now actually causing exclusions. This contradicts Kuyper's efforts, which were precisely intended to bring the excluded groups of his day into the public domain.

Thirdly this updated version of the ideal of a Dutch Christian society is, unlike the Kuyperian source, missing a normative core. It is conservative in nature, while Kuyper also could be very critical of conservatism. An element of randomness is found in all conservatism: a specific historical phase is made absolute. Admittedly, it provides a counterweight to progressive historicism in which each new moment denies the previous one. At the same time, it can not escape such a historicist structure itself. Christians who adopt this strategy in response to secularization are choosing a backward-looking approach in which they play down the rift with the Christian past. Conservative ideals have the character of a final defence, which sooner or later has to be abandoned in order to find another ideological position in which to make a last stand or to surrender and capitulate to onrushing developments. It seems more appropriate to aptly respond to the direction in which context changes.

Principled Pluralism
Such a response is, in a certain way, provided by another late-modern adaptation of Neo-Calvinism known as "principled pluralism". Kuyper's original model is still recognizable in it.[82] Different religious traditions

---

[82] Lugo, *Pluralism*; Richard J. Mouw, Sander Griffioen, *Pluralisms and Horizons: An Essay in Christian Public Philosophy* (Grand Rapids: Eerdmans, 1993); James W. Skillen, *Recharging the American Experiment: Principled Pluralism for Genuine Civic Community* (Grand Rapids: Baker Books, 1994).

organized on their own basis and from their own conviction operate with equal rights in the public domain. Through mutual discussion, they achieve a resulting political equilibrium. Compared to Kuyper, this plural interchange is no longer built on a Christian background shared by all parties. The goal attempting to be accomplished is also set lower from the outset. The public domain must remain plural until the coming of Christ. A Christian Netherlands shall only be perceivable on the horizon of history. It does not lead to normative idealism, as it does for the school around Schilder. Principled pluralism causes greater realism and greater willingness to compromise.

This point is made even clearer in some variants of the pluralist model. For instance, Gerrit de Kruijf, partly under the inspiration of Kuyper's acceptance of democracy, argues that a Christian should exercise double think, maintaining high aspirations within the context of the church and engaging in the task of living with others in a pluralistic political society. The second consideration should involve the determination of a political objective that is practically feasible and that is preferably influenced by an assessment of what is attainable in the concrete situation of society and in public debate.[83] Stefan Paas and Erik Borgman direct attention to an additional factor. They suggest that Christians themselves do not yet fully know the truth, especially with regard to concrete political problems. Because they are thus involved with non-Christians in a joint search for political truth, the only suitable approach is a pluralist one that affords others the greatest possible space. This requires a Christian form of moral multilingualism. Christians must be able to switch between the language of their own world view and that of others.[84] Supporters of principled pluralism like to point to the biblical parable in which wheat and tares grow up together as long as Christ's judgement stays out. Therefore, Christians are not allowed to translate their faith in Christ's reigns into an exclusive claim on society. As long as this dispensation lasts, plurality and tolerance are indispensable.[85] This feature renders principled pluralism more at-

---

[83] G.G. de Kruijf, *Waakzaam en nuchter: over christelijke ethiek in een democratie* (Baarn: Ten Have, 1994).

[84] Erik Borgman, *Overlopen naar de barbaren: het publieke belang van religie en christendom* (Kampen: Klement, 2009); Paas, *Vrede*, 76, 138, 398, 418. The idea of multilingualism is derived from American political philosopher Jean Bethke Elshtain. She uses the term "bilingual" (in: Budziszewski, *Evangelicals*, 202).

[85] J.W. Skillen, "Public justice and true tolerance", in: H. Hart *et al.*, *Confessing Christ in Doing Politics: Essays on Christian Political Thought and Action* (Orientation; Potchefstroom: International Circular of the Potchefstroom University for Higher

tractive to Evangelicals who, at this point, have a classic Anabaptist objection to Christian political participation. According to this, no one without personal conviction can be forced into a Christian vision or to display Christian behaviour. If, in this model, the public domain attains more or less a Christian character, this shall be the result from the pluralistic and equal exchange. It need not be interpreted as disguised theocratic coercion.

To a great extent, this principled pluralism provides a response to the changing secular context. And yet it remains recognizably Neo-Calvinist. No wonder others also embrace it. Particularly in the Anglo-Saxon world, this model is proposed as an alternative to the existing situation.[86] Its proponents even include individuals sympathetic to the anti-Constantinian Anabaptist option.[87] In the Anglo-Saxon world, there is, however, a certain uniform religious tradition that can function as a backdrop to political activity. In England, it is the tradition of the established Church of England. The United States has built its strict separation of church and state precisely on an Enlightened Christian identity for the entire nation. In the Anglo-Saxon context therefore, principled pluralism constitutes a real and still untried alternative. It also offers Christians a third way, apart from theocratic ideals or adaptation to the liberal canon. The Netherlands, however, has been implementing an ideologically organized pillarization model for decades. Partly due to Kuyper's input, this model was already functioning as an updated strategy for continuing the ancient Christian ideal. The ongoing secularization in the Netherlands therefore at the same time includes a final departure from the pillarization model itself. Therefore, if this pluralist model is still fruitful in the Netherlands as an instrument for Christian political participation is questionable.

We should not, however, conclude too soon that such a pluralist model will work even elsewhere. Although the late modern context is more pluralist than ever, it really is not an ideological pluralism of *groups* but a plurality tinted by emotivist and voluntaristic tendencies among *individuals*. Fixed sub-communities are giving way to frequently changing networks. Political movements are no longer understood as ideologically organized pillars. They draw their support on other grounds. Furthermore, they no longer constitute public bodies for ra-

---

Christian Education, 1995), 348–355, 348, 350.

[86] Stephen Monsma, Christoffer J. Soper, *The Challenge of Pluralism: Church and State in Five Democracies* (Lanham, New York: Rowman & Littlefield 1997).

[87] Stuart Murray, *Post-Christendom*, 246v.

tional exchange, but bundles of power. They offer individuals the opportunity (or suggestion thereof) that they can realize their will with regard to all sorts of issues. They are bound to a party not by deeper visions or rational arguments but by the recognition of the appearance and attitude of the politicians themselves. Once the other players in the political arena no longer engage in the plural game of ideologies, this strategy will become less effective for Christians. Even the phenomenon of the "Christian organization" (or in the Anglo-Saxon context "Faith Based Initiative") must be subject to question. It no longer offers Christians an obvious operating base in society that is recognized by others. Christian organizations are increasingly required to become open and modernized. As a result, they are less a "home" where Christians may dwell and survive in a secular context. Whoever wants to guard his Christian identity while participating in the current sociopolitical environment should look for a more appropriate home, an alternative localization of Christian life. In this respect, the concrete community of the church congregation constitutes an obvious candidate. We saw that both Kuyper, for certain circumstances, and contemporary Anabaptists have such communities in mind. Although a great deal of principled pluralism does justice to many features of late modern secularism, it remains blind to precisely this problem.

That some Dutch Evangelicals converted to this variant of Neo-Calvinism, which has been adapted to a secular context, is understandable. However, their still strongly present ideal of a Christian Dutch state does not really suit the extensively plural feature of this model. Moreover, this transition also contains a greater problem. Even this contemporary variant of Neo-Calvinism is insufficiently able to really respond to late modern secularism. Meanwhile, in accepting the Neo-Calvinist model, these Evangelical Christians have abandoned the emphasis on the church as the locus where subjects of the heavenly kingdom can "survive" in the earthly realm, a view that was often typical of their tradition, and that turns out to be very important for Christian responsibility in the present context.

4.2. *The Anabaptist Option and Current Political Theology*

The following concluding step in my argument will demonstrate that an "Anabaptist" option holds a key position in the current politico-theological debate. If Reformed Christians and Evangelicals (in the narrower sense) wish to arrive at an appropriate theological rationale for their possible political mission in the late modern age, they will have to participate in this debate. Evangelical Christians with an Anabaptist background should not simply abandon what characterized them, but bring it to this debate.

Political Theology Today
Recent decades have seen a revival of the classic theological genre of "political theology".[88] Similar re-awakenings have also occurred twice before in the twentieth century. In the 1930s, developments in Nazi Germany led to theological reflection on politics. Carl Schmidt wrote his controversial *Politische Theologie* and Karl Barth developed the concept of a "politischer Gottesdienst".[89] In the 1960s and 70s, theology tried to demonstrate its contemporary relevance in the wake of (neo-)Marxist ideas by contributing to social change and liberation.[90] The current revival of "political theology" reflection dates from the 1980s and 90s and still shows no signs of having passed its peak. This latest revival originates in what it is characterized as "the end of the Constantinian era".[91]

In this way, the field of "political theology" has, in a certain way, gone back to its roots. Oliver O'Donovan has shown that this type of theology has been extensively practised throughout much of the Christian tradition. This involves almost the entire period from Irenaeus to the Enlightenment. The relationship between religious and political authority has been of especially urgent concern since the conversion of Constantine the Great. In the "Christian era", both forms of author-

---

[88] Stephan van Erp, "Openbaring en tolerantie: actualiteit en toekomst van de politieke theologie", *TTh* 48/2 (2008), (who is critical about the particularist approach that contributes to the revival of political theology without abandoning the marginalization of the field); W.L. Dekker, "Politieke theologie een ander geluid (I)", *In de Waagschaal* 36.8 (June 2007), http://www.karlbarth.nl (22-12-2010); for example, the online scholarly journal *Political Theology* has been in existence since 1999 (www.politicaltheology.com).

[89] Carl Schmitt, *Politische Theologie I–II* (Berlin: Duncker & Humblott, 1934-1970); Karl Barth, *Gotteserkenntnis und Gottesdienst nach reformierter Lehre: 20 Vorlesungen (Gifford Lectures) über das Schottische Bekenntnis von 1560, gehalten an der Universität Aberdeen im Frühjahr 1937 und 1938* (Zollikon: Evangelischer Verlag, 1938), 203–216.

[90] See, for example, Jürgen Moltmann, *Politische Theologie—politische Ethik* (Munich: Kaiser, 1984).

[91] Malcolm Muggeridge, *The End of Christendom* (Grand Rapids: Eerdmans, 1980); Douglas John Hall, *The End of Christendom and the Future of Christianity* (Valley Forge, PA: Trinity Press, 1997); Feitse Boerwinkel, *Einde of nieuw begin: onze maatschappij op de breuklijn; een informatie- en werkboek* (Bilthoven: Ambo, ⁴1974); Arend Th. van Leeuwen, *Het christendom in de wereldgeschiedenis* (Amsterdam: Ten Have, 1966); G. J. van der Heide, *Christendom en politiek in de tijd van keizer Constantijn de Grote* (Kampen: Kok, 1979), 127.

ity ultimately involve institutions that claim to represent the authority of Christ. The Enlightenment privatized religion and theology lost its prominent place in the canon of knowledge. Reflection on political reality became secular and took place in philosophy and the social sciences (e.g., political science). At first, there emerged a new synthesis between Christian tradition and modern culture. Ongoing secularization, however, also put this new configuration under pressure, causing Christians and the church to again be confronted with an urgent challenge concerning their position in a no longer Christian society.[92] That led to the current revival of political theology, which entered into an emphatic dialogue with the classical tradition and also with Christian reflection from the period before Constantine.[93]

The structure of this new political and theological debate can be understood by distinguishing the two major fronts involved in it.[94] Facing each other on these fronts are four main opposing viewpoints. At the same time, there are intermediary positions that have developed on each battlefield. They can in turn be combined in various ways.

(a) The first front is fundamental. It provides a place where the traditional theocratic (a1) and the modern liberal (a2) views face each other. The liberal separation of church and state and the consequent privatization of denominational religion as a matter of fact is a reaction to the theocratic dominance of a certain confessional tradition within the state.

(b) The second front involves a confrontation between an updated Christian "civil religion" (b1) and the Anabaptist or anti-Constantinian (b2) approach. This second front developed because clashes on the first front have, since the nineteenth century, created the alternative of a "civil religion". This view proposed to establish an intermediary position between theocracy and secular liberalism by changing Christian public involvement. The Enlightened society cannot exist without a religious centre and, in the Western world, the Christian religion makes a non-negligible contribution in this regard. The aforementioned focus on the Judeo-Christian-humanist tradition is a contemporary interpretation of this input.[95] The Anabaptist or anti-Constantinian option in this de-

---

[92] Taylor, *Secular*, 423f., 427, 473.
[93] Oliver O'Donovan, Joan Lockwood O'Donovan (eds.), *From Ireneaus to Grotius: A Source book in Christian Political Thought* (Grand Rapids: Eerdmans, 1999).
[94] De Bruijne, *Levend*, 11–21, 27f., 202–261.
[95] Ad Verbrugge, *Tijd van onbehagen; filosofische essays over een cultuur op drift* (Amsterdam: Sun, 2004); B.C. Labuschagne (red.), *Religie als bron van sociale cohesie in de democratische rechtstaat? Godsdienst, overheid en civiele religie in een post-geseculari-*

bate is primarily a reaction against this type of "civil religion" adapted to modernity, especially in an American form. At the same time, this option reacts against the two forces of the previously mentioned confrontation. It shares the emphasis placed on the church by the theocratic approach, but this latter approach is simultaneously held responsible for the slippage in the direction of a "civil religion". The church is allied in theocracy with power and is not willing therefore to abandon its influence. Like liberalism, an Anabaptist approach advocates the separation of church and state. It differs from liberalism, however, in not accepting a modified place for religion and church in the private sphere. The church is in its message and way of life a public community of contrast. More radically than all other options, this approach accepts and brings about the new post-Christian context.

In the meantime, another front dominates public debate, namely that between liberalism and "civil religion". The first position denies any public significance to religion, while the second calls for precisely such public acknowledgement of the value of religion.[96] Many ordinary Christians and sometimes even theologians become entangled in this duality. Usually they then opt for a "civil religion" position. Theologically speaking, however, the debate must only then begin. Not many Christians simply opt for either a theocratic or liberal alternative. In the present context, the opposition between "civil religion" and the Anabaptist option, theologically speaking, is precisely what keeps the debate on edge. Is a modified form of public Christianity conceivable in late modern society or should Christians retreat from the political sphere and operate in society from within the church as a public alternative?

The "civil religion" approach has the most support among Christians because it also receives attention in the debate involving society as a whole. This is especially true when we also more or less associate it with related positions like Neo-Calvinism, principled pluralism and even the recent political theology of Oliver O'Donovan (see below). Although they differ substantially from a pure "civil religion" approach, they structurally aspire to a similar purpose. They seek a way

---

seerde samenleving (Leiden: E.M. Meijers Instituut, 2004).

[96] Mary C. Segers, Ted G. Jelen, *A Wall of Separation? Debating the Public Role of Religion* (Lanham, Boulder, New York, Oxford: Rowman & Littlefield, 1998); Henk Vroom, Henk Woldring (red.), *Religies in het publieke domein* (Zoetermeer: Meinema, 2002); Ton Bernts (red.), *Boodschap aan de kerken? Religie als sociaal en moreel kapitaal* (Zoetermeer: Meinema, 2004); Anton van Harskamp, *Van fundi's, spirituelen en moralisten: over civil society en religie* (Kampen: Kok, 2003); Wibren van der Burg, *Over religie, moraal en politiek: een vrijzinnig alternatief* (Baarn: Ten Have, 2005).

to accept the modern liberal context while maintaining some of the traditional theocratic fervour. To a greater or lesser extent, they ally God's kingdom with the earthly realm and will therefore, as Christians, assume political responsibility. In light of this analysis, the "Anabaptist or anti-Constantinian option" is the only one that is separate from and, in a certain sense, opposed to all the others. Just because it consistently takes the post-Christian context into account and distances itself from the synthesis of church and state that has existed for centuries, it becomes the wick from which the contemporary politico-theological debate takes flame.

This central conceptual position is confirmed by the actual roots of the current upswing in the politico-theological debate. These origins are mainly traceable to American theologian Stanley Hauerwas.[97] That William T. Cavanaugh, an editor of a recent standard work in this area, expresses ideas that are clearly derived from Hauerwas, is no surprise. In addition, John Milbank, who has developed his own position in this debate, places an emphasis on nonviolence in a way that comes close to Hauerwas.[98] At the same time, it should not be forgotten that Hauerwas also borrowed ideas from Mennonite theologian John Howard Yoder, who has been offering a political interpretation of Jesus' kingship and the church since the 1960s.[99] By this, he was not, during this period, referring to existing political ideals in which the church tries to demonstrate its social relevance. For Yoder, the stress on the political character of the gospel was based on the insight that Jesus' kingship, God's kingdom, the church and all of Christian ethics bore a distinctive political character of its own. This politics of the kingdom is real politics, not a metaphor for spiritual reality. This creates confrontation between two rival political entities; the kingdom of God and the earthly realm collide. The politics of the church and the politics of the state oppose each other. The classical Anabaptist contrast between the two realms is readily discernible in this position. This contrast is returning to the modern political stage and is playing a major role in the current debate.

At the same time, the current debate makes it clear that this opposi-

---

[97] Peter Scott, William T. Cavanaugh (eds.), *The Blackwell Companion to Political Theology* (Oxford: Blackwell, 2004); William T. Cavanaugh, *Theopolitical Imagination* (London: T&T Clark, 2002); William Cavanaugh, "Stan the Man: A Thoroughly Biased Account of a Completely Unobjective Person", in: Berkman, *Reader*, 17–32.

[98] John Milbank, *Theology and Social Theory: Beyond Secular Reason* (Oxford: Blackwell, 1990), 5f., 9, 387ff., 398, 419.

[99] Yoder, *Politics*; idem, *The Priestly Kingdom: Social Ethics as Gospel* (Notre Dame: University of Notre Dame Press, 1984); Wright, *Disavowing Constantine*.

tion is not exclusively Anabaptist. We also encounter this duality earlier in the Bible (e.g., John's *Revelation)* and in the Early Church. Augustine also maintained it, although he also accepted political participation of Christians in the period after Constantine, admittedly in a cautious and conditional manner. Oliver O'Donovan and others have shown that this contrast has existed since Augustine and was present even during the Constantinian period, and is therefore noticeable in the political theology that takes root in this period. During the Reformation, all traditions ultimately chose the more comprehensive and less dualistic idea of one harmonious kingdom of Christ that was furthermore manifest in two spheres ("regiments"). Only the Anabaptists maintained the traditional contrast, and they associated it with different conceptions, particularly their dualist view of the relationship between creation and recreation. For this reason, this classical approach became burdened with the odium of being "Anabaptist". In reality, however, the Anabaptist tradition preserved an older classical line of theological thought in regard to this point. It consequently plays a key role in re-introducing this historical notion into theological debate in response to the rupture that becomes visible in the late-modern age.

O'Donovan's political theology illustrates that no one can simply overlook its role. O'Donovan is one of the most important contributors to contemporary politico-theological discourse. As mentioned, he too eventually arrives at a position that accepts the separation of church and state, while continuing to discern a public role for the church and to facilitate Christian political responsibility. As an Anglican, he even shows sympathy for the "establishment" situation. Yet, his thinking also demonstrates how the Anabaptist option dominates the current debate. Challenged by the thinking of Yoder and Hauerwas, he devotes much of his ground-breaking work, *The Desire of the Nations,* to a profound confrontation with the Anabaptist option. Moreover, extensive Biblical and theological analysis leads him to adopt a political interpretation of the kingdom of God comparable to the two other thinkers. In line with Augustine, he also subsequently describes a tension between the heavenly kingdom and the earthly realm. His views on Christian political responsibility also therefore incorporate this tension and the post-Constantinian context of today.[100]

---

[100] De Bruijne, *Levend*, 36–44, 64–69, 77–81; Oliver O'Donovan, *The Desire of the Nations: Rediscovering the Roots of Political Theology* (Cambridge: Cambridge University Press, 1996); idem, *The Ways of Judgement: The Bampton Lectures 2003* (Grand Rapids, Cambridge: Eerdmans, 2005); idem, *Irenaeus*; Augustinus, *De Stad van God* (vert.

The rediscovery of eschatology in the nineteenth and twentieth centuries and its incorporation in the dialectic tradition also have roles to play in this movement.[101] Yoder was a student of Barth for a while, and there was good reason for him to become the translator of Hendrikus Berkhof's *Christ and the Powers*.[102] Exactly this eschatological theological innovation uncovers one of the reasons why Neo-Calvinist political reflection requires renewal. Its work often still bears the stamp of the nineteenth-century emphasis on creation and history, and has insufficiently adopted the eschatological twist. As a result, Neo-Calvinism operates too easily in assuming continuity between God's kingdom and the earthly realm. It is precisely with regard to this point that the new duality between the two realms preserved in the Anabaptist tradition is so important. This again illustrates the irony that inflicts Evangelicals in the late modern era who dismiss the Anabaptist duality in order to move closer to Neo-Calvinism. The duality being abandoned is precisely the element that should stimulate necessary renewal of Neo-Calvinism.

Evangelical Christians and Current Political Theology
This current political and theological debate is given little attention by Evangelical and Reformed Christians.[103] For example, the recent political theology of American Baptist Wayne Grudem virtually ignores it. He advocates an approach that tends to principled pluralism. While he does not aspire for Christianization of the nation, he nevertheless seeks to promote Christian influence of the public domain. Political indifference among Christians is dismissed by him. Furthermore, his specific political choices share to a great extent a conservative political agenda in which America's interests lie in close proximity to the interests of

G. Wijdeveld; Baarn: Ambo, 1983), I, Inleiding; V, 1, 19, 25; XI, 1; XVII, 21; XVIII, 18, 22. 48f., 51, 54; IX, 17; Oliver O'Donovan, Joan Lockwood O'Donovan, *Bonds of Imperfection: Christian Politics Past and Present* (Grand Rapids: Eerdmans, 2004), 48–72; Van 't Spijker, *Gereformeerden*.

[101] Gerard den Hertog, *De passie van de hoop: over de verhouding van eschatologie en ethiek* (Zoetermeer: Boekencentrum, 2007).

[102] De Bruijne, *Levend*, 193; Hendrikus Berkhof, *Christ and the Powers* (transl. John Howard Yoder, PA: Herald Press, ²1977).

[103] Illustrative is the fact that the recent Christian Encyclopaedia appears to be unaware to this latter revival (Theo Witvliet, s.v. *Politieke theologie*, in: G. Harinck *et al.* (ed.), *Christelijke Encyclopedie* (Kampen: Kok, 2005). In the United States a new movement of "Younger Evangelicals" has developed. They adopt anti-Constantinian positions and develop a new local way of being church in society. Nevertheless they only seem to select some aspects from the new political theology that suits their agenda without participation in the underlying politico-theological discussions (Webber, *Younger Evangelicals*, 110, 113f., 117–122).

Christians. A confrontation with Stanley Hauerwas' school cannot be avoided on both points, especially since another important Baptist theologian, James McClendon, also belongs to this school.[104] After all, this school argues for a form of political detachment, not as the unreflective traditional Evangelical position renounced by Grudem but based on a contextually aware political theology. Moreover, Hauerwas provides the sharpest critique of the contemporary American synthesis between Christianity and the nation. In this light, it is incomprehensible that Grudem chooses the position that he does without entering into dialogue with Hauerwas or relating to him as a thinker. He certainly identifies a few other contributors to the politico-theological debate (for instance, he points to O'Donovan's work), but never really incorporates any of their material ideas. In effect, the entire current politico-theological debate is left outside his comprehensive study entirely.

In this way, Grudem illustrates what I also suggested about the Dutch Evangelicals who joined the tradition of the later *ChristenUnie*. Many Evangelical theologians also operate based on the mindset of "Christendom" and consequently they too easily join approaches about which they could at least pose fruitful critical questions based on their own tradition. For example De Vries finds it particularly important to warn against the tendency to be insulated from culture. Do not become Amish, he tells his readers. This contrasts strikingly with the sympathy for exactly the Amish with which Hauerwas now recommends the Anabaptist option as an alternative.[105]

Sometimes that Anabaptist option remains discernible. For instance, Cees Verharen repeats a warning first issued by Peter Kuzmic, a Croatian, while engaged in a process of Evangelical reflection on a united Europe. Kuzmic points to the Eastern Churches and warns churches against a Constantinian model of cooperation with the state. On the other hand, Verharen joins with those who emphasize "values", a stance that is often typical of a modernized Christian political contribution such as "civil religion". [106]

Dutch Baptist Henk Bakker operates explicitly on the basis of the Anabaptist tradition, while simultaneously participating in the Christian political tradition of the *ChristenUnie*. He expresses, for example, reservations about much thinking in Christian politics that turns out to be based on majority options. He engages in dialogue with Hauer-

---

[104] McClendon, *Ethics*.
[105] De Vries, "Flexibiliteit", 39.
[106] Verharen, "Hele kerk", 39f.

was, although, for Bakker, this remains only an isolated appeal. The broader politico-theological debate is overlooked. When dealing with major points in the debate, he fails to engage in the relevant discussions between Hauerwas and other approaches. This obscures his own position; sometimes he even seems to return to the view of a church setup to be of service and therefore adapted to society, albeit from a position in the margin. As a peacemaker, this church will make a difference in the world of nations. In this view, I do not recognize the uncompromised, prophetic element that characterizes the Anabaptist option. In Hauerwas' approach, the peace that the church wants to establish is not automatically recognized as the peace for which society awaits. For this peace, society must first learn to look and think from within the narrative tradition of the church itself.[107]

A similar observation applies to some publications by the theologian Bernard Reitsma, who belongs to the reformed tradition but remains receptive to Anabaptist ideas on this point.[108] He also emphasizes the minority position of the church on the margin and opposes a Christian connection to political power. At the same time, he also fails to make any link to the existing politico-theological debate. Even the related position of Hauerwas receives little or no consideration. The same is also true of Reitsma's teacher Bram van de Beek. Starting with an entirely different (Reformed) background, he comes to conclusions similar to those of Hauerwas. He does not, however, operate within the larger politico-theological debate of the moment.[109]

Theologians such as Bakker and Reitsma represent the movements that I now regard as necessary: an Evangelical theologian who remains himself while participating in the existing Neo-Calvinist political tradition, and a Reformation theologian who is not ashamed to take traditional Anabaptist ideas seriously. Nevertheless, explicit commitment to the broader politico-theological debate is desirable here.

Especially in this borderland between Evangelical (in the narrower

---

[107] Bakker, *Weg*, 235–250; Henk Bakker, "Bijdrage Hauerwas Symposium Vrije Universiteit 26-02-2009" (unpublished); Henk Bakker, "Groeiende bomen en diepe wortels: over de McDonaldisering van het geloof", Bezinningsavond IZB Nijkerk, 16–05–2006.

[108] Bernhard Reitsma, "De kerk in de context van de Islam: macht of minderheid", *Soteria* 25/3 (2008); idem, "De kerk als missionaire minderheid: hoe kan de kerk als minderheid getuigend aanwezig zijn in een multireligieuze samenleving?", *Soteria* 26/2 (2009), 6–17.

[109] For example A. van de Beek, *God doet recht: eschatologie als christologie* (Zoetermeer: Meinema, 2008).

sense) and Reformed is where O'Donovan's ideas may prove fruitful. His basic ideas match Hauerwas' views because, in his case, the kingdom of God is a political reality that is coming to dissolve the earth's kingdoms. However, his approach arrives at a different outcome. The emergence of Christ's kingdom does not immediately bring the dissolution of existing history (the "saeculum") and its political authorities and structures. Nor does the church then become immediately recognizable as a political alternative. Because Christ's kingdom is still hidden, governments retain the task of maintaining provisional justice in anticipation of Christ's final judgement. At the same time, the church can not exist independently of these vanishing structures of political authority and human communality. On the basis of the gospels, the church should beckon all authorities to recognize the imminent end of their reign and to submit to Christ. Refusal to make such submission constitutes a threat to their political authority. This contrasts with a Neo-Calvinist approach which views politics as a created area of life and which regards a choice against Christ as only a problem of direction, and not the cause of a crisis for political structures as such. Like Augustine (and Kuyper!), O'Donovan sees political authority as an unnatural emergency measure in response to sin. Political authorities that do not recognize Christ are therefore occupying positions that do not really belong to them and live under the threat of the wrath of God, such as Psalm 2 indicates. Apart from Christ's kingdom, political reality is indeed an infected area, although it continues to serve Christ for the time being. O'Donovan is close to the Anabaptist option at this point. But when political authorities respond to the Gospel that the Church proclaims and recognize Christ's kingship, O'Donovan sees more opportunities than Anabaptists do. He does not go so far as to include their earthly realm in Christ's kingdom once they, as individuals, have joined the church and entered into this kingdom. Worldly power remains a temporary structure that will disappear. However, the way that they fulfil this for some time, while still maintaining worldly responsibility, is now inevitably affected by their new Christian convictions and life-style.

For the ideal of a Christian society, this means that such a society can never become an independent aim as such. A Christian society can only be brought indirectly into existence, as a blessing accompanying missionary success. The greater the number of Christians in a society, the greater is the chance that the features of that society become in a certain way Christian. As increasingly more political authorities become Christian, there is a stronger possibility that their works indirectly change the character of a society in a Christian direction. For O'Donovan, it cannot be a direct goal of Christian political engagement to strive for a Christian society. Christian political activity is more modest and limited, a characteristic that enables it to endure more persuasively in the current, no longer Christian context. Politically, Christians must cooperate to achieve the provisional justice and the provisional stability required in the earthly realm as long as Christ's final judgement has not yet occurred.

More than the Anabaptist option and more than Bakker's variant, O'Donovan also takes into account that the post-Christian Western society is not directly comparable to the pre-Christian society from the period of the Early Church. The specific mission of Christian political engagement today is that its adherents must speak and act in a society that, viewed historically, once displayed a Christian identity, or at least some derivatives thereof. All kinds of phenomena have been influenced by the Gospel. These historical features can be positively valued despite the many failures. In late modernity, Western society tried and is still trying to undertake a harsh separation from this history, but it cannot undo its own past. This paradox precisely is what underlies many current political issues (e.g., in dealing with suffering and death). Christians therefore have a special possibility and opportunity to make specific contributions to the resolution of this paradox by prophetically exposing and clarifying the background of many discussions, and by simultaneously assuming practical responsibility. Even if they serve another king and belong to another kingdom, they do not operate from outside, from an alternative contrasting society. They act from within. Viewed historically, the Western society, partly formed by the Christian tradition, also constitutes their society. Moreover, the church before the *Eschaton* occurs does not have a locus of its own. Basically, the church can be considered the true society, the society of the future. However, it can still not detach itself from the existing society and exist independently. It remains, to a large extent, dependant on the existing societies and should operate, especially in the Western post-Christian situation, from the inside. O'Donovan therefore argues for a continued public role for the church, not only in acts of service but also by means of prophetic disclosures and clarifications.

The above shows even more clearly why the shift of certain Dutch Evangelicals to the Neo-Calvinist political tradition cannot just simply be appreciated as something positive. I pointed out earlier that they abandon typical Anabaptist features at three points. They do not operate from within a dualist two-kingdom doctrine. They henceforth see the political atmosphere as one of the areas of creation that in themselves are good. And they also try to avert secularization by ostensibly political means. Exactly with regard to these three points, however, the Neo-Calvinist tradition requires a certain Anabaptist correction in the face of the late modern secular context. In O'Donovan's approach we see a way in which this might occur. He offers a model in which Christians no less than those in the Neo-Calvinist tradition can bear political responsibility in the changed context. Not without reason Peter Heslam characterizes him as someone in whom you recognize the Kuyperian spirit.[110] At the same time, O'Donovan allows for a sharp duality between God's kingdom and the earthly realm. He also does not readily declare the political sphere to be a created domain that in its structural dimension can be unquestionably accepted. Moreover, he frees Christians from all types of re-christianization ideals, without, at the same time, principally condemning a Christianized society or a Christianized state as such. His views therefore offer Neo-Calvinism an opportunity to rediscover the contextual component that was still crucial for Kuyper. This opens the possibility for more realistic, and in the current Dutch context for more fitting, Christian political objectives.

5. Final Remarks

Promising examples already exist elsewhere in the world on which to model the necessary dialogue between Evangelicals (in the narrower sense) and Dutch Reformed Christians.[111] Moore even notes (somewhat too optimistically) that meanwhile all American Evangelicals (he also means Reformed Christians) have learned to put God's eschatological kingdom at the centre of all their political reflection. He sees them together facing the challenge of elaborating this emphasis. In so doing, the dispensational views of Evangelicals must not be abandoned, but brought into dialogue with the emphasis on the covenant among Re-

---

[110] Heslam, Creating, 8.143.
[111] E.g. in Budziszewski, *Evangelicals*. Also in the appropriation of the Kuyperian tradition by Vincent E. Bacote, a Baptist theologian (*The Spirit in Public Theology: Appropriating the Legacy of Abraham Kuyper*, Grand Rapids: Baker Academic, 2005). On the other side attention is paid to the Anabaptist tradition by Reformed thinkers like Richard J. Mouw, *God*, 150–175 (wants to integrate Kuyperian and Anabaptist moralities) and Mark A. Noll, *Adding Cross to Crown: The Political Significance of Christ's Passion* (Grand Rapids: Baker Books, 1996).

formed Christians. This exchange might clarify the fact that, and the ways in which, the kingdom of God is already active, though not obviously visible or ostentatiously triumphant. Moore speaks of a "Reformed dispensationalism" that should simultaneously be an "apocalyptic Kuyperianism". But he warns about new points of difference (e.g., around the authority of Scripture or the doctrine of God). These divisions, however, are not so much factors distinguishing "Evangelicals" from "Reformed", but occur within each of these traditions themselves. The resulting divisions may frustrate joint public reflection.[112]

In any event, it is high time that Evangelical and Reformed Christians in the Netherlands fully participate in the current politico-theological debate. Such involvement is precisely what will guarantee their respective identities and mutual conversation and optimally mobilize them for the political mission in the late modern secular Netherlands.

---

[112] Moore, *Kingdom*, 175f. 183f.

Chapter Five

Ecclesiology in Context:
Urban Church Planting in the Netherlands

Stefan Paas

1. Introduction

Evangelicals have always been known for their missionary zeal. Usually, this went together with a pragmatic or even dismissive attitude towards ecclesiology. However, in a late-modern urban context ecclesiological questions are inevitable when Christians set out for mission. These questions will be the main subject of this chapter.[1]

Christian community formation is part of the answer that human beings give to the Gospel—we may say their "conversion". This answer will always be culture-specific, because the "ideal", a-contextual respondent does not exist.[2] Therefore, in its organisation and life together the church will always reflect characteristics of the broader culture to which it belongs. This was so in the New Testament and it will always be that way.[3] Gradually, the fact that late-modern Europeans, if the Gospel affects them, choose different types of community than their ancestors, is gaining attention. In several countries one can witness the emergence of mostly small, fluid, flexible, eclectic Christian communities, in which a new generation seems to feel better at home than in the traditional "congregation".[4] This seems to be especially true for younger city dwellers. This observation is the point of departure for this article.

---

[1] I have dealt with some preliminary questions in: Stefan Paas, "Kerken vormen: de gemeenschappelijke structuur van het Evangelie anno nu", *Soteria* 23/1 (2006), 6–26.

[2] Cf. Andrew F. Walls, "Culture and Conversion in Christian History", in: idem, *The Missionary Movement in Christian History: Studies in the Transmission of Faith* (New York: Orbis Books, 1996), 43–46.

[3] For the relationship between "secular" community types and church planting in the New Testament, cf. Andrew D. Clarke, *Serve the Community of Christ: Christians as Leaders and Ministers* (Grand Rapids: Eerdmans, 2000), 11–141.

[4] A rapidly growing number of websites are exploring this phenomenon. E.g., http://emergingchurch.info, www.freshexpressions.org.uk, www.encountersontheedge.org.uk, etc.

Here, I reflect in particular on some experiences with new church formation in the Netherlands; and I ask what can be its contribution to theological thinking about the church.

For me, this is no theoretical question. From January 2006 until December 2008 I have been working professionally in a church plant in Amsterdam, called Via Nova (www.vianova-amsterdam.nl). This new church, planted by the Christian Reformed Church in the Netherlands, is particularly focused on young professionals in Amsterdam.[5] More than other segments of society this group consists of people who represent a late-modern Western view of life. As such, they are a good "control group" as to questions about the future of the church in a post-Christian and post-secular society.[6] In the preparatory stage of the new church plant, we have dealt intensively with matters of church planting and community formation among this social group. How do they respond to the Gospel in terms of their own life? This question will be my guiding light in the remainder of this article. Without even trying to be exhaustive, I will describe three ecclesiological shifts that I observe in our practice of church formation: (1) from monopoly to marketing, (2) from the congregation to a network church, and (3) from an emphasis on confessional foundations to an emphasis on mission and values. In my opinion these shifts are crucial for *ecclesiogenesis* in a secular and individualistic context. Before discussing them further, however, I will first present some details of this context.

2. *Young Urban Professionals in Amsterdam*

In 2003 and 2004, a team of the Christian Reformed Church in Amsterdam conducted dozens of semi-structured interviews with young, unchurched professionals or "knowledge workers".[7] This group consists of people, born between ca. 1970 and 1985, who have consciously chosen the city as a place to work, to find friends and to be in touch with cultural resources. They are highly educated and many of them are making a lot of money or expect to do so in the near future. These people have a

---

[5] Via Nova has been described in several Dutch studies. See, e.g., Gerrit Noort et al., *Als een kerk opnieuw begint: handboek voor missionaire gemeenschapsvorming* (Zoetermeer: Boekencentrum, 2008), 136–146.

[6] I have discussed these terms in: Stefan Paas, "Post-Christian, Post-Christendom, and Post-Modern Europe: Towards the Interaction of Missiology and the Social Sciences", *MisSt* 28 (2011), 3–25.

[7] *Resultaten van de interviews onder niet-kerkelijke jonge hoger opgeleide Amsterdammers* (Amsterdam 2004).

high degree of autonomy and many daily options are available to them. They are creative, career focused, materialistic, hedonistic, flexible, ambitious, outspoken, and competitive. Church and (Christian) faith are not very much in the picture, although many of them are willing to discuss faith-related subjects. Regarding belief in God, we could call most of these young career people "agnostic". Usually, they do not have clear ideas about God or the divine, but they do not have strong objections either. Overall, this subject is one in which they are not very interested. Their image of the church is ambiguous. They acknowledge that the church has some use for certain people groups (elderly, lonely) and as a public service (weddings and funerals), but that is where it stops. When asked what kind of church would be interesting for them, they answer that this church should have a lot of room for debate and questions. It must be "informal and warm" (probably the best translation of Dutch *gezellig*) and it must not be too dogmatic about truth and morals. On the other hand, this church must have a clear religious profile: spiritual questions must be central. It should be about faith and religion.

This profile is very different from that of the average churchgoing Dutchman. Almost everything that is valued by church people is frightening for this group—and vice versa. Recent research into regular churchgoers (at least once in two weeks) in the Netherlands confirms that this group (approximately 5–10% of the Dutch population) is the opposite of these young Amsterdammers in almost every respect. For example, the core support group of the Evangelical broadcasting organisation in the Netherlands (*Evangelische Omroep*) reveals itself as an example of traditional, community-focused values, with an emphasis on loyalty and duty.[8] Other studies confirm this opposition between church members and Via Nova's "target group". An investigation of Dutch values and lifestyles, *Mentality*, by the marketing bureau Motivaction (www.motivaction.nl) distinguishes eight different social milieus in the Netherlands. Church people can be found primarily among "traditional citizens" (18% of the Dutch population). This group is characterised by conservatism and attachment to the status quo. These people are duty bound, they trust institutions, avoid risks and are involved with the care of ethnic minorities and environmental issues. Family values are very important for this group that consists of relatively more women and fewer younger and highly educated people.

---

[8] W.H. Dekker, W. Vollbehr, *De verlegenheid voorbij: onderzoek ter gelegenheid van het 40-jarig bestaan van de Evangelische Omroep* (Ede: Christelijke Hogeschool Ede, 2007).

The profile of younger "knowledge workers" in Amsterdam, however, is more consistent with the lifestyle types "cosmopolites" (10% of the general population), "upwardly mobiles" (13%), and, to a lesser degree, "postmodern hedonists" (10%). All these groups are influenced to a high degree by modern and postmodern values, with self-development, individualism and freedom as linking pins. In an important study of the Scientific Council for Government Policy (Wetenschappelijke Raad voor het Regeringsbeleid), *Geloven in het publieke domein*, the Motivaction typology is refined further and complemented with other analyses. On this basis the SCGP distinguishes six lifestyles, defined by their different strategies to give meaning to life.[9] Two lifestyles are dominating the "target group" of young professionals in Amsterdam: "non-religious and humanistic" (NRH; 12% of the Dutch population) and "non-affiliated spiritual people" (NAS; 26%). The group called NRH experiences meaning in life primarily through relatives and friends. Pleasure and fun are important goals in life, with respect and tolerance as most important life conditions. This group consists of people who are flexible, have broad cultural appetites, want to keep control over their own lives, are eager to perform, and have a pragmatic attitude to life. From a religious perspective they are omnivores: they like to keep their options open, but are not especially interested in religion.

The other lifestyle group, NAS, looks the same as the first group in many respects, but is clearly much more interested in transcendence and spirituality. Within this context, its emphasis is on enrichment of life, pleasure and responsibility, rather than on rules of life and obedience. Autonomy and self-development are important values for this group as well. When these conditions are satisfied, people are open to forms of spirituality that are not (too obviously) connected to institutions and doctrines. So, this group too is very different from the "Christian" lifestyle (ca. 25% of the general population). All of this leads to the reasonable assumption that this group will find it hard to find its way in existing churches. Basically, there is a lack of "natural bridges" between the majority of church members and this group of young, secular urbanites. For us, this has been the most important missionary motivation to plant a new church, with a focus on this group. This motivation is confirmed by the reactions of attendees of services in Via Nova. One of the most frequently heard is this: "Nice to see so many people like

---

[9] W.B.H.J. van de Donk et al. (eds.), *Geloven in het publieke domein: verkenningen van een dubbele transformatie* (Amsterdam: Amsterdam University Press, 2006), 171–207.

me".

The group of young "knowledge workers" in Amsterdam belongs to the first generations that have been raised in a country where most people are no (longer) members of a church. Most of them come from non-religious backgrounds, with only vague memories of church and Christianity. As a consequence, they have only a very superficial knowledge of Christian beliefs. Moreover, they are real individualists; they are used to making their own choices and are allergic to every attempt from others to make decisions for them. Control of their own lives is crucial for them. In many respects they are the archetypes of late-modern man: critical, insecure, consumerist, very sensitive to matters of identity, with a great need of control, hedonistic, etcetera. Whenever Christian community formation takes place among this group, we can learn something about the future of the church in cities of the West in general and in the Netherlands in particular.

Now I shall turn to the description of three important shifts that to my opinion are characteristic of this future.

3. *From Monopoly to Marketing*

In his masterpiece *Transforming Mission* David Bosch (following Hans Küng) describes six historic missiological paradigms, beginning with the Early Church and ending with an emerging "ecumenical" paradigm.[10] This concept of consecutive paradigms is interesting when we consider the missionary context in the Netherlands. We can characterise this context in one sentence like this: people usually do have a certain interest for "religion", but not for "church". For many, faith and spirituality have received a place in their personal project of self-development. However, personal autonomy is the core condition of this project.[11] Which missiological paradigm would fit best this reality? In my opinion a *marketing* paradigm deserves serious consideration here. A market is an intermediary between supply and demand. The underlying assumption of the marketing metaphor implies that there is still

---

[10] David J. Bosch, *Transforming Mission: Paradigm Shifts in Theology of Mission*, (Maryknoll: Orbis Books, 1991, ¹⁸2003), 179ff.

[11] The relationship between a shift towards (post)modern values and changes in the religious outlook of Europeans is described by Ronald Inglehart, *Modernization and Postmodernization: Cultural, Economic, and Political Change in 43 Societies* (Princeton: Princeton University Press, 1997). For a case study, cf. Paul Heelas, Linda Woodhead et al., *The Spiritual Revolution: Why Religion is Giving Way to Spirituality* (Oxford: Blackwell, 2005).

an unaltered demand for religious meaning in the Netherlands.[12] However, on the supply side things have changed: the religious monopoly of the church has been broken. People have lots of options and they use them at will. Therefore, suppliers have to distinguish themselves; they must present their products as visibly and attractively as possible, without forgetting their core objectives. In a recent study, the Dutch sociologist of religion Erik Sengers has thought through this market metaphor, with a view towards mission in the Netherlands.[13] In this book he points out the importance of a clear mission statement, good publicity, and an effective use of resources. Our contemporary situation is so complex and multidimensional that it has simply become impossible to be all things to all people at the same time and in the same place. This is particularly true in the context of one of the most multi-ethnic cities of the planet—Amsterdam.[14]

Marketing is severely criticized in the church. Very good reasons can exist to do so, but it is important to emphasize: we are talking about a *metaphor*, nothing less or more than that. Christian mission is not identical with marketing, but it serves our purpose to look at it from a marketing perspective. In this way dimensions can come into view that would not have been visible otherwise. Also, a comparison with other missiological approaches and metaphors in history can be instructive. When the Netherlands was christianized, in the age of Charlemagne and his successors, mission was—at least to a great extent—equal with *conquest*, i.e. the subjection of pagans. During the Reformation era the emphasis was on *education*—the progressive evangelization of nominal Christians. In the nineteenth century the mission of the church in the Netherlands was defined as the *elevation of the masses*, whereas in the twentieth century the missionary task was first seen as *evangelism*

---

[12] Of course, this assumption of unchanging religious needs is an acknowledged weak spot of this paradigm. For a criticism of "rational choice" explanations of the religious situation in Europe, see e.g., Grace Davie, *Europe, the Exceptional Case: Parameters of Faith in the Modern World* (London: Darton, Longman & Todd, 2002, ²2007); Grace Davie et al. (eds.), *Predicting Religion: Christian, Secular and Alternative Futures* (Aldershot: Ashgate, 2003). However, even if this assumption is not true (something I consider very probable), I think a modest application of marketing philosophy in a church context still possible. For this, see also Norman Shawchuck et al., *Marketing for Congregations: Choosing to Serve People More Effectively* (Nashville: Abingdon, 1992).

[13] Erik Sengers, *Aantrekkelijke kerk: nieuwe bewegingen in kerkelijk Nederland op de religieuze markt* (Delft: Eburon, 2006).

[14] Per 1-1-2009 Amsterdam had 177 nationalities within its territory. With a population of 756,347, this makes the city one of the most multicultural, but also one of the most fragmented cities in the world. Source: www.amsterdam.nl.

(regaining the lost sheep) and thereafter as *service* (or *presence*). These metaphors were all inspired by changing circumstances. All of them contain certain disadvantages, some more than others. However, in a consumer's society like ours the marketing paradigm quickly jumps on the stage, and why would we reject this immediately?

In his book Sengers only discusses missionary activities in existing congregations and Christian organizations. However, the marketing metaphor comes into view mostly in church planting projects. As an example I want to discuss the phenomenon of the "target group". Whoever wants to start a missionary project, must think about what he or she exactly wants to achieve, with whom, and about the resources that are available. Thus, in the practice of church planting, having a "target group" is almost inevitable. Deciding on a specific target group is not so much inspired by a desire for efficiency and success, as is sometimes suggested by Dutch critics.[15] It is motivated by church planters with an appeal to *missionary* reasons—they have, as it were, integrated the marketing metaphor in their missiological reflection. From my own situation I only mention the question of language. In a city with 177 different ethnic groups, as is the case in Amsterdam, the choice for Dutch as *lingua franca* in church is not neutral. Irrevocably we exclude people by preaching in Dutch. Anyone can imagine that the same is true for choices in areas of venue, music, decoration, emotional intensity and the like. Given limited resources and the vulnerability in general of a new project, that it would be possible to make choices in all of these areas with different people groups in view is hard to imagine. A new project like Via Nova must therefore focus on a target group. In our context this means that the choices we make are accounted for with respect to a certain "calibration group", in our case: young, secular, career focused people. In no way do we want to refuse other people, but we fine-tune our choices with this particular group in view. Crucial to note, therefore, is that this focus on a specific group is not the same as excluding people. Rather, it is a matter of choosing a point of entry in the complex tapestry of the city. The big question projects like these face is: how can we gradually broaden our community, how can this community become more inclusive and become more of a reflection of the city itself? What is inevitable in *starting* a church—a certain exclusivity—is a sin in *being* a church. This tension is the territory in which many church plants have to work.

---

[15] Like Sake Stoppels, "Kerkplanting", in: Rein Brouwer et al., *Levend lichaam: dynamiek van christelijke geloofsgemeenschappen in Nederland* (Kampen: Kok, 2007), 94–95.

The marketing metaphor requires some theological reflection, however. I want to give two suggestions, one starting with the incarnation, the other with the cross. As for the first suggestion: whenever the Gospel enters a new culture, making choices is necessary. From Abraham's election to the incarnation of Christ salvation always started in particularity, only to end in universality. Jesus became a *man*; he did not become humanity. We might say that the incarnation meant a choice for a "limited reach". Salvation is from the Jews; it started in a small area in Israel, among a circumscribed group of people. But that is not where it stayed. Thus, the incarnation can be used as a confirmation and as a critique of "target group" thinking: universal salvation can only start in a particular way, but always keeps the whole of creation in view.

Regarding the second suggestion, we must consider what Paul writes in 1 Corinthians 1 and 2 about the cross as a sign of God's preference for what is weak and foolish. Just like it pleased God to save the world through the seeming failure of the Jewish Messiah, he works today through that which has no status or power. Paul applies this to his own life: he came to the Corinthians in fear and insecurity, without a respectful position. My impression is that the marketing metaphor can help churches to understand what it means to be "weak". If we can see the recipient of the Gospel no longer as someone to be conquered, educated or relieved, but as a (critical) "customer" or "consumer", the balance of power between preacher and hearer starts to shift. It is remarkable that Paul's speech about the foolishness of preaching and his own weakness is used in many churches to reinforce the traditional preacher instead of "weakening" him or her. It has been used as an excuse for a manner of preaching or evangelizing that does not seriously study the questions of modern people, for finding a power basis in theological knowledge, thus keeping the recipient in dependence. However, when the hearer does not have a high opinion of our knowledge and is not very eager to hear what we have to tell, then we will be "weak" indeed. I think that a position like that is reached primarily when a small group of Christians steps out of its "comfort zone" and sets out to plant a church among people who do not know the Gospel. Seen from this perspective church planting is a vulnerable practice in every respect—theologically, financially, and in matters of organisation and human resource. These are the precise contexts in which creative and innovative theology is born. This may be another confirmation that mission is the mother of theology, and the church its maternity ward.

4. From the Congregation to a Network Church

For many Christians being church is equal to being a congregation. Also in this article I use these terms as rough equivalents. However, strictly speaking, the congregation as we know it is an institutional representation of the church, with a specific structure and origin.[16] According to some—among them many church planters—the congregation even is an institutional fossilization of something that originally started as a movement of disciples of Jesus.[17] In this context there is often a reference to the *network* as a typical urban, late-modern, flexible and "liquid" form of community. For people who live in a network it is typical that geographic location is less important to them than social location. "To live in one place no longer means to live together, and living together no longer means living in the same place" (Ulrich Beck).[18] To city-dwellers terms like "neighbourhood" or "district" are less determining for their identity than their (self-chosen) relationships with others. They hardly know their neighbours, if they know them at all. Those with whom they feel related and for whom they feel responsible, probably live somewhere else in the city. For many urbanites networks are far more important to their identity than their family, place of living or social class. This is especially true for the highly individualized group among which Via Nova is working. One should expect that community formation in this context will have many network characteristics.

Pete Ward mentions four advantages of such a "network church":[19] (1) informal relationships are more important for being church than the institutional and organisational dimensions of church, structured meetings, etcetera; (2) in a globalized world, determined by economical laws, new religious "products" will be easier to access for every congregation (e.g., the latest worship songs). Through this, countless Christians all over the world can profit from each other's creativity, which will enrich congregational life considerably; (3) the leadership of the church is no longer able to control or even suffocate promising new developments on a local level. Everything will take place with far

---

[16] See Israel Galindo, *The Hidden Lives of Congregations: Discerning Church Dynamics* (Herndon: Alban Institute, 2004), 21–22.

[17] E.g., Michael Frost, Alan Hirsch, *The Shaping of Things to Come: Innovation and Mission for the 21st-Century Church* (Peabody, MA: Hendrickson, 2003). A Dutch example is Daniël de Wolf, *Jezus in de Millinx: woorden én daden in een Rotterdamse achterstandswijk* (Kampen: Kok, 2006), 41–57.

[18] Ulrich Beck, *What is Globalization?* (Cambridge: Polity, 2000), 74.

[19] Pete Ward, *Liquid Church: A Bold Vision How to Be God's People in Worship and Mission—A Flexible, Fluid Way of Being Church* (Peabody, MA: Hendrickson, 2002).

less possibilities for control. Through this the church can easily spread out in various social groups; (4) the borders of the church will become less defined and formal. Instead of membership lists churches will have a communication network and relationships in which Christian love and mutual support will be ingredients of a continuing "stream". Thus, the church can establish contacts with outsiders more easily, and in this way more people may be involved in the network called "church".

I recognize many of these characteristics in the practice of church formation. However, it may be a little bit naïve of Ward only to put these bright sides forward. Critical questions can be asked at every point of these advantages. For example, Third World churches do not have access at all to those networks in which the latest worship songs circulate. Poor inner city dwellers have little opportunity to build their own network. It would not be difficult (and not quite incorrect) to label this view as a typical middle class ecclesiology. However, this is not yet a theological assessment of a church that operates as a network. Here, I suggest two theological considerations, which are important in my opinion. The first can be used to support a network ecclesiology, the second to assess it critically.

From a missiological perspective the new situation in the Netherlands is unique. Every previous missionary movement in this country—Willibrord and Boniface, the Reformation, the nineteenth-century Reveil movement—could rely on a certain sympathy or even support from the ruling powers. Besides, the last two movements worked in a nominal Christian context. All of this has changed now. Therefore, I think that we, when we try to find historical models to be church in a culture that is by and large alienated from church life, as we know it, must not find wisdom in those ecclesial traditions that were supported by the powers that be. We will have to look in the margins of history. Especially, I think of the "free church" tradition—early Puritans and Anabaptists.[20] In my opinion ecclesiological notions have been devel-

---

[20] By putting these two groups together I do not want to suggest that these church traditions were completely similar. The emphasis on free church formation by Mennonites and early Baptists [cf. Nigel Wright, *Free Church, Free State: The Positive Baptist Vision* (Leicester: Authentic, 2005)] originated in the context of Luther's two Kingdom theology and was influenced by the jesuology of humanists like Erasmus of Rotterdam. Free church formation by the 16th Century Puritans was far more linked to Reformed covenant theology, especially in Bullinger's version [for this, see C. Graafland, *Van Calvijn tot Comrie: oorsprong en ontwikkeling van de leer van het verbond in het Gereformeerd Protestantisme* (Zoetermeer: Boekencentrum, 1994), 313–314]. Here, God's initiative in the covenant of grace was more emphasised as the context and source of the

oped here, that can be of use now. These churches share some important characteristics that can be very relevant in a modern network society.[21]

First, they see the congregation as a *voluntary community of believers*.[22] They reject the distinction between a visible and an invisible church as an artificial one, developed so that people could be seen as church members, even if they did not show any willingness to follow Jesus. With regard to the covenant, their covenantal theology has developed more along the lines of contract philosophy ("covenanting"): people decide to form a community in the presence of God and they oblige themselves to be accountable towards each other. This may be a model that can be of use in church planting in a modern city, in which voluntary community formation is the only way in which a church can emerge. For example, we can think of different consecutive stages of commitment, with vows or even signing contracts.[23]

Secondly, they have an *egalitarian structure*. This implies among other things a "low" theology of the offices. Having said this, a closer look at the Reformed tradition to which most Dutch churches belong would be instructive. The true church is, according to Nicaea, one, holy, catholic and apostolic. But how do we know whether somewhere in the Netherlands (say, Amsterdam) a true church is taking shape? To answer this question the Reformation has given us some specific *notae ecclesiae*: pure preaching of the Word, pure administration of the sacraments, and the exercise of church discipline (*Confessio Belgica*, 29). John Howard Yoder points to the fact that these *notae* first and foremost are responsibilities of the *offices*. Their application does not concern the church as a community called by Christ, but their "superstructure". When someone wants to see whether a certain church is "true", he or she must listen to the pastor preaching, check the Eucharist, and evaluate the disciplinary procedures. But the question how many people attend worship, the intensity of their listening to sermons, the

---

human decision for community. However, these two traditions were much more comparable in their underlining of the human will as an important aspect of community formation, in their accent on sanctification (not happy with the distinction between an invisible and a visible church), and in their confessed independence of worldly powers.

[21] See also Stefan Paas, *Vrede stichten: politieke meditaties* (Zoetermeer: Boekencentrum, 2007), 253–262.

[22] For criticism on *choice* as a constitutive criterion of church formation, see Oliver O'Donovan, *The Desire of the Nations: Rediscovering the Roots of Political Theology* (Cambridge: Cambridge University Press, 1996), 223–224.

[23] I have elaborated upon this in Stefan Paas, *De werkers van het laatste uur: de inwijding van nieuwkomers in het christelijk geloof en in de christelijke gemeente* (Zoetermeer: Boekencentrum, 2003), chapters 5–9.

question whether they can forgive their neighbours, the testimony of changed lives—apparently all of this does not belong to the definition of a true church.[24] Presently we can witness attempts to "repair" this by underlining notions like sharing the Gospel, service and community. In this way attention can be focused again on the actual *quality* of being church. For church formation in a major city the relevance of all this is evident. Modern networks are egalitarian and they consist of self-conscious people. Church formation implies that we must stimulate people to be accountable towards each other and it requires a strong emphasis on discipleship.[25]

Thirdly, "free churches" are usually *not organised in denominations*. I do not want to be an advocate of congregationalism here, but I do believe that denominations cannot be so strictly organised as they used to be—at least in the Netherlands. My country has become so fragmented and pluralistic that local churches from one denomination will face very different questions in different areas of the country. There will be far fewer opportunities to arrange matters from a central location, and perhaps we should not wish to do so. The first Christians were very reluctant to be centralists, as we can read in Acts 15. From a missionary perspective, making a new project accountable to denominational headquarters in every detail is not very helpful.

In a church-planting project many of these elements speak for themselves. An urgent matter for me is that the theological climate in the Netherlands be enriched by serious ecclesiological contributions from an "Anabaptist" or free-church angle. This will further the discussion and increase our resources to respond fundamentally to a changing missionary situation.

So, this first theological consideration may be used to support network thinking in an ecclesiological context. My second theological consideration is of a more critical nature. A network is usually seen as a complex of mutual relationships. As such it is an exchange of services. From this point of view it is primarily accessible for those people who can offer something. However, what about those who have nothing to offer? Jesus said that it is not hard to love your friends (Luke 6:32–35), but the core characteristic of Christian community is the *non-mutuality* of service. The prime example of this is love for those outside

---

[24] John Howard Yoder, "A People in the World", in: idem, *The Royal Priesthood: Essays Ecclesiological and Ecumenical* (Grand Rapids: Herald Press, 1994), 76.

[25] Cf. Wilbert R. Shenk, "Believing without Belonging? Reflections on the Consultation", *IRM* 92/365 (2003), 234–235.

("enemies"), as well as inside, the community. The first Christians "had everything in common", but this did not exclude that some of them gave more and others received more. A network that also wants to be a church must show who Jesus is. This means that there is a surplus of love: there is more to give than to receive. He, who did not come to be served but to serve, is the highest model of this unmutual love that is the characteristic of a Christian. Therefore, a new church in a city like Amsterdam must be a network to the extent that it relies on personal relationships and an egalitarian structure, with an emphasis on expertise and personal charisma rather than traditional authority.[26] However, this is only one side of the matter. A church that wants to be a network will be different than usual: typical of this network is that all relationships are triangular relationships—Christ mediates them. It is a network of people who have been liberated from their idols and who consider other people not as a means to their own ends. They have received more than any human being can give them.

How can we break through this almost natural mutuality of a network community? I mention two examples. First, from the very outset a strong diaconal emphasis should belong to every initiative of church planting. Attention within such an initiative cannot only be focused on people who attend its meetings. The inevitable decision for a "target group" must also lead to "local rootedness"—a vision for the place where one lives and gathers in worship.[27] Only in this way one can get involved in the lives of people who cannot afford the luxury of a network. Secondly, giving without an ulterior motive also means something for counselling. Especially new churches tend to attract all kinds of people with a sad ecclesial history. There is a real risk that those people will absorb all your time and energy, and you will drown in caring for people. When this happens, an important mindset to have is: "I will give these people only part of my time and attention. I do this without creating obligations. They do not have to pay me back in whatever respect". Doing this also helps you to create boundaries for *yourself* and thus protect yourself. A leader, especially in church, must

---

[26] Cf. Henk Witte, "Van systeem naar netwerken: de sociale gestalte van de oecumene", *WeZ* 33/2 (2004), 19.

[27] Commission on Urban Life and Faith, *Faithful Cities: A Call for Celebration, Vision and Justice* (Peterborough: Methodist Publishing House, 2006), 3: "[T]here are still many 'churches of place' with strong local connections. This local rootedness is often very longstanding, encouraging a commitment to people that is tolerant of slow progress and assigns importance to particular relationships and the needs of specific people and groups".

be free from the need to let his or her confidence be bolstered by people who *need* you so much. Pioneering is a vulnerable job and leads to constant attacks on your sense of comfort and security. There is a huge temptation to let yourself be confirmed by people who admire you and seek your attention. The consequence of this is a structure in which leaders and followers keep a firm grip on each other and drain each other slowly. However, when I give my time *freely*, without expecting attention, admiration or respect in return, I can also limit this relationship. I can process the possible anger or disappointment of the other person, when I let him or her know that I do not have time now or that other tasks need priority. Whenever the other is aware that he or she does not have any *power* over the leader, a deep awareness can grow of grace—what it means really to receive and really to give. Free leaders have free followers. This freedom can be lacking in a network. Often modern people experience that they can only gain their freedom by breaking out of mutual obligations. I believe that a Christian network community can show what freedom is within the field of relationships: freedom as bonds that are lovingly accepted. The key to this lies in the unconditional gift.

5. From Confessional Foundations to Mission and Values

In our contemporary missionary context, and particularly in the practice of church planting, we also see another ecclesiological shift—from an accent on foundations to an accent on vision and values. At its core this concerns questions like: "What is a Christian? In which way are Christian practices all over the world related to each other?" In church history such questions have often been applied to even more specific matters: "What does it mean to be Reformed? How do Protestants and Catholics differ?" These questions have always been asked, but their answers are changing. Kathryn Tanner points to the fact that Christians usually gave answers that defined certain *contents* and *practices*. Christians believe different things than non-Christians, and they have different customs. Tanner shows that those answers seem very logical, but on further reflection they cannot be sustained easily. Christians very rarely agree on what they believe, even when they acknowledge each other as Christians. Moreover, Christian standpoints shift in the course of history. For example, was Cyprian's view of conversion the same as Billy Graham's? And what about their opinions of the last things? If they would not agree, how then can we determine whether a theology of the eschaton is "Christian" at all? Regarding practices, we can ask: are there truly things that can only be done by Christians and not by anyone else? Even if this would be true: is it possible to define such Christian cultural characteristics, apart from the context in which Christians live? Is, for example, eating beef "Christian"? Perhaps in India, where eating beef can be a strong symbol of Christian freedom for someone who is converted from Hinduism. But in the Netherlands this practice is obviously not Christian at all. Some would say, on the contrary. Tanner thinks that views of Christianity that present it as a clearly bounded group identity with its "own" practices are typically modern. It is impossible to render her very sophisticated statement here, but it is interesting to see where she seeks the typical "Christian" identity of postmodern Christians. For her, this identity is a matter of *style* rather than *content*. Christians distinguish themselves by a particular way of dealing with creation and each other and by a shared interest in items as the cross, the sacraments, and etcetera. However, they do not necessarily think the same about these shared objects of interest. Christian identity "is more a matter of how than of what".[28] Thus, this identity is not something solid and eternal, but it needs elaboration and reshaping on the road.

For many church planters this is familiar (and not only for them). Our age is the age of post-Evangelicals, post-Reformed, etcetera.[29] This is partly due to a general cultural shift to a more contingent and fragmentary worldview. But in terms of church planting, it is also due to the two previous shifts I mentioned. The dominance of the marketing metaphor makes it more important to agree on targets and a mission to be achieved than on foundations or a point of departure. The shift to a network ecclesiology renders relationships and social skills more important than knowledge and confessional solidity. Therefore, in new church types more energy is invested in defining a clear mission statement and some values than in a detailed confessional statement. The emphasis is more (although not exclusively) on "how?" and "whereto?" than on "what?" and "from where?" Someone I know, from a strict Calvinistic background, works in a flourishing church planting project in Rotterdam. This church explicitly links itself to the Reformed tradition.

---

[28] Kathryn Tanner, *Theories of Culture: A New Agenda for Theology* (Guides to Theological Inquiry; Minneapolis, MN: Augsburg Fortress 1997), 112.
[29] A good example is Brian D. McLaren, *A Generous Orthodoxy* (Grand Rapids: Zondervan, 2004). Cf. also Noort et al., *Als een kerk opnieuw begint*, 278–281 ("Is the denomination passé?").

However, he wrote to me: "In my opinion a larger urban network in our time can hardly consist of people who cross the same doctrinal *t*'s and dot the same doctrinal *i*'s. In our church I am aware of a multitude of theological opinions, especially in the minor points. We clearly distinguish type-A truths and type-B truths. Unity is kept by a common vision on the major points of creation, fall, salvation by Christ, the work of the Spirit, expectation of God's future. But on details of the last days, theology of baptism, healing by prayer etc. we think differently and we let this happen. We even encourage it, in order to teach people to look for tolerance and love, rather than similarity and uniformity". This is very familiar in our own community in Amsterdam. New participants give a brief vow. The text of this promise does refer to a theological core content (basically the Apostolic Creed), but most of it is filled with specific references to the style we expect members to cherish in their relationships with the Bible and with each other. What is central is not what someone believes exactly about the Bible, but everyone promises to be accountable on a Biblical basis. This means that everyone will take arguments from the Bible very seriously; he or she will not stop conversation on this point. As for mutual relationships, this is not about avoiding conflicts, but about what one will do when conflicts happen (and they will happen!). The vow contains promises referring to a culture of peace, dialogue and reconciliation, but not so much to a culture of agreement on all kinds of issues.

In my opinion, the strength of a traditional congregation is exactly this large extent of agreement and a certain uniformity. This means stability and clarity. However, the dark side of this is a regular lack of loving relationships, because of the eagerness to define who is or is not "Reformed", "Evangelical", or "Bible believing". Traditional congregations often find it hard to deal with the "other", with someone who is different. Another downside is that many congregations can easily tell what they believe exactly about a number of issues, but they find it much more difficult to say where exactly they are going. We could say that there is a lack of evangelical style and Kingdom-oriented mission. Perhaps traditional churches can learn something here from missionary pioneer projects. As long as everyone must agree on all possible points of argument, the church will not move forward. A common search for a shared goal, with the explicit intention to further Christian virtues of grace, humility, dialogue and forgiveness, will not solve every difference, but enables movement.

6. Conclusion

Missionary pioneering in cities such as Amsterdam and Rotterdam is important. In order to theologize creatively we must make ourselves vulnerable. We have to enter new contexts in which old, well-known answers are not so relevant anymore. I am convinced that we, to stay fresh and inspired, need to look very purposefully for those contexts, to live and work there. Seen from this perspective, church planting is the Research & Development department of the church. Eventually, there can be a unique contribution to the global church. It appears that Western individualism will determine our world more and more, especially in the cities. If this is true, it is crucial for the church—in the Netherlands and in other countries—to attempt seriously the contextualization of the Christian faith in this urban culture.

Chapter Six

The Impact of Liquid Church Discourse in Dutch Evangelical Churches: A Practical-Theological Analysis

René Erwich

1. Introduction

This article considers the current state of Liquid Church discourse and seeks to relate this to the impact Liquid Church thinking has in Dutch Evangelical churches and circles. The influence of Pete Ward's book *Liquid Church* has been considerable.[1] Initially it seemed to be a reaction against the more rational and teleological concepts of church development (e.g. Purpose Driven Church, Natural Church Development). Looking more carefully at these developments leads to a different direction in which Evangelical church structures suffer from the same erosion as in other institutional churches. The quest for newer forms of church directs itself to a deeper consideration and theological reflection on "shapes of liquid" and the related ecclesiological themes. The article looks at this development from a practical-theological point of view. I will argue that Evangelical churches and movements are struggling with the transformation of their heritage into a postmodern climate. A lack of clear and explicit ecclesiological reflection may lure them into various manifestations of Liquid Church and may lead to an increase of ecclesiological pragmatism. In my analysis I use Richard R. Osmer's model of the four tasks of practical theology.[2]

2. Four Tasks of Practical Theology

In his recent book Richard Osmer introduced a helpful way to stimulate practical-theological reflection. He defines four tasks for practical

---

[1] P. Ward, *Liquid Church: A Bold Vision of How to Be God's People in Worship and Mission. A Flexible, Fluid Way of Being Church* (Carlisle: Paternoster, 2002).
[2] R.R. Osmer, *Practical Theology: An Introduction* (Grand Rapids: Eerdmans, 2008).

theology, besides a thorough methodological basis. The hermeneutical work practical theology should do consists of four core tasks in their intricate relationship.

First, Osmer discerns a *descriptive-empirical task* starting with the question: what is going on? Within this task we are invited to discern, to collect data and to look for patterns that may emerge in specific events, situations and contexts. This practical-theological task is informed by different types of research and methodology with the purpose of listening well and postponing judgment. This task is inspired by the *habitus* of priestly listening and a spirituality of presence.

Second, Osmer refers to the *interpretive task* focused by the question: Why is this going on? After performing well arranged research the practical-theological work of the search for explanations and theories that can explain and clarify specific conditions is necessary. The researcher looks for theories that can reframe the researched context and data. This implies the ability to test theories on the basis of adequate rules and validation procedures.

Third, the practical theologian should perform the *normative task* by answering the question: What should be going on? In order to enable us to interpret events, situations and patterns we need a normative frame of reference, theological and ethical theories. Prophetic discernment is here at stake as an important *habitus*.

Fourth, and finally, Osmer defines the *pragmatic task:* How should we react? This task focuses on the conditions needed to reformulate an improved practice and should be inspired by serving leadership. I will now use these four tasks to sequence my line of thinking in this article.

3. *What Is Going On? Interest in Practice: Implicit and Imbalanced Ecclesiology*

Church practice and the development of a missionary church is "hot" and high on the agenda of mainline Evangelical churches in the Netherlands. Publications with direct or indirect links to this theme are numerous, both in church-news magazines and in more popular theological journals.[3] A quick internet survey shows thousands of hits on such terms as "church growth", "church development" and "church planting". Both churches and Evangelical organizations (e.g. *Evangelische Alliantie, Evangelische Omroep*) show, for various reasons, great interest, but

---

[3] Cf. the more popular Evangelical-theological journal *Soteria*.

as it seems with one goal: the search for the development of missionary churches, churches that mediate the gospel to a post-Christian nation, caught in economic and political turmoil after the 2010 elections and subsequent delay in forming a new government. These latter developments are not causing a growth of interest in church renewal (this interest is older), but illuminate the climate in which they are present.

Most of the attempts breathe very positive attitudes towards the possibilities of developing new churches with new forms as well. Within Evangelical churches and networks a variety of experiments with ecclesial forms pass by with characteristics implying familiarity with Liquid Church thinking.[4] The first to coin the term 'liquid' was the sociologist

---

[4] R. Erwich, *Veelkleurig Verlangen: wegen van misisonair gemeente-zijn* (Boekencentrum: Zoetermeer, 2008); Ward, *Liquid Church*, and idem, *Participation and Mediation. A Practical Theology for the Liquid Church* (London: SCM, 2008). Even outside Evangelical circles Ward receives quite some attention and in the same context of theological reflection concerning the church. Cf. http://www.peternissen.nl/lezingen/lezingen-in-2009/55-kerk-in-limburg-na-de-vanzelfsprekendheid.html, accessed June 19, 2010, translation RE): "If we would grant the church in Limburg a new future, beyond naturalness, we must be prepared to let her be born again. In order to succeed we need a willingness to leave the old behind; we must show the courage to move out of the Pharao's house, away from Egypt. The British theologian Stuart Murray compares leaving Christendom and the classic folk church with leaving the Titanic. People do not like that, rather they reposition the chairs on the deck, knowing that the ship is sinking. They resist trading the seeming safety of the ocean liner for an insecure small boat. These new liquid communities will not be big ocean liners, no world church, but rather vulnerable rowing-boats. They will not be large communities and they will not have lots of power and prestige ... they work in the margins of society and culture, without a lot of institutional luggage and status. They will be more like a movement than an institution. But they are open for the blowing of the Spirit, the Spirit of Pentecost, who takes them forward, beyond what seemed so natural". Cf. also http://www.dsts.nl/Zondervan_lezing.html, accessed June 19, 2010, translation RE): "An interesting attempt to such a critical correlation is the attempt of the Evangelical theologian Pete Ward. In his book 'Liquid church' he reworks Castell's sociological theory about the network society to a church theory of a liquid church. The core problem with this book is the following: no single structure can be totally liquid. Metaphorically speaking every liquid finds itself in a container, in a space that contains the liquid. The question is: in what kind of container do we find the liquid church? Ward's answer would be that 'the individuals and groups the liquid church consists of must limit themselves to embrace an orthodoxy which is rooted in confessions and traditions of the church'. I question this type of critical correlation. The relevance of confessions and the tradition of the church cannot be assumed but has to be object of critical review. Ward's answers neglects the fact one important fact I have in mind. Allowing yourself to be limited by an ecclesial orthodoxy assumes confidence and knowledge of the church and her tradition. The latter is not present with young people nowadays. For them the church is no longer the natural setting to search for God's presence. For most of them the church and her language and rituals has lost its plausibility. They live in a sociocultural environment in which religion becomes plausible in new ways. It is impossible to visualize

Zygmunt Bauman.⁵ He distinguishes between *solid modernity* and *liquid modernity*. The first indicates a massive constituency by which the political, economic and ecclesial life and structures were regulated. The latter reflects the current phase of modernisation: a fluid, liquid society in which nothing is fixated, everything is characterized by movement.⁶ Pete Ward was the first to connect a variation of Bauman's conceptualization of solid and liquid to theological reflection about the church.⁷ He believes that the solid church has failed to respond adequately to the changes underway. He comments that solid modernity has led to a solid form of church and this church has uncritically taken for granted the central values of modernity. In his perception churches have accepted, across denominations and in various types of ecclesiologies, patterns that have decreased genuine mission, ignored cultural change and could therefore not respond to people's spiritual hunger. Solid church "mutated" and has become either a heritage site, a refuge or a nostalgic community.⁸ Ward pleads for a liquid church, characterized by a flow of religious communication through smaller and larger networks. As such Ward is correctly described by De Groot: being a church is not solely a matter of gathering on Sundays, but of individuals related to Christ, participating in the liquid dance of the Triune God.⁹

Liquid Church should not be seen as a phenomenon in itself but as part of the larger Emergent Church movement. The term reflects the way in which new communities of mission and discipleship are being constructed as they evolve out of inherited models of church. New communities are more developed as communicative projects, rather than structures. This movement shows itself to be of highly experimental nature and has a positive attitude towards postmodern culture and is assessed differently.¹⁰ Liquid Church is in contrast with Solid Church.

---

this starting from orthodox convictions. Tradition and contemporary experience must be joined otherwise". Compare as well Erwich, *Veelkleurig verlangen*.

⁵ Z. Bauman, *Liquid Modernity* (Cambridge: Polity, 2000).

⁶ Bauman, *Liquid Modernity*, 2: "These are the reasons to consider 'fluidity' or 'liquidity' as fitting metaphors when we wish to grasp the nature of the present, in many ways novel, phase in the history of modernity".

⁷ Ward, *Liquid Church*.

⁸ Ward, *Liquid Church*, 13-30.

⁹ R. Brouwer, C.N. de Groot, H. de Roest, E. Sengers en S. Stoppels, *Levend Lichaam: dynamiek van christelijke geloofsgemeenschappen in Nederland* (Kampen: Kok, 2007), 240-280. De Groot questions the assumptions: how can people participate if there is hardly any religious socialization, which is almost unthinkable without local communities?

¹⁰ For a brief overview of major characteristics compare R. Doornenbal, "Een

Within the solid paradigm the emphasis is on formal growth and influence in the local community; rules and regulations are of great importance; one finds fixed patterns of leadership and authority. Within the liquid paradigm the focus is not on formal institutional business but on the informal "flowing" communication between believers.[11] The liquid community consists of networks of believers and is geared towards spiritual activities.[12] The related community must not necessarily have the form of a weekly worship on Sundays but may have the form of a decentralised network of spiritual exercises.[13]

By means of illustration I present three examples of familiarity with Liquid Church thinking as a help on our way to answer our first question, *What is going on?*

3.1. *The Evangelical Community Elim*

The first example comes from a Dutch Evangelical community called *Elim*, a platform for base-communities with an evangelical orientation. Elim has a set of activities, varying from worship meetings to supporting international diaconal projects in Asia.[14] The website shows the development through the years and gives interesting insights in some theological lines of thinking and specifically with regard to Liquid Church.[15] The site is affirmative to the questions that are raised by Pete

---

complex en fascinerend fenomeen: een karakterisering van de Emerging Church Beweging", *TheolD* 3/3 (2008), 18–24. See also D.A. Carson, *Becoming Conversant with the Emerging Church: Understanding a Movement and Its Implications* (Grand Rapids: Zondervan, 2005).

[11] Cf. G. Delanty, *Community* (London: Routledge, 2003). Delanty contends that community is constructed in communicative processes, rather than in institutional structures, spaces or even in symbolic forms of meaning. Compare as well H. de Roest, *Een huis voor de ziel: gedachten over de kerk voor binnen en buiten* (Zoetermeer: Meinema, 2010).

[12] Compare G. Heitink, *Een kerk met karakter: tijd voor heroriëntatie* (Kampen: Kok, 2007), 166–167. Heitink writes: "New forms of community get more and more the shape of network. The old concept of cohesion is replaced by the modern concept of network. The individualized persons builds carefully a network of relationships which extends further than the close circle of family, friends and neighbours ... in this setting the new church type that fits with our times is called 'liquid church'. Boundaries and shapes become liquid. Membership is no longer connected to church attendance. Believers meet each other no longer only in the context of a church. Led by the Spirit they search their own way. They meet each other while they sport or in a reading club. I think this is a an extensive form of adaptation to modern culture." (translation RE)

[13] For more detailed characteristics see Ward, *Liquid Church,* and idem, *Participation and Mediation*.

[14] http://www.elim.nl (accessed June 19, 2010).

[15] http://www.elim.nl/nl/lifestylevloeibare-kerk.html (accessed June 19, 2010).

Ward and the author of the text connects, rather uncritically, Ward's assumptions with the situation of their community. According to the author their way of community life and outreach are what Ward intended.[16] Fluidity is one of the characteristics and at the same time he claims the necessity of solidity as the community develops through the years. In his text he moves between the "safe frame of tradition" and "flexible vulnerability" of a "fluid organization ". He finalizes his essay with the following sentences (translation RE):

> We must not lock the gold of the tradition behind the safe church walls where inflation devalues it. It is time to purify the gold of tradition of its contamination by melting it. Once it is liquid, we may use it in a changing society. Only if we keep the gold of tradition warm by mutual love and gifts and fruits of the Spirit, to prevent it from solidifying, we can keep growing ... communities do not solidify! Keep the 2000 year old principles of Acts 2 liquid in Jesus name![17]

This is an intriguing quote and full of play of metaphor. The gold of tradition? What is meant by this? And: how to melt this gold and what should be taken out of it in order to purify it? The essay betrays the struggle between traditional ways of being church and the more experimental way this community has existed so far in time. It shows a kind of being caught in the middle between (if I may use this terminology) "solid" and "liquid". In fact there is a constant dynamic between "flexibility" and "institutionalizing". Besides the play with metaphor it seems there is a tendency to create a false dualism between church as a "movement" and church as an "institution". Doing so, emergent church leaders run the risk of perpetuating one of modernity's characteristics in the way they speak and write about church.

3.2 *Choose a Church – No Church*

The second example I have taken from a public lecture with the Dutch title *De vloeibare kerk: Kies een kerk—geen kerk* [*The Liquid Church. Choose a Church—No Church*, translation RE], by Matthijs Vlaardingerbroek given at the *Youth for Christ Flevo Festival* in August 2006.[18] Vlaardingerbroek, himself a devoted pioneer of alternative forms of

---

[16] We might argue that Ward is far more critical to the ideas of "liquid" than generally is assumed. Cf. Ward, *Participation and Mediation*.
[17] http://www.elim.nl/nl/lifestylevloeibare-kerk.html (accessed December 21, 2010).
[18] M. Vlaardingerbroek, *De vloeibare kerk: kies een kerk—geen kerk* (2006). Accessed through the website http://www.stadopeenberg.nl/downloads/gemeente/vloeibarekerk.pdf (June 19, 2010).

church and mainly inspired by church planter Stuart Murray, admits that many people no longer fit in the traditional churches. He predicts that in the coming years the number of people who seek alternative ways of being and belonging to church will increase. In his analysis he takes for granted the post-Christendom thesis of Stuart Murray with a strong and negative judgement of the events that led to the merger of state and church in the fourth century known as the Constantinian turn. The church, according to Vlaardingerbroek should be "searching, finding and following Christ and his Kingdom". As a consequence older forms of church are full of risks if they do not get beyond meetings and drinking coffee. In his attempt to formulate newer forms of church he turns the term church into a verb: we church, you church etc. He is cautious and warns people not to leave their own church where they may experience growth as well, but he concludes:

> Where people are members of different networks, in which they search, find and follow Jesus and his Kingdom, where they are members of groups strong in worship, mission and community, there is what Pete Ward calls "liquid church".[19]

Again, I appreciate this work but questions also arise: to what extent is the interpretation of the Constantinian turn not an over-interpretation based on a specific and shallow reading of historical data? And: how does community really take shape in these various networks of which people are members? There is no long-term empirical evidence that pioneer situations will not undergo similar institutional crises as their "solid" predecessors experienced. Such statements seem, again, to be a quick and rather superficial affirmation of the Liquid theses.

3.3. *Dutch Baptist Churches*

My third and final example relates to my own Baptist church context. Within the Baptist churches of the Dutch Baptist Union the debate about the relationship between baptism and membership has emerged in the last ten years. Various churches notice a growing influx of believers from more institutional churches, mainly from a Reformed background. Most of the time people choose a Baptist church because of the middle position the churches take between the more charismatic and reformed churches. Classically membership in our churches is linked to baptism, only those baptized (through immersion) are members. In

---

[19] http://www.stadopeenberg.nl/downloads/gemeente/vloeibarekerk.pdf (accessed December 21, 2010).

the baptismal service the believer becomes a member through the baptism performed. This has been much in debate lately as many other Evangelical churches have adopted the same form of baptism. Baptists felt they were no longer unique in their emphasis on this identity marker and this led to reflection on the relationship between baptism and membership in many local churches.

The discussion was strongly influenced by elements of the Liquid-Church discourse. Baptists have always been very much concerned with the visibility of the local church and its believers. They struggle with the idea that in fact *commodification* leads to more spiritual *fluidity*. In the Liquid discourse believers are seen more as consumers who, being part of several networks, travel and "shop" for meaning and spirituality without a commitment in terms of formal membership. According to Ward the liquid community should gather herself around spiritual consumers.[20] This forces Baptist communities to reconsider their ecclesiology and the way they think and act concerning membership and baptism and therefore also reflect deeper on their perception of community. The "centred set" option as a possible way forward with membership divided into core members and those who are moving in the direction of Christ (without formal membership) is in fact close to accepting the liquid church thesis, at least partially.[21] This typology was developed by Hiebert.[22] He discovered that older overseas churches were putting a lot of energy into maintaining boundaries. As time went on these boundaries became characteristics of the true church. Those people who came in had to pass these boundaries. This characterizes a "bounded set" mentality, as opposed to the "centred set". The community believes that when they lose the qualities belonging to these boundaries, the entire identity gets lost. Consequently this leads to a new intensified effort to safeguard the same boundaries.

I now come to a conclusion concerning the first part of this article. *What is going on?* I collect my findings and observations so far, as follows.

There seems to be a fair struggle concerning the form of churches, both in terms of content and structures. The Liquid Church discourse infused and stimulated reflection on these themes and impacted the clash between the traditional church and newer forms of church. At the

---

[20] Ward, *Participation*.
[21] Erwich, *Veelkleurig Verlangen*.
[22] Paul G. Hiebert, "The Category 'Christian' in the Mission Task", *IRM* 72 (1983), 421–27.

same time there is much insecurity as to the direction churches have to take concerning identity markers and ecclesiology. Striking are either implicit ecclesiological assumptions or shallow ecclesiological thinking related to the current shifts.

4. Why Is This Going On? Unresolved Tensions and Heritage, Theology and Culture Issues

We now come to our second practical-theological task, an attempt to find adequate clarifications of our questions. In my view two issues are at stake and they are interrelated. The first is the mere absence of serious ecclesiological reflection-in-context. The second issue is the subsequent *pragmatism* and preoccupation with (undefined) practice. Let me start with a brief analysis of the church in Evangelical theology.

That Evangelicalism lacks a well grounded ecclesiology is no secret. I agree with Leanne Van Dyk that the historical foundations of Evangelicalism have contributed to this.[23] The development of the movement characterized itself by disillusionment with church structures, anti-institutional (dualistic?) tendencies and strong emphases on personal (inner) experiences. Very often individual choices (if people disagree with certain practices in churches) are presented as solutions (leaving and changing the church) to ecclesial problems. It has been attested more than once that Evangelicals are very sensitive to the surrounding culture and have surrendered too easily to modernity and its benefits. While some speak of the betrayal of Evangelical core values using "market tools", others are more nuanced in their critique and talk about "marginalized ecclesiology".[24] Yet, the accusation remains firm. Van Dyk quotes David F. Wells who stated that the evangelical world has lost its radicalism along the lines of a severe accommodation to modernity.[25]

Several solutions have been proposed, varying from taking up the "right doctrine" to reframing and relating the original heritage to the current culture in a more valid way. The first measure became popular and seemingly the best. Within conservative Evangelical circles many contend that as long as there is a right orientation towards the teaching about God, churches will regain their vitality. A doctrinal solution

---

[23] L. van Dyk, "The Church in Evangelical Theology and Practice", in: T. Larsen, D.J. Treier (eds.), *The Cambridge Companion to Evangelical Theology* (Cambridge: Cambridge University Press, 2007), 125ff.
[24] Van Dyk, "The Church in Evangelical Theology".
[25] Van Dyk, "The Church in Evangelical Theology", 129.

does not seem to be the only remedy against a lack of ecclesiological thinking, let alone a cure for the apparent erosion and liquefaction of institutional structures. The attempt Miroslav Volf undertook is widely acknowledged, even with the criticism he received about his reasons for the church starting from a social-trinitarian perspective. In my perception his attempt is a serious one, compared to many other more popular writings.[26] Help might be found through a serious and in-depth study of the Emergent Church movement as a whole. The independence and the flexibility of this movement might sustain serious theological work and wider conversations about this important topic.

Fair enough, this brief analysis shows that the Evangelical heritage apparently runs behind in her theological reflection on the church in society and has not been adequately retransformed for the current culture[27]. At the same time the perception of culture itself is an important factor in defining a valid ecclesiology in whatever direction. In fact the unresolved theological issues and a tension-filled relation with culture lures Evangelical churches into experiments with "liquid" with the effect of sliding into all kinds of pragmatism. We cannot be totally sure here, but it may be the case that many Evangelical churches use "liquid" language to hide the classical low-church ecclesiology.

This brings us to a second point, related to this first one. It seems that as a consequence of (the lack of) a clear ecclesiological reflection church practices become gradually "the one and only thing churches need". Churches leap into extreme pragmatism. The separation of practice and norms puts valid growth (both in quality of faith and in number of believers) of the church at risk. I have once and again pointed to this problem in the context of congregational development.[28] Church models and newer approaches of church development are implemented with good intentions but with hardly any reflection as to the match with content and church theology of the local church. Healy has in a somewhat different perspective pointed to this same fact:

> Over the last decade or so there have been signs of a shift away from the highly systematic and ideal ecclesiologies of the twentieth century, those described, for example, in Avery Dulles's classic study, *Models of*

---

[26] Cf. M. Volf, *After Our Likeness* (Grand Rapids: Eerdmans, 1998). Volf's concept has not been fully developed into an more practical-theological ecclesiology. Compare as well R. Erwich, "Ecclesiologie van de participatie: de ecclesiologie van Miroslav Volf", *Soteria*, 22/4 (2005), 8–16.

[27] Cf. Corey E. Labanow, *Evangelicalism and the Emerging Church: A Congregational Study of a Vineyard Church* (Farnham: Ashgate, 2009).

[28] Cf. R. Erwich, "Gemeenteopbouw en ecclesiologie", *Soteria* 22/4 (2005), 2–4.

the Church. Increasingly, theologians have turned their attention to the concrete church, to its activities and distinctive functions.[29]

Practices of the church are the focus of what Healy calls the "new ecclesiology". Healy notices a lack of *definition* of practice. What is practice and how is it used? A practice is not right by itself and needs to be tested and normative data, ecclesiology and pneumatology play an important role in this testing. Ecclesiology seems highly related to the doctrine of God and this part of theological reflection cannot be omitted in this discourse. And this is exactly, in addition to my earlier point, the case. There is a need for more balanced ecclesiological reflection, taking practice and (constructed) norms into account. Recently I was engaged with students in a course on ecclesiology, and teasing them a bit we started with the question: "Tell me about your concept of God and I will tell you what concept of the church you have!"

5. *What Should Be Going On? Ecclesiological Balance and Informed Critical Dialogue*

We do need wisdom to cope with the current situation. My analysis does not lead to a quick-fix route to success. All serious participants are aware of the difficulties: clashes of older and newer forms of church, a lack of ecclesiology-in-context and consequential pragmatism. In search for a normative direction for Evangelical churches there are a number of reflections I would like to make.[30] For our purpose I would like to underline the importance of *ecclesiological balance*. By this I mean several things.

5.1. *Learning from Newer Movements*

First, I am strongly convinced that we need to be willing to learn from newer movements such as the Emergent Church, including their use of historical traditions on liturgy, worship and sacraments. The good

---

[29] Nicholas M. Healy, "Practices and the New Ecclesiology: Misplaced Concreteness?", *IJSTh* 5 (2003), 287–308. New approaches to church revitalization tend to assume that there is a basic complementarity of various approaches without serious investigation into the underlying church theories and ecclesiologies. Compare as an example the way the Australian NCLS Research contends the equality of Purpose Driven Church (Warren) and Natural Church Development (Schwarz).

[30] Generally I agree with the proposal Van Dyk gives. Evangelical ecclesiology should be of incarnational, trinitarian, sacramental, proclamatory and eschatological nature.

practices that have been developed in this movement are vital to further learning experiences. This involves as well the willingness to use (early) church tradition as a valid source next to Scripture as unifying norm. It will not suffice to judge the Emergent Church movement as Carson did.[31]

5.2. *Theology, Culture and Evangelical Churches*

Second, we will need a more in-depth dialogue concerning the relationship between theology, culture and church. There are two important issues I am more than concerned about in this respect. One is the extent to which churches are able to consider the positive value of perceiving themselves on a continuum between "solid" and "liquid". Doing this would enable them to use the two sides of the ecclesial coin. In fact I agree with De Groot who contests that "liquid" and "solid" religion are entangled in an ongoing interplay.[32] There is no clear separation line between these two and more examples could illustrate this easily.[33] Liquid and solid manifestations of church live as inseparable twins, with possibly the same genetic codes but with different outlook and manifestations. De Groot: "It is not sociologically inevitable that this liquid church will mix with other religious traditions and vanish as something unidentifiable, unless there is a solid church that supports it".[34] The other concern is the lack of reflection on the relationship between church and predominant culture. As De Groot has shown in his analysis of Bauman,[35] Bauman's social theory can be helpful in analysing the church's stance in society and hence help the *reformulation* of the mission of the church. I agree fully with Barry Harvey when he writes:

> [In like manner] the problem for the body of Christ is not that we do not know precisely what to believe, say or do when confronted with new

---

[31] Carson, *Becoming Conversant*.
[32] C.N. de Groot, "Three Types of Liquid Religion", in: *Implicit Religion* 11 (2008), 277–296. Compare as well his "Fluide vormen van kerk-zijn", in: R. Brouwer, et al. (eds.), *Levend Lichaam,* 240-280. De Groot describes three liquid variations of church: (a) churches in a "reli-culture": youth churches, Mary devotion, Roman Catholic World Youth Days and other newer flexible movements like *Focolare*; (b) categorial churches, local forms of church in a secular setting: hospitals, prisons, television communities; (c) secular-religious phenomena: business spirituality, theatre, musea, public events. Many of these raise questions concerning the definitions of church. De Groot acknowledges this (253).
[33] De Groot, "Three Types of Liquid Religion", 277–296.
[34] C.N. de Groot, "The Church in Liquid Modernity: A Sociological and Theological Exploration of a Liquid Church", *IJSCC* 6 (2006), 91–103.
[35] De Groot, "The Church in Liquid Modernity", 91–103.

or puzzling circumstances ... this is a time of real testing for the viability and flexibility of the church's tradition, as Christians struggle to discover whether there is any sense in which the other languages we are working with can be faithfully incorporated in our theology. The difficulty is rather that the shared practices, judgments, and institutions that once allowed Christians to interact with the world about them and engage in meaningful transactions with one another have eroded to the point that we no longer know how to proceed ... it affects virtually every aspect of Christ's body.[36]

This reformulation is needed for Evangelical churches in the direction Harvey points out. It concerns integration of different types of languages, spiritual, theological, cultural and missiological, that will enable profound missionary engagement in this world. Evangelical churches would therefore benefit from a more critical analysis of the cultural climate with its growing insecurity, inequality etc. There is hardly any evidence of serious attempts to read the predominant culture in Evangelical circles. Even when churches use popular trend-watchers, these trends are hardly incorporated in a contextual theology for the church. Developing a more *diaconal* theology might balance one-sided soteriological thinking, since the emphasis on diaconal presence frees the local church from her "sacred egocentricity".[37] This could be seen as a partial correction, but a more fully developed normative missional ecclesiology would be needed as well. Classical Evangelicalism (proclaim the Word more vigorously than before) would not work as a recipe without reviewing its major assumptions.

I do present this here as a *norm* under the heading of this third practical-theological task. Without profound rethinking of these aspects mentioned I am afraid many young churches of whatever form will not be able to contribute to the mission of the church. They will either implicitly disconnect and create a new subculture or they will affirm uncritically the predominant culture within their church practice. Both seem to be not desirable.

---

[36] Barry Harvey, *Can These Bones Live? A Catholic Baptist Engagement With Ecclesiology, Hermeneutics, and Social Theory* (Grand Rapids: Brazos, 2008), 42–47. Harvey offers many insightful and provoking lines of thought in this brilliant essay.

[37] D. Guder, *The Continuing Conversion of the Church* (Grand Rapids: Eerdmans, 2000).

6. How Should We React? Empirical Research and Reformulation of Core Values

What should we do? In the end we want to improve practice and generate new(er) strategies. In my view a new practice entails (at least) the following.

(1) *More long-term empirical research in Evangelical churches in which "grassroot ecclesiology" can be developed and monitored over a number of years.*

I know of hardly any current projects of in-depth research focusing on the development of ecclesiology-in-context in Evangelical communities. A good example of local research, based on the methods of *congregational studies* we found in *Geloven in Gemeenschap: het verhaal van een protestantse geloofsgemeenschap* [Eng. *Believing in Community: The Story of a Protestant Community of Faith*] by Rein Brouwer.[38] In this study, which does not focus on an Evangelical church, there is a qualified attempt to connect context research with practical-theological ecclesiology. Adopting several Evangelical churches and working with a research group would be a good way forward. Both qualitative and quantitative methods could be combined and assure more long-term insights and monitor the development of communities. Research could look at concepts like vitality, participation, church culture, leadership etc. The assumption is that Evangelical churches have to offer a specific contribution to the development of newer forms of church. They bring their own still implicit views on the church in mission in their practices. These practices might prove to be potential additions to the wider ecclesiological discourse in which we find ourselves engaged.

(2) *Stimulating study groups in churches and outside churches concerning faith, theology and culture.*

One of the recurring themes in social studies is the emphasis on group learning. Instead of various new activities in local Evangelical churches I would like to stress the underestimated power of group learning, of course under specific conditions. It has been attested more than once that transforming thought patterns (and subsequent changes in behaviour) is more likely to succeed in group work. It would be worthwhile to set up a pilot in several Evangelical churches in which attenders and

---

[38] Brouwer, *Geloven in Gemeenschap*.

members are invited to participate in serious study groups on Evangelical identity, attitude towards culture etc. The assumption would be that there is a well-prepared proposal describing Evangelical core values, or simply reading a book together to stimulate awareness on important issues regarding the church. It seems to me that the experience of learning about culture and the way culture manifests itself in our way of *doing church* is of utmost importance.

(3) *Reformulating the Evangelical heritage linked with the mentioned long-term empirical research (increasing congregational studies).*

One of the difficulties in the Evangelical wing is that most of the churches are "solo-players". The connection, let alone some exceptions, with other partner churches is poor. This is a serious threat for the future. Volf, in his attempt to define a Free Church ecclesiology, has pointed more than once to the importance of belonging and participation to networks of churches.[39] This principle of interdependency is of great importance for Evangelical churches in the current climate. This working together could stimulate rethinking a valuable heritage in close connection with good empirical testing of concepts and practices. Besides cooperative theological reflection, working together would already be a positive thing.

(4) *Encouraging guided experiments with alternative forms of church combined with creating platforms to evaluate these.*

In combination with my earlier suggestion of research involvement, we would need guided experiments with newer forms of church. This is an addition to research in existing churches and this should get more attention. The Evangelical world is full of church planting initiatives, yet without solid evaluation on specific platforms. The *Incarnate Network* is a good example of such a platform where all sorts of initiatives are evaluated.[40] Theologically speaking, we might expect the Spirit to use faithful experiments and bless both old and new churches.

(5) *Groups of theologians and church leaders who are committed to these tasks together for the sake of the churches.*

A final point in designing strategy would be the bringing together of

---

[39] Volf, *After our Likeness*.
[40] This is the organisation Dr. Stuart Murray is involved in. For more information look at http://incarnate-network.eu (accessed December 13, 2010).

theologians and practitioners. This involves sacrifices on both sides of the spectrum. By bringing the two together we envision a mutual conception of creativity that is so much needed in this time of transition. The mutual awareness of what is urgent and necessary will help to reflect on the one and only thing that is needed for passionate involvement of the church in the mission of God's Kingdom. According to Evangelicals, the church is not the ultimate goal, the Kingdom of God is.

These are only a few modest attempts to keep this important discourse going and to improve the quality of the practices of the churches we serve. Much depends in terms of research on the willingness of local churches to participate and their openness to learning. In my experience this is hard work, but worthwhile as they experience working with more joy and effect after elements of practice have been improved and create openness for the Spirit to do the work.

Chapter Seven

Health, Wealth and Prosperity: A Biblical-Theological Reflection

Bernhard J.G. Reitsma

1. *Introduction: Health, Wealth and Prosperity Gospel*

Is there an Evangelical perspective on suffering and persecution? That question increasingly challenges Evangelical theology, not only because more and more Evangelical Christians are living in the so-called developing, less affluent, parts of the world, or because there is a growing awareness of the worldwide persecution of Christians for their faith, but more importantly because increasingly Evangelical Christians are attracted by the so-called "Health, Wealth and Prosperity Gospel". This appears as a new trend in Evangelicalism. In the past health and prosperity thinking was more at home in Pentecostal/Charismatic circles.[1] It is true that classic Pentecostalism has always been critical of this movement,[2] yet most of the radical health, wealth and prosperity preachers, like Oral Roberts, Kenneth Hagin, Kenneth Copeland and Joseph Prince, are clearly Charismatic.

Evangelicals have been and are less sympathetic to health and prosperity theology. Many key-figures have denounced it as unbiblical.[3]

---

[1] Cf. D. Lioy, "The Heart of the Prosperity Gospel: Self or Savior?" *Conspectus* 4/1 (march 2007), 41–64, 42: blending "Pentecostal revivalism with elements of positive thinking" (quoting S. Coleman); A. Anderson, *An Introduction to Pentecostalism: Global Charismatic Christianity* (Introduction to Religion; Cambridge 2004), 157; Stanley M. Burgess, Gary B. McGee (eds.), *Dictionary of Pentecostal and Charismatic movements* (Grand Rapids [7]1995), 372, 373. Many Evangelical systematic theologies mention the health, wealth and prosperity thinking only as a side-thought or not at all. It is never an important topic.

[2] Cf. Walter J. Hollenweger, *Pentecostalism: Origins and Developments Worldwide* (Peabody 1997), 228–233; Burgess, McGee (eds.), *Dictionary of Pentecostal and Charismatic Movements*, 372, 373.

[3] Cf. very explicitly John Piper, "Prosperity Preaching: Deceitful and Deadly" (www.desiringgod.org/resource-library/taste-see-articles/prosperity-preaching-deceitful-and-deadly), and in a variety of posts and blogs (www.desiringgod.org); Gordon D. Fee, *The Disease of the Health and Wealth Gospels* (Vancouver [2]2006). In the Netherlands by

Evidently Evangelical theology has accepted the supernatural power of God and His miraculous interventions[4]—God is a God who heals his people and sustains them in the most difficult and (financially) challenging situations—but it has never claimed that God would heal all Christians or that Christians would be more prosperous than other people. On a more popular level, however, it seems that health and prosperity thinking has swept beyond its charismatic base into more "buttoned-down Evangelical churches" and even into more liberal congregations.[5] Many Evangelical Christians in Europe are very open to elements of health, wealth and prosperity teaching[6] and a majority of (Evangelical) Christians in parts of Africa and Asia associates itself with health and prosperity faith.[7]

All of this justifies a renewed Evangelical reflection on questions of health, wealth and suffering. Even though most Evangelicals will probably not adhere to a radical and pure form of health and prosperity

---

example a very large Charismatic movement called *Opwekking* (Revival), which at Pentecost every year organizes a Pentecostal conference visited by approximately 40,000 people, has openly distanced itself from outright prosperity teaching as presented by pastor Joseph Prince from Singapore. The conclusion seems justified that the health, wealth and prosperity gospel is not a major dogma of faith for (European) Evangelical theology.

[4] Cf. Roger E. Olson, *A-Z of Evangelical Theology* (London 2005), 233.

[5] Lioy, "Heart of the Prosperity Gospel", 46. Of course this raises the issues of how to define Pentecostal/Charismatic on the one hand and Evangelical on the other. Hollenweger, *Pentecostalism*, 1–5, esp. 2, identifies three forms of the Charismatic Pentecostal movement: classic Pentecostal Churches (originating in the Azusa-street revival in Los Angeles at the beginning of the twentieth century), the Charismatic Movement (from the sixties and seventies of the twentieth century in the traditional churches), the (relatively young) Non-White Indigenous Churches. Hollenweger considers the so called Signs and Wonders movement of John Wimber (interpreted by C. Peter Wagner as the third kind of Pentecostalism) to be a newer form of the second kind. Some would include this last movement in the Evangelical tradition, while others use the term Evangelical to describe the pietistic movement that can be associated with Pietism and Puritanism. Gary J. Dorrien, *The Remaking of Evangelical Theology* (Louisville 1998), characterizes even Reformed Calvinists such as A. Kuyper, H. Bavinck, G.C. Berkouwer and H.N. Ridderbos as Evangelicals.

[6] Over the years different movements have drawn attention in the Netherlands, like the Vineyard Movement, the so-called Toronto blessing (named after some extraordinary signs and wonders in a Vineyard Church in Toronto), and the more recent Lakeland Revival movement associated with Todd Bentley. Many Evangelical churches have split over these movements. There is a growing interest in the Netherlands in healing and a ministry of deliverance and exorcism. Prosperity does not seem to be a very important topic of faith, although Joseph Prince from Singapore has some influence in some churches.

[7] Especially in Nigeria, South Africa and Kenya, cf. Lioy, "Heart of the Prosperity Gospel", 42.

thinking and would be prone to pick and choose what is most beneficial to them, it is nevertheless justified to take our starting point in the distinct health, wealth and prosperity gospel. Its extreme character exposes more clearly than a balanced and nuanced theology the core issues concerning Christian faith and suffering.

My intention is not to offer here a comprehensive and exhaustive overview of the teaching of the health and prosperity movement. It can even be questioned whether it is a movement at all. Probably it is better to speak of different movements in which health and prosperity receive varied emphases.[8] Nevertheless a number of ideas and thoughts are recurring. We could define the health, wealth and prosperity gospel as a theology, which claims that a true believer in Christ can count on being blessed by God in all areas of life. Accordingly, a believer

 a. should not have to be sick;[9]
 b. will be prosperous and lead a long life;[10]
 c. will be wealthy.[11]

In other words, healing, prosperity and wealth are the normal features of the Christian life in this age. Believers can taste heaven on earth.

The key to receiving these blessings is faith, which almost serves as a supernatural force through which believers get whatever form of personal success they want.[12] Faith is often closely associated with positive thinking and visualization. Health and prosperity need to be believed, visualized and then spoken into reality. A believer has to name and claim the promise by faith. [13]

---

[8] Fee speaks in the plural of *The Disease of the Health and Wealth Gospels*. For different aspects of these theologies, cf. the various articles on the websites of among others Kenneth Copeland (www.kcm.org), Kenneth Hagin (www.rhema.org), The Lakeland Revival (www.thelakelandrevival.com), Todd Bentley (www.freshfire.ca) and Joseph Prince (www.josephprince.org).

[9] Reference here is e.g. to Isa. 53:4 and 5 ("he carried our sicknesses and our pain", "by his stripes we are healed"; since our iniquity was on Him and since He will bear our sins), Isa 53:6, 11. The assumption is that for the believer in Christ the consequences of sin have either disappeared as well or should no longer be there. Cf. Matt. 8:17, 1 Pet. 2:24.

[10] Cf. 3 John 2, John 10:10.

[11] Cf. Ps. 23 (lack nothing), Deut. 7:12–26; Josh. 14:9; Mal. 3:10, Mark 10:29, 30

[12] Lioy, "Heart of the Prosperity Gospel", 42.

[13] Cf. Lioy, "Heart of the Prosperity Gospel", 43; this kind of theology is therefore also called a "name it and claim it" theology, or "the word of faith theology". Kenneth Hagin is the father of this movement, and his theology can be called "rhematology", a theology of the spoken word. Important elements are "positive confession and sensory denial and implicit rejection of medical science", and visualisation and positive confessions, *Dictionary of Pentecostal and Charismatic Movements*, 372, 373.

Adherents of this kind of theology do not ignore that there are Christians in the world who suffer and do not prosper. Different reasons are provided for this, like lack of faith, either of the believer or of the church, specific and continuous sin, possession by evil spirits or continuing influence of the devil, lack of perseverance in visualizing or believing prosperity into existence and failing to claim healing and prosperity. Some would admit, as a last explanation, that God in his sovereignty has other plans or that lack of healing and prosperity is simply a mystery. Usually this is only considered as a last option, when no other explanation will do.[14]

My intention in this article is to test the core claims of the health, wealth and prosperity gospel by interacting with Paul's paradigm in Romans 8. In this chapter Paul does not only discuss the issue of suffering and persecution (Rom. 8:17, 18, 23, 35, 36), but he does so in an overall perspective of the Christian life in the actual world. This interaction must help us to answer the question how suffering, health and prosperity relate to each other in the Christian life.[15] We do not use Romans 8 as proof-text, nor Paul's worldview as a model that can simply be transferred to a modern context. Mainly it will be used for interaction in order to develop an Evangelical Theology of suffering and persecution.

2. *Suffering with Christ (Rom. 8:17); God's Plan and Paul's Vision*

Paul emphasizes that those who are in Christ are presently suffering

---

Gloria Copeland emphasizes that the Bible should be used daily (almost magically) as a medicine that makes one literally and physically well, for the Bible is the divine word of life, cf. Gloria Copeland, "Live Long, Live Strong", (www.kcm.org/real-help/article/live-long-live-strong).

[14] In this way, Willem J. Ouweneel, *Geneest de zieken!* (Vaassen 2003), 378, 379. The so-called Signs and Wonders movement (or "Third Wave") does not promise total healing nor prosperity for every believer; John Wimber, one of the founders of the movement, himself died of cancer while he was still very young. Cf. John Wimber (with K. Springer), *Power Healing* (London, Sydney, Auckland, Toronto ³1987), 159–178.

[15] It would be interesting to explore whether the shift in focus in Evangelical/Charismatic thinking towards health, wealth and prosperity parallels a shift in modern (Western) culture from the transcendent future to the workaday present, from theocentric providence to anthropocentric prosperity, cf. Lioy, "Heart of the Prosperity Gospel", 48, 49. Until the second half of the nineteenth century it seems health, wealth and prosperity were no issue at all. The focus was more on eternity and saving souls. At the end of the nineteenth century we see a kind of shift in focus, from eternity to reality. At least some of the prosperity movements emphasize that believing could lead to experiencing heaven on earth.

with Christ in order to be glorified with Him (8:17).[16] That seems to suggest that there is an intrinsic link between the future glorification of the believer and his present suffering. Even more, to suffer with Christ now seems to be a precondition for being glorified with Him in the future. If this is what Paul intends to say, it has significant implications for our understanding of Evangelical Theology in relation to the health, wealth and prosperity gospel. So what is Paul trying to say? How does the wider context of Romans 8 help us to understand Paul's theology of suffering?

2.1 *Christ the Climax of the Covenant (Romans 8)*[17]

The first thing we observe in Romans is the strong dualism between the past and the present, between then and now, between old and new.[18] The coming of Christ, his death and resurrection, mark a turning point in history. In Christ, God has acted decisively for His people and in Him a whole new era has begun. This new era in Christ stands in stark contrast to the past. The time before Christ was the time of Adam, marked by the powers of sin and death. Through Adam sin entered the world and through sin death; and because all people have sinned just like Adam (Rom. 3:10, 11; 5:12), death has come over the world like a tsunami. Sin has taken up residence in the actual and tangible reality of human life in this world (Rom. 7:17 "sin dwells in me") and dominates human life. Together with the flesh[19] and death, sin has established a deadly and powerful alliance that dominates the old age. This alliance is so strong that not even the law of God was able to break its power.[20] Although the law is God's expression of the basic principles of the righteousness of the covenant—good and holy (Rom. 7:12)—it nevertheless

---

[16] Εἴπερ as fulfilled condition [cf. F. Blass, A. Debrunner, F. Rehkopf, *Grammatik des neutestamentlichen Griechisch* (Göttingen ¹⁷1990), § 454.2₂]: "If, as is the case right now, you are suffering with Christ...". Cf. Joseph A. Fitzmyer, *Romans* (AncB 33; New York 1993), 502 "if indeed". Literally Paul writes: "you are co-suffering (συμπάσχω)", which in the light of the preceding "co-heirs" with Christ (συγκληρονόμοι δὲ Χριστοῦ) can only be interpreted as suffering with Christ.

[17] This is taken from the title of the book of N.T. Wright, *Christ, the Climax of the Covenant: Christ and the Law in Pauline Theology* (London, New York ³2003), cf. 241.

[18] Cf. Rom. 3:26; 5:9, 11; 6:19; 6:21, 22; then – now, Rom. 8:1, 18, 22; 11:5, 30, 31; 13;11; 16:26, cf. in Paul also: 2 Cor 5:16; 6:2; Gal. 2:20; 4:9, 25, 29.

[19] The flesh here is used by Paul as an indication of the human life under the authority of sin, cf. Bernhard J.G. Reitsma, *Geest en schepping: een bijbels theologische bijdrage aan de systematische doordenking van de verhouding van de Geest van God tot de geschapen werkelijkheid* (Zoetermeer 1997), 73

[20] Reitsma, *Geest en schepping*, 74.

is an instrument of death (cf. Rom. 7:11). As long as the power of sin has not been broken and sin has not been removed from this world, as long as "there is no one righteous, not even one" (Rom. 3:10 NIV), "no one who does good, not even one" (Rom. 3:12 NIV), the only thing the law can do is to point out human transgression and sentence humanity to death.[21]

> In contrast to this old age of Adam, the new era in Christ Jesus is marked by righteousness and life. Through Christ the grace of God has entered the world, to be abundant for many (Rom. 5:15). In order to deal with sin,[22] God sent his own Son into the world, in the likeness of the flesh of sin, to do what the law was unable to do. Since the law was weak as a result of the power of the flesh—the dominion of sin—God condemned sin in the flesh in Christ (Rom. 8:3); the condemnation (κατάκριμα *katakrima*) that was so distinctive of the life "in Adam" (cf. Rom. 5:16, 18) has been eliminated (Rom. 8:1) and the power of sin has been broken. Therefore the just requirement of the law (δικαίωμα), that could not be fulfilled under the old regime of sin, is now being fulfilled in those who walk according to the Spirit (Rom. 8:4).[23] During the old regime the law was an instrument of sin and death, with the new regime it is under the authority of the Spirit of life (Rom. 8:2). The Spirit is the inaugurator and the controlling power of the new era. He has replaced sin and now dwells in the believer (cf. Rom. 7:20 and 8:9, 11) and guarantees that the new life will be really lived. By being baptized the believers have died with Christ to the powers of the old age so that, just as Christ was raised from the dead by the glory of the Father, they too might walk in newness of life (Rom. 6:4). They should consider themselves dead to sin and alive to God (Rom. 6:11). Instead of serving in the old way of the written code ("the letter") they now serve in the new way of the life of the Spirit (Rom. 7:6).

Distinguishing these era's is not just a matter of history or chronology, but is first of all a question of authority. The different ages are distinct

---

[21] In Romans 7, Paul explains how it is possible that the holy, just and good law of God has sided with the powers of the old aeon. The reason is the supremacy of sin in the old aeon. All who are of the flesh (7:14) may be able to wish to do good (7:18), but are not able to really act on this desire. Even the law of God is not able to break the dominion of sin (cf. 7:24). It can only point out the trespasses and accordingly proclaim the just judgment, which is the death sentence (Rom. 6:23). Cf. Reitsma, *Geest en Schepping*, 71–73.

[22] As NRSV translates περί ἁμαρτίας *peri hamartias* (Rom. 8:3); literally: "for" or "for the sake of sin".

[23] The passive voice in the context most likely points to the Spirit as the one that fulfills the just requirement in the believer, cf. Reitsma, *Geest en Schepping*, 77. This implies a kind of liberation of the law itself as well, since the law was imprisoned by the powers of the old age.

because of their opposing powers. The old age of Adam is qualified by the domination of the flesh, the regime of sin and death, the new age is marked by the power of the Spirit, which is life (Rom. 8:6, 10).[24] In Christ, a change of regimes has taken place and Paul painstakingly makes clear that these two regimes mutually exclude each other. A person is either a slave of sin and free in regard to righteousness or free from sin and through Christ a slave of God (cf. Rom. 6:20–22).

Significant is the fact that Paul in Romans 8 speaks about this new time period in Christ in a manner almost verbally identical to those passages in the Septuagint that speak about the promise of a new covenant.[25] That the law is being fulfilled in those who walk according to the Spirit (Rom. 8:4) reminds us of Jeremiah 38 (31):33, where God pledges to write the law in the hearts of his people when the covenant will be established.[26] In Ezekiel 36:27 God promises to put his Spirit within his people, a promise that returns in Romans 8:9 (cf. Ezek. 11:19). The result of the presence of the Spirit according to both Romans and Ezekiel is a life in obedience to God's commands and statutes. Those references underline that Paul clearly considers the coming of Christ to be the beginning of the long expected time of salvation for Israel.

This is further supported by the fact that the Spirit, who in Paul is the mark, power and inaugurator of the new age, according to several Old Testament passages is promised as gift of the eschaton, the Day of the Lord.[27] Likewise in the literature of the Second Temple Period, the Spirit of God is the Spirit of Holiness, which will be given to Israel at the end of the world.[28] For Paul, the coming of the Spirit is therefore the sign that the last days have begun.[29]

---

[24] For this interpretation cf. Reitsma, *Geest en schepping*, 82.

[25] Cf. Jer. 38(31):31–34; Ezek. 11:17–20, 36:27. Cf. Isa. 59:21, 61:8. In other passages there is a similar expectation of a new age of salvation, cf. Isa. 11; 30:20vv.

[26] "Serving in the new way of the Spirit (7:6) reminds us of "the new covenant" [Jer. 38 (31):31]. In both Romans and Jeremiah, the new covenant is also based upon the removal of sin and unrighteousness, cf. Jer. 38 (31):34 with Rom. 4:7,8; 6:13; 8:1, 3. The link with Jeremiah is the more likely, since Paul is also quoting (from) Jer. 38 (31):33, 34 in Rom. 2:15, 33 and Rom. 11:27.

[27] In Joel 3:1–5 (2:28–32) by example the gift of the Spirit on all flesh is promised "in those days", i.e. the day of the Lord, which in Acts 2:17 is interpreted as: "in the last days".

[28] We find a similar expectation that the Spirit of God—which at present had ceased to operate—would be poured out in the last days, in the literature of the Second Temple period, cf. Reitsma, *Geest en Schepping*, 79, 80, for references.

[29] In some more apocalyptic manuscripts of this period we find an explicit dualism between this present age and the age to come (*ha olam hazzè* and *ha olam haba*). This age is the age of sin corruption and suffering, the age to come is the age in which God will deliver Israel, punish his enemies and vindicate himself in glory. Paul does

In general, in the literature of post-exilic Judaism we find an expectation that God would act in history to inaugurate a whole new age of salvation for his people.[30] This would finally and truly mark the end of the exile and could be considered a new exodus.[31] Even though Israel had physically returned from the exile, still foreign powers occupied the land and ruled the nation; the great promises of God in the TeNaCh concerning the new covenant had not yet fully materialized.[32] In this context Paul's emphasis on the newness of life in Christ implies that the salvation for Israel has arrived in Jesus Christ. God's righteousness, his covenant faithfulness, has been revealed in the gospel of Christ (Rom. 1:16, 17); the reality of what God had intended for his people during the old covenant has been ultimately and fully realized through the work of Christ.[33]

2.2 *Eschatological Reservation*

Paul's strong belief that in Christ the new age of salvation has come, does not make him close his eyes to the fact that the old age of Adam is in a certain way still making itself felt. There is an eschatological reservation concerning the presence of the new age. It has not been realized to its full extent. According to Paul this can been seen in two ways:

First, although those who are in Christ have received the Spirit of life, and ought to consider themselves dead to sin and alive to God through Jesus Christ (Rom. 6:11)[34], their bodies are still dead (Rom. 8:10) and

---

not explicitly use the same terminology, and avoids the same systematic division. The remarkable difference between Paul and Judaism of his days is that for Paul this new age has already come while for Judaism it is still expected

[30] Vgl. N.T. Wright, *Jesus and the Victory of God* (COQG 2; London 1996), 615–624; despite its diversity, all Judaism shared the Faith in one God, the single chosen nation, interest in the land, the central place of the law and an eschatological hope for the future of land and nation, cf. W.D. Davies, "Reflections on Aspects of the Jewish Background of the Gospel of John" in: R.A. Culpepper, C.C. Black (eds.), *Exploring the Gospel of John* (In Honor of D.M. Smith; Louisville, 1996), 43–64, 46. Some groups were more apocalyptic in outlook, emphasizing the immanence of salvation.

[31] Cf. A.C. Brunson, *Psalm 118 in the Gospel of John: An Intertextual Study on the New Exodus Pattern in the Theology of John* (WUNT 2. Reihe, Tübingen 2003), 380, quoting Wright, *Victory*, 477. The expectation of a new exodus is, according to Brunson, marked by three elements: the return from exile, the defeat of Israel's enemies, and the return of YHWH to live among and rule over his people.

[32] Cf. N.T. Wright, *The New Testament and the People of God* (COQG 1; London ³1996), 268–270, 299–301; Brunson, *Psalm 118*, 284.

[33] Cf. Bernhard J.G. Reitsma, *Wie is onze God? Arabische Christenen, Israël en de aard van God* (Zoetermeer 2006), 52, 53; cf. Wright, *Climax*, 242, 243.

[34] The dative τῇ ἁμαρτίᾳ in Rom. 6:11 can be read as: "to sin" or as "by sin". The best

mortal (Rom. 8:11). This can only be understood as the continuing influence of the powers of the age of Adam, sin and death. Although there is no condemnation for those who are in Christ, and although they do not have to experience death as the wages of sin (cf. Rom. 6:23), they still live in a world that has not fully been redeemed yet. Through their bodies they share in the condition of this world,[35] which has been subjected to futility and still is in bondage to decay. Therefore they are still looking forward to the full redemption in which their bodies will also share (Rom. 8:23); they will be raised to life, for which the Spirit is the guarantee and promise (Rom. 8:11, cf. 1 Cor. 15).[36]

Second, all who are being led by the Spirit are children of God and that implies being heirs with God (Rom. 8:14, 17). With Christ they will share in God's inheritance. However, although this inheritance is rightfully theirs, they have not yet received it. That is why they are looking forward to it, when they will be glorified with Christ (Rom. 8:17). Those who are in Christ have received the Spirit of "sonship" (υἱοθεσία, Rom. 8:15), they have become children of God, yet this sonship is subject to further expectation as well (ἀπεκδέχομαι, Rom. 8:23). This only makes sense when the expected sonship is the fullness of what the believers have already received. According to Romans 8:23 this will be the redemption of their bodies, which can only be understood as a reference to the resurrection of which Paul spoke before (Rom. 8:11).

Paul does not describe in detail what this future glory will be like, but in this context it can only stand for the full disappearance of the powers of the old age. In Christ they have already been defeated, their power has been broken, in the future they will completely cease to exist. At that point the glory of God will be fully revealed and realized (Rom. 8:18), which will result not just in the redemption of the children of God, but of the whole creation as well. The whole creation will be set free from the bondage to decay and corruption to share in the freedom

---

interpretation in the context would be: dead *to* sin, cf. the argumentation in Reitsma, *Geest en schepping*, 80, 81 and footnote 79.

[35] The body is the reality of mankind in this world. With the body a person acts and participates in this world. That is why Paul makes a certain connection between the future of the creation and the body of the believer in 8:18–23, cf. Reitsma, *Geest en schepping*, 81, footnote 84, 110, 111 and footnote 273.

[36] Since Paul is expecting the resurrection of the body (Rom. 8:11), the genitive in 8:23 cannot be a genitive of separation but is most likely an objective genitive. The children of God will not be delivered from their bodies, but their bodies will be delivered. Nevertheless we still find a separative element here, since the body will be really and radically separated from the conditions of the old aeon. The body of death (7:24) will be transformed into the delivered body, cf. Reitsma, *Geest en Schepping*, 108–110.

of the glory of the children of God (Rom. 8:21). To understand this as a simple restoration of creation, a subtraction of corrupted creation minus the powers of the old age, is impossible. In 1 Corinthians 15 Paul emphasizes that the resurrection of the body is a complete renewal of reality, a transformation that is as thorough as the transformation of a kernel of wheat into full grown grain; the realities differ from each other as much as what is perishable from imperishable, as much as shame from honour and weakness from power. Therefore we can conclude that the expected fullness of glory entails a completely new creation. On the one hand this includes continuity: it is the present creation that will be renewed. At the same time there is also discontinuity, for the new creation will be completely *new*.[37]

2.3 *Suffering at the Crossroads of the Present Time (καιρός, kairos)*

From what we have seen so far we can conclude that suffering with Christ (Rom. 8:17) is a suffering at a very crucial moment. It is suffering that takes place at the crossroads of the old age of Adam and the new age of Christ. Paul calls it the suffering of *ho nun kairos* (ὁ νῦν καιρός, "this present time" (Rom. 8:18). *Kairos* usually indicates a specific moment, a critical point in time.[38] In Romans 8:18 it is not just a chronological, but primarily a theological qualification. It qualifies the time in relation to God and his work in history. In that relation it is a significant and critical moment in history.[39] It is the time between the Christ-event—His being sent into the likeness of the sinful flesh (Rom. 8:3), his death and resurrection (Rom. 8:11)—and the future of the fullness of God's glory. It is the *transition* from the old age of Adam to the new age of Christ. Spoken from a historical perspective, this might be considered a time *period*, lasting now for over 2000 years, theologically, however, it is merely a *point* in time.[40] The decisive victory over the

---

[37] Cf. Reitsma, *Geest en schepping*, 119, 120.

[38] Cf. Rom. 5:6.

[39] Cf. O. Christoffersson, *The Earnest Expectation of the Creature: The Flood-Tradition as Matrix of Romans 8:18–27* (CB.NT 23; Stockholm 1990), 128: "the decisive moment". The metaphor of labour-pains (birth-pangs), that Paul introduces in v. 22, points in the same direction. Labour-pain indicates a crucial moment in the delivery of a baby (for the meaning of that metaphor, see below).

[40] Important to underline is that Paul does not speak about *ho nun aioon*, but about *ho nun kairos*; likewise he does not speak about *hè melloon aioon*, but about *hè melloon doxa*. That difference is significant, cf. Reitsma, *Geest en schepping*, 87, n.124. Paul uses *aioon* in 12:2 and Gal. 1:4. Here he emphasizes the transition between the ages. J.C. Beker, *Paul the Apostle* (Edinburgh 1989), 146, talks about a proleptic presence of the new age in the old.

powers of sin and death has been gained and the believers are now simply waiting for the consummation of this victory. Whatever will take place adds nothing essential to the victory; it will basically be a materializing of what has already been achieved.[41]

When Paul describes the Spirit as the "first fruits" (Rom. 8:23),[42] he is exactly trying to grasp this dual character of the present time. In the Septuagint the expression "first fruits" is used to indicate the first part of the harvest, which at the Festival of Harvest had to be brought into the Temple.[43] These first fruits in a certain way represent the full harvest, but cannot be identified with it. The fullness is still awaited. In using this expression for the Spirit that the believers have received, Paul emphatically describes it as the first part and manifestation of the inheritance of the believers, the glory to come (cf. Rom. 8:17, 18, 23). The future glory somehow is already present in the Spirit, the end *has* come. At the same time, however, the expression "first fruits" indicates that there is something being represented. The full manifestation of the glory is still awaiting. Only then, the old age will completely cease to exist.[44]

Those who are in Christ and have received the first fruits of the Spirit suffer with Christ particularly at *this* point in time (Rom. 8:17). This suffering is qualified both by the reality of the new age and by the continuing presence of the old.

(1) First of all suffering with Christ is the consequence of the con-

---

[41] Cf. Reitsma, *Geest en schepping*, 87. Therefore the future glory will be revealed; it is already present, waiting to be revealed. At the same time that revelation implies a realization of the fullness of the glory, which is not yet a present reality in the same sense of the word.

[42] There is difference of opinion whether Paul uses the genitive as an explicative genitive (the first fruits which is the Spirit) or as a partitive genitive (the first fruits as part of the Spirit). In the LXX and in Paul the genitive is usually used in the latter sense (cf. Ex. 23:19; Lev. 23:10; Rom. 11:16; 1 Cor. 15:20). In Romans 8, however, this would mean that the believers have received only part of the Spirit, while awaiting the rest of the Spirit to come at a later point. Although not impossible, in the context of the expectation of the future glory it seems more suitable to read the genitive as explicative genitive. There is also no indication in Romans 8 that the Spirit is present in a partial way. The Spirit is the first part of the future glory. At the same time however, it is difficult to imagine that the Spirit will not be able to work in a much fuller way when the fullness of God's glory has arrived. So the partitive element is not completely absent.

[43] Cf. Ex. 23:16–19; Lev. 2:12; 23:10; Num. 15:17–21; 18:12; Deut. 18:4; 26:2, 10. In other passages ἀπαρχή is a technical term for offering, cf. Ex. 25:2, 3; 35:5, 6; Lev. 22:12; Num. 5:9; 18:8; Deut. 12:6.

[44] Cf. Bernhard J.G. Reitsma, "The Power of the Spirit: Parameters of an Ecumenical Pneumatology in the 21st Century", *NESTTR* 23/1 (April, 2002), 3–26, 18.

tinuing presence of the old age. According to Romans 6 believers have been united with Christ through baptism and participate in what has happened to him. All who have been baptized into Christ Jesus have been baptized into his death and have been buried with him (Rom. 6:3, 4), in order that just as Jesus was raised to new life they might walk in newness of life. In this context suffering *with* Christ can only be related to Christ's suffering and death on the cross.[45] In Philippians 3:10 Paul makes a similar connection between sharing in the suffering of Christ and becoming like him in His death. Suffering with Christ is therefore suffering as a result of the power of death that is still manifesting itself as mark of the old age; it is the consequence of what Paul wrote in Romans 8:10 that the bodies of the believers are still dead and therefore mortal. Death manifests its power in suffering.[46]

When we understand suffering with Christ in this way, we cannot limit this suffering to persecution, as some interpreters do.[47] The argument for that interpretation is that the rest of the New Testament usually refers to persecution as suffering for Christ. However, there are two main objections to this line of reasoning.

First, Paul never describes the persecution of the body of Christ as *suffering with Christ*. Paul prefers forms of the verb διώκω (Rom. 8:35; 1 Cor. 4:12; 2 Cor. 4:9; Gal. 1:13, 23; Phil. 3:6).[48] *Sumpascho* (συμπάσχω) does not appear in the rest of the New Testament and is only used by Paul once more in 1 Corinthians 12:26 to indicate the joint suffering of different members of the one body of Christ.[49] The emphasis with *sumpascho* (συμπάσχω) is on the similarity in suffering: the one is affected by the same thing as the other. It never designates suffering on behalf or because of the other. In all other instances where Paul uses the word *sun* (σύν) in connection with Christ it always relates either to the crucifixion and death of Christ or to his resurrection and the future glori-

---

[45] Cf. Fitzmyer, *Romans*, 502.

[46] Wright, *Jusitification: God's Plan and Paul's Vision* (London 2009), 207: "'Salvation' is from death itself, and all that leads to it and shares its destructive character (tribulation, hardship, persecution, famine, neediness, danger, weaponry) and all the powers that use these things to oppress humans and deface God's world".

[47] Cf. e.g. G.M. Penner, *In the Shadow of the Cross: A Biblical Theology of Persecution and Discipleship* (Bartlesville 2004), 197–202.

[48] Cf. Matt. 5:11, 12; here and elsewhere persecution is connected with reproach, speaking bad about etc. Nowhere, however is the word *(sum)pascho* used for being persecuted with Christ. When Paul speaks about trouble, tribulation, hardship etc., it is without "with Christ" or "for the sake of Christ".

[49] It does not appear in the rest of the New Testament and in classical Greek it is rare, cf. LSJ a.l.

fication.⁵⁰ Whenever the New Testament speaks about persecution of believers it uses different expressions, like "suffering because of (ἕνεκα or ὑπέρ) Christ" or "Christ's name".⁵¹

Second, the context of Romans 8 points in a different direction. The suffering of the believers is set within the wider perspective of the suffering of the whole creation (8:18–22). The suffering of the believers with Christ (8:17) is characterized as the suffering of this present time. This suffering has affected the whole creation: it is subjected to futility and decay and therefore is groaning in birth pain, eagerly awaiting its liberation (Rom. 8:20, 22). This suffering is distinct from persecution and can only be explained as the continuing influence of death as the power of the old age, that has entered the world through the sin of one man (Rom. 5:12, 17). Therefore the suffering of the believer likewise must encompass more than just persecution.

According to Romans 8:35, suffering includes or encompasses all kinds of suffering: tribulation or hardship (θλῖψις), distress (στενοχωρία), persecution (διωγμός), famine (λιμός), nakedness (γυμνότης), danger (κίνδυνος) and the sword (μάχαιρα); all of them are presented as different aspects of the suffering of the present time. One of these clearly is persecution,⁵² but it is not the only one. In 2 Corinthians 12:9, 10 likewise Paul puts different kinds of suffering together, when he states that the weakness of the present age—in which the power of Christ is made perfect or full—is expressed both in weaknesses, insults, hardships en persecution and difficulties or calamities.

We can conclude that with *sumpascho* Paul does not want to distinguish meticulously between persecution and other kinds of suffering; he presents an overall and inclusive concept of suffering with Christ, which is the result of the continuing presence of the old age. Suffering includes both suffering in general, like sickness, poverty and hardship, *and* persecution. This is further supported by the fact that *pascho* (πάσχω) without *sun* (σύν) can be used in the New Testament for both

---

⁵⁰ This could be "with Christ" (in Paul: Rom. 6:8, 2 Cor. 4:14; 6:1; 13:4; Phil. 1:23 and further in Col. 2:20; 3:3) or "with Him" (Rom. 8:32, cf. 8:17, referring to the future glorification with Christ; 2 Cor. 3:14; 1 Thess. 4:14, 17; 5:10) or composites with *sun* (Rom. 4–6, 8; Phil. 3:10, where suffering and death are mentioned in one sentence in a context where Paul also mentions future glorification with Christ in 3:21; Gal. 2:19).

⁵¹ Cf. ἕνεκα Matt. 5:10, 11; 10:18 (Mark 13:9, Luke 21:12); Matt. 10:39 (cf. Mark 8:35; Luke 9:24); ὑπέρ: Acts. 5:41; 9:16; 15:26; 21:13; cf. Eph. 3:1.

⁵² Cf. Rom. 8:36: Paul quotes Ps. 44:23, that the people of God are being killed for God's sake all the time, accounted as sheep to be slaughtered.

suffering in general[53] and for persecution.[54]

(2) Second, suffering with Christ is determined by the reality of the power of the new age in Christ, the Spirit of life. Paul underlines that the powers of the old age are now—in this *kairos*—no longer present in the same way as before the coming of Christ. The bodies of the believers are not yet fully delivered, but the Spirit of Him who raised Christ from the dead is already at work in them, and therefore the future resurrection of the body is guaranteed by the Spirit (Rom. 8:11). Therefore suffering with Christ is not a suffering in death pain, but in birth pain. It already announces the fullness of the new life. In no way is the suffering a sign that the new age might still be defeated. On the contrary, the suffering has come to serve the coming glorification with Christ. "We suffer with Christ *so that* we will share in his glory" (Rom. 8:17). For the believers the only road to the inheritance with Christ is the path of suffering. As there was no other way for Christ to glorification than through suffering, there is no other way for those who are in Him to share in the blessings of the new age than by suffering, dying and rising with Christ (cf. Rom. 6). In this way, however, the future glory is in a certain way already present in the suffering with Christ. It is about to break through and therefore eagerly expected. The sufferings have changed into announcements of the fast approaching glory; suffering is suffering in hope.[55]

This observation of Paul is far-reaching. It implies that even though people in the world may experience similar kinds of suffering and persecution, for those who belong to Christ the quality and character of suffering has changed. Suffering has been transformed into a sign of the glory that is about to come, in the same way that birth pangs announce new life. Those who have died with Christ through the Spirit already belong to the new glory and therefore their suffering is pointing to the fullness of what they have already received. The same cannot necessarily be said of those who do not belong to Christ.[56]

---

[53] Cf. Phil. 3:10; Matt. 17:15; 27:19; Acts 28:5; even the suffering of Christ (cf. Matt. 16:21) is more than just persecution. The same goes for the subst. *pathèma* (πάθημα).

[54] Cf. 2 Cor. 1:52; Thess. 1:5; Acts 9:16 speaks about suffering with the meaning of persecution as apostle of Christ, but explicitly uses the expression for the sake of the name (ὑπὲρ τοῦ ὀνόματός) of Christ and not "suffering with Christ".

[55] In 2 Cor. 1:22 Paul speaks of the Spirit as deposit (ἀρραβών), emphasizing the element of certainty and promise that the full payment will come. In Eph. 1:13 and 4:30 the image is of the Spirit as seal, also underlining the certainty of the promise of the future salvation.

[56] A comparison can be made with 2 Cor. 2:15, 16, where the same smell of Christ

In sum, Paul's paradigm is marked by the strong conviction that in Christ the long-awaited and promised new age of salvation has come for Israel and the nations. At the same time however, he emphasizes that this new life is not an extrapolation of the present world order. The new life sharply contrasts with the old age of sin and death and is waiting eagerly for the fullness of God's glory. In the present age, living in a broken world, this tension between the present and the future implies that Christians suffer with Christ; that is the only way they can also be glorified with him. That glory, that awaits them, is so magnificent that it outweighs all present suffering. This situation qualifies and transforms the suffering of the believer in this world. Even though believers might physically go through similar experiences as those who do not belong to Christ, it is nevertheless different in character. It is no longer a sign of death, but has become a pointer to the future glory of the new life in Christ. It is no longer qualified as "death-pain" alone, but as birth pain, an indication that the new life is imminent. Both kinds of pain result in similar physical responses but differ substantially because of what they are leading to. The confirmation of this reality for the believer is the Holy Spirit, who as the first-fruits represents the future glory in the present. In and amidst the suffering therefore through the presence and the gifts of the Holy Spirit, believers already and truly experience the glory of the new life in Christ.

3. Conclusion

When we try to look at the consequences of Paul's paradigm for an Evangelical theology of health, wealth and prosperity the following can be said.

(1) The Health, Wealth and Prosperity gospel rightly draws attention to the close relationship between what Christ has achieved and the physical reality of mankind. Paul underlines that what God has done in Christ has direct implications for the physical life of the believers in Christ. Even though they are still mortal and die, their bodies will in the future be raised with Christ. Salvation is not just the deliverance of a non-material, eternal soul, but embraces the physical life as well. A renewed body implies life without sickness and death. So prosperity theology rightly claims, that when the reality of sin leads to suffering, grace as the eradication of sin will lead to the disappearance of suffer-

---

that the believers spread has a different outworking for different people.

ing (as the consequence of sin). Moreover, salvation is not just something believers will individually experience, it implies a renewal of the whole creation. The defeat of the powers of sin and death result in a renewed and glorified creation, where there will be no more suffering and disease. The health, wealth and prosperity gospel is right in underlining that God intended for the world life, joy and happiness. The new creation is a life in which God's purposes for mankind are being fulfilled and in which God's honour and glory are complete.

(2) Despite seeing this relationship between the salvation of Christ and health and prosperity, the health, wealth and prosperity theology derails in two ways, with respect to time and with respect to quality.

(a) *With respect to time.* The health, wealth and prosperity gospel fails to notice the special quality of the present time as a "kairos" moment. It is a decisive and unique time-period between the first and the second coming of Christ. Although the new life, salvation and deliverance from sin, is a reality, it has not been completed yet. In this respect prosperity theology overlooks that there is an eschatological reservation in the work of Christ. The present salvation is pointing to the future fullness of redemption. Therefore the health, wealth and prosperity theology fails to see what Paul is continuously stressing, that we are suffering with Christ, not just as a result of unbelief, lack of faith, sin, unwillingness to break with sin or lack of perseverance, but specifically as a consequence of the fact that the new life is present in a reality that is still marked by death.

In this reality, Christians are not detached from a broken world; the laws of a broken nature are not simply suspended for those who belong to Christ, whether they are flying in a crashing air plane or being affected by the HIV virus, falling from a roof, being in the path of a lethal hurricane, too close to an erupting volcano or present in the midst of ethnic violence. Sometimes people are miraculously saved, sometimes people are unintelligibly killed.

For those suffering Christians the health, wealth and prosperity gospel has no message. It cannot provide a coherent Christian worldview that accounts for suffering and persecution. Pastorally this theological model is in many ways very harsh. It easily brings guilt and condemnation to those who truly believe but are not healed or do not prosper. It creates the impression that God is no longer for them but against them.[57] Even if it theoretically could be possible to explain this reality of

---

[57] Cf. Craig L. Blomberg, *Neither Poverty nor Riches: A Biblical Theology of Possessions* (New Studies in Biblical Theology 7; Nottingham 1999), 25: the failure of the

suffering believers by referring to unbelief of the community,[58] sin, not claiming salvation or the reality of the devil, that is no longer possible for the predicament of the persecuted Church. Persecuted Christians are precisely suffering because of their allegiance and commitment to Christ; because they do not want to give up their faith in him, they suffer, lose their jobs, are being harassed or thrown in prison. Exactly because of believing in Christ many Christians in the world will never prosper materially. Unbelief, compromising their faith in Christ as the only Saviour, would immediately end their ordeal. Calling Caesar Lord is the quickest remedy for persecution. The prosperity gospel can therefore not account for the faithful martyrs of the past and present.

(b) *With respect to quality*. What the health, wealth and prosperity gospel promises as God's blessing remains primarily within the parameters of the present creation. The vision of God's salvation does not rise above the restoration of life under the conditions of the old age. It envisions material wealth as one of the ultimate blessings of God and physical healing of this mortal body as one of the highest objectives for which to strive. Apart from the fact that this does not reckon with the reality of death, it also thinks too small of God and his gifts. It fails to acknowledge that God's salvation is of a completely different quality than life as we know it now. For Paul, the new creation is a total renewal of the present creation. That implies on the one hand that it will be the same creation that is going to be renewed, but at the same time that it will be so completely new, that it can hardly be recognized as this creation. The renewed creation is as similar and different to the old creation as the grain of wheat is similar and different to the kernel. The health, wealth and prosperity gospel mainly thinks in terms of the kernel and overlooks the magnificent newness of the glory of God. That glory outweighs everything and makes reality look dim. What God has in store for his people surpasses our understanding. "What no eye has seen, no ear has heard, in no heart arose, that is what God has prepared for those who love him" (1 Cor. 2:9).

Concluding we must emphasize that in trying to understand suffering and persecution in relation to God Evangelical theology has to take into consideration that the victory of Christ does not yet exclude suffering for those who belong to Christ. On the contrary; suffering could in the present time even be called inherent to the Christian life.

---

health, wealth and prosperity theology leads to "great guilt complexes" or "disillusionment with Christianity".

[58] Cf. Ouweneel, *Geneest de zieken*, 373.

If Christians would not be experiencing some kind of suffering in this present age, Paul would assume that the newness of their life has lost its essential character, so that the tension between the new life of Christ and the old life of sin and death has evaporated. That implies that Evangelical theology can only be very critical of any form of health, wealth and prosperity theology. On the other hand, renouncing health, wealth and prosperity thinking can only be done in the light of the approaching fullness of the new life, when all believers will prosper and with the whole creation reach their destiny; then "God will be all in all and shall the earth be filled with the knowledge of the glory of the Lord as the waters cover the sea" (Hab. 2:14).

Chapter Eight

Creative Love Theism: The Doctrine of God in Reformed and Evangelical Theology

Cornelis van der Kooi

1. Introduction

Creative love theism—the theological model presented in the book *Unbounded Love*, written a number of years ago by Clark H. Pinnock (1937–2010) in collaboration with Robert C. Brow[1]—aims to offer theology in its narrowest sense, i.e. a doctrine of God. It touches the core of Christian theology. The question, "Who or what is the ultimate reality with which humankind is faced?" plays in the background of many aspects of the dialogue between Reformed and Evangelical spirituality. Our view of the world, the church and its mission, our view of the work of the Holy Spirit and of the hope that Christianity can offer the world, are all directly linked to the debate about the doctrine of God. Decisions made in this area are of eminent importance to the demand for an Evangelical-Reformed theology. A common characteristic of current theological models is that God's relationality is emphasized. What characterizes God in the first place, according to contemporary theology, is not his absoluteness or his total independence from this world, but his involvement in our world and history.[2] This leads straightaway to an important question: How does this preference for a relational image of God tie in with the traditional emphasis in Reformed theology on God's independence and majesty, in other words, his sovereignty? It

---
[1] C.H. Pinnock, R.C. Brow, *Unbounded Love: A Good News Theology for the 21st Century* (Leicester: InterVarsity, 1994); translated in Dutch under the dubious title *Ontketende liefde: Een evangelische theologie voor de 21ste eeuw* (Gorinchem: Ekklesia, 2001).

[2] See for example H. Jansen, *Relationality and the Concept of God* (Amsterdam, Atlanta, GA: Rodopi, 1994), and W.M. Dekker, *De relationaliteit van God: onafhankelijkheid en relatie in de godsleer en ontologie van Francesco Turrettini en Eberhard Jüngel*, (Zoetermeer: Boekencentrum, 2008).

also leads to questions about methodology. Which route do we take in our attempt to obtain a critical review of the doctrine of God, and what role do Bible and philosophy play in this review?

The choice for Pinnock's model as a subject of research into the elementary differences between Reformed and Evangelical is not self-evident. The main objection that can be raised against this choice is that Pinnock was a controversial figure in Evangelical circles during his lifetime. At the start of this millennium some even attempted to have him expelled from the Evangelical Theological Society. Moreover, the book *Unbounded Love*, which he co-authored with R.C. Brow, was an important publication, but not his best. Those who look for more robust research should read *Most Moved Mover. A Theology of God's Openness*,[3] which was written in response to the debate and is more concise and better researched.

Nevertheless, the choice for Pinnock as a figure who represents a particular development in the wider Evangelical world, i.e. a shift to a consistently relational doctrine of God, is justifiable. This shift, again, is not self-evident. Evangelical spirituality, which historically developed from eighteenth-century Methodism and the holiness movement in the nineteenth century, and which was strongly influenced by fundamentalism at the start of the twentieth century, is characterized by a remarkable paradox, namely that of great openness to contemporary culture in religious expression on the one hand and stubborn theological conservatism on the other. The theological content or doctrine is mainly taken from Protestant orthodoxy. I do not claim that in the domain of systematic theology, "Evangelical" simply means that people take what they like from Protestant tradition and add to that a number of characteristics such as the special emphasis on the communication of the Gospel or on personal religious experience. After all, the typical elements of Evangelical tradition and spirituality result in quite a number of differences compared to the Reformed faith. If the accents are being shifted one at a time, the centre of gravity will eventually shift as well. In short, as a result of the focus on the individual and his response, man has obtained a much more important place in nearly all areas. This change will become more evident as we continue our study of creative love theism.

In presenting the subject of open theism, Pinnock seems to presume that it offers an Evangelical theological model with which we can face

---

[3] C.H. Pinnock, *Most Moved Mover: A Theology of God's Openness* (Carlisle: Paternoster, 2001).

contemporary humankind and from which unnecessary obstructions have been removed. The openness to a relationship with contemporary culture goes much further than just style and form, it touches the substance of theology. Pinnock radicalizes several essential theological notions that have always been important in Arminian tradition. The God of the Bible should not be identified with a God who leaves no room for human freedom; God leaves a lot of room for humankind and focuses on relationships. When we link this to a parable told by Christ, the Parable of the Lost Son (Luke 15:11-32), we see that the image of the father who is passionately waiting and involved is presented to us as a concept that still needs to be integrated into Christian theology.[4] Christian theology needs to shake off the unnecessary feathers of determinism and dare to fly on the wings of the relational image of God.

This theological proposition seems to me to deserve at least some merit. What Pinnock says is not very new, and it is open to some serious criticism. The relational image of God is not new at all. Those of us who have some knowledge of the theological landscape will find in his model an amalgamation of the debate of the past seventy years about christology, doctrine of election, doctrine of the social trinity and process theology. However, that does not nullify the merit. Pinnock makes the Evangelical world aware of the question to what extent the image of God it often works with, either secretly or openly, is really based on the Bible. He forces an answer to the question to what extent we should take more distance from classical theism. Creative love theism believes that it can use the Bible to make decisions that have not been made in classical theology and that are so complicated that they cause unnecessary frustration.

In this article I like to give a short presentation of some of the relevant themes. I shall ask whether creative love theism really offers building blocks for an Evangelical theology or whether we are in fact in danger of losing biblical substance in accepting its proposition. Before we start, however, we need to make a number of preliminary remarks, first about the concept "evangelical" and then about the "communitarian turn".

2. *The Term "Evangelical"*

For many years, theological discourse in Evangelical circles was dominated by the debate about the Bible. The big difference between Liberal

---

[4] Pinnock, *Most Moved Mover*, 3–4.

and Evangelical, at least in the English-speaking world, was found in the position, infallibility and authority of the Bible.⁵ The attitude toward the Bible as the book that contains God's will and message for doctrine and practice was the common denominator for a wide range of movements. On that basis, what was called "orthodox" in the European context was often labelled as "evangelical" in the United Kingdom and the United States. Let us call this the wider definition of the term "evangelical". A narrower and probably more accurate description of this term can be obtained by adding a number of other characteristics to this definition. Apart from what we have just seen—the reliability of the Bible as an authoritative Book on life and doctrine (1)—we should also mention the central place of Christ (2), the focus on conversion and personal religious experience (3), and the focus on communicating the Gospel (4).⁶ The English term "evangelical" therefore has a wider scope than the term *evangelicaal* in the Netherlands. And in the German-speaking world, *evangelikal* has a narrower scope than *evangelisch*. Evangelicals can be Baptists, Methodists, but also people who were originally Calvinists. What they have in common is the wealth of songs and hymns brought forth by Methodism, which have had a lasting effect on many believers.

Essentially, the definition of "evangelical" refers to a stronger proposition. The wider Evangelical tradition always appeals to its sources, to the Gospel itself. It is in the light of that proposition that we will discuss some of the themes of open theism as well as the question regarding what makes a theology Evangelical.

3. *From Bible to Church*

A notable trend in the current Evangelical world is that the debate about the reliability of the Bible seems to have eased and there is now more emphasis on the church as a community. The Evangelicals seem to have taken what Stanley Grenz calls a "communitarian turn".⁷ Church and

---

⁵ For an overview, see William V. Trollinger, "Protestantism and Fundamentalism", in: Alister E. Mcgrath, Darren C. Marks, *The Blackwell Companion to Protestantism* (Oxford: Blackwell, 2004), 344–356; George Marshden, *Fundamentalism and American Culture: The Shaping of Twentieth-Century Evangelicalism, 1870–1925* (Oxford, New York: Oxford University Press, 1980).

⁶ See, for example, David W. Bebbington, *Evangelicalism in Modern Britain: A History from the 1730s to the 1980s* (London: Unwin Hyman, 1989).

⁷ Stanley J. Grenz, *Renewing the Center: Evangelical Theology in a Post-Theological Era* (Grand Rapids: Baker Academic, 2001), 21, 201, 281.

contemporary society now play a more important role in finding and discovering God's truth. The Bible as God's Word is a book that is inextricably connected with the community of faith. This shift to the community is also present in Pinnock's model. The debate about the truth of Christian faith has changed from a debate about the Bible to a debate about the relationship between God and humankind, about salvation and damnation.

This shift from Bible to church, to the positioning of Christian theology in the faith community is probably inconceivable without the postmodern climate in which we live. In the same way that modernity demands an absolute foundation for human knowledge, the recognition of the historical embedding of faith into a confessing community corresponds with postmodern thinking.

This leads us to the question about the basis on which the debate about the doctrine of God should be held. Will the discussion be held as a philosophical debate about the consistency of concepts and models? The debate about free will that is currently taking place in the English-speaking Evangelical world is being fought with the weapons of analytical philosophy. This is useful, but from a theological viewpoint philosophical discourse has important limitations. Analytical-philosophical discourse concerns the question in what measure certain faith concepts are conceivable, consistent, and coherent, and in what measure the truth of expressions of faith can be guaranteed. It is about the *warrant of belief*.[8] Again, these questions are important to theology, because they are part of the intellectual debate with the surrounding culture. However, analytical reflection is not sufficient for systematic theology. Again and again, systematic theology will need to reconsider the content of the Christian faith, and to keep translating this into new situations, always on the basis of its sources. The dialogue with exegesis can teach us that those sources do not offer ready-made concepts, but are the result of a debate about God's relationship with humankind that has been held in earlier generations. For current theology this means that Biblical studies are an important interlocutor and that the search for a responsible doctrine of God needs to be the result of an ongoing interaction with these textual sources.

---

[8] For an example and model for high-calibre academic debate, I refer to the works of Alvin Plantinga, *Warrant and Proper Function* (New York, Oxford: Oxford University Press 1993), idem, *Warrant: The Current Debate* (New York, Oxford: Oxford University Press, 1993); idem, *Warranted Christian Belief* (New York, Oxford: Oxford University Press, 2000).

I make these remarks about the partnership with systematic theology in view of the debate about open theism. Open theism as represented by Pinnock has an outspoken opinion about the classical doctrine of God. It claims that it is closed and deterministic. I shall for now ignore the question whether this qualification is justified or whether it rests on a gross distortion.[9] Interestingly, the partnership with philosophy as an interlocutor is hardly at issue. Pinnock argues for the necessity to overcome our pagan legacy.

What is his criticism of classic theism? In classical theism, the absoluteness and independence of God's being in relation to the world, or God's *aseitas,* is emphasized. According to Thomas, God is *ipsum esse subsistens,* or "subsistent Being itself".[10] This means that God contains all *being* in Himself. Lutheran and Reformed orthodoxy have followed him in this choice, as can be seen in the *Reformed Dogmatics* of H. Bavinck, to mention but one example. God's being is perfect life (*vita*) or pure act (*actus purissimus et simplicissimus*). Any form of composition, limitation or change in God as the highest being must be denied. This means that the most accurate way of describing God is by his absolute or non-transferable attributes. The Latin terms for these attributes are *independentia, simplicitas, infinitas (aeternitas et immensitas)* and *immutabilitas.*[11] In spite of the many *dicta probantia* brought forward by, for example, Bavinck, the question is what meaning is given to these terms. And are these meanings based on exegesis, or mainly on classical metaphysics? If the latter is the case, the Christian concept of God is made to depend on a general ontology. Within this hierarchical idea of "being", God is the highest being and his being is defined on the basis of what is known of "being" and existence. Moreover, Platonic or Aristotelian tradition has become the dominant factor.

In contrast with this classical model of thought about being, we find that the supporters of open theism use "relationship" and "relationality" as their keywords. Who or what God is, is defined as love. In this regard, Pinnock is looking for the meaning that the Bible will have for a metaphysics of love.[12] Is that beneficial? At first sight it is. It means

---

[9] On the contribution of Antonie Vos and others in the Utrecht School, see Dolf te Velde, *Paths Beyond Tracing Out: The Connection of Method and Content in the Doctrine of God, Examined in Reformed Orthodoxy, Karl Barth and the Utrecht School* (Delft: Eburon, 2010), 415–456.

[10] Thomas Aquinas, *Summa Theologiae* I.4.2.

[11] H. Heppe, *Die Dogmatik der evangelisch-reformierten Kirche* (hg. v. E. Bizer; Neukirchen: Neukirchener, 1958), 47.

[12] Pinnock, *Most Moved Mover,* 113–151.

that a paradigm is being used that is closer to the modern experience of truth. But to what extent the shift to a different paradigm constitutes a methodological benefit is questionable. In both cases, contemporary philosophy is the main interlocutor and a very close connection is made between the doctrine of God and an existing ontology that can easily develop into a real dependency. Karl Barth especially criticized the dependency of the Christian doctrine of God on metaphysics during the twentieth century. He tried to avoid it, and his attempts to practice methodologically consistent *revelation* theology seem impossible to abandon. To what extent he was successful is another question, but the methodological approach is crucial here. It means that Christian theology keeps having to ask, on the basis of the Bible as a compilation of concrete texts, what God's revelation and its own presuppositions need to recapture. This continuous recapture is in keeping with the deeply Reformed conviction that Scripture needs to be our guide and norm. And as I remarked earlier, it is also in keeping with the Evangelical tradition that returns to its source again and again in order to be able to face its surrounding culture. In short, we continuously need to return to the Biblical canon as the record and proof of the history of God's relationship with Israel and with Jesus Christ.

4. *The Central Problem: The Weight of Time vs. the Weight of Eternity*

Creative love theism can best be understood as a model that deals once and for all with a problem that has played an important role in theology, especially in the past few centuries. What is the division of roles between God and man? Can God be characterized as the ultimate cause? Or is he determined by relationality? The first option is the most well-known, and it traditionally determines the Christian concept of God. What can we say about God? We can point to article 1 of the Dutch Confession of Faith:

> We all believe with our hearts and confess with our mouths that there is one single spiritual being who we call God: eternal, unfathomable, invisible, unchanging, unending, all-powerful, perfect in wisdom, righteous, good, and a richly overflowing fountain of everything that is good.[13]

Especially the first and transcendent attributes seem to determine the

---

[13] "Wij geloven allen met het hart en belijden met de mond, dat er een enig en eenvoudig geestelijk wezen is, dat wij God noemen: eeuwig, onbegrijpelijk, onzichtbaar, onveranderlijk, oneindig, almachtig, volkomen wijs, rechtvaardig, goed en een zeer overvloedige fontein van al het goede."

popular image of God. Even those who turned away from God a long time ago are convinced that if there is a highest power called "god", he is involved in everything and there is nothing that is outside his will, knowledge or power. In other words, the well-known starting point is that God is an ever-present, omniscient power. This means that everything that happens in time can only be considered as the unfolding of a plan that was made and determined before time began. God's counsel is all-encompassing. In theological language: the order of eternity rules over the order of time. Time and eternity are played off against one another.

Open theism is modern in the sense that this paradox, that has caused a lot of problems in classical doctrine, is solved by consistently taking the order of time as a starting point. Whatever happens inside time, in our history, in our choices, is taken utterly seriously. The concept of openness is used in two ways. First, openness is linked with the statement that God is love. If God is love, he is inherently open to relationships and looks for fellowship with people. Secondly, there is another meaning of the term "openness". In this sense of the word, whether God's attempt to have fellowship with people will succeed is not certain in advance. The outcome is essentially open. Whether God will succeed in having a relationship with an individual depends on the response of that individual. God will not force it, because that would contradict man's freedom and God's love. In this respect, God is not all-powerful. As a loving being he decides not to force himself on us and leaves us room to make our own decisions and respond in the way we want. In creative love theism this means that God is not omniscient. His knowledge consists of things that have already happened and are happening now, but he does not know what each human being will do in the future.

As we have seen, creative love theism starts from the order of time and the decisions made there. In fact it only sees one order, where people and God meet and where that meeting is decisive. By working in this way, Pinnock attempts to give human history, the way in which people respond to God's invitation, its full weight. The weight of human decisions and actions are not crushed by the decrees of an eternal divine counsel. Human decisions count. This view meets the need for a conviction that the human choice should be taken seriously. What I do, matters. People who wilfully refuse God's salvation, will not have it forced upon them. In the words of Dutch poet Hendrik Marsman (1899–1940):

Neem mijn laatste bezit mij niet af.
Mijn zonden gaan mee in *mijn* graf."

("Do not take away my last possession.
My sins will go with me into *my* grave.")[14]

Is there anything else we can say about this? What is the ultimate consequence of what open theism says? Should we allow ourselves to be forced into the dilemma that open theism offers, i.e. the choice between determinism and freedom? The solution for the dilemma of human responsibility and divine power is found in many places in this model. Let us therefore look at a number of subjects. In each case there is a dilemma, a situation where we are faced with two options that are mutually exclusive. After describing each dilemma, I shall offer a suggestion that admittedly does not entirely solve it, but that will help us to deal with it.

5. *First Dilemma: Salvation for All or Only for a Limited Group?*

Is salvation in Christ a privilege for an elect group of people, or is it available to all? Let us take a brief look at the debate about grace and double predestination. In Augustine's doctrine of grace we find an outspoken doctrine of predestination in which God's initiative plays a decisive role. After the Synod of Orange in 529, the doctrine of God's gracious initiative was elevated to a dogma, but it was only during the Reformation, especially with Calvin, that the doctrine of double predestination was given a prominent place centre-stage. Calvinism was, from an ecumenical viewpoint, isolated by the Canons of Dort.[15]

The debate about this subject has found a preliminary conclusion, as I see it, in Barth's view of election. Christ is God's "yes" to all people. In Christ, God chooses to refuse to exist without humankind.[16] With this proposition of Christ as both the means and the end of election, we have found one of the main building blocks for an inherently Evangelical theology, i.e. a theology focussed on the Gospel. This way, the message of the church really is good news. Since Jesus Christ, God can-

---

[14] H. Marsman, 'Verzet', *Verzamelde Gedichten* (Amsterdam: Querido, 1971), 89.

[15] See the eloquent papers of H.A. Oberman, *De erfenis van Calvijn: grootheid en grenzen* (Kampen: Kok, 1988), especially 36–51. See also C. van der Kooi, *Als in een spiegel: God kennen volgens Calvijn en Barth. Een tweeluik* (Kampen: Kok, 2002), 326–342; transl. *As in a Mirror: John Calvin and Karl Barth on Knowing God. A Diptych* (StHCT 120; transl. D. Mader; Leiden, Boston: Brill, 2005), 363–380.

[16] K. Barth, *Die Kirchliche Dogmatik*, II/2, (Zürich: Theologischer, 1942).

not be considered without the name of Christ. God has pinned himself down on everything that is contained in that name and its history. As such, salvation is in principle universal. It is not destined for a small selection of people only, but it is aimed at all who have chosen for Christ.

With this reconstruction of the doctrine of salvation, Barth attempted to remove the shadow hanging over the doctrine of grace in Calvinism. He shares this aim with the heirs of the Arminian tradition and we also see it with Pinnock as a representative of open theism. But the two parties solve the dilemma in distinctly different ways.

Let us return to the beginning. The dilemma is about how man is eventually saved. Is the redemption from alienation based on our own free decision to believe, or is our "yes" really only one side of the coin and were we, as soon as we started considering our "yes" to God, persuaded, changed and moved as God changed our hearts? Reformed theologians who were forced to choose, chose for God and spoke of His eternal counsel. Theological reflection about grace is here nearing the boundary of God as the all-determining power. According to the Canons of Dort it is not only true that God foresees the choices that people make, but also that he takes a decisive role in their actions, although the Canons immediately add that God's will is not involved with unbelief in the same way as it is with belief. God's election and rejection are viewed as asymmetrical opposites. Interestingly, the formulation is cautious and the Canons defend the spiritual importance of election. The reason for this is that the sovereignty of God's grace is at stake.[17] If we reduce that to its simplest core, we see that it is important that *God's surprising grace is emphasized.*

This emphasis on God's gracious intervention has a number of implications. Even though it should be maintained that, historically, these theologians attempted to emphasize the freedom of God's approach of humankind and the surprise that becoming a child of God involves, in practice the doctrine of election has developed into a theological and pastoral burden. If God only elects a certain number of people and saves them in his eternal love, where do all the others go? Can we escape the conclusion that God, by not electing so many others, in fact makes a negative choice and rejects them? Speaking about God becomes problematic when one of the coordinates we find in the Bible is made into an absolute, into a central theme. We see here the struggle between various groups within the Reformed spectrum, and the di-

---

[17] See, for example, the *Canons of Dort*, I, 5.

lemma has reared its head many times and in countless variations. For whom is God's grace intended? Can we avoid the conclusion that God does not wish all people to be saved?[18] In that case, is God capricious? Are his actions morally flawed?

Creative love theism suggests that Christian theology can be freed from this scandal and burden once and for all. It claims that it would be immoral if God would offer his communion only to a limited number of people. God would be failing in his love as a Father if we were to think of Him that way. That is why it takes as its starting points the invitation of the prophets to the whole nation and Christ's offer of the kingdom to all. It fixates on the resurrection. The Resurrected One does not represent a limited offer of salvation. No, in Him the whole world is offered a part in the fellowship of love that characterizes the Father, Son and Holy Spirit.

I believe that in this emphasis on the general offer of God's grace in Christ, something else plays a role apart from the appeal to the Bible. Contemporary theology reveals its modernity by the fact that it does not only apply the equality of all people before God to the fact that they are all equal in His eyes as his creation. This principle of equality has, via Calvinism, and especially via the New England Puritans, penetrated into the American declaration of independence. On the European continent, this principle of equality was incorporated into the principles of the French revolution. In the twentieth century we find it in the universal declaration of human rights. The idea that we are also equal in God's eyes when it comes to our eternal salvation appeared in theology at a much later stage. In Protestant theology it was Karl Barth who gave it theological consideration. Jesus Christ is God's "yes" to all fellow human beings of Christ. In Christ we see God's "yes", His grace for all.

Let us return to open theism. In Pinnock's theological model, the universality of salvation is of central importance. The invitation to come to Christ goes out to all people. The invitation to become a child of God, to live in communion with Him and to change through Him, is not limited by "ifs and buts", and is freely offered to all. God's love is accessible, the trinity circle is open as an invitation to us all.

As we saw before, this focus on Christ contains a building block for an Evangelical theology. God's invitation to have fellowship with Him is real and unconditional. The Gospel is good news for everyone. Since

---

[18] See, for example, the passionate discussion of this problem by J. Bonda, *The One Purpose of God: An Answer to the Doctrine of Eternal Punishment* (Grand Rapids: Eerdmans 1998).

Christ, each and every person can and should be considered in the light of the fact that He, the Living One, has come close to us. But in what measure does this saving truth really take effect? In this, open theism takes a much more decisive, and I would say a more "closed" view than Karl Barth, whom we discussed earlier. According to open theism the effectiveness of God's grace depends on the response that each person gives individually. As part of human freedom, the individual can refuse God's offer of salvation. In creative love theism God is utterly creative in choosing ways of convincing us of his love, but his effectiveness in convincing us is limited by human freedom. God's grace is only effective in those who choose to accept his invitation.

This leads us to another dilemma. How free are we to refuse God's love? Or are we so entirely alienated from our origins that we are not free at all?

6. *Second Dilemma: Freedom or Uncertainty?*

Are we free to choose for God? Creative love theism makes a clear choice. It says that we are free to say yes or no. No one is excluded from salvation, except those who exclude themselves. As we saw earlier, this model takes history, or the order of time, as its starting point. The human decision is taken utterly seriously. That is also the choice that is made at a theological level in Molinism, Arminianism[19], and Methodism, in fact in large parts of the Evangelical world. Each person has a choice. What he or she chooses, is not determined by God. People either choose for God or against him. Arminius said, thereby following Molina, that God knows what choice the person will make, but this does not negate the fact that the person is free to choose. In the open theism that Pinnock and his followers advocate, God's omniscience and prescience cannot be maintained. In creating the individual, God chooses to take a step back and to offer this individual his own space and autonomy. In Pinnock's model, God's foreknowledge would imply the absence of freedom.

Finding biblical support for this view is not difficult. There are many examples in biblical narrative where the human choice is decisive. In Deuteronomy 30:15-20 people are offered a choice. Keeping the com-

---

[19] See, for example, E. Dekker, *Rijker dan Midas: vrijheid, genade en predestinatie in de theologie van Jacobus Arminius (1559-1609)* (Zoetermeer: Boekencentrum 1993), and W. den Boer, *Duplex Amor Dei: contextuele karakteristiek van de theologie van Jacobus Arminius (1559–1609)* (Apeldoorn: Instituut voor Reformatieonderzoek, 2008).

mandments will lead to life, disobedience will lead to death. Blessing and curse are the results of people's own choice. In Matthew 11:28 the invitation implies real freedom: "Come to me, all you that are weary and are carrying heavy burdens." The invitation, the choice that needs to be made is not a game, it should be taken very seriously and it implies freedom of choice.

As regards our own responsibility and our freedom of choice there is no real difference with what can be found with Calvin and with the best representatives of Calvinist tradition. They too maintain the reality of human responsibility. There is no compulsion to sin. The difference between the classical doctrine of God and open theism concerns the scope of God's grace. When Pinnock uses the term "openness" in its second meaning, it does not mean that everything is determined by God. Man and his autonomy are given the last word. In speaking about God and man, freedom and human responsibility do not have the function of a boundary, but that of the central theme. Pinnock seems to take God's foreknowledge out of the equation. To him, God does not know beforehand whether a person will accept or refuse his offer. The result is uncertain, even to God. Pinnock explicitly denies God's foreknowledge, and in doing so he radicalizes the Arminian position.[20] The Arminians maintain both free will and God's omniscience, but the *Openness of God movement* has abandoned God's omniscience. Thus, openness has become a gap, and their position is very close to that of process theology, which claims that the future depends on the human response. History is open as well, in the sense that the individual can say no, thereby excluding himself. God is powerless if a person refuses to allow God to take control.

On the surface, this solution looks reasonable. Open theism is appealing to the extent that it tries to prevent history from becoming a system in which each human action and each human choice has been determined by God's foreknowledge. The person is not forced, but invited. One is essentially free to say "yes" and God as a father waits for his child to invite him in. This leads to some important questions. In what measure is God submitted to humankind and time in this model? Better still, in what measure has a particular concept of relationality become decisive here? In what measure does this "solution" stay within

---

[20] For Arminian theology, especially the idea of a *scientia media*, see Richard A. Muller, *God, Creation and Providence in the Thought of Jacob Arminius: Sources and Directions of Scholastic Protestantism in the Era of Early Orthodoxy* (Grand Rapids: Baker, 1991), 154–158.

the scope of the biblical drama of Israel's disobedience and the ignorance of the nations on the one hand and divine grace as we find it in the Biblical canon on the other hand? Is God in this model still the Lord, the *Kurios*, who can relate to all the dimensions of his created reality? In this model the future, including humankind's future actions, is approached as a number of separate events or factualities. It seems to me that if we want to think theologically sound, we need to start from the biblical fact that God is Lord of his creation and that He is close to his creation and to humankind and our history. That would mean that no event or future prospect is out of God's reach. Open theism starts from the other end of the spectrum, where the individual has his own space, and where there are aspects of the future that are out of God's reach and outside his knowledge. Let me say it more clearly. This point where Pinnock fully agrees with modern autonomy, also shows us the cruel side of his theological model. Part of God's creation is out of his reach, he has definitely lost it. The Father is powerless against the choice of his stubborn child. Is this really the direction into which the Gospel is taking us? Or does open theism change the Gospel into a wonderful offer that only stupid and thoughtless people will refuse?

Pinnock decides the dilemma of human freedom versus God's omnipotence firmly in favour of human freedom. I believe there is only one possible response to that. If Evangelical theology uses this model as a building block, it will slide into a cheapness that makes salvation in Christ into the attractive offer we have just discussed. At this point, the Reformation looks further and holds treasures that should not be abandoned. The idea that the individual is not as free as he thinks but is confused in his alienation of himself and God, and that faith is still a question of grace and surprise, is not or not sufficiently acknowledged in open theism. Election is a word that gives hope. It means that God has not finished talking when people have. It seems to me, this is to what the biblical texts refer.

The proposition that humankind is called to respond and that this response should be taken very seriously, does contain a building block for Evangelical theology. It even has a strong point here in comparison to a position that is in fact deterministic. But the question remains whether this alternative is correct and the concept of freedom has not become too superficial. How free are we really? Of course I am completely free to take a left or a right turn when driving, to hang my coat in one place or another. I do not mean that trivial kind of freedom of choice, and the Reformation never meant that when it spoke about the unfree will. This is about a freedom that concerns our deepest being. I mean the freedom we experience when we are "in our element", when we are free to do what fits our character and destination. It is the experience of freedom a windsurfer has when responding to the wind and waves. He feels essentially free, in his element. When we apply this meaning of freedom to theology, the person who feels really free is the one who worships God and who can abandon himself to his worship. At such moments, freedom is not a formal freedom, not a freedom of choice but a material freedom, a fulfilled freedom. The deepest experience of freedom is one that enables. Being able to walk the street and go somewhere after being ill for a few days, that is freedom. Essential freedom is the possibility to do the thing you are meant to do. Let us apply that to the question about God. Are we free to choose for God? I believe that when it comes to God's kingdom we are not really that free and we have to be saved before we are free to choose.

Let us assume that God would indeed take our choice seriously in that superficial sense. That would be terrible. The Gospel tells us that God has not finished talking to us when we refuse him. "Flesh and blood has not revealed this to you, but my Father in heaven", Christ said to Peter when he confessed him as Messiah and Son of God (Matthew 16:17 NRSV). The Gospel of John talks about the mistakes and blindness that characterize us as people. The light needs to shine into our darkness. The history of Christ shows that God goes his own sovereign way with human refusal and stubbornness.

What is most problematic about Pinnock's vision is not that he overestimates human decisions, but that he underestimates God's lordship and glory. To put it into more theological words: in creative love theism God's sovereignty and human autonomy are drawn into one and the same realm, where they are played out against each other, and the result is that the latter wins. But Pinnock seems to have lost sight of the fact that God is still Lord in the face of human powerlessness, alienation and refusal. To put it into terms that can be explained by using the books of Deuteronomy and Isaiah: the creative love model takes the covenant of Sinai as a starting point and also as a condition for life. This covenant was based on a core covenant containing certain obligations, and should be distinguished from God's covenant with Abraham. Time and again the prophets appeal to the Abrahamic covenant, in which God takes the initiative and which is therefore more one-sided.

The starting point and building block for an Evangelical theology must be that we do not allow our speaking and our thinking to be trapped in the dilemma between determinism on one hand and relationality or freedom of choice on the other. If Evangelical theology allows itself to be governed by this dilemma, it gives in to the same dilemma that has paralysed the debate in classical theology from time to time and of which the dogma of double predestination is a result. Double predestination in a rigid form is after all a result of this model in which the person is forced to choose for God as the first cause. Open theism only makes the opposite extreme into its central theme. It makes God the prisoner of our idea of relationality.

7. Third Dilemma: Absolute Principle or Person?

Is God a person or an absolute principle? In this dilemma we find an element that is a building block for Evangelical theology. God is a person, he is approachable, he sees us and wants to be in fellowship with us. The creative love model has obviously chosen for God as a person. God is a person who cares about people, who wants to be in fellowship with them. He should not secretly be regarded as an absolute principle that is the cause of everything. The creative love model argues that when God is regarded as a principle, this will lead to despair and fatalism, and I agree. This is definitely a reason why classical theology and its definitions of omnipotence, omnipresence and omniscience can no longer be maintained. It discusses God's being in terms of a problem with his creation. Eternity, omnipotence, omnipresence and omniscience are regarded as negations of human limitation. We will need to loosen theology from the grip of general ontology. We will need to derive the attributes of God's being from the contingent revelation of God in Jesus Christ.

The decisive choice that creative love theism makes for the proposition that God is a person, deserves our approval. God wants to meet us. It fits with the theology that sees God as the one who knows fellowship within himself and who invites us to be part of that. It all sounds very good, very contemporary, and it fits in with the best traditions of fellowship thinking. However, I do have a point of critique. In my view, personalism and relationalism are too limiting in this model. They work as a new kind of metaphysics that starts from the "being" with which we are familiar. God is now considered in analogy with man as a person, in analogy with human relationship, and this has a limiting effect. God becomes an individual who is subject to all the limitations of human "being" from the very start. God does not know what will come from his relationship with the individual. This is an implication of God's "openness". But can we still pray the words of Psalm 139 when we think of God in analogy with a human person? What we can say with certainty is that verse 15-16 will then be difficult for us: "My frame was not hidden from you, when I was being made in secret, intricately woven in the depths of the earth. Your eyes beheld my unformed substance. In your book were written all the days that were formed for me, when none of them as yet existed" (NRSV). In the traditional doctrine of God these verses take the function of *dicta probantia* for the concept of God's omniscience. If God's omniscience is denied in open theism because his personhood is considered in analogy with a human person, we have not gained much. One model has simply been replaced with another one. We need to read these doxological expressions of faith in God's presence as references to God's lordship. As Lord he is capable of being near his creation. Omnipresence is one of the characteristics of God's freedom, because it means he can be close to his creation.[21]

8. Fourth Dilemma: Father or Judge?

Even if the third dilemma is solved in the favour of God as a person, we still have another problem. Our fourth dilemma, which is also presented by Pinnock and Brow, is the choice between the image of God as a father and that of God as a judge. Here too, creative love theism offers a lot of good as it focuses on the image of family and fellowship. The image of God as Father is deeply rooted in biblical thinking. But is it contradicted by the image of Christ as judge? In the New Testament we find the explicit statement that Christ will act as a judge at the Final Judgement. But again we see that the meaning of these concepts should not be derived *in abstracto*. What Pinnock writes about God as judge is highly caricatural. In his view, God as a judge is far removed from humankind, cold and distant. Perhaps this is how many pious people experience God, and if that is the case, the caricature may be useful as a broom with which the church can be swept clean. Pinnock seems to suggest that Anselm and Calvin believed that God needs to be appeased before he can be gracious. We first need to meet God's righteousness, his need for satisfaction, before there is room for God's love and mercy. Thus God becomes a difficult person to deal with; someone who, if he were a man, we would urgently send to a therapist.

---

[21] Cf. Barth, *KD* II/1, 521; ET 461–463.

Let me respond by simply saying that the idea that God should be appeased first, is historically incorrect. Anselm's doctrine of satisfaction has nothing to do with a God who should first be appeased. Satisfaction is about man being restored to communion with God, it is about the restoration of a relationship in order to have fellowship with him and to know him.[22] Pinnock's solution makes sense in so far as it says that God's judgement is not an extreme in God, a "pole" opposite his love and mercy. God's judgement serves salvation and restoration. However, we are already aware of this from Barth's doctrine of God and from biblical theology.[23]

9. Fifth Dilemma: Heaven and Hell, Two Opposite Exits from Life?

The fifth dilemma that I should like to discuss, is in some sense a result of something we have discussed earlier. What is man's role in the relationship between God and man? What is the power and strength of human refusal? Can man prevent God from reaching his goals by being foolish, alienated and turned away from him? In other words: is there a real hell, a place where man's "no" reigns and where people live outside God's fellowship? Pinnock does two things that fit in with the Methodist tradition. He defends the weight of human decisions and the possibility of hell. But he also states that hell is not a permanent place. Man is conditionally immortal. He appears to support the doctrine of annihilation. Those who refuse, those who do not want to have fellowship with God, will eventually be annihilated. They will cease to exist. What can we say about this? Is this a form of defeat for God's love, for God's desire to have fellowship with people and to save them? In this context, we need to remind ourselves of the fact that to Anselm, this goal of glorification or *beatitudo* is the driving cause for the way of satisfaction. The price for human autonomy, for man's "no", is that God will let go of some of the work that his hand once started. How can this be reconciled with the father heart of God? Does it not mean that our (and God's) sadness about those who are lost will be eternal? Can we say, with the prophet Jeremiah, that "Rachel will cry for her children for ever"? Can God as a mother forget her children? The biblical desire

---

[22] G. Plasger, *Die Notwendigkeit der Gerechtigkeit: Eine Interpretation zu "Cur Deus homo" von Anselmus von Canterbury* (München: Aschendorf, 1993), 120–126. See also Stephan Schaede, *Stellvertretung: Begriffsgeschichtliche Studien zur Soteriologie* (BHTh 126; Tübingen: Mohr Siebeck, 2004), 286–293.

[23] The Heidelberg Catechism did indeed feed the thought that righteousness and mercy are two separate attributes. See question and answer 11.

to lead creation, including the lost, back to God, seems to me to be too deep, too strong, too powerful and too creative for us to theologically embrace the rational solution of annihilation. Would it not be better — without belittling the human power to refuse God's offer—not to regard any individual *in abstracto*, as an autonomous being, since God has chosen in Christ to live in close proximity of this sinful person? If that is true, our refusal is not the last horizon, but the deepest secret of life is God in Christ.

10. *A Third Way?*

We have looked at a number of dilemmas that the model of creative love theism solves in a one-sided way. In each dilemma, we see the importance of human responsibility played out against God's power and sovereignty. Earlier on, we looked at Deuteronomy 30. In verses 15-20 the nation is confronted with a clear choice. Keeping the commandments will lead to life, disobedience will lead to death. Blessing and curse are the results of our own choice. Also in Christ's teachings we find the often recurring theme of the appeal to Israel and its leaders. The parable of the workers in the vineyard in Matthew 21:33-46 is an appeal to Israel's leaders. The parable is not about an unavoidable tragedy. The future is principally open. But we can also find a different thread that seems to support God's immutability. Numbers 23:19 is a well-known example. "God is not a human being, that he should lie, or a mortal, that he should change his mind. Has he promised, and will he not do it? Has he spoken, and will he not fulfil it?" (NRSV). Also 1 Samuel 15:29 seems to support the view that God's will cannot be changed: "The Glory of Israel will not recant or change his mind; for he is not a mortal, that he should change his mind." (NRSV) There are many more texts that can be used to support this idea. We are faced with the idea of two boundaries within which God works: his immutability and his relationality. Those who put all their money on God's immutability, interpret the verses about the importance of man as anthropomorphic accommodations. Those who give priority to relationality, interpret the statements about God's immutable will as signs of an immature or incomplete image of God. Do we have to choose between these two extremes, or is there a way for systematic theology to stay closer to the biblical texts without being driven by philosophical conceptuality?

I believe that the only practical course of action is to stay close to the biblical narrative, close to the history of salvation, to the *oikonomia* of

God's great deeds as revealed to us in the biblical canon. Only here do we learn how God interacts with his people and how he reveals himself as Lord, *Kurios*. This communion as described in the Old Testament and continued in the New, is a history of conflict, denial, and unexpected continuity. Time and again the history of the covenant seems to come to an end as a result of Israel's unfaithfulness, but then God takes the initiative to hallow his name and continue this history. In other words, God proves by his actions that he is the Lord, that he takes the initiative and finds a reason to continue with his people and to redeem them. We see that the history of God's dealings with humankind is played out as a drama in which history seems to come to a halt every now and then. But then God confirms that he is God by intervening in Israel's history. If we have to position the word "freedom" somewhere theologically, we will need to place it in the depth of God's own being. God is free to find a continuation, a way of accomplishing salvation for Jerusalem and the nations. Sometimes he needs to be reminded by a mediator—such as Moses after the event with the golden calf—but there is always a way out. The Parable of the Lost Son gives the impression that the Father needs to reinvent his parental role in relation to his youngest son. But he does find a way, there is reconciliation. In the face of the drama played out in the biblical texts handed down to us, I see that God's lordship, his Godhead has often mistakenly and misleadingly been translated in terms of omnipotence and omniscience. These totalitarian qualifications seem to suggest that we could speculate *in abstracto* about God's power and knowledge. But those who want to stay close to the source of the Christian knowledge of God, choose a different path. They find a way by holding on to God's confirmation of his lordship in the history of Israel and of Jesus Christ. What is inherent to his power, freedom and knowledge needs to be derived from this history, not *in abstracto*, that is, apart from this salvation history.

Is it possible that an Evangelical-Reformed approach can prevent us from taking either of the two extremes or boundaries that we have just discussed as a central thread for our thinking about God? I suggest that we take as a starting point what theologians call the *oikonomia*, the total sum of God's interaction with his creation, with Israel, the sending of Christ and the outpouring of the Holy Spirit. When we follow history, we become witnesses of the drama of the interaction between God and man, in which God acts and man is continually invited to respond. The recurring problem in this history is that man with his limitations, his suspicion or stubbornness, keeps running away and the history of the covenant is continually in danger of coming to a dead end. Time and again God refuses to be frustrated by human unfaithfulness and provides continuity. God and man both play their own role in this drama, and the terms *responsibility* and *sovereignty* are explained. A theology is Evangelical to the degree that it succeeds in ascribing meaning to the terms that it uses and that reflect the way God interacts with his people. In the light of the New Testament this means that the norm must not be our contemporary metaphysics of love, but God's dealings with us through Christ and the Holy Spirit. Only this history makes clear how God in Christ chooses to confirm his choice to live with his people and with all nations. By doing this, God confirms his own being in a sovereign way.

Chapter Nine

John Wesley
On Salvation, Necessity and Freedom

Antonie Vos

1. Introduction

In several strands of religious life in the Dutch speaking world Evangelical and Reformed traditions now meet, and contributing to this interaction in theological and theology-historical ways is a happy and fortunate challenge. However, how can they come together? Have we not learned from our teachers—and many of us from their parents—that Evangelicalism being mainly Arminian and Wesleyan embraces a heresy profoundly felt in the Dutch and Reformed tradition? And does "Reformed" not mean Calvinist and are the Calvinists not subscribing to a strict determinism? How can they go together? Clark Pinnock, who died in the summer of 2010, formulated his own sharp answer. He said goodbye to the harsh determinism of the Calvinism of his youth, as he saw it himself, and became the inspired protagonist of his own "open theism". He replaced his hero Calvin by his new hero Wesley.

For Pinnock much was at stake, for he was convinced that the history of Christian theology has substantially been infected and threatened by paganism. Here, Pinnock follows the liberal *Dogmengeschichte*, and Harnack in particular. Harnack's verdict is that alien powers influenced Christianity. Gnostic Christianity is the acute Hellenization of Christianity and Catholic Christianity suffered from chronical Hellenization. Both damaged the biblical focus.[1] According to Clark Pinnock, this her-

---

[1] See Adolf Harnack, *Das Wesen des Christentums* (Leipzig: Hinrich, 1900, ^{10}1903), 119-128. This crucial point is central in Harnack, *Lehrbuch der Dogmengeschichte* 1 (Freiburg and Leipzig: Mohr Siebeck, ^{3}1894), 590-647. This view had already been refuted by Isaäc van Dijk, "Christendom en Historie", in: Maarten van Rhijn et al. (eds.), *Gezamenlijke Geschriften van Dr. Is. van Dijk* 2 (Groningen: Noordhoff, 1917, ^{3}1924), 304-339. Cf. A. Vos, *Johannes Duns Scotus* (Leiden: Groen, 1994), 118-120. To my mind, a marriage between Evangelical theology and the German *Dogmengeschichte*, as can be observed with Clark Pinnock and Alister McGrath, is an unwanted, but also an unhappy marriage.

itage has to be undone and he considers himself to be the prophet of this renewal, for the theology of the Church betrayed the Gospel:

> A package of divine attributes has been constructed which leans in the direction of immobility and hyper-transcendence, particularly because of the influence of the Hellenistic category of unchangeableness.[2]

So, how can they go together? That is only possible, if such assumptions are mistaken. But how can that be after centuries of interaction and almost two centuries of historical studies? However, let us see. We start with the general historical background of John Wesley (§2), and the first stages of his long life (§3). Predestination lurks in the background and we pay attention to the distinction between *Calvinist* and *Arminian Methodists* (§4), and continue with Wesley on *free grace* and *predestination* (§5). The usage of the word "Arminian" in seventeenth-century English is a long story to be told, but now I face another riddle: Wesleyanism is commonly called "Arminian". But what has Wesley's work to do with the theology of the historical Arminius? By the way, there is not much British interest in the theology of the historical Arminius, nor in the historical Arminius himself. However, the fact that we can spell out Wesley's view on free will in a precise manner, is due to a philosophical clash (§6), for in the 1770s Wesley intervened in the British debate about philosophical determinism. How does the view of Wesley relate to Arminius' theory of freedom and will systematically (§7), and to the classic Reformed tradition (§8)? Finally, some concluding remarks in §9 will offer an evaluation.

2. John Wesley: General Background

George Eliot's *Adam Bede* (1859) draws a lovely portrait of the lay preacher Dinah Morris, which is based on historical memories when George's aunt was a little girl:

> It was just such a sort of evening as this, when I was a little girl, and my aunt brought me up, took me to hear a good man preach out of doors, just as we are here. I remember his face well: he was a very old man, and had very long white hair; his voice was very soft and beautiful, not like any voice I had ever heard before. I was a little girl and scarcely knew anything, and this old man seemed to me such a difference sort of man from anybody I had ever seen before.[3]

---

[2] Clark H. Pinnock, *Most Moved Mover: A Theology of God's Openness* (Carlisle: Paternoster Press, 2001), 65 (65–111).

[3] George Eliot, *Adam Bede* (London: Everyman's Library 59, 1992), 23. Cf. H.M. van

That man of God was Mr. Wesley. The voices of Whitefield and Wesley have been famous. They were melodious and still able to reach thousands of people. These preachers changed eighteenth-century England. The century between the Massacre of St. Bartholomew in Paris (1572) and the Revocation of the Edict of Nantes (1685) might be called *the Age of Zeal*. There was the zeal of the princes and the kings and their zeal cost millions of lives. There was also the zeal of serious Christians anxious to be saved. John Wesley detested the zeal which killed innumerable people. He himself was also a man of zeal: he was unable to do things halfway. In general, the Wesleys were unable to be *halfhearted*. The wonderful Susanna Wesley-Annesley taught her numerous children:

> Resolve to make religion the business of your life.

The Wesley grandparents had been Puritans and their generations had suffered a lot for their cause and eventually they had lost. *Dort* (1618–19) means that in the Dutch situation the Reformed and Puritan movements had won. The result was cultural and academic stability and dynamics for almost two centuries. Reformed thought flourished at many universities, but after the death of Cromwell, the light of this theological tradition was dashed in England. Owen, Twisse and Rutherford had no successors. The Puritans were dispelled from the pulpits and from the academic chairs. They suffered immensely.

The reign of Charles II (1660–1685) makes clear that the Puritans had become second-rate citizens and even after King William III there was little tolerance. I provide one odd example of such painful intolerance. During a long stay of her husband in London, Susanna Wesley did not admire the preaching of the curate replacing her husband and she arranged simple services for her children at home. These meetings attracted more and more people, even criminal people who stopped sinning publicly, until about 200 people gathered in the vicarage. However, irregular meetings with more than five people were forbidden and the curate almost brought her to trial.

Samuel and Susanna Wesley were very independent individuals. They revolted as young folks against their nonconformist upbringing. By then they had already left the irregular cause of Dissent and had wholeheartedly chosen for the Established Church and the royalist party.[4] They were people of rules themselves and we observe that the young

---

Nes, *John Wesley* (Nijkerk: Callenbach, 1907), 5–6.

[4] See Henry D. Rack, *Reasonable Enthusiast: John Wesley and the Rise of Methodism*

John was also obsessed by rules, as, to the Dutch mind, Englishmen still are. At any rate, his failure in Georgia (1735–1737) was partly caused by his stiff High Churchmanship.

3. John Wesley (1703–1738)

John Wesley (1703–91) was born 17 June 1703 in Epworth (Lincolnshire). He entered Christ Church (Oxford) in 1720 where he took his M.A. in 1725. In 1728 he was ordained a priest. From 1726 to 1751 he was a Fellow of Lincoln College. He did not study theology. So, when the literature stresses that Wesley was no *systematic* theologian, we may simply add that, like John Calvin, he was no academic theologian at all, although both were self-made theologians of genius.

In the course of his student years, John became very serious, looking for salvation in every spot. Every new initiative was also related to his personal problem: Am I saved? He joined the study club of his brother Charles and helped the group to grow in numbers, although it never became a big movement. They were derisively called the Methodists, and also the Holy Club and holiness would remain one of his great doctrines for the whole of his life. For Wesley, repentance was the porch to religion, faith the door, but holiness was religion itself.

Back in England in 1737 after his Georgia failure he also joined some Moravians in London. On Wednesday 24 May 1738, in Aldersgate Street, during a meeting composed largely of Moravians under the auspices of the Church of England, Wesley's intellectual conviction transformed into a personal experience while Luther's preface to his *Commentary on the Letter to the Romans* was being read. Wesley's *Journal* tells us:

> In the evening I went very unwillingly to a society in Aldersgate Street, where one was reading Luther's Preface to the Epistle to the Romans. About a quarter before nine, while he was describing the change which God works in the heart through faith in Christ, I felt my heart strangely warmed. I felt I did trust in Christ, Christ alone, for salvation; and an assurance was given me that he had taken away my sins, even mine, and saved me from the law of sin and death.[5]

From this stage onward, at the age of 35, Wesley viewed his mission in life as one of proclaiming the good news of salvation by faith and he did so until he eventually died as an honoured figure in the British Isles in

---

(London: Epworth Press, 1989), 45–60, cf. 1 ff.
    [5] *The London Journal*, in: Albert C. Outler (ed.), *John Wesley* (New York: Oxford University Press, 1964, ²1980), 66 (53–69: "The Aldersgate Experience").

London on 2 March 1791, almost 88 years of age. He preached almost 50.000 sermons and travelled about 400.000 kilometres. By doing so he changed the Christian scene. "The work of the Wesleys represents a turning point in the history of Christianity. The adjustments they made have influenced the life and mission of the Protestant churches".[6] We may add that although John Wesley was no systematic theologian, he was certainly the most outstanding practical theologian of the eighteenth century, because he solved the problem of presenting the issue of living the *human life* in early modernity.

His lifelong mission mirrors the result of the long journey looking desperately for peace and joy. Wesley was also a formidable debater and was able to defend his case in a reasonable way. We read his defence of faith in his first *An Earnest Appeal to Men of Reason and Religion* (1743). Faith is such a wonderful gift that no reasonable person can resist it:

> By faith we are saved from all uneasiness of mind, from the anguish of a wounded spirit, from discontent, from fear, and sorrow of heart, from that inexpressible listlessness and weariness, both of the world and of ourselves, which we had so helplessly laboured under for many years, especially when we were out of the hurry of the world, and sunk into calm reflection. In this we find that love of God and of all mankind which we had elsewhere sought in vain. This we know and feel—and therefore cannot but declare—saves everyone that partakes of it both from sin and misery, from every unhappy and every unholy temper.

> *Soft peace she brings, wherever she arrives.*
> *She builds our quiet as she forms our lives;*
> *Lays the rough paths of peevish nature even,*
> *And opens in each breast a little heaven.*[7]

4. *Calvinist and Arminian Methodists*

Terminology is a risky landscape. In some cases, we are aware that what we are saying is anachronistic, but when we realize that *Anglican* is a nineteenth-century term, like *Evangelical*, and so on, we become aware that our historical figures talked quite differently about the themes in which we are interested. For the moment, we use our key terms as empty labels.

---

[6] Clark H. Pinnock, *The Beauty of God: John Wesley's Reform and its Aftermath*, 1, (Lecture at the Occasion of Wesley's 300th Birth Anniversary; Nassau, The Bahamas, January 2003).

[7] John Wesley, "An Earnest Appeal to Men of Reason and Religion", in: Gerald R. Cragg (ed.), *The Works of John Wesley* 11 (Nashville: Abingdon Press, 1975), 47.

Calvinist criticisms of the Wesley position came from within. They were held in the area of Revivalism itself. There, we find Whitefield who continuously tried to moderate the debate. For Wesley, it was his sternest challenge. Fortunately, the conflict between Wesley and Whitefield in 1741 was of short duration. However, Wesley eventually took his stand in *The Lord Our Righteousness* in 1765: Christ's death is the meritorious cause of our justification. He shattered the uneasy truce five years later (1770) when Whitefield died. After 1770, Wesley's new stress was on *holy living*—in opposition to its distortions by other Evangelicals, as he saw them. It is easy to forget that both parents of the Wesleys were converts to Anglicanism. They had consciously said goodbye to Nonconformity. They shared a horror of anarchy.

> John Wesley was bred up [...] to a theological position not fairly labeled "Arminian" or "Laudian" and certainly not "latitudinarian".[8]

The young Wesley had inherited from both his mother Susanna and his father Samuel an inborn aversion to the doctrine of predestination, an aversion prevalent in the patristic and meditative theology of the representative divines of the Caroline Established Church, including the Cambridge Platonists.

During the last stage of his career Wesley was caught up in polemic against the Calvinist view. *The Arminian Magazine* was only established in 1778. The title is simply the pejorative label that the Calvinists had pinned on him, like *Methodist* was pinned on him in earlier days. Through the lenses of the Calvinists, one is an *Arminian* if one is not a Calvinist. Remember that there were more *Calvinist* Methodists than *Arminian* ones, and Lady Huntingdon had chosen for the Whitefield wing and expelled the Arminian teachers from her College. However, have Wesley's "Arminian" thoughts historically anything to do with *Arminianism*? The other question that arises is what the eighteenth-century Calvinist view in Britain has to do with the classic Reformed doctrine of predestination.[9] At any rate, Jacobus Arminius does not appear in *The Christian Library* where Wesley parades most of his theological favourites.[10]

---

[8] Albert C. Outler, "The Place of Wesley in the Christian Tradition", in: Kenneth E. Rowe (ed.), *The Place of Wesley in the Christian Tradition: Essays Delivered at Drew University in Celebration of the Commencement of the Publication of the Oxford Edition of* The Works of John Wesley (Metuchen, NJ: Scarecrow Press, 1976), 19 (11–38).

[9] See Vos, *Johannes Duns Scotus*, Chapter 7: "Predestinatie".

[10] See Outler, "The Place of Wesley", 26–27. *The Arminian Magazine* only has Bertius's funeral sermon and a pro-Remonstrant history of Dort.

5. Wesley on Free Grace and Predestination

John Wesley conceives of justification as the pardon and acceptance of a sinner by God by means of *faith alone*.[11] By his pure acceptance, God receives us into his favour. God's grace is the source of justification. If Wesley's *sola fide* is clear, in fact, he also accepts the T of *TULIP*, that is, the T of Total Depravity of Mankind. Salvation occurs to a depraved sinner. Wesley and Whitefield share the same foundation, continuously mirrored in the innumerable conversions of their thousands and thousands of sermons during endless campaigns.

However, according to Wesley, saving grace is not restricted. It is not particular and it does not rest on the principle of election and predestination. God freely loves the world. Christ died for the ungodly and everybody is ungodly. So, Christ died for all.[12] *Verily, FREE GRACE is all in all, and FREE for all.*

What then does Wesley as an "Arminian" dislike? He loves many Calvinists, but he does not love their opinions. He does not believe what they term *the truths of God*, including the doctrine of absolute predestination. He did not believe them for one hour, but of what does the Wesleyan interpretation of this doctrine consist? Wesley's answer is crystal-clear. Salvation is freely offered to some, but many are lost too, but why? Many are lost, because God condemns to destruction. They are not lost because they do not believe—they simply do not believe, because God eternally decided that they do not believe—but because they have already been condemned. I note that this was not Whitefield's view: his view states that some are lost, because God permits them to remain in their sins: He lets it be. However, for Wesley, an eternal decree is a *mandatory* decision. Salvation history is only the temporal execution of an eternal blueprint.[13]

Although Wesley was certainly unaware of it, here, he shares a point with Arminius: God's decision is as such *made mandatory*. However, while Arminius' reaction consists in bracketing divine will, Wesley is convinced that a necessary will is simply impossible, and likewise a neutral will of God. For Wesley, in life and in life's activity *will* is crucial, both with respect to God and with respect to human individu-

---

[11] See Martin Luther, *Werke* (*Weimarer Ausgabe*), II 13–14 and 427, VIII 106–11, XXII 138 and 248 and XIII 238, and John Calvin, *Institutio* III 11.2 and 13, and III 14.11.

[12] Wesley's notion of *universal redemption* is in need of closer inspection.

[13] See Albert Outler, "The Struggle with the Calvinists", in: Outler (ed.), *John Wesley*, 425–426, and John Wesley, "Predestination Calmly Considered", in: Outler (ed.), *John Wesley*, 427–471, and Rack on the 1760s and the 1770s in *Reasonable Enthusiast*.

als. Although Wesley was definitely no latitudinarian, he joins them in interpreting the Reformed doctrine of predestination as a determinist decree; and because of the contacts between the Cambridge Platonists and some latitudinarians, we may conclude that this interpretation has an Arminian bias. Wesley developed his criticisms on this basis and they are serious ones.[14] This doctrine makes preaching redundant and vain. It closes the gate of holiness and tends to fill its adherents with pride. It destroys the comfort of religion. It is incompatible with God's mercy, and, in fact, with all divine attributes.

6. *Wesley on Freedom and Necessity*

The 1770s were a theological battleground for John Wesley. In 1774 Wesley published his essay *Thoughts upon Necessity*. This essay carried him far into the arcanum of scholarly theology. He wrote a first draft in 1774 and its occasion was the predestinarian conflict. After having studied Henry Home's *Essay on Liberty and Necessity* Wesley published an enlarged version and a second edition appeared in 1775. So, the wider context was the vigorous debate between the great British philosophers of the day: David Hume, Henry Home, Richard Price, James Beattie, Thomas Reid and Joseph Priestly.[15] The determinism of some of these philosophers and the theological determinism of Jonathan Edwards' *Freedom of the Will* (1754) had alarmed Wesley:

> I cannot believe the noblest creature in the visible world to be only a fine piece of clockwork.[16]

Wesley was particularly opposed to the statement of a radical deterministic theory brought forward by Henry Home (Lord Kames) in his *Essay on Liberty and Necessity* (1751). According to Home, man's sense of freedom is an illusion:

> I had finished what I designed to say on this subject when the *Essay on Liberty and Necessity* fell into my hands, a most elaborate piece, touched and retouched with all possible care. This has occasioned a considerable enlargement of the following tract.[17]

---

[14] See William Ragsdale Cannon, *The Theology of John Wesley: With Special Reference to the Doctrine of Justification* (New York: Oxford University Press, 1946), 90–102.

[15] See Frederick Copleston, *A History of Philosophy* 5 (London: Search Press, 1959), 361–374.

[16] John Wesley, "To the Reader", in: Outler (ed.), *John Wesley*, 474. In idem, *John Wesley*, 472–474, the editor offers a helpful introduction to *Thoughts upon Necessity*.

[17] Wesley, "To the Reader", in: Outler (ed.), *John Wesley*, 474.

Wesley was critical of Henry Home's philosophy, but he felt himself also challenged by this bold necessitarianism. Moreover, in particular, Wesley was very critical of David Hume, "the most insolent despiser of truth and virtue that ever appeared in the world".[18] In the spring of 1772 Wesley travelled in Scotland and informs us that on his journey from Aberdeen to Arbroath, he read

> Dr. Beattie's ingenious *Inquiry After Truth*. He is a writer equal to his subject and far above the match of all the "minute philosophers".[19]

The affinities between Wesley's counter-attack and the refutation of Hume by the Scottish common sense realists are obvious. Wesley's language is never woolly language and his formulations of the issues at stake here are clear too:

> Is man a *free agent*, or is he not? Are his actions *free* or *necessary*? Is he self-determined in acting or is he determined by some other being? Is the principle which determines him to act in himself or in another? This is the question I want to consider. And is it not an important one? Surely there is not one of greater importance in the whole nature of things. For what is there that more nearly concerns all that are born of women? What can be conceived which more deeply affects, not some only, but every child or man?[20]

According to Wesley, determinism is an exceedingly ancient opinion. Adam was the first determinist (Gen. 3:12). The Manichaeans, the Stoics and many others have followed that sway. In §3.9 Wesley presents his own logic of freedom and free will. There are the human faculties of understanding, will and affections. *Will* presupposes freedom or liberty, the faculty of choosing,

> either to do or not to do (commonly called the *liberty of contradiction*), or to do this or the contrary, good or evil (commonly called *liberty of contrariety*). Without the former at least, there can be nothing good or evil, rewardable or punishable. But it is plain, the doctrine of necessity

---

[18] Wesley, *Journal* 5:458.

[19] Wesley, *Journal* 5:458. James Beattie's *An Essay on the Nature and Immutability of Truth in Opposition to Sophistry and Superstition* (Edinburgh 1771), is meant. On Beattie, see Elmer Sprague, "James Beattie", *The Encyclopedia of Philosophy* 1 (London/New York: Macmillan, 1967), 262–263, and Patricia Kitcher, "James Beattie", in: Robert Audi (ed.), *The Cambridge Dictionary of Philosophy* (Cambridge: Cambridge University Press, 1995), 65–6. Cf. Jerome B. Schneewind, "Scottish Common Sense Philosophy", in: Audi (ed.), *Cambridge Dictionary*, 719.

[20] Wesley, "To the Reader", the Preface of Wesley, *Thoughts upon Necessity*, in: Outler (ed.), *John Wesley*, 474. The essay *Thoughts upon Necessity* is to be found in Outler (ed.), *John Wesley*, 474–491.

as taught either by ancient heathens or by moderns (whether deists or Christians), destroy both.[21]

The *libertas contradictionis* or the liberty or freedom of contradiction rests on the fact that

> it is possible "either to do or not to do" something,[22]

but what does this exactly mean? This first kind of *freedom* is formulated with the help of a contradiction and a contradiction is a conjunction of the form *p and not-p*. We see this in the contradictory pair *act and not-act*. The ontological position is that if I am doing something, it is *possible* at that same time *that* I do *not* do so. I am free in talking about Wesley and this freedom rests on the fact that at the time when I am talking, freedom presupposes the pattern that it is possible that I do *not* write at the time when I write. In early modern scholasticism this freedom is called *libertas contradictionis*.[23] In contrast with other concepts of *freedom* I call this freedom *synchronic freedom*, or synchronic liberty.[24]

Moreover, John Wesley mentions another kind of freedom: the *libertas contrarietatis*, or the *liberty* or *freedom of contrariety*, for he also writes, that it is also possible

> to do this or the contrary, good or evil (commonly called *liberty of contrariety*),[25]

but, again, what does this exactly mean? If I write, then it is possible that I do not write, but one can also say: it is possible that you are now on the phone or that you open the door for your daughter. Then we contrast an act with *another act*, and not with its own denial. However, this situation presupposes the first kind of situation when we combine

---

[21] Wesley, *Thoughts upon Necessity*, in Outler (ed.), *John Wesley*, 486.
[22] Wesley, *Thoughts upon Necessity*, in Outler (ed.), *John Wesley*, 486.
[23] For the notion of *libertas contradictionis*, see Eef Dekker, *Rijker dan Midas: vrijheid, genade en predestinatie in de theologie van Jacobus Arminius (1559-1609)* (Zoetermeer: Boekencentrum, 1993), 135-136. Here, the *libertas contradictionis* is called the *libertas quoad exercitium*. Cf. Willem J. van Asselt, J. Martin Bac and Roelf T. te Velde (eds.), *Reformed Thought on Freedom* (Grand Rapids: Baker Book House, 2010), 128-129 and 154-155. Dekker's dissertation offers a comprehensive survey and critical analysis of the basics of Arminius' theology and philosophy.
[24] For Duns Scotus' concept of *synchronic freedom*, see A. Vos, H. Veldhuis, A.H. Looman-Graaskamp, E. Dekker and N.W. den Bok, *John Duns Scotus: Contingency and Freedom. Lectura I 39* (Dordrecht, Boston: Kluwer, 1994), 26-28 and 123-128, and Vos, *The Philosophy of John Duns Scotus* (Edinburgh: Edinburgh University Press, 2006), 413-430.
[25] Wesley, *Thoughts upon Necessity*, in: Outler (ed.), *John Wesley*, 486.

an act and the possibility of not-doing so. Now, the opposites are not contradictory, but contrary. Thus, this kind of freedom is called *libertas contrarietatis*.²⁶ It is based on the first kind of freedom, *synchronic freedom* in the strict sense; *libertas contradictionis* and *libertas contrarietatis* together constitute *synchronic freedom* in the broad sense.

This Wesleyan notion of *synchronic freedom* presupposes the concept of *synchronic contingency*. From the systematic point of view, Wesley stands squarely in the classic Reformed tradition.²⁷ Thus, where John Wesley stands in the whole of the Western tradition of theology and philosophy is clear: in the *AA*-line of Augustine and Anselm, in the Middle Ages continued by the Victorines and Bonaventure, Henry of Ghent and John Duns Scotus, and in the early modern age by Reformed and Puritan Scholasticism, in particular. But how is Arminius' theology related to this tradition?

7. Arminius on Necessity and Freedom

Arminius' theology of predestination and grace rests on his doctrine of the will of God, for God's decree of predestination and his decision to give grace are acts of his will. The Christian doctrine of God in particular deals with God's essence, knowledge, will and agency. The nature of the interrelationship between God's essence, knowledge, will and activity (*potentia*) defines the model to which a certain doctrine of God adheres. When Arminius gives his definition of *divine will* in his doctorate thesis (1603), he immediately comments on the relationship between God's nature and intellect, and his will. God's basic faculty is his intellect. Since God is essentially God, He is knowing and omniscient and He necessarily knows everything knowable. His nature entails his knowledge. Arminius' doctrine of God is essence-based, and knowledge-based.²⁸ His view is also evident from his *direct-indirect will* distinction. In order to understand this distinction we have to know how Arminius uses "necessary" (*necessarius*) and "contingent" (*contingens*).²⁹

---

²⁶ For the notion of *libertas contrarietatis*, see Dekker, *Rijker dan Midas*, 136–138. Here, the *libertas contrarietatis* is called the *libertas quoad speciem actionis*. With Gomarus the same usage is found. Cf. Van Asselt, Bac and Te Velde (eds.), *Reformed Thought on Freedom*, 129–130 and 155–156.

²⁷ For this notion of *synchronic contingency*, see Vos, et al., *Contingency and Freedom*, 25–28, 30–36, 113–117 and 123–129, and Vos, *The Philosophy of John Duns Scotus*, 224–232 and chapters 7, 14 and 16.

²⁸ See Dekker, *Rijker dan Midas*, Chapter 4: "The Doctrine of Divine Knowledge".

²⁹ The remarkable fact is that Arminius deviates from the logical tradition.

Arminius elaborates on the following distinctions: first, he distinguishes between "absolute necessity" (*necessitas absoluta*) and "hypothetical necessity" (*necessitas ex hypothesi*). Second, he adds a further distinction, distinguishing between two kinds of "hypothetical necessity".[30] First, we look at the first distinction:

> I. *necessitas absoluta*: if "absolute necessity" is at stake, then the opposite is intrinsically impossible.[31] Here, Arminius only refers to necessary truths concerning God and essential attributes of his.
> II. *necessitas ex hypothesi*: if the "hypothetical necessity" of a proposition p is at stake, p is not necessary by itself—as in the case of I—but then p is necessary on the basis of something else. A *hypo*thesis is a foundation that supports and builds up something.[32]

Let us explain this basic distinction in an informal way. The crucial difference between *necessity* I and *necessity* II is based on the notion of *consequence* (*consequentia*): something *follows* (*sequitur*) from something else and if this is *not* the case, it rests on itself. Then, we have *necessitas absoluta*. Here, *absolutus* does not have the modern metaphysical or political meanings, but it possesses the traditional grammatical meaning. If something is *absolved*, then it is untied and set free. It does not depend on something else any more. It stands on itself. It is "zelfstandig".[33] If it is necessary, although it is not necessary *in itself*, it is so in virtue of *something else*: it is hypothetically necessary.

A further distinction is applied by Arminius at the second kind of necessity:

> IIA. *necessitas ex hypothesi consequentis*: hypothetical necessity of the consequent. Arminius' example is: "God does not necessarily create the world. Yet, if He creates the world, it necessarily exists by that action".[34]

---

[30] See Dekker, *Rijker dan Midas*, §3.2: "Kinds of Necessity and Contingency" (55–60) in Chapter 3: "Modality and Degrees of Freedom" (54–75).

[31] See Dekker, *Rijker dan Midas*, 55. The formal translation runs: we take a variable proposition p and if p is absolutely necessary, then *not-p* cannot be true on the basis of its own content.

[32] The letters p, q, and r, ..., are variables for propositions—a proposition is the content of a statement or an assertion—, just as, in algebra, x, y, and z, ..., are variables for numbers.

[33] Compare the Latin translations of the sentences: "When mother is ill, mother still goes to church" and "When father is ill, mother still goes to church". These sentences are to be translated into Latin as follows: *Mater aegra vadit in ecclesiam* and *Patre aegro* (ablativus absolutus) *mater vadit in ecclesiam!* The illness of father is not intrinsically connected with mother going to church: it stands on itself, it is 'absolute.'

[34] J. Arminius, *Examen Perkinsiani*, 708–709 (see Dekker, *Rijker dan Midas*, 56 n.9):

II B. *necessitas ex hypothesi consequentiae* (hypothetical necessity of the consequence). Here, Arminius refers to deductive reasoning.

Let us comment on this distinction between two kinds of "hypothetical necessity" in a somewhat more technical way. What is a *consequentia*? Knowing what modern logic understands by an *implication* is helpful. An *implication* or *conditional proposition* is a compound proposition of the form: *if ... , then ...* . We take a famous medieval example:

(S) If Socrates is running (p), then he moves (q).[35]

In (S) we observe four elements (*a-d*):

a) (S) itself—the whole of the compound proposition: this compound *if/ als/si ..., then/dan/igitur ...* proposition is called an *implication* or *entailment* (*consequentia*).

We have the two propositions which make up the compound proposition (I), first:

b) the first proposition—the *if...* proposition—is the proposition *Socrates is running*. This proposition is called the *antecedent* (Latin: *antecedens*).

And we have the second composing proposition:

c) the second proposition—the *then ...* proposition—is the proposition *Socrates moves*. This proposition is called the *consequent* (Latin: *consequens*).

The fourth element is the logical element:

d) the logical connective: *if ... , then ...* (formally: ... → ...).

Now, we bridge the distance to Arminius. A *consequentia* is either an *implication* or a *deductive argument*. We meet the first aspect with Arminius' *necessitas ex hypothesi consequentis* (II A), and the second with his *necessitas ex hypothesi consequentiae* (II B).

First, we tackle the *necessitas ex hypothesi consequentiae*. A simple example can easily make clear what the *necessitas ex hypothesi consequentiae* is about by assuming the premise:

2 x 2 = 4.

The conclusion

"Deus non creat necessario mundum, si tamen creat, *necessario* mundus ex illa actione existit".

[35] Formally: $p \to q$. This formalization is also to be applied at a Dutch example: "Als Socrates rent (p), dan loopt hij (q)". It reads: $p \to q$. As the Dutch reader sees without any doubt, the crucial move rests on the semantical fact that "rennen" means "hard lopen".

$4 \times 4 = 16$

validly follows from the basis of the given premiss. We deductively derive a true conclusion from a true premise. This aptly illustrates the Arminian *necessitas ex hypothesi consequentiae*.[36]

Last, but not least, Arminius' *necessitas ex hypothesi consequentis* is at stake. Here, causality is what matters. Something is brought about. This act is not necessary, but according to Arminius it still causes a necessary effect. Bringing about, including willing, leads to necessity: it is a property necessarily made. Arminius' treatments of *logical deductivity* and *causality* run parallel to each other.

God's *will and activity*

These tools must be used to explain some of Arminius' key notions. We assume that God acts—He creates or elicits one or another act. If God does something, He does so by willing it. Then, God brings something about. He does not do so in a necessary way. His action does not follow the line of *necessity* I, nor the deductive pattern of *necessity* II B. Here, *necessity* II A applies and then there is a necessary effect. To Arminius' mind, what *follows* from something is as such necessary. *Following* [*(con)sequi*] is *necessity* making! Moreover, in Arminian language, if something is necessary, it is *irresistible*, but if something is irresistible, then freedom is excluded. Now, we have reached the point where we can understand in which sense Arminius is a *freedom* thinker.

God's *direct and indirect will*

At this point, the distinction between *direct-indirect will* comes in. If God acts properly and in his own divine way, what He is doing, is irresistible and such an activity of God excludes human freedom. However, although God can perform things necessarily, He decides not to do so. He freely refrains from it. He is too nice to overwhelm us. Human freedom presupposes *resistibility* and the effect of these moves on Arminius' part is that he creates a rather personal and idiosyncratic terminology. He links tightly:

> causality—necessity—irresistibility—abolishment of freedom. Cf. deductivity (premiss // cause)—necessity—irresistibility.

Moreover, the parallel upshot consists of the following links:

---

[36] By the way, notice that all components are necessarily true: they cannot be untrue.

denial of necessity—contingency—resistibility—freedom, connected with God's indirect will.

Arminius' logical and ontological moves imply the heart of his doctrine of God's will from which his doctrines of predestination, grace and freedom flow. For these reasons, God withholds his will. He does not will that his irresistible action destroys human freedom.[37] That He wills and acts *directly* is possible, but He decides not to do so. He allows humans to be free. Eventually, for Arminius, freedom entails *neutral will*.[38] *Direct will* is: compulsion. In this sense, Arminius is a *freedom* thinker, and at the same time an *autonomy* thinker.[39]

According to this model, the will is not a new and structural function in God's activity in addition to God's foreknowledge. God provides for the circumstances. His policy is not related to the concrete, contingent deeds of individual persons. It is none of his business. Then He would keep after us. An Arminian is afraid that God is closing in too much on our skin and soul. We have to feel ourselves free. Arminian theology is a theology of tolerance; "Hollish" tolerance is the lifestyle of not interfering with one another: Do not meddle in someone's affairs.[40]

However, Puritans, Evangelicals and people of the *Nadere Reformatie* are busybodies, but, according to the Remonstrants, faith must not be too personal. Arminius still uses salvation-historical language, but it is transferred to a higher and abstract level. It is the level of the things which are there and we can make use of them in our own ways:

> That is to say that the decree does not interfere directly with the actuality of contingent human deeds.[41]

---

[37] Compare Wtenbogaert's reaction to Gomarus' protest against the thesis that God's will is not determinately related to our reality, as reported in G.P. van Itterzon, *Franciscus Gomarus* ('s-Gravenhage: Nijhoff, 1929), 89: "Wtenbogaert vond het echter in het geheel niet goddeloos om te zeggen, dat God geenszins die dingen bepaalde, die Hijzelf niet bepalen wilde. Arminius zou voor die uitspraken zijn goede redenen wel weten te geven".

[38] That is: no interference with one another—the famous Holland way of *letting one another free*! However, *letting free* does not constitute freedom. It is laziness and indifference.

[39] Consult the important sections in Dekker, *Rijker dan Midas*, §5.3: "Will, Contingency and Middle Knowledge" (110–112) and §5.5: "The relations between effective, indirect and direct will" (119–123).

[40] For the not-existing adjective "Hollish", compare England-English with Holland-"Hollish". Apart from Zeeland, Holland is the Western part of the Netherlands.

[41] Dekker, *Rijker dan Midas*, 111: "Dat wil zeggen, dat het decreet met het feitelijke zus of zo zijn van de contingente menselijke daden geen rechtstreekse bemoeienis heeft". The individuals do not fall under the range of God's activity.

Since God's will is not actively and directly related to the life and activities of individual human persons, free will is an independent will. The costs of this independence approach are high. The price is the cost of an indirectly necessitarian view of reality.[42]

8. Moral: The Alternative Orthodox Stance

Classic Reformed theology shows a lucid pattern. This pattern rests on the classic Christian doctrine of God which is based on the duality of necessity and contingency, as it found its expression in late medieval theology. The threefold duality structuring the knowledge, will and agency of God is built on the logical and ontological distinctions between necessity and contingency, for when we apply this fundamental distinction to divine knowledge, will and agency, we arrive at the basic structure of the necessary and contingent knowledge, the necessary and contingent will and the necessary and contingent activity of God, which are called in Latin, respectively, *scientia necessaria* and *libera*, *voluntas necessaria* and *contingens*, and *potentia absoluta* and *ordinata*.

The tradition of Reformed scholasticism constitutes an historical reality quite different from what we find in the traditional literature on the subject, because this thought is based on the *necessity-contingency* distinction.[43] The discovery that classic Reformed scholasticism offers us a theology of contingency and individuality, goodness and will, freedom and grace can be a shock, but it is a present.[44] Here we find truth, strength and beauty and rediscovering such a comforting historical re-

---

[42] Although Muller presents a somewhat alternative tradition-historical diagnosis, he also detects a necessitarian approach to reality with Arminius, but he seems to be less upset by this discovery. He is more unhappy with its intellectualism, but necessitarianism and intellectualism are hand in glove. See Richard A. Muller, *God, Creation, and Providence in the Thought of Jacob Arminius* (Grand Rapids: Baker Book House, 1991), part IV: "The Divine Knowledge and Will". The consequences of necessitarianism are much more far-reaching, for necessitarianism entails atheism, although I do not assert that all necessitarians are atheists. Apparently, necessitarians who are not atheist, miss the entailment of atheism. They are fortunately incoherent. See also A. Vos, "Geboeid door Arminius", *Soteria* 27/4 (2010), 46–52.

[43] See A. Vos, "De kern van de klassiek gereformeerde theologie", *KeTh* 47 (1996), 106–125.

[44] See Van Asselt, Bac and Te Velde, "Introduction", in: *Reformed Thought on Freedom*, 17 (15–17): "In the present book, the reader will certainly find the most important results of Vos' innovative research project". Cf. Maarten Wisse and Marcel Sarot, "Introduction", in Maarten Wisse, Marcel Sarot and Willemien Otten (eds.), *Scholasticism Reformed* (STAR 14; Leiden: Brill, 2010), 1–15, and Roelf T. te Velde, *Paths Beyond Tracing Out* (Delft: Eburon, 2010), part III.

ality is a gift and a joy. In the 1990s, I trained my research students and members of the Research Group "Oude Gereformeerde Theologie" (*Reformed Scholasticism*), which I had already founded in the autumn of 1982, for years in this new style of research. In the first half of the 1990s, the first fruits were master theses, Dekker's *Arminius*-dissertation: *Rijker dan Midas* (1993) and Van Asselt and Dekker (eds.), *De scholastieke Voetius* (1995).[45] Some colleagues belonging to *the Old School*—the phrase is Van Asselt's—became angry, when they were confronted with this scientifically historical revolution, because they thought that Reformed scholasticism was a well-known area. After years, Kees Graafland, the leading representative in the line of decline ideology in the last quarter of the twentieth century, told me: "Antoon, probably you have not noticed it, but when you told your story for the first time, I fell almost literally off my chair".[46]

9. Assessment: Seven Theses on the Predestination Conflict

Precisely the newly rediscovered historical reality of classic Reformed thought is the key to the reconciliation of Evangelical and Reformed traditions in their garments before 1800. Wesleyanism is not Arminian, and the classic Reformed tradition before 1800 is not necessitarian, nor determinist. In these terms we can state succinctly the position of the defenders of the main Reformed tradition (Gomarus, Dort):[47]

> a) God's *will* is intrinsically connected with *contingency*: the assertion that *will* entails *necessity*, presents a contradiction, and
> b) Reality is essentially divine will-based: based on God's contingent will, intrinsically linked with the contingency of human freewill.

---

[45] In 1996 I codified the crucial structures of this perspective in a series of brief contributions: Vos, "Klassiek hervormd: de omweg is de kortste weg", *KeTh* 47 (1996), 54–61, idem, "Review of Paul Helm, *Divine Providence*", *KeTh* 47 (1996), 86–87, idem, "De kern van de klassieke gereformeerde theologie", *KeTh* 47 (1996), 106–125, and idem, "Review of E. P. Meijering, *Reformierte Scholastik und Patristische Theologie*", *KeTh* 47 (1996), 168–169.

[46] Oral communication at the Conference on the occasion of Willem J. van Asselt and Eef Dekker (eds.), *De scholastieke Voetius* (Zoetermeer: Boekencentrum, 1995), March 1996. Cf. A. Vos, "Wie is op heden groter, wie oprechter?", in Marco Batenburg, Arjan Markus and Roelof de Wit (eds.), *De erfenis van Voetius* (Utrecht, 1996), 35–38.

[47] Be aware of the fact that this view opposing Arminius' alternative is the orthodox main tradition, having already maintained itself for centuries and centuries. The paradoxical effect of Renaissance *autonomy* philosophy is that it partially, but substantially falls back on necessitarian patterns of ancient philosophy. This Renaissance *autonomy* philosophy is diametrically opposed to the Reformation.

We summarize the field of forces:

First, the Wesleyan *predestination conflict* was a conflict within the ranks of Methodism itself. It was a rather late conflict. The 1770s—a rather troubled decade for Wesley—were also the 70s of his own life.

Second, the Wesleys were converts *from* Puritanism, although Puritan spirituality continued to put a mark on them, but the Puritan past affected the so-called Calvinist circles more powerfully.

Third, in addition to the Puritan tension, the predestination issue also constituted an inconsistency in Wesley's theology itself. He embraced the *Thirty-Nine Articles* as a Church of England man, but these Articles are unequivocal on predestination.

Fourth, the predestination conflict shows that in England the university dimension of Reformed and Puritan theology (*scholasticism*) had already virtually collapsed at the end of the seventeenth century. In the Dutch Republic it only collapsed at the end of the eighteenth century.

Fifth, there is also a language shift to be observed and this language shift deserves more attention, because it has a great impact on such crucial terms as grace, freedom, and predestination. According to the strict Calvinism of the nineteenth and twentieth centuries, Arminius is the arch-heretic. In the sixteenth century the standard orthodox accusation was: *Pelagian*, then it became: *Arminian*. Arminians believe in free will, but—according to strict modern Calvinism—there is no free will, for determinism excludes free will. The paradoxical feature of this criticism is that these Calvinists embrace the picture of the Reformed position construed by the Arminians. Already Arminius himself painted Gomarus' supralapsarianism with dark determinist colours, but Gomarus never accepted that picture. However, both the modern Calvinists and the Arminians are mistaken: not only is the traditional view on the classic Reformed position not true, the traditional view on Arminius and Remonstrant theology is also false.

It is not helpful to say that *a* or *b* denies free will, or that *a* or *b* believes in predestination. The first questions to be answered are: What do *a* and *b* understand by 'free will' or by 'predestination'? Now, we turn to Wesley and Arminianism. The standard view is that the theology of Wesley is Arminian and that the Arminian view embraces free will. But which position did the historical Arminius adhere to?

Arminius' theology rests on a specific logic and on a specific theory of action. He is convinced that doing so and so makes so and so necessary at the moment when it is done. So, if God causes that p, then p is necessary. Arminius calls this the *necessitas ex hypothesi consequentis*.

However, God is the Creator of everything. Then, it seems to be that human freedom is excluded. At this point, Arminius introduces his own notion of *freedom*: *being free* means that I am left free, because the other is so kind and agreeable that he does not intermingle with my life and God is the most kind of all: He is no busybody. He neutralizes his own will so that we can make up our mind without being disturbed by his interventions. God is 'tolerant.' Arminian freedom is based on a neutral will. This Arminian notion of *freedom* differs markedly from traditional freedom (= the absence of compulsion or coercion), Augustinian or perfect freedom (= being open for God and his redemption and salvation), freedom as happiness (= the absence of misery), Counter-Reformational freedom (= semi-autonomous freedom), Enlightenment freedom (= being free in the sense of being entirely autonomous), and true freedom (= ontological freedom: = if a wills that p, then it is possible that a does not will that p).[48]

This kind of Arminian *freedom* I call *Hollish freedom*.[49] It is just the opposite of the Wesleyan attitude. He rides on the back of his horses day and night to intervene and to hinder people—to hinder them with the power of the Gospel in the hope that they will be saved. John Wesley is the arch-evangelist, Arminianism, in my view, is neither evangelical nor evangelistic. Arminianism defends one great virtue: Please: Let me free. Do not intermingle with my life. Let me alone. Wesley could answer: Then, you will never become free.

What is then the source of this fundamental misunderstanding? The source is the common opposition of both Arminianism and Wesleyanism against predestination. The Wesleys continued to cherish profound elements of Puritan spirituality, but they also shared a radical opposition to the Puritan doctrine of eternal predestination with the Latitudinarians of the Established Church: Wesley was convinced that an eternal act of God's will makes the object of will necessary. He also concluded that this necessity not only excludes freedom of will, but that it also destroys the possibility that it makes sense to preach: "Repent! Convert yourself".

We have seen that Wesley wholeheartedly accepted the notion of

---

[48] This is the kind of freedom we have discussed above (*libertas contradictionis* and *libertas contrarietatis*). This Scotian freedom on which Reformed scholasticism is based, was embraced by John Wesley.

[49] Just as *English* is to be derived from England, 'Hollish' is from Holland: the Western part of the Netherlands which was the patrician part of the Netherland, dominated by an oligarchic system.

synchronic freedom, and Gomarus did the same, but this only applies to human freedom, but what Wesley did not know, was that—in contrast with Arminius—Gomarus and the Dort tradition also utilized the notions of *synchronic freedom* and *synchronic contingency* with respect to divine freedom: God acts freely and contingently. Grace is free grace, but eternal grace is also free grace and God's radical grace does not imply necessity, but can only imply contingency. The classic Reformed tradition is a tradition of grace and forgiveness and God acts contingently and freely in this reality of grace and forgiveness, and the human person also acts contingently and freely in this reality of grace and forgiveness. The openness of reality means that the reality of salvation is also open reality. Because of this ontological openness, and its contingency, will and freedom the Wesleyan legacy and the classic Reformed tradition can be reconciled, and Wesleyanism and Arminianism cannot. The same Gospel of the good news elicits acceptance and rejection. The same cause can have opposite effects. That is the quintessence of *contingency*. It presupposes freedom on both sides—on the human side and on God's side, and Arminius could know that Gomarus also defended the last aspect, although Wesley could not.

Sixth, the label *Arminian* is utterly misleading, because Arminianism is a position simply excluded by Wesley's theology. The theology of the historical Arminius, based on necessitarianism and the notion of a *neutral divine will*, is quite a different phenomenon. The contingency and free will tradition of Reformed scholasticism seems to have escaped the attention of both parties, but this scholastic tradition is just the key to reconciling the Evangelical and Reformed traditions, and, at the same time, the foundation of alternative, tenable systematic theology.

Finally, we finish with John Wesley himself. As an old man Wesley preached in Cornwall in the Gwennap Pit, with his back to the last rays of a setting sun, in the quiet of an English summer evening, where not a breath, not a leaf, not one of thousands of humans stirred. All melted into one in the growing darkness as they hung on the lips of one who commended his Saviour—how right faith is, how solemn and majestic.

Wesley spent his last days in London where we see him go, bareheaded on four bitter winter mornings, begging from door to door, his feet always immersed in melting snow. He did not rest until he had collected £ 200 with which to feed and to clothe his poor.[50]

---

[50] See Gordon Rupp, "Son of Samuel: John Wesley", in: Rowe (ed.), *The Place of Wesley in the Christian Tradition*, 61–62.

Chapter Ten

The Wesleyan Quadrilateral Reconsidered: Wesley Meets Gadamer

Arie W. Zwiep

1. *Introduction. Setting the Scene*

The purpose of my contribution is to explore the boundaries and intersections of Wesleyan theology (or at least an aspect of it) in the light of current trends in biblical hermeneutics and Evangelical theology. Although I am not a Wesleyan scholar, I do strongly sympathize with many Wesleyan and Arminian concerns, and, alternately, from a hermeneutical perspective, I see a number of issues in Wesleyan theology that may be fruitfully assimilated in a broader hermeneutical program and thus may help us to come to a clearer understanding of what biblical faith entails.[1]

In this article, I take Hans-Georg Gadamer (1900–2002), the most influential hermeneutical thinker of the twentieth century next to Paul Ricoeur and Jacques Derrida, as my main conversation partner, and my question is, What would happen when Wesley met Gadamer? They would, to begin with, most probably arrange a meeting in a debaters' club. After all, Wesley's special liking of "conferences" as a means to exchange knowledge and achieve common understanding comes close to Gadamer's preference for conversation and dialogue as the primary hermeneutical tools to come to understanding (*Verstehen*). They would appreciate their common indebtedness to Plato and Aristotle, and they would share the conviction that reason and scientific method have their limitations. They would both agree that there can be no finality in our systems. Wesley, I believe, would especially like Gadamer's notion of

---

[1] This article originates from a paper delivered at a symposium on Wesleyan Theology (A Theology of Renewal) at the VU University Amsterdam, organized by the Center of Evangelical and Reformation Theology (CERT), in cooperation with the Church of the Nazarene the Netherlands, 5 April 2007. I am grateful for a number of helpful comments by colleagues and students from both Amsterdam and Ede.

application (*Applikation*) as an essential part of the interpretative process. Hence, the odds are fairly favourable that their rendezvous could be a success. So let's give it a try!

2. The Wesleyan Quadrilateral

In today's Wesleyan theology the so-called "quadrilateral" plays an important role. In brief, the quadrilateral stands for four complementary sources of religious authority to guide the interpreter in his or her quest for (religious) truth. They are Scripture, tradition, reason and experience, usually in that order. The quadrilateral is, in the words of Don Thorsen, who devoted an important book to this topic, "a heuristic tool," a method of doing theology.[2]

In current hermeneutical terms the Wesleyan quadrilateral is a typical expression of a *local* or regional hermeneutic, that is, a hermeneutic the validity of which extends to a limited area of relevancy. In what follows I will try to lift the quadrilateral from its time-bound, historical and confessional confines, to provide a basis for a broader application in biblical and theological hermeneutics. In line with Anthony Thiselton, whose work I highly respect as a major source of inspiration for my own hermeneutical thinking,[3] my aim is to find out the metahermeneutical potential of the Wesleyan quadrilateral. Does it provide biblical expositors and biblical theologians with a sufficiently stable and trustworthy instrument to discover what faith in Jesus means, not only then but now? And does it enable us to avoid the pitfall of "sociopragmatic hermeneutics" (in the Thiseltonian sense of the word), that is, does it help us to avoid reading the Bible to find confirmation of what one already believes or expects to find? And does it have trans-

---

[2] Don Thorsen, *The Wesleyan Quadrilateral: Scripture, Tradition, Reason, and Experience as a Model of Evangelical Theology* (Grand Rapids: Zondervan, 1990; Lexington, KY: Emeth Press, 2005), vii, 6. See also W. Stephen Gunter *et al.*, *Wesley and the Quadrilateral: Renewing the Conversation* (Nashville: Abingdon Press, 1997).

[3] See, e.g., Anthony C. Thiselton, *The Two Horizons: New Testament Hermeneutics and Philosophical Description with Special Reference to Heidegger, Bultmann, Gadamer, and Wittgenstein* (Exeter: Paternoster, 1980); idem, *New Horizons in Hermeneutics: The Theory and Practice of Transforming Biblical Reading* (London: HarperCollins; Grand Rapids: Zondervan, 1992); idem, *Interpreting God and the Postmodern Self: On Meaning, Manipulation and Promise* (Edinburgh: T.&T. Clark; Grand Rapids: Eerdmans, 1995); idem, *Thiselton on Hermeneutics: The Collected Works and New Essays of Anthony Thiselton* (Ashgate Contemporary Thinkers on Religion; Aldershot: Ashgate, 2006); idem, *The Hermeneutics of Doctrine* (Grand Rapids, Cambridge: Eerdmans, 2007); idem, *Hermeneutics: An Introduction* (Grand Rapids, Cambridge: Eerdmans, 2009).

formative power? At the outset, I have to admit that the odds are somewhat unfavourable, since Mr Wesley himself clearly thought in terms of accumulating evidence to corroborate orthodox, historical Christian faith, especially when the four sources of religious authority concurred. Now, a "restoration theology" that has to be legitimized by a conservative majority standpoint is not always the best guarantee for renewal and transformation. But, hopefully, I am mistaken (and, knowing the conclusion to this paper already, I *know* I am).

First, then, I will briefly sketch the historical and social context of the quadrilateral in Wesley, briefly because other scholars have done that already and my concern here is not so much with historical knowledge as such but with its hermeneutical application and deployment in the present.

Second, I will review the four components of the quadrilateral to tackle some current hermeneutical issues and see to what extent they contain promises for broader hermeneutic theory. Granted that the quadrilateral worked in the (pre)modern age (that, of course, remains to be seen but is not my present concern), how can it work in our postmodern age, for instance in the case of religiously motivated violence, with which we all have become so familiar these days?

Third, a final preliminary remark before we embark upon our short journey. Hermeneutics is all about perspectives. "What You See Is What You Get" is not only a quality of every modern word processor, it is also an adequate description of how biblical interpretation often works. Although I am fully aware of the religious diversity in our society and in the academic world, in this paper I write from an internal Christian (Evangelical, whatever that means) perspective, at any rate, from what we nowadays call a faith-based (non-secular) hermeneutic. That God, the Father of Jesus Christ, somehow spoke *and still speaks* through the ancient documents we call the Scriptures (the *Christian* Scriptures, that is), I take for granted in the most literal sense of the word. Such a position is, at any rate, the natural habitat of the Christian believer and at this point I do not feel the need to apologize for it.[4] It belongs, as Gadamer would put it, to the "legitimate prejudices" (*legitime Vorurteile*) of interpretation.[5] Further investigation will of course be needed to es-

---

[4] Cf. James D.G. Dunn, *The Living Word* (Philadelphia: Fortress, 1988, ²2009); Paul J. Achtemeier, *Inspiration and Authority: Nature and Function of Christian Scripture* (Peabody, MA: Hendrickson, 1999).

[5] Hans-Georg Gadamer, *Wahrheit und Methode: Grundzüge einer philosophischen Hermeneutik* (GW 1; Tübingen: Mohr Siebeck, 1960, ⁶1990) 275, 281; idem, *Truth and*

tablish whether this is an adequate and appropriate prejudice, but for now it seems to suffice for our purposes.[6]

3. The Wesleyan Quadrilateral – Background Matters

The term quadrilateral is not from Mr Wesley himself. Albert C. Outler was the first to use it in the late sixties of the last century (and later on regretted that he did).[7] However, the idea runs throughout Wesley's writings, as all Wesley scholars that I have read hasten to affirm. Historically, the term has been coined by Outler after the analogy of the Lambeth quadrilateral (1888), which was a fourfold statement of Anglican identity, encapsulating Scripture, the Creeds, the sacraments of Baptism and Holy Communion, and the historic episcopate.[8]

Outler, Thorsen and other Wesley scholars speak of the four *sources* of (religious) authority. But this terminology may create unnecessary confusion and from a hermeneutical perspective does not help very much, since it leaves their interdependence unexplained and their precise referent undefined. There is much to be said for taking the four

---

Method (transl. J. Weinsheimer, D.G. Marshall; London, New York: Continuum, [1975] ²2004), 273, 278.

[6] On Gadamer's hermeneutics, see Richard E. Palmer, *Hermeneutics: Interpretation Theory in Schleiermacher, Dilthey, Heidegger, and Gadamer* (NUStPEPh; Evanston, IL: Northwestern University Press, 1969); Louise D. Derksen, *On Universal Hermeneutics: A Study in the Philosophy of Hans-Georg Gadamer* (Proefschrift Vrije Universiteit; Amsterdam: VU Boekhandel/Uitgeverij, 1983); Joel C. Weinsheimer, *Gadamer's Hermeneutics* (New Haven, London: Yale University, 1985); Werner G. Jeanrond, *Text und Interpretation als Kategorien theologischen Denkens* (HUTh 23; Tübingen: Mohr Siebeck, 1986); Georgia Warnke, *Gadamer: Hermeneutics, Tradition, and Reason* (Key Contemporary Thinkers; Stanford: Stanford University Press, 1987); Anthony C. Thiselton, *The Two Horizons*, 24–47, 293–356; idem, *New Horizons*; Jean Grondin (ed.), Gadamer Lesebuch (UTB 1972; Tübingen: Mohr Siebeck, 1997); C.R. Ringma, *Gadamer's Dialogical Hermeneutic: The Hermeneutics of Bultmann, of the New Testament Sociologists, and of the Social Theologians in Dialogue with Gadamer's Hermeneutic* (Heidelberg: Universitätsverlag C. Winter, 1999); Jean Grondin, *Einführung zu Gadamer* (UTB 2139; Tübingen: Mohr Siebeck, 2000); Robert J. Dostal (ed.), *The Cambridge Companion to Gadamer* (Cambridge: Cambridge University Press, 2002); Donatella Di Cesare, *Gadamer. Ein philosophisches Porträt* (Tübingen: Mohr Siebeck, [Ital. 2007] 2009); David P. Parris, *Reception Theory and Biblical Hermeneutics* (PTMS 107; Eugene, OR: Pickwick, 2009), 1–115; Andrzej Wierciński (ed.), *Gadamer's Hermeneutics and the Art of Conversation* (ISHPh 2; Berlin, Münster: Lit, 2011); Arie W. Zwiep, *Tussen tekst en lezer: een historische inleiding in de bijbelse hermeneutiek 2* (Amsterdam: VU University Press, forthcoming)

[7] See Albert C. Outler, "The Wesleyan Quadrilateral in John Wesley," *WTJ* 20/1 (1985), [7]; Thorsen, *Quadrilateral*, 5–7.

[8] Thorsen, *Quadrilateral*, 38.

elements in a more *instrumental* way: Scripture, tradition, reason and experience are four avenues into the reality of faith, although admittedly even this sounds somewhat static. Perhaps "icon" is an appropriate metaphor, as it points to the referential or "window" character of the four items.[9] My point, at any rate, is that there may be many other sources that have, to varying degrees, (religious) authority, not least God himself, Jesus, the Spirit, the church, creation, the arts, etc. etc.[10]

4. *The Medieval Fourfold Sense of Scripture*

The quadrilateral is not a Wesleyan novelty. A distant yet instructive analogy may be found in the medieval theory of the fourfold sense of Scripture.[11] According to a famous verse attributed to Nicholas of Lyra (1270-1349) but going back to as early as the fourth century CE, the meaning of biblical texts could be sought at four different levels of interpretation:

> The literal meaning teaches what happened (*Littera gesta docet*)
> The allegorical meaning teaches what to believe (*quid credas allegoria*)
> The moral meaning teaches how to act (*moralis quid agas*)
> The anagogical meaning teaches what to hope for (*quo tendas anagogia*).[12]

Thus, an average medieval interpreter of Scripture would read an Old Testament verse about Jerusalem, e.g. in the book of Psalms, first, as a

---

[9] This suggestion was made to me by Dr K. Steve McKormick in an oral communication d.d. 5 April 2007.

[10] Gadamer, for one, has important things to say on the arts as a source of truth. Gadamer, *Wahrheit und Methode*, 103: "Kunst ist Erkenntnis und die Erfahrung des Kunstwerks macht dieser Erkenntnis teilhaftig (...) Soll in der Kunst keine Erkenntnis liegen? Liegt nicht in der Erfahrung der Kunst ein Anspruch auf Wahrheit, der von dem der Wissenschaft gewiß verschieden, aber ebenso gewiß ihm nicht unterlegen ist?"; *Truth and Method*, 84: "[A]rt is knowledge and experiencing an artwork means sharing in that knowledge (...) Is there to be no knowledge in art? Does not the experience of art contain a claim to truth which is certainly different from that of science, but just as certainly is not inferior to it?" Cf. Palmer, *Hermeneutics*, 167–176.

[11] See Arie W. Zwiep, *Tussen tekst en lezer. Een historische inleiding in de bijbelse hermeneutiek 1: De vroege kerk–Schleiermacher* (Amsterdam: VU University Press, 2009, ²2010) 235–238.

[12] Nicolas of Lyra, *Prologus de commendatione Sacrae Scripturae*; PL 113:28. Beryl Smalley, *The Study of the Bible in the Middle Ages* (Notre Dame: University of Notre Dame, [1941], ³1983), xiii, traces the rule to Augustine of Denmark (c. 1260). Cf. the freer rendering of Robert M. Grant, David Tracey, *A Short History of the Interpretation of the Bible* (Philadelphia, PA: Fortress, 1963, ²1984), 85: "The letter shows us what God and our fathers did; The allegory shows us where our faith is hid; The moral meaning gives us rules of daily life; The anagogy shows us where we end our strife."

literal description of the historical city on Mount Zion, second, as an allegory of the Church Militant on earth. He would take, third, the moral sense of Jerusalem to refer to the human soul, to a good conscience or to the state, and, fourth, the anagogical meaning to refer to the Church Triumphant in heaven.[13]

This multiple reading strategy, as we would nowadays call it, enhanced the hermeneutical potential of Scripture and enabled the interpreter to enlarge its *functionality* and *applicability*. Most significantly, it enabled the interpreter to break away from the constraints of history and bridge the gap between then and now, between text and reader.[14] It was a most convenient tool to provide an answer to the burning question that Origen once had when he wrote a sermon on the book of Jeremiah: "What has this history to do *with me?*"[15]

The medieval model of the fourfold sense of Scripture was admittedly driven by a different motif. The four components did not *corroborate* but *expand* the meaning of the text. But the concern for multiple perspectives to guide and enrich exegesis and theology *combined with* the intention to delimit the possibilities of exegesis (there is, after all, a limit to what one can make of texts),[16] seem to be very similar.[17] In fact, Origen and Augustine had already established this dual concern as a matter of principle to guide exegesis.[18] Perhaps rabbinic theology,

---

[13] This particular example has been taken from Nicolas of Lyra, *Prologus*; PL 113:28–29.

[14] Cf. Brian E. Daley, "Is Patristic Exegesis Still Usable?," in: Ellen F. Davis, Richard B. Hays (eds.), *The Art of Reading Scripture* (Grand Rapids, Cambridge: Eerdmans, 2003), 69–88.

[15] Origen, *Homiliae in Jeremiae* 1.2; ed. Pierre Husson, Pierre Nautin, *Origène. Homélies sur Jérémie. Traduction, édition, introduction et notes* (SC 232; Paris: Cerf, 1976), 198–99: τὶ οὖν πρὸς ἐμὲ αὐτὴ ἡ ἱστορία; (italics mine).

[16] So rightly Umberto Eco, *The Limits of Interpretation* (Advances in Semiotics; Bloomington, Indianapolis: Indiana University Press, 1990; First Midland Book Edition 1994). A different position is taken by Stanley E. Fish, *Is There a Text in This Class? The Authority of Interpretive Communities* (Cambridge, London: Harvard University, 1980); idem, *Doing What Comes Naturally. Change, Rhetoric, and the Practice of Theory in Literary and Legal Studies* (Post-Contemporary Interventions; Durham, NC, London: Duke University Press, 1989, ⁴1999).

[17] See Smalley, *Study*; Henri de Lubac, *Exégèse médiévale: Les quatres sens de l'Ecriture* (1959–1964), 4 vols.; Gillian R. Evans, *The Language and Logic of the Bible: The Earlier Middle Ages* (Cambridge, New York: Cambridge University Press, 1984); idem, *The Language and Logic of the Bible: The Road to the Reformation* (Cambridge, New York: Cambridge University Press, 1985); Zwiep, *Tussen tekst en lezer*, 228–260.

[18] Richard P.C. Hanson, *Allegory and Event: A Study of the Sources and Significance of Origen's Interpretation of Scripture* (London: SCM, 1959; repr. Louisville, London: Westminster John Knox, 2002); Bertrand de Margerie, *Introduction à l'histoire de*

with its stress on the application of rules (e.g. the seven rules of Hillel) and its conviction of the unfathomable depths of Scripture provides another parallel.[19] At any rate, I believe a convincing case can be made for the suggestion that the quadrilateral is just a local expression of what biblical theologians have been doing from the beginnings of biblical faith, including, I think, the typically Wesleyan emphasis on the role of experience.

But let's start at the beginning. In the following sections of my paper I will review the four components of the quadrilateral (Scripture, tradition, reason, experience) and briefly comment on each of them. What are the issues under debate and how can they deepen and expand our understanding of Scripture and faith?

5. Scripture – sola Scriptura or prima Scriptura?

The first and, according to most Wesleyan scholars, most important (authoritative) component of the quadrilateral is *Scripture*.[20] To start with Scripture is of course a Christian truism. Without the writings of the Old and New Testament it would be impossible to do Christian theology and to produce knowledge of such central theological convictions about salvation, the work of Christ, the Holy Spirit, and so on. I will of course resist the temptation to quote Wesley's famous and much quoted (and misquoted) dictum that he considered himself to be "a man of one book" (*homo unius libri*),[21] but whatever it meant to him, at

---

l'exégèse 3. Saint Augustin (ICA; Paris: Cerf, 1983); Zwiep, *Tussen tekst en lezer*, 158–171 (Origen), 202–224 (Augustine).

[19] Martin Jan Mulder (ed.), *Mikra: Text, Translation, Reading and Interpretation of the Hebrew Bible in Ancient Judaism and Early Christianity* (CRINT II.1; Assen: Van Gorcum, 1988; Philadelphia, PA: Fortress, 1990); Günter Stemberger, "Schriftauslegung I. Judentum," in: Gerhard Müller (Hrsg.), *Theologische Realenzyklopädie* 30 (Berlin, New York: Walter de Gruyter, 1999), 442–457; Zwiep, *Tussen tekst en lezer*, 79–122.

[20] H. Ray Dunning, *Grace, Faith, and Holiness: A Wesleyan Systematic Theology* (Kansas City, MS: Beacon Hill Press, 1988), 55–76; Thorsen, *Quadrilateral*, 75–91; Stephen J. Jones, "The Rule of Scripture," in: Gunter, *Quadrilateral*, 39–61. Typically, the unique position of Scripture within the quadrilateral is graphically depicted in a diagram on the front cover of Thorsen's book on the quadrilateral: the triad Tradition, Reason and Experience are subsumed under the heading Scripture. See also Dunning, whose prolegomena include separate chapters on the Sources of Theology, one on the Bible (55–76), one on Tradition, Reason and Experience (77–94). He writes: 'These (= the "four foundation stones commonly referred to as the Wesleyan Quadrilateral") are not of equal authority. (...) In fact, properly understood, the three auxiliary sources directly support the priority of biblical authority' (77).

[21] The various references are found in Thorsen, *Quadrilateral*, 174 n.17.

least it suggests that he had a high esteem for the Scriptures and took them as *sine qua non* for theological reflection and Christian living.

There is, however, an ongoing debate on the particular role of Scripture compared to the other three components of the quadrilateral. Most Wesleyan scholars, I think, regard Scripture as the main source of authority and consider the other sources to have secondary, derived authority. In the words of Thorsen, the quadrilateral stands for "the primacy of scriptural authority with the complementary sources of authority found in tradition, reason, and experience."[22]

That said, however, another issue comes up. According to some interpreters, the Wesleyan quadrilateral stands in sharp contrast to the Reformation principle of *sola Scriptura*, "Scripture alone." I think Mr Wesley himself would not agree, seeing that he makes constant reference to the authority of Scripture in his works.[23] However, the objection is a serious one and demands careful attention. Is there a conflict with *sola Scriptura*? And would it perhaps not be more accurate to speak in terms of the *primacy* of Scripture, as some Wesleyan scholars suggest? *Prima Scriptura* (Scripture first) rather than *sola Scriptura* (Scripture alone)?

The context of Wesley was that of an Anglican-Puritan dispute over the role of Scripture, especially about its range of authority and applicability. For Anglicans, Scripture was the norm for faith and morality, while for Puritans it had authority for *all* ecclesial and personal life, including the details of liturgical and administrative matters.[24] Hence, they admitted no other authorities to guide their exegesis and theology, at least in theory.[25]

But this is not, I think, what the Reformers meant when they stood up for the principle of *sola Scriptura* in their controversies with Rome. The Reformers' practice is decidedly against it. When Luther and Calvin rediscovered the Scriptures, they availed themselves of the entire humanistic tradition with its emphasis on philological research, classical and patristic studies, and this is exactly what Wesley also does in his writings. For him, *sola Scriptura* does imply a recognition of scriptural authority, but it does not mean an exclusive role for the Bible.[26]

---

[22] Thorsen, *Quadrilateral*, 1, 5 and *passim*.
[23] Thorsen, *Quadrilateral*, 82–83.
[24] Gunter, *Quadrilateral*, 29–37.
[25] Cf. Heinrich Heppe, *Die Dogmatik der evangelisch-reformierten Kirche dargestellt und aus den Quellen belegt* (hg. v. Ernst Bizer, Neukirchen: Neukirchener, [1861] ²1958), 10–33.
[26] Albert C. Outler (ed.), *The Works of John Wesley, vol. 1. Sermons I, 1–33* (Bicen-

The Wesleyan Quadrilateral   231

I would like to suggest a slightly different understanding or application of the principle of *sola Scriptura*.[27] Honesty requires me to say that I am not quite sure whether the Reformers themselves would agree with my interpretation (or with my reinterpretation, if you like), but I like to think that they would if they were living in our time. And I think they should.

The background of the Reformers' appeal to the *sola Scriptura* principle is the power struggle with Rome. In whose hands was the interpretation of the Bible safest? The Roman Catholic hierarchy of the time argued that the Bible was a difficult book and that the expertise of professionals and the wisdom of the ages was needed to guide the believing community into the true exposition of the Scriptures and to prevent ordinary believers from misinterpretation by either ignorance or heresy. And to a large extent they were right, of course. Professionals have been trained in exegesis and biblical interpretation and know by profession what they are talking about, and we do well to learn from the wisdom of those who went before us.

The Reformers, however, argued on a more basic level. They protested against the claim that the interpretation of Scripture was the prerogative of an elite group, to the exclusion of others. And they refused to believe that God's word was to be mediated by mediators, because of their firm belief in "the priesthood of all believers." In their view the Scriptures were and should be accessible to everyone and the search of their meaning a public matter. Scriptural interpretation was a community affair, to be exercised "in the community of the saints."[28]

So far so good. Up to here I do not think I have expressed any heresy. But let's turn to a present-day application of the Reformers' principle. In my view, this is what is at stake if we want to remain loyal to the *sola Scriptura* principle: Scripture does not need *my* support or confirmation by any of its readers, for that matter: it can stand on its own feet. Scripture is an *independent* conversation partner that is not to be over-

---

tennial Edition; Nashville, TN: Abingdon, 1984), 57–58: "There was never a thought that he should restrict his reading to the biblical text alone. It was, instead, a matter of hermeneutical principle that Scripture would be his court of first and last resort in faith and morals. This was the entire Scripture, too, and not just a biblical anthology; his view of the canon (not excluding the Apocrypha) was of a whole and integral revelation, inspired by the same Holy Spirit who continues to guide all serious readers into / its unfathomable truth, parts and whole together." Also Thorsen, *Quadrilateral*, 82.

[27] See also Zwiep, *Tussen tekst en lezer*, 272–275, 297–298.

[28] Cf. Richard A. Muller, *Post-Reformation Dogmatics 2: Holy Scripture. The Cognitive Foundation of Theology* (Grand Rapids: Baker, 1993), 471–487.

ruled by church officials and theologians *nor by its present-day readers*. There is (and there should be) a distance between text and reader that should be respected. Knowing the perspective of the biblical writers does not yet settle the matter. It does not automatically evolve into a normative perspective, that is. After all, their perspectives are largely uninformed by tradition, critical reason, and experience to the degree that ours is. Only in a later stage of the hermeneutical process may the horizon of the text "fuse" with the horizon of the reader, to use Gadamer's term, but this should not take place prematurely, lest the text be silenced by the modern reader. A fusion of horizons in Gadamer's terms is the experience of the conversation partners that they "relate" and are grasped by a third party (in Gadamer's terms: *die Sache*), even when they may still disagree in their positions, to be sure: it is not the victory of one of the conversation partners over the other.[29]

Such a distance is essential if we are to avoid reading the Bible as a ventriloquist and to be prevented from a disastrous *sacrificium intellectus*. I *need*, in other words, that distance not only to maintain my intellectual integrity, but also as expression of my respect for the otherness of Scripture. My voice is not identical with the biblical writer's voice (which is, of course, a basic principle in exegesis). He will sometimes differ from mine and I differ from his. I should not refashion the findings of exegesis (unwelcome as they sometimes may be) according to my own image and likeness.

Let us go to an application and see if all this can help us in a current debate on religious violence in the Bible.[30] The question is this: must I submit unconditionally to the perspective of the biblical text or author (*Roma locuta, causa finita*) or am I allowed to distance myself

---

[29] On Gadamer's concept of *Horizontverschmelzung*, see Gadamer, *Wahrheit und Methode*, 307–312; *Truth and Method*, 301–306. Later on he writes: "Wie einer sich mit seinem Gesprächspartner über eine Sache verständigt, so versteht auch der Interpret die ihm vom Text gesagte Sache. (...) Verständigung im Gespräch ist nicht ein bloßes Sichausspielen und Durchsetzen des eigenen Standpunktes, sondern eine Verwandlung ins Gemeinsame hin, in der man nicht bleibt, was man war" (*Wahrheit und Methode*, 384); "Just as each interlocutor is trying to reach agreement on some subject with his partner, so also the interpreter is trying to understand what the text is saying (...) To reach an understanding in a dialogue is not merely a matter of putting oneself forward and successfully asserting one's own point of view, but being transformed into a communion in which we do not remain what we were" (*Truth and Method*, 370, 371).

[30] I am referring here in particular (but not exclusively) to the debate on Sam Janse, *De tegenstem van Jezus: Over geweld in het Nieuwe Testament* (Boekencentrum Essay; Zoetermeer: Boekencentrum, 2006); cf. H.G.L. Peels, "Liever langer luisteren: Antwoord aan dr. S. Janse," *Wapenveld* 56/6 (2006), 24–29.

from what we nowadays call "texts of terror"? In his book on *Divine Discourse* Nicholas Wolterstorff makes a fruitful distinction between human and divine discourse in Scripture.³¹ To use his terminology, the actual historical documents written by the human authors are "human authorial / appropriate discourse." This human discourse is "appropriated" as it were by God as medium through which divine communication takes place. Scripture as a whole is "appropriated divine discourse," that is, the book we have may be rightly termed the Word of God because it is authenticated as it were by God. Yet this does not make Him the immediate cause of each and every utterance that his employees and secretaries decided to put on paper: human appropriate discourse and divine appropriated discourse overlap to a large extent but they are not identical. The interpreter is expected to discern God's words *in these human words*. A few quotations from Wolterstorff may elucidate what is at issue and how he thinks we must proceed:

> [I]nterpretation of a biblical passage for the divine mediating discourse cannot proceed without the interpreter appealing to convictions she has as to what God would and would not be likely to have intended to say by appropriating this passage within the whole text of the Bible. *And such convictions ... will depend crucially on what the interpreter believes about the nature and purposes of God.*³²
>
> ... there may be various things said or suggested in the appropriated discourse of which the appropriator doesn't want to say even some equivalent. He wants to embrace the main point but not all the incidentals. Thus to get from the propositional content of the appropriated discourse to that of the appropriating discourse requires subtlety and sensitivity in interpretation. In appropriating, we refashion, not always, but often.³³

Elsewhere I have suggested that this distinction may be fruitfully applied to the issue of violence in the Bible.³⁴ Wolterstorff himself took the last words of Psalm 137 as an example ("Happy shall they be who take your little ones and dash them against the rock!," NRSV),³⁵ but I

---

³¹ Nicholas Wolterstorff, *Divine Discourse: Philosophical Reflections on the Claim that God Speaks* (Cambridge: Cambridge University Press, 1995). For a summary and critique, see Maarten Wisse, "From Cover to Cover? A Critique of Wolterstorff's Theory of the Bible as Divine Discourse," *IJPR* 92 (2002), 159–173. I read Wolterstorff slightly different from Wisse. While Wisse thinks Wolterstorff is trying to argue that the entire Bible is the Word of God "from cover to cover," I think Wolterstorff tries to avoid such a wooden interpretation by distinguishing human and divine discourse.
³² Wolterstorff, *Divine Discourse*, 221; italics mine.
³³ Wolterstorff, *Divine Discourse*, 53.
³⁴ Arie W. Zwiep, "Jezus, geweld en politiek?," *TheolD* 4.1 (2007), 33–36.
³⁵ Wolterstorff, *Divine Discourse*, 211–212.

think the principle can be applied more widely, even though Wolterstorff probably did not realize (or would not agree as to) the possible implications of his approach. As a critical principle the distinction between human words and the Word of God allows the interpreter to make ethical judgements, informed, to be sure, by and based on the central message of Jesus as found especially (and paradigmatically) in the Sermon on the Mount, without obliging the interpreter to ascribe to what we in our time regard unethical material. Did God really command the slaughter of the entire population of Canaan (Deut. 7:1–4)? Did He really command death penalty for violation of the Sabbath (Ex. 35:2), a stubborn and rebellious son (Deut. 21:18–21), adultery (Lev. 20:10ff.), homosexuality (Lev. 20:13)? I would suggest that we sometimes could better distance ourselves from such "texts of terror" as being incidental to and conflicting with the larger message of the Bible and with the nature of God as revealed elsewhere in the Scriptures than that we refashion the texts (e.g. through allegorical interpretation) to make them fit our perspective. This, I submit, is not as radical as some may think, since it amounts to no more than a modern day application of the principle "to interpret Scripture with Scripture" in line with the Reformed and Wesleyan focus on the scope (*scopus*) and the totality of Scripture (*tota Scriptura*).[36] It forces us, at any rate, all the more to be clear on what the Christian gospel is really all about. The Gospel, in my view, is not about violence, revenge, injustice; it is essentially *good* news, about salvation, from an essentially *good* and righteous God.[37]

6. Tradition – The Wisdom of the Ages

Back to Wesley and the quadrilateral. The second component of the quadrilateral is tradition.[38] By tradition we mean ancient authorities that help to shape our understanding of what Scripture and Christian life are all about. In the case of Wesley, this is the entire corpus of Christian antiquity, with a particular focus on the early Church Fathers and the early history of the Church of England.[39] Our self-understanding is

---

[36] Wesley's favourite term for this was the "analogy of faith" (*analogia fidei*); see Thorsen, *Quadrilateral*, 86–88; Jones, "Rule of Scripture," 52–57.

[37] See on this problematic also Wes Morriston, "What If God Commanded Something Terrible? A Worry for Divine-Command Meta-Ethics," *TS* 45 (2009) 249–267.

[38] Dunning, *Grace*, 77–83; Thorsen, *Quadrilateral*, 93–105; T.A. Campbell, "The Interpretive Role of Tradition," in: Gunter, *Quadrilateral*, 63–75.

[39] Thorsen, *Quadrilateral*, 11–32. Outler, *Works*, 66–96, mentions Holy Scripture (69–70), the Classics (71–73), Christian Antiquity (74–76), the Anglican and Puritan

not only *informed* by tradition but is *shaped* by it. Tradition has to do with identity matters. It makes who we are.

At this point we need to bring in the particular contribution of Hans-Georg Gadamer to our conversation. In his work, tradition plays a major role.[40] Against the Cartesian rejection of all authority outside the thinking subject and against the existentialist rejection of history by Rudolf Bultmann, he fervently called for the rehabilitation of authority and tradition. This at first sight seems to conflict with the principle of *sola Scriptura* and with the role of reason, but I think the conflict is apparent and superficial. Gadamer refuses to draw a sharp contrast between individual judgement and tradition (= a community's judgement).[41] The self-awareness of the individual "is only a flickering in the closed circuits of historical life."[42] The focus on subjectivity is "a distorting mirror" (*ein Zerrspiegel*).[43] Listening to what has been handed down and filtered through a succession of community experiences and community judgements is "based," says Gadamer, "not on the subjection and abdication of reason but on an act of acknowledgment and knowledge—the knowledge that the other is superior to oneself in judgment and insight and that for this reason his judgment takes precedence."[44] Tradition in this sense should be valued as an act of reason itself. It has nothing to do with blind obedience and irrational submission to

---

traditions (79–88), contemporary culture (88–96) as sources of Wesley.

[40] Gadamer, *Wahrheit und Methode*, 281–290; *Truth and Method*, 278–85; Warnke, *Gadamer*, 75–82; Anthony C. Thiselton, *A Concise Encyclopedia of the Philosophy of Religion* (Grand Rapids: Baker, 2002), 309–310, *s.v.* Tradition; Parris, *Reception Theory*, 2–11.

[41] Gadamer, *Wahrheit und Methode*, 287: "Am Anfang aller historischen Hermeneutik muß ... die *Auflösung des abstrakten Gegensatzes zwischen Tradition und Historie, zwischen Geschichte und Wissen von ihr stehen*. Die Wirkung der fortlebenden Tradition und die Wirkung der historischen Forschung bilden eine Wirkungseinheit, deren Analyse immer nur ein Geflecht von Wechselwirkungen anzutreffen vermöchte" (his italics); *Truth and Method*, 283–284: "At the beginning of all historical hermeneutics, then, *the abstract antithesis between tradition and historical research, between history and the knowledge of it, must be discarded*. The effect (Wirkung) of a living tradition and the effect of historical study must constitute a unity of effect, the analysis of which would / reveal only a texture of reciprocal effects" (his italics).

[42] Gadamer, *Wahrheit und Methode*, 281; *Truth and Method*, 278.

[43] Gadamer, *Wahrheit und Methode*, 281; *Truth and Method*, 278.

[44] Gadamer, *Wahrheit und Methode*, 284: "Die Autorität von Personen hat aber ihren letzten Grund nicht in einem Akte der Unterwerfung und der Abdikation der Vernunft, sondern in einem Akt der Anerkennung und der Erkenntnis - der Erkenntnis nämlich, daß der andere einem an Urteil und Einsicht überlegen ist und daß daher sein Urteil vorgeht, d.h. vor dem eigenen Urteil den Vorrang hat"; *Truth and Method*, 281.

authorities,[45] since the authority of tradition must be earned, affirmed, embraced, cultivated (all Gadamer's words! all verbs in the active!).[46] It is the simple and humble acknowledgment that other perspectives may be more legitimate, better informed, more appropriate than one's own. The fact that they have come down to us and have stood the test of time, is significant in itself. Says Gadamer: "Thus, acknowledging authority is always connected with the idea that what the authority says is not irrational and arbitrary but can, in principle, be discovered to be true. This is the essence of the authority claimed by the teacher, the superior, the expert."[47]

At this point, it appears to me, Gadamer and Wesley are close allies: they both reject the autonomous self of modernity as a fiction, a distortion of reality, while not giving up the rationality of human discourse. The appeal to tradition is a call for humbleness and critical self-reflection.[48]

Now, Gadamer has not made himself popular with his plea for the rehabilitation of tradition. Some of his opponents, e.g. Jürgen Habermas, Karl-Otto Apel and Richard Rorty, have accused him of a naive, uncritical acceptance of tradition.[49] How can we be sure that the truth we receive from tradition is not distorted truth? The only answer that Gadamer can give is: keep on dialoguing, keep the conversation go-

---

[45] Gadamer, *Wahrheit und Methode*, 284 uses strong terminology: "der blinde Gehorsam" (blind obedience, *Truth and Method*, 281), "blinde[m] Kommandogehorsam" (blind obedience to commands, *Truth and Method*, 281).

[46] Gadamer, *Wahrheit und Methode*, 284 (*erworben*); Tradition "bedarf der Bejahung, der Ergreifung und der Pflege" (286); *Truth and Method*, 281, 282.

[47] Gadamer, *Wahrheit und Methode*, 285: "So ist die Anerkennung von Autorität immer mit dem Gedanken verbunden, daß das, was die Autorität sagt, nicht unvernünftige Willkür ist, sondern im Prinzip eingesehen werden kann. Das Wesen der Autorität, die der Erzieher, der Vorgesetzte, der Fachmann in Anspruch nehmen, besteht darin"; *Truth and Method*, 281.

[48] See on the constructive-formative role of tradition from a historical point the instructive article about the fourteenth/fifteenth-century theologian Jean Gerson and his emphasis on the *sensus a sanctis patribus traditus*: Mark S. Burrows, "Jean Gerson on the 'Traditioned Sense' of Scripture as an Argument for an Ecclesial Hermeneutic," in: Mark S. Burrows, Paul Rorem (eds.), *Biblical Hermeneutics in Historical Perspective: Studies in Honor of Karlfried Froehlich on His Sixtieth Birthday* (Grand Rapids: Eerdmans, 1991) 152–172. Burrows also makes a comparison with Gadamer (167ff.).

[49] See the assessment by Warnke, *Gadamer*, 107–138 (Habermas and Apel, with a discussion of Gadamer's response); 139–166 (Rorty). See further Karl-Otto Apel *et al.*, *Hermeneutik und Ideologiekritik. Theorie-Diskussion* (Frankfurt am Main: Suhrkamp, 1971); Ulrich Nassen, "Hans-Georg Gadamer und Jürgen Habermas. Hermeneutik, Ideologiekritik und Diskurs", in: idem (Hrsg.), *Klassiker der Hermeneutik* (UTB 1176; Paderborn: Ferdinand Schöningh, 1982), 301–321.

ing on and keep trying to find a common language, being all the more aware of your own ideological and critical biases.[50]

7. Reason – The Rationality of Faith

The third component of the quadrilateral is reason, critical reason.[51] In our postmodern age, the role of reason and the rationality of faith are under dispute, not least because of the collapse of global ideologies and the failure of rational man to create a world without evil and violence. Wesley lived in the age of transition from the precritical approach to the Bible to the critical approach, although he did not live to see the full development of the historical-critical method.[52] In his time he used what we would call the best of biblical scholarship that helped him to understand the message of Scripture.

Again, Gadamer may help us to clarify matters a little and prevent us from an application of Wesley that is inadequate and counterproductive.

Looking with hindsight, we can easily see that Descartes and the Enlightenment thinkers, living in the Age of Reason, were overly optimistic about the role of reason.[53] Wesley was surely under their spell to a large degree, especially through the philosophical empiricism of John Locke (1632–1704).[54] Wesley had a rather positivistic understanding of reason and the natural sciences. Under the influence of the three "masters of suspicion," Friedrich Nietzsche, Karl Marx and Sigmund Freud, we have come to realize that reason is not an objective tool and that the human mind is susceptible to manipulation, self-deception, and illusion.[55] Reason, therefore, should be "handled with care." But that *every*

---

[50] Gadamer, "Selbstdarstellung Hans-Georg Gadamers (1975)", in: *Wahrheit und Methode (GW II)* 2:497: "Wo Verständigung unmöglich scheint, weil man 'verschiedene Sprachen spricht', ist die Hermeneutik nicht etwa am Ende. Dort stellt sich die hermeneutische Aufgabe vielmehr gerade in ihrem vollen Ernst, nämlich als die Aufgabe, die gemeinsame Sprache zu finden".

[51] Dunning, *Grace*, 83–87; Thorsen, *Quadrilateral*, 107–128; Rebekah L. Miles, "The Instrumental Role of Reason," in: Gunter, *Quadrilateral*, 77–106.

[52] See the various entries in Donald K. McKim (ed.), *Dicionary of Major Biblical Interpreters* (Downers Grove, IL, Leicester: InterVarsity, [1998] 2007), 45–66, and the contribution on the hermeneutics of John Wesley by S.J. Jones on 1034–8. See further Henning Graf Reventlow, *Epochen der Bibelauslegung IV: Von der Aufklärung bis zum 20. Jahrhundert* (Munich: C.H. Beck, 2001).

[53] See Zwiep, *Tussen tekst en lezer*, 334–397.

[54] Cf. Thiselton, *Encyclopedia*, 71–74 (Empiricism); 170–2 (John Locke).

[55] Cf. Paul Ricoeur, *Philosophie de la volonté 1. Le Voluntaire et l'Involuntaire* (Préface J. Greisch; Points 622; Paris: Points, [1949] 2009); idem, *Philosophie de la volonté 2. Finitude et Culpabilité* (Préface J. Greisch; Points 623; Paris: Points, [1960] 2009); idem,

act of reason is illusionary and manipulative is simply *not* true. It is possible, as Thiselton has argued so perceptively, to move beyond the level of self-affirmation and give way to a non-manipulative interpretation.[56] That is why reason and rationality should never be given up.

Despite misgivings to the contrary, Gadamer is not against method as such, but he argues that the human sciences (*Geisteswissenschaften*) have their own method, one that cannot and should not be copied from the natural sciences.[57] And this would be, I guess, precisely his objection to Wesley: Wesley still thinks too much in terms of the objective and the empirical. Gadamer's dislike of scientific method as a tool for the human sciences sharply contrasts with Wesley's attraction to experimental theology. In fact, Wesley believed that there was a clear analogy between the empirical senses of science and natural knowledge and the spiritual senses of faith.[58] In this respect, he was too much under the aegis of seventeenth-century natural sciences. This, I think, is no longer an option for us. In addition to the collapse of Western Enlightenment ideology, globalization has to a large degree contested the monopoly of critical reason. After all, a Latin-American peasant or an African teenage mother is not helped by a rational explanation of their predicament, nor by an ecclesial or divine statement on how things are, but by a real change of her socioeconomic circumstances, "a cup of water in the name of the Lord" rather than right doctrine, so to speak. This calls for a new rationality, the contours of which we can hardly see.

Personal convictions are constantly on the move. What one believed ten years ago, is not necessarily what one believes today or tomorrow. But scholarly opinions are also on the move. Yesterday's ground-break-

---

De l'interprétation. Essai sur Freud (Points 298; Paris: Seuil, 1965, 1995).

[56] See esp. Thiselton, *Interpreting God and the Postmodern Self.*

[57] I am not sure that the title of Gadamer's *Truth and Method* is to be taken ironically, as is suggested by Palmer, *Hermeneutics*, 163 ("method is not the way to truth"), Anthony C. Thiselton, *Hermeneutics. An Introduction*, 2, 210 (Truth and method "in ironic apposition"), and other Gadamer interpreters. After all, the title is not *Truth* or *Method* (*pace* Thiselton). Gadamer's point is that the human sciences have their own "method." See esp. Gadamer, *Wahrheit und Methode*, 1: "[E]s geht um Erkenntnis und um Wahrheit auch hier (*sc.* in the human sciences)" ("it too is concerned with knowledge and with truth," *Truth and Method*, xx); *Wahrheit und Methode*, 47: "... geht es an, den Begriff der Wahrheit der begrifflichen Erkenntnis vorzubehalten?" (*Truth and Method*, 37: "... is it right to reserve the concept of truth for conceptual knowledge?"). Cf. also Warnke, *Gadamer*, 137: "[I]n calling his book *Truth and Method* Gadamer insists that he does not mean to contrast the recognition of truth with methodical social science, but merely to show the extent to which such methodical social inquiry is itself hermeneutic" (her italics).

[58] See Thorsen, *Quadrilateral*, 115–119.

ing studies are tomorrow's revered tradition. He who likes to stand, hermeneutically speaking, on firm and immovable ground, will surely be disappointed, since everything is on the move, as the Greek philosopher Heraclitus in the fifth century BCE already knew ("Everything flows," πάντα ῥεῖ). Archimedes' wish to be given a place to stand on, where he could move the earth,[59] is pure fiction: there is no such a place for us mere mortals.

For this reason classic foundationalism, the theory that everything can be reduced to rational propositions, has lost its attraction and has had to give way to more realistic (pragmatic) approaches, in which coherency and consistency are higher values than the demands of verifiability and objectivity: the more data fit into what we know already, the more credible a theory is.[60]

The collapse of foundationalism in favour of coherentism does not automatically mean that we fall victim to subjectivism or that we can no longer make truth claims on the basis of Scripture or that universal statements are altogether impossible. But one has to realize that theological statements have their own "grammar" (in the Wittgensteinian sense of the word). Theological statements are usually not "one-to-one" descriptions of states of affairs or universal truths ("x = y"), but context-dependent judgements and value-laden interpretations. The theological statement that "God is love," for instance, is part of a larger repertoire of affirmations about God (*Christian* affirmations about God) that cannot be applied in each and every case without qualification. However, that does not make the affirmation useless for theological conversation: "x" may very well *count as* "y" ("x counts as y"). "God is love" is not a mathematically verifiable statement, but is sufficiently stable by which to proceed and to live. As in real life: I do not need to know all the details of my wife's inner thoughts to give her my love and affection.

---

[59] Archimedes, as quoted by Pappus of Alexandria. See http://www.math.nyu.edu/~crorres/Archimedes/Lever/LeverIntro.html, for sources and variant translations of this text.

[60] See Stanley J. Grenz, John R. Franke, *Beyond Foundationalism: Shaping Theology in a Postmodern Context* (Louisville: Westminster John Knox, 2000, ³2002); Grenz, "Evangelical Theological Method after the Demise of Foundationalism," in: idem, *Renewing the Center: Evangelical Theology in a Post-Theological Era* (Grand Rapids: Baker, 2000), 184–217, and "Theology and Science after the Demise of Realism," 218–248. See also Clark H. Pinnock, "Evangelical Theologians Facing the Future. An Ancient and a Future Paradigm," *WTJ* 33/2 (1998), 7–28; Arie W. Zwiep, "Onderweg naar morgen. Hermeneutische bespiegelingen vanuit een post-conservatieve Evangelical perspectief," in: Gerard C. den Hertog, Cornelis van der Kooi (red.), *Tussen leer en lezen: de spanning tussen bijbelwetenschap en geloofsleer* (Kampen: Kok, 2007), 33–54.

All this is fully in line with Gadamer, although some interpreters (e.g. Richard Rorty) like to give a different interpretation.[61] Gadamer's acknowledgment of the subjective character of interpretation did not lead him to deny the possibility of knowledge, not even of supernatural knowledge, for that matter: "The possibility of supernatural truth can remain entirely open," he said explicitly.[62] For him, the hermeneutical circle is a spiral; it is not a closed circle, at any rate.[63] Understanding is possible.[64]

Theological statements, then, need to comply with the criterion of coherency (they need to cohere with as many data as possible), not with the criterion of scientific verification (that is, they need not necessarily cohere with each and every detail before one can proceed). In this way, one does not fall prey to naive objectivism and positivism and it becomes possible to take the biblical truth claims seriously as a basis for one's life. According to Thiselton, precisely this was the issue under debate between Luther and Erasmus in their dispute on the clarity of Scripture (*claritas Scripturae*).[65]

8. *Experience – The Rootedness of Faith in Life*

The fourth component of the quadrilateral is experience.[66] According to Albert Outler this is Wesley's distinctive contribution to the traditional triad of Scripture, tradition and reason of Anglican theology, an

---

[61] On the various Gadamer receptions, see Thiselton, *New Horizons*.

[62] Gadamer, *Wahrheit und Methode*, 282 (in response to Spinoza's radical critique of religion): "Vielmehr kann die Möglichkeit übernatürlicher Wahrheit durchaus offenbleiben"; *Truth and Method*, 279.

[63] See Jean Grondin, "Gadamer's Basic Understanding of Understanding," in: Dostal (ed.), *Cambridge Companion to Gadamer*, 36–51; Brice Wachterhauser, "Getting it Right: Relativism, Realism and Truth," in: Dostal (ed.), *Gadamer*, 52–78.

[64] On this point Gadamer has been fiercely criticized, e.g., by Emilio Betti, *Allgemeine Auslegungslehre als Methodik der Geisteswissenschaften* (Tübingen: Mohr Siebeck, 1967); idem, *Die Hermeneutik als allgemeine Methodik der Geisteswissenschaften* (PhG 78–79; Tübingen: Mohr Siebeck, 1962, ²1972), who accused Gadamer of subjectivism. On the Betti-Gadamer controversy, see Palmer, *Hermeneutics*, 46–65; J. Vandenbulcke, "Betti-Gadamer. Een hermeneutische kontroverse," *TFil* 32 (1970) 105–113. Gadamer was convinced that, had Betti been given more time to live, they would have come to a common understanding, see Betti, *Zur Grundlegung einer allgemeinen Auslegungslehre* (mit einem Nachwort von H.-G. Gadamer; Tübingen: Mohr Siebeck, [1954] 1988), 93–98. The controversy is largely based on misunderstanding and communication at two different levels.

[65] Thiselton, *New Horizons*, 179–185.

[66] Dunning, *Grace*, 87–93; Thorsen, *Quadrilateral*, 129–145; Randy L. Maddox, "The Enriching Role of Experience," in: Gunter, *Quadrilateral*, 107–127.

attempt to add vitality to church theology of his time without altering its substance.[67] Wesley's concern was for the religion of the heart in place of nominal Christian orthodoxy. Now, the term "experience" is ambiguous, and Wesley seems to use it in various shades of meaning, so let me focus on one particular aspect of it.

Wesley believed that the famous experience he had had at Aldersgate Street on May 24, 1738, which had given him assurance of his own salvation, was an important privilege that *all* believers should have.[68] Hence, there is a tendency in Wesley and Wesleyans to focus on personal experience and on the spiritual life of individual believers. We need only be reminded of the (paradigmatic) importance Wesley attached to what he liked to call "true, inward religion" and "heart-religion."[69] We need not question the authenticity and validity of such private experiences; on the contrary, they are vital if one is to avoid successfully being locked up in the past. In our individualistic and bureaucratic society Wesleyan theologians' stress on the need of personal involvement is more than welcome. But as a hermeneutical tool, I think, there is more to be said about it.

Today we are more impressed by the *social* context of experience.[70] Again, I think, Gadamer may help us to put this in perspective, especially with his notion of *Erfahrung*, which plays such an important role in his hermeneutics.[71] Experience as understood by Gadamer is *not* some mystical inner-light experience that enables the interpreter to get information that is otherwise inaccessible by the conventional means of communication. It is *not* some mysterious spiritual guidance unavailable to less inspired and less mystically attuned readers. And it is *not* gnostic knowledge for the enlightened few only *nor* is it what we in the Netherlands call *bevindelijkheid*. Experience in the Gadamerian sense of the word is the dynamic encounter in the public domain, cultivated by the wisdom of the ages (the Aristotelian concept of

---

[67] Outler, "Quadrilateral" [3].
[68] Jones, "Wesley," 386; Thorsen, *Quadrilateral*, 141.
[69] References can be easily found in the subject index to Thorsen, *Quadrilateral*, 225, *s.v.* Heart-Religion.
[70] Cf. for a critique of an over-individualistic understanding of religious experience, my "Luke's Understanding of Baptism in the Holy Spirit. An Evangelical Perspective," *PentecoStudies* 6/2 (2007), 127–49; repr. in: Arie W. Zwiep, *Christ, the Spirit and the Community of God. Essays on the Acts of the Apostles* (WUNT 2. Reihe 293; Tübingen: Morh Siebeck, 2010), 100–119.
[71] Gadamer, *Wahrheit und Methode*, 270–346; *Truth and Method*, 268–336; Palmer, *Hermeneutics*, 194–198; Thiselton, *On Hermeneutics*, 292, 421–422.

phronesis),⁷² inspired by authority figures (wisdom teachers), and having stood the test of time. The hermeneutical key values for Gadamer are *Bildung* (culture), *sensus communis*, judgement (*Urteilskraft*) and taste (*Geschmack*).⁷³ These qualities cannot be learned by techniques and scientific method, but are to be cultivated in the stream of life.⁷⁴

Experience is always grounded in a particular situation within history and tradition, and, importantly, for Gadamer experience is first and foremost the experience of human finitude: "The truly experienced man knows that he is master neither of time nor of the future."⁷⁵ Hermeneutical experience in Gadamer's sense is a basic openness for tradition and openness for the other. It is being grasped by a reality "from beyond" to which one commits oneself at a certain risk, as in a real conversation, where the outcome is always unpredictable.

In a simile Gadamer elucidates what is at issue.⁷⁶ Someone who plays a game, say a game of chess, enters (or better, creates) a distinctive "world of experience." For the time being the player obeys all the rules of the game and consciously accepts restrictions that he or she would never accept in real life. The spectator, alternately, may know all about the rules of the game and observe the moves of the players and describe the various pieces of the game accurately (this is of course what exegetes should do, after all, as Wittgenstein said, "one learns the game by watching how others play"),⁷⁷ but he or she is not caught up in the experience of the game. The players *are* by having entered the world of the game: they have adopted the presuppositions, attitudes and re-

---

⁷² Gadamer, *Wahrheit und Methode*, 25–27; *Truth and Method*, 18–19. On the role of *phronesis* in Gadamer, see further Paul Schuchman, 'Aristotle's Phronesis and Gadamer's Hermeneutics', *PhTo* 23 (1979), 41–50; Günter Figal, 'Phronesis as Understanding. Situating Philosophical Hermeneutics', in: Lawrence K. Schmidt (ed.), *The Specter of Relativism. Truth, Dialogue, and Phronesis in Philosophical Hermeneutics* (NUSPhEPh; Evanston: Northwestern University Press, 1995), 236–247; Fred Lawrence, 'Gadamer, the Hermeneutic Revolution, and Theology', in: Dostal (ed.), *Cambridge Companion to Gadamer*, 169–183; Di Cesare, *Gadamer*, 140–145.

⁷³ Gadamer, *Wahrheit und Methode*, 15–47; *Truth and Method*, 8–37.

⁷⁴ See also Palmer, *Hermeneutics*, 242–246.

⁷⁵ Gadamer, *Wahrheit und Methode*, 363: "Die eigentliche Erfahrung ist diejenige, in der sich der Mensch seiner Endlichkeit bewußt wird. An ihr findet das Machenkönnen und das Selbstbewußtsein seiner planenden Vernunft seine Grenze"; *Truth and Method*, 351.

⁷⁶ For what follows, see Gadamer, *Wahrheit und Methode*, 107–139; *Truth and Method*, 102–30.

⁷⁷ Ludwig Wittgenstein, *Philosophische Untersuchungen/Philosophical Investigations: The German Text, with a Revised English Translation* (transl. G.E.M. Anscombe; Malden, MA, Oxford: Blackwell, 1953, ³2001), sect. 54.

strictions that go with playing this particular game; for a while, they are seized by (they have let themselves be seized by) another reality.

Private experiences, such as dreams, visions, or "the heart strangely warmed," do not lend themselves easily to objective verification by spectators. Yet this does not make these experiences less real. A little child feels pain without being able to articulate its sensations in rational speech. This is why Anthony Thiselton turns to the linguistic philosophy of Wittgenstein and calls for *public criteria of meaning*. When Jesus, Paul and the early Christians proclaimed salvation, they did so not with reference to inward religion, "the heart strangely warmed," or in the tradition of Schleiermacher to "a feeling of being utterly dependent upon God,"[78] but with appeal to the Hebrew Scriptures, that is, to the publicly accessible tradition of Israel with its testimonies of creation, the exodus, the exile, and so on. This provided them with a language to express their experiences in rational and communicative terms.

Such an understanding of experience makes experience open to investigation. In the field of New Testament studies, Larry Hurtado's work on early Christian devotion to Jesus is a promising line of research.[79] This goes equally for studies in what is nowadays called empirical hermeneutics,[80] and for the recent emergence of *autobiographical literary criticism*, also called *autobibliocriticism*.[81] In these new methods the

---

[78] Cf. Friedrich D.E. Schleiermacher, *Der christliche Glaube nach den Grundsätzen der evangelischen Kirche im Zusammenhange dargestellt* (KG I/13; Berlin, New York: Walter de Gruyter, [1821–1822] 2003), vol. 1, § 4 ("schlechthinniges Abhängigkeitsgefühl").

[79] Larry W. Hurtado, *Lord Jesus Christ: Devotion to Jesus in Earliest Christianity* (Grand Rapids, Cambridge: Eerdmans, 2003); idem, "Religious Experience and Religious Innovation in the New Testament," *JR* 80 (2000), 183–205.

[80] As, e.g., in Hans de Wit *et al.* (eds.), *Through the Eyes of Another: Intercultural Reading of the Bible* (Elkhart, IN: Institute for Mennonite Studies; Vrije Universiteit Amsterdam, 2004).

[81] Nancy K. Miller, *Getting Personal: Feminist Occasions and Other Autobiographical Acts* (New York: Routledge, 1991); Diane P. Freedman, Olivia Frey, Francis Murphy Zauhar (eds.), *The Intimate Critique: Autobiographical Literary Criticism* (Durham, NC: Duke University, 1993); Jeffrey L. Staley, *Reading with a Passion: Rhetoric, Autobiography, and the American West in the Gospel of John* (New York: Continuum, 1995); J. Capel Anderson, Jeffrey L. Staley (eds.), *Taking It Personally: Autobiographical Biblical Criticism* (Sem. 72; Atlanta: Scholars, 1995); H. Aram Veeser (ed.), *Confessions of the Critics* (New York: Routledge, 1996); Ingrid Rosa Kitzberger (ed.), *The Personal Voice in Biblical Interpretation* (London: Routledge, 1999); idem (ed.), *Autobiographical Biblical Criticism: Between Text and Self* (Leiden: Deo Publishing, 2003); Eve-Marie Becker (Hrsg.), *Neutestamentliche Wissenschaft: Autobiographische Essays aus der evangelischen Theologie* (UTB 2475; Tübingen, Basel: Francke, 2003); William R. Tate, "Autobiographical Literary Criticism", in: idem, *Interpreting the Bible. A Handbook of Terms and Methods* (Peabody, MA: Hendrickson, 2006) 31–36.

interpreter is wholly engaged in his field of research without giving up rational discourse. In biblical studies no neutrality is possible, no neutrality needed, and, put more strongly, perhaps personal involvement may even stimulate creative understanding.

9. Some Further Considerations

Now that we have reviewed the four components of the quadrilateral, let's turn back to our initial question. Is the concept of the quadrilateral intrinsically socio-pragmatic? Is it just another way of searching for what the interpreter wishes to find? In some cases (perhaps in many cases) it surely is. You can easily prove any theological point you like by picking elements from each of the four components of the quadrilateral or by playing off the various components against each other.[82] To avoid this, Wesley strived for the united testimony of the four components, not unlike the medieval rule of Vincent of Lerins (fifth century). According to Vincent, the interpretation of Scripture should be in agreement with "what has been believed everywhere, always, by everyone" (*quod ubique, quod semper, quod ab omnibus creditum est*).[83] At first sight, this may sound somewhat naive. There is no hard rule that the majority is always on the right track. And what if reason contradicts Scripture (e.g. Josh 10:1–15)? Nowadays we are more impressed by the tensions, hidden agenda's, conflicts of interests that may arise when the various components of the quadrilateral are brought into play, and we may therefore like to stress the dynamic, or better dialectical interaction of the various components. But perhaps the analogy of modern science may shed a different light on it. Modern science works with the principle of consensus based on experiments. Everyone is free to depart from the scholarly consensus, but if one is to do that successfully one has to bring forward cogent arguments. That is not impossible, but it takes good reasoning to do so. By analogy, there may be good reasons to depart from the wisdom of the ages, but one has to have good reasons to do so.

---

[82] Cf. the famous example of "voting out" the Bible in: Thorsen, *Quadrilateral*, 38; Jones, "Rule," 42–43.
[83] Vincent of Lerins, *Commonitoria* 2.2 (3); PL 50:640. On Vincent, see further: Martin Parmentier, "Vinzenz von Lérins", TRE 35 (2003), 109–111; Thomas G. Guarino, "Tradition and Doctrinal Development: Can Vincent of Lérins Still Teach the Church?", TS 67 (2006), 34–72; Zwiep, *Tussen tekst en lezer*, 233–235.

10. Concluding Remarks

What, then, is the lasting value of the Wesleyan quadrilateral? I think it is this: the quadrilateral is an attempt to take seriously both the open-ended nature of theology and hermeneutics and, at the same time, to recognize the limits of interpretation: we need *perspectives*, we need *multiple* perspectives. The late Stanley Grenz argued for a threefold model,[84] and Ted Campbell toys with the idea of a five-fold understanding.[85] It seems to me that what is at issue in these models is *plurality*. Our current situation, at any rate, demands us to go beyond local (confessional) hermeneutics and show real openness to the other. The best perspectives are those that have stood the test of time, that are anchored in a broad tradition of faith and scholarship, and that bring the liberating and transforming power of the gospel into the lives of men and women.

Theology (God-talk) is not a matter of construing statements and articles of belief as wooden positions, but is engaging in a dialogue or, if I may coin what I think is a new term in English, a "multilogue," for which we need an *explorer's mentality* rather than a *crusader's mentality*.

All this, needless to say, presupposes a firm belief in rationality and the rational character of reality, yet at the same time it requires us to recognize the boundaries of what reason can achieve. As Anthony Thiselton argues, contemporary theology "requires a multiform grammar of truth that, while recognizing the limits of reason, does not thereby reduce it to the merely local or instrumental or rhetorical. It will also respect history, traditions and wisdom."[86] In the words of Blaise Pascal: "Le coeur a ses raisons, que la raison ne connaît point," "the heart has its reasons of which reason knows nothing."[87] I think both Wesley and Gadamer would fully agree.

The last words are for Gadamer, but I'm sure he speaks on behalf of Wesley. In the Afterword to *Truth and Method* he wrote: "But I will stop

---

[84] E.g. in: Stanley J. Grenz, *Revisioning Evangelical Theology: A Fresh Agenda for the 21st Century* (Downers Grove, IL: InterVarsity, 1993), 87–108. As the three pillars of theology he mentions "(1) the biblical message, (2) the theological heritage of the church and (3) the thought-forms of the historical-cultural context in which the contemporary people of God seek to speak, live and act" (93).

[85] Campbell, "Interpretive Role," 65: "[A] case can be made that in place of the Quadrilateral we should understand Wesley as embracing a five-fold understanding of authority including Scripture, Christian antiquity, the early Church of England, reason, and experience."

[86] Thiselton, *On Hermeneutics*, 600, Thesis 6a.

[87] Blaise Pascal, *Pensées* (éd. L. Brunschicg; Paris: Le livre de poche, 1972), 134 (277).

here. The ongoing dialogue permits no final conclusion. It would be a poor hermeneuticist who thought he could have, or had to have, the last word."[88] Nothing closer to the truth could be said indeed!

---

[88] Gadamer, *Truth and Method*, 581; *Wahrheit und Methode: Ergänzungen*, 478: "Doch ich brech ab. Das Gespräch, das im Gange ist, entzieht sich der Festlegung. Ein schlechter Hermeneutiker, der sich einbildet, er könnte oder er müßte das letzte Wort behalten."

Index of Authors

Aalberse, P.J.M   81
Aalders, J.C.   69, 74, 75
Aalders, M.J.   68
Achtemeier, P.J.   225
Allen, G.F.   74
Anderson, A.   164
Anderson, J.C.   243
Anderson, R.S.   2
Anscombe, G.E.M.   242
Apel, K.-O.   236
Arminius, J.   204, 208, 209, 212, 213, 214, 215, 216, 217, 218, 219, 222
Asselt, W.J. van   212, 213, 218, 219
Audi, R.   211
Augustijn, C.   110

Bac, J.M.   212, 213, 218
Bacote, V.E.   129
Bakhuizen van den Brink, J.N.   34
Bakker, H.A.   15, 20, 23, 35, 58, 60, 97, 125, 126, 128
Balke, W.   18
Barnhoorn, J.G.   17
Bartelink, G.J.M.   20
Barth, K.   74, 75, 83, 84, 112, 119, 124
Bartholomew, C.   93
Batenburg, M.   219
Bauckham, R.J.   60
Bauman, Z.   151, 159
Bavinck, H.   165
Beattie, J.   210, 211
Bebbington, D.W.   3, 34, 35, 36, 38
Becker, E.-M.   243
Becker, J.   16
Beck, U.   139
Beek, A. van de   22, 126
Beeke, J.R.   36
Beelaerts van Blokland, F.   81
Beerens, J.F.   80
Begbie, H.   74

Beker, J.C.   173
Bekkum, K. van   17
Belt, H. van den   95
Bentinck, J.   76
Bentley, T.   165, 166
Bercken, W. van den   29
Berg, J. van den   34
Berkhof, H.   124
Berkman, J.   107, 122
Berkouwer, G.C.   2, 165
Berlin, I.   40, 62, 65
Bernts, T.   5, 26, 121
Bethge, E.   34
Bethge, R.   34
Betti, E.   240
Bizer, E.   230
Black, C.C.   171
Blass, F.   168
Blomberg, C.L.   179
Blumhardt, J.C.   69
Bod, R.   58
Boersema, P.R.   20, 21, 22, 24, 31, 93, 100, 101, 102
Boer, W. den   95, 97
Boerwinkel, F.   119
Bok, N.W. den   212
Bolt, J.   110
Bonhoeffer, D.   18, 34
Borgman, E.   116
Borg, M.B. ter   32
Bosch, D.A. van den   71
Bosch, D.J.   135
Boschma, H.   80
Bras, K.   59
Brink, G. van den   61
Brink, H.C. van den   71
Brinkman, M.E.   112
Broeyer, F.G.M.   17
Brouwer, R.   137, 151, 159, 161
Brow, C.H.   7

Brown, C. 100
Brow, R.C. 7
Bruce, S. 21, 22
Brueggemann, W. 44, 53, 55, 56, 57, 58, 59, 61
Bruijne, A. de 87, 100, 120, 123, 124
Bruijne, O. de 52, 27, 28, 53, 3, 27
Brunner, E. 70, 73, 77, 78, 79, 84
Brunschicg, L. 245
Brunson, A.C. 171
Buchman, F.N.D. 69, 70, 71, 74, 75, 76, 77, 81, 84, 85
Budziszewski, J. 89, 93, 96, 100, 101, 102, 116, 129
Buijs, G. 32
Bultmann, R. 235
Burgess, S.M. 164
Burg, W. van der 121
Burrows, M.S. 236
Buskes, J.J. 76, 77, 78, 81, 83, 84

Cairns, D. 73
Calvin, J. 209
Campbell, T.A. 234, 245
Cannon, W.R. 210
Carson, D.A. 152, 159
Cartwright, M. 107
Castellio, S. 48
Cavanaugh, W.T. 122
Christoffersson, O. 173
Clark, D.K. 105
Clarke, A.D. 131
Coffey, I. 19
Coffey, J. 36
Coleman, S. 164
Commons, rev. 73
Constandse, A.L. 17
Copeland, G. 167
Copeland, K. 164, 166
Copleston, F. 210
Corts, S.D.C. 20
Costa, Isaäc da 17, 20
Cragg, G.R. 207
Cranfield, C.E.B. 18
Creutzberg 70
Culpepper, R.A. 171

Daley, B.F. 228
Dankbaar, W.F. 34
Davie, G. 136
Davies, W.D. 171
Davis, E.F. 228
Dayton, D. 17
Debrunner, A. 168
Deemter, R. van 76
Dekker, E. 212, 213, 214, 217, 219
Dekker, G. 5
Dekker, J.R.A. 21
Dekker, W.H. 133
Dekker, W.L. 110, 119
Delanty, G. 152
Derksen, L.D. 226
Derrida, J. 223
Descartes, R. 237
Deth, A. van 82
Deth, G.W. van 71, 72, 74, 75, 76, 80, 82, 83, 84
Di Cesare, D. 226, 242
Diepenhorst, I.N.Th. 73
Diepenhorst, P.A. 73
Diepersloot 79, 82, 83, 84
Dijk, Isaäc van 203
Dijk, J.W. van 69
Dippel, C.J. 112
Dirkse, W. 80
Dobson, E. 93
Dolejšová, I. 19
Donk, W.B.H.J. van de 26, 16
Doornenbal, R. 151
Dorrien, G.J. 165
Dostal, R.J. 226, 240, 242
Douma, J. 113
Driel, L. van 18
Dulles, A. 157
Dunning, H.R. 229, 234, 237, 240
Dunn, J.D.G. 18
Dussen, A. van der 61
Dyk, L. Van 156, 158

Eco, U. 228
Edwards, J. 35, 210
Eisenstadt, S.N. 40, 42, 44, 53
Eliot, G. 204

Index of Authors

Elshtain, J.B. 89, 116
Erp, S. van 119
Erwich, R. 150, 155, 157
Essen, Th. van 106
Evans, G.R. 228
Evans, R. 69, 70
Exalto, J. 69
Exalto, K. 18

Fagel, P. 83
Fee, G.D. 164, 166
Feith, R. 81
Fernhout, J.G. 76
Figal, G. 242
Fish, S.E. 228
Fitzmyer, J.A. 168, 175
Fokkelman, J. 58, 63
Ford, D.F. 2
Francke, J. 98
Franke, J.R. 239
Freedman, D.P. 243
Freud, S. 237
Frey, O. 243
Frinsel, J.J. 88, 89, 90, 91, 95, 99
Froehlich, K. 236
Frost, M. 139

Gadamer, H.-G. 223, 225, 226, 227, 232, 235, 236, 237, 238, 240, 241, 242, 245, 246
Galindo, I. 139
Galipeau, C.J. 62
Geelkerken, J.G. 68, 73, 74, 75, 79, 80, 83, 84
Geisler, N.L. 42
Gerleman, G. 48
Gibbs, E. 19
Gomarus, F. 217, 219
Gordon, R. 60
Graafland, C. 140, 219
Graham, B. 20
Grant, R.M. 227
Greisch, J. 237
Gremmels, C. 34
Grenz, S.J. 3, 17, 18, 35, 60, 239, 245
Greschat, M. 100

Griffioen, S. 115
Groen, E. 95
Groenhuijsen, C. 56
Groen van Prinsterer, G. 17, 20
Grondin, J. 226, 240
Groot, C.N. de 151, 159
Grudem, W.A. 94, 124, 125
Guarino, T.G. 244
Guder, D. 160
Gunter, W.S. 224, 229, 230, 234, 237, 240
Guroian, V. 100

Habermas, J. 236
Haeringen, C.B. 70
Hagin, K. 164, 166
Hall, D.J. 119
Hanson, R.P.C. 228
Harinck, G. 68, 124
Harnack, A. 33, 203
Harskamp, A. van 121
Hart, H. 116
Hart, J. de 5, 16
Hart, J.W. 78
Harvey, B. 159, 160
Hauerwas, S. 55, 107, 122, 123, 125, 126, 127
Haykin, M.A.G. 35, 36
Hays, R.B. 228
H. de 77
Healy, N.M. 157, 158
Heeckeren van Kell, van 70
Heelas, P. 135
Heer, J. de 15
Heide, G.J. van der 119
Heidema, S.T. 78, 79, 84
Heijne, B. 54
Heitink, G. 41, 44, 46, 47, 59, 152
Helm, P. 219
Henry, C.F.H. 46, 93, 96, 101
Heppe, H. 230
Herder, J.G. von 49
Herik, J. van den 43, 52
Hertog, G.C. den 55, 97, 124
Heslam, P. 110, 129
Hiebert, P.G. 155

Hirsch, A.   139
Hoekendijk, B.   101, 105
Hoek, J.   89
Hoek, J.A.   78, 79
Hollenweger, W.J.   164, 165
Holvast, R.   89
Home, H.   210, 211
Horley, D.   106
Houtman, C.   60, 63, 64, 65
Hoven van Genderen, H.A. van den   71
Hume, D.   210, 211
Huntingdon, lady   208
Hurtado, L.W.   243
Husson, P.   228
Huttinga, W.   87

Inglehart, R.   135
Israel, J.I.   40, 56, 58
Itterzon, G.P. van   217

Jagt, J. van der   113
Janse, S.   232
Jeanrond, W.G.   226
Jelen, T.G.   121
Jinkins, M.   65
Jones, S.J.   229, 234, 237, 241
Jong, G. de   26
Jonkers, A.P.   16

Kaajan, H.J.Ph.G.   71
Kagchelland, A.   17
Kagchelland, M.   17
Kendall Soulen, R.   56
Kennedy, J.   87
Kierkegaard, S.   112
Kitchen, J.   74
Kitcher, P.   211
Kitzberger, I.R.   243
Klaver, M.   5, 8, 26, 48
Klei, E.H.   86, 99
Koch, J.   110
Kooi, C. van der   47, 55, 58, 60, 239
Koopmans, J.   80
Koppen, C. van   110
Kronjee, G.J.   16

Kruijf, G.G. de   116
Kuiper, D.Th.   , 68, 17
Kuiper, R.   113
Kuitert, H.M.   51, 52
Küng, H.   135
Kunst, J.G.   76
Kuyper, A.   86, 93, 95, 102, 108, 109, 110, 111, 112, 113, 115, 117, 127, 129, 165
Kuzmic, P.   125

Laar, W. van   104
Labanow, C.E.   157
Labuschagne, B.C.   120
Lagemaat, T. van de   23
Lanczkowski, G.   20, 38
Larsen, T.   156
Lawrence, F.   242
Lazarus, S.   93, 94, 102
Lean, G.   69
Leer, N. van der   103
Leer, T. van der   35, 92, 95, 97
Leeuwen, A.Th. van   119
Lewis, C.S.   51
Lindijer, C.H.   51, 62
Lindsey, H.   15
Lioy, D.   164, 165, 166, 167
Locke, J.   35, 237
Lont, Y.   87
Loofs, F.   33
Looman-Graaskamp, A.H.   212
Loor, H.D. de   69, 70, 71, 75, 76, 78, 81, 82, 83
Lubac, H. de   228
Lugo, L.E.   110, 115
Lugt, P. van der   63
Luther, M.   209

Maddox, R.L.   240
Mader, D.   190
Margerie, B. de   228
Markham, I.S.   114
Markus, A.   219
Marshall, D.G.   226
Marsman, H.   189, 190
Marty, M.E.   114

Index of Authors

Marx, K.   237
McClendon, J.   60, 97, 125
McConville, G.   60
McGee, G.B.   164
McGee, M.C.   25
McGrath, A.E.   32, 33, 34, 60, 58, 38
McKim, D.K.   237
McKormick, K.S.   227
McLaren, B.D.   145
McLeod, H.   100
Mead, S.E.   114
Meijering, E.P.   51, 219
Meulen, H.C. van der   32
Meyer, L.   56
Migliore, D.L.   47
Milbank, J.   122
Miles, R.L.   237
Miller, N.K.   243
Mink, G.   17
Miskotte, K.H.   71, 112
Molendijk, A.L.   17, 107
Moltmann, J.   119
Monsma, S.   117
Moore, R.D.   93, 95, 129, 130
Morris, D.   204
Morriston, W.   234
Mott, J.   69
Mouw, R.J.   98, 115
Mowinckel, S.   75
Muggeridge, M.   119
Mulder, M.J.   229
Müller, G.   229
Muller, P.H.   82
Muller, R.A.   218, 231
Muns, C.   76
Murray, J.   18
Murray, S.   154, 107, 117

Nassen, U.   236, 237
Nauta, R.   16, 32
Nautin, P.   228
Nes, H.M. van   205
Neuhaus, R.J.   114
Nie, J.A. van   71
Nietzsche, F.   112, 237
Nieuwpoort   79

Noll, M.A.   31, 35, 92, 129
Noort, G.   15, 132, 145

O'Donovan, J.L.   120, 124
O'Donovan, O.   119, 120, 121, 123, 124, 125, 127, 128, 129, 123
Oldham, J.H.   100
Olson, R.E.   165
Osmer, R.R.   148, 149
Otten, W.   218
Ouden, W.H. den   46
Oud, P.J.   81
Outler, A.C.   206, 208, 209, 210, 211, 212, 226, 230, 234, 240, 241
Ouweneel, W.J.   47, 88, 90, 99, 167, 180

Paas, S.   15, 60, 87, 116, 131, 141, 99, 116
Palmer, R.E.   226, 227, 238, 240, 241, 242
Parmentier, M.   244
Parris, D.P.   226, 235
Parry, R.   93
Pascal, B.   245
Paul, H.   32, 55
Paul, M.J.   20
Peels, H.G.L.   232
Penner, G.M.   175
Penn-Lewis, J.   69
Perkins, M.A.   100, 114
Pierson, A.   17
Pinnock, C.H.   7, 203, 204, 207, 239
Piper, J.   105
Pit, P.   3, 27
Plum, R.J.J.M.   16
Poll, E.W. van de   103, 104
Poorthuis, M.   114
Potok, Ch.   53
Prenter, R.   78
Preus, R.D.   42
Price, R.   210
Priestly, J.   210
Prince, J.   164, 165, 166
Prins, J.H.   110
Rack, H.D.   205, 209

Radmacher, E.D.   42
Rakestraw, R.V.   105
Randall, I.   18, 26
Ratzinger, J.   61
Rauschenbusch, W.   96
Rehkopf, F.   168
Reid, T.   210
Reitsma, B.J.G.   126, 168, 169, 170, 171, 172, 173, 174, 126
Reventlow, H.G.   237
Rhijn, M. van   70, 203
Ricoeur, P.   38, 223, 237
Ridderbos, H.N.   165
Ringma, C.R.   226
Roberts, O.   164
Roeland, J.   5
Roeland, J.H.   26, 45, 48, 56, 57
Roest, H. de   15, 30, 33, 151, 152
Rooden, P. van   30
Rorem, P.   236
Rorty, R.   236, 240
Rose, C.   79
Roukema, R.   63
Rouner, L.S.   114
Rowe, K.E.   208, 222
Ruiter, J.J. de   114
Ruler, A.A. van   99
Runia, K.   104
Rupp, G.   222
Russel, A.J.   72
Ruys, G.   76

Salemink, Th.   114
Sant, W. van 't   76
Sarot, M.   49, 54, 218
Sasse, H.   76
Schans, A.A. van der   106
Schepens, T.   16
Schilder, K.   112, 113, 116
Schinkelshoek, D.   51, 87
Schleiermacher, F.D.E.   243
Schmal, J.J.R.   73, 75, 79, 83
Schmidt, L.K.   242
Schmitt, C.   119
Schneewind, J.B.   211
Scholte, H.P.   98

Schothorst, H. van   70
Schouwenburg, N.G.J. van   75, 76
Schuchman, P.   242
Schutte, G.J.   113
Schwarz, C.A.   158
Scott, P.   122
Seeberg, R.   33
Segers, M.C.   121
Selderhuis, H.   17
Sengers, E.   31, 92, 136, 137, 151
Shawchuck, N.   136
Shaw, I.J.   36
Shenk, W.R.   142
Sider, R.J.   31, 93, 95, 103
Sillevis Smitt, P.A.E.   69, 74, 79
Skillen, J.W.   93, 115, 116
Slotemaker de Bruine, G.H.   82
Smalley, B.   227
Smelik, E.L.   69, 72, 73, 74
Smith, C.   93
Song, R.   100
Soper, C.J.   117
Soulen, R.N.   56
Spijker, G.-J.   87
Spijker, W. van 't   18, 124
Spinoza, B. de   58, 240
Spoerri, T.   81
Sprague, E.   211
Springer, K.   167
Staalduine-Sulman, E. van   40, 63
Staley, J.L.   243
Stapert, J.   104
Stavleu, C.C.   88, 91, 92
Stemberger, G.   229
Steward, K.J.   35, 36
Stoffels, H.C.   10, 29, 21, 92, 95, 26, 100, 101, 102, 103
Stoppels, S.   15, 30, 137, 151
Stott, J.   60, 92

Talstra, E.   64
Tanner, K.   145
Tate, W.R.   243
Taylor, C.   42, 44, 45, 47, 48, 49, 50, 111, 120
Taylor. C.   44

Index of Authors

Temple, W.   100
Thiselton, A.C.   60, 224, 226, 235, 237, 238, 240, 241, 242, 243, 245
Thomas, C.   93
Thomas, W.   105
Thorsen, D.A.D.   224, 226, 229, 230, 231, 234, 237, 238, 240, 241, 244
Thurneysen, E.   73, 74
Tidball, D.J.   92
Tieleman, H.   16
Timmerman, K.   3, 27
Tolkien, J.R.R.   51
Top, C.M.   76
Tracey, D.   227
Treier, D.J.   156
Trembath, K.R.   56
Trimp, C.   113
Troeltsch, E.   107
Tromp, D.   71, 76

Ubbink, G.   79, 81, 84
Uitman, J.M.Ph.   77
Ustorf, W.   100

Vandenbulcke, J.   240
Veeser, H. Aram   243
Velde, R.T. te   212, 213, 218
Veldhuis, H.   212
Veling, K.   113
Vellenga, S.J.   24, 30, 31
Verbrugge, A.   120
Verbrugh, A.J.   113
Verharen, C.J.   104, 125
Verhoeff, M.   20
Vermaat, C.   68, 69, 79
Versteeg, P.   5
Versteeg, P.G.A.   26
Vigilax   82
Visser, H.A.   83
Vlaardingerbroek, M.   153, 154
Vliet, W.G.F. van   92
Vold, K.   75
Volf, M.   60, 157, 162
Vollbehr, W.   133
Vos, A.   16, 17, 33, 57, 203, 208, 212, 213, 218, 219

Vries, O.H. de   15, 60, 37, 59, 60, 20, 92, 94, 95, 96, 97, 100, 125
Vroom, H.   121

Wachterhauser, B.   240
Wagner, C.P.   165
Wallace, M.I.   59
Wallet, B.   43, 55
Wallis, J.   103
Walls, A.F.   131
Ward, P.   139, 148, 150, 151, 152, 153, 155
Warnke, G.   226, 235, 236, 238
Warren, R.   158
Wassenaer van Catwijk, G. van   70, 81
Webber, R.E.   92, 95, 103, 124
Weinsheimer, J.C.   226
Wells, D.F.   156
Wenham, G.   60
Wentsel, B.   16, 19
Weren, W.   58, 63
Wesley-Annesley, S.   205
Wesley, J.   35, 203, 204, 205, 206, 207, 208, 209, 210, 211, 212, 213, 220, 222, 223, 226, 20, 229, 230, 234, 235, 236, 237, 238, 241, 244, 245
Wesley, Samuel   205, 208
Wesley, Susanna   205
West, A.   93
Whitefield, G.   35, 205, 20, 208
Wiercinski, A.   226
Wijdeveld, G.   124
Williams, G.   36
Williamson, H.   60
Wimber, J.   165, 167
Wisse, M.   218, 233
Wit, J.H. de   243
Wit, R. de   219
Witte, H.   143
Wittgenstein, L.   239, 242, 243
Witvliet, Th.   124
Woelderink, J.G.   99
Wolde, E. van   62
Woldring, H.E.S.   110, 114, 121

Wolf, D. de   139
Wolterstorff, N.   233, 234
Woodhead, L.   135
Wright, C.J.H.   46, 65
Wright, N.   140
Wright, N.G.   104, 122
Wright, N.T.   60, 168, 171, 175
Wumkes, G.A.   17

Yar, H.   26

Yoder, J.H.   142, 107, 122, 123, 124, 124

Zandbergen, M.   57
Zauhar, F.M.   243
Zimmer, S.   42, 43, 62, 63, 64, 65
Zuidema, S.U.   111, 112
Zwaag, W. van der   17
Zwiep, A.W.   58, 60, 65, 227, 228, 229, 231, 237, 239, 241, 243, 244